Better Homes and Gardens

fresh

RECIPES FOR ENJOYING INGREDIENTS AT THEIR PEAK

Houghton Mifflin Harcourt
Boston New York 2013

Better Homes and Gardens® *Fresh*

Editor: Jan Miller

Project Editor and Writer: Lisa Kingsley, Waterbury Publications, Inc.

Contributing Editor: Mary Williams, Waterbury Publications, Inc.

Contributing Copy Editors: Terri Fredrickson, Gretchen Kauffman

Contributing Writer: Karen Weir-Jimerson, Studio G

Recipe Development: Lisa Holderness-Brown, Jill Lust, Deborah Wagman, Charlie Worthington, Caroline Wright

Recipe Testing: *Better Homes and Gardens®* Test Kitchen

Contributing Photographers: Jason Donnelly, Andy Lyons, Kritsada Panichgul

Contributing Stylists: Greg Luna, Jill Lust, Sue Mitchell, Jennifer Peterson, Charlie Worthington

Houghton Mifflin Harcourt

Publisher: Natalie Chapman

Editorial Director: Cindy Kitchel

Executive Editor: Anne Ficklen

Editorial Associate: Heather Dabah

Manufacturing Manager: Tom Hyland

Design Director: Ken Carlson, Waterbury Publications, Inc.

Associate Design Director: Doug Samuelson, Waterbury Publications, Inc.

Production Assistants: Mindy Samuelson, Waterbury Publications, Inc.

Our seal assures you that every recipe in *Better Homes and Gardens® Fresh* has been tested in the Better Homes and Gardens® Test Kitchen. This means that each recipe is practical and reliable and meets our high standards of taste appeal. We guarantee your satisfaction with this book for as long as you own it.

contents

8 Introduction

Dive into eating the freshest, best produce of the season.

10 Breakfast & Brunch

Start the day with something fresh and fabulous.

36 Appetizers, Snacks & Drinks

Enjoy fresh-ingredient nibbles, noshes, and sips all year.

68 Main Dishes

Peak-season produce is the star ingredient in these entrées.

164 Big Salads

Tossed or arranged, these hearty salads are a whole meal.

198 Soups, Sandwiches & Pizzas

Enter the fork-free zone with this fresh and casual fare.

240 Little Salads & Sides

Fruits and veggies shine in these accompaniments.

282 Desserts

Fruit, barely embellished, satisfies the sweet tooth.

328 Produce Guide

Learn what to buy when and how to store and prepare it.

388 Index

400 Metric

introduction

Fresh is a flavor you can taste. Whether it's the peppery first radishes of spring, a perfectly ripe summer peach that sends juice cascading down your chin, or a sublimely crisp, sweet-tart fall apple, there is no doubt that eating fresh produce at its peak makes it taste better—and makes it better for you too. That's what *Fresh* celebrates.

The growing number of home gardeners, farmers' markets, food cooperatives, and CSAs (community supported agriculture) points to an increased interest in eating fresh, in-season foods. Fruits and vegetables are allowed to ripen naturally on the bush, vine, tree, or underground and are eaten soon after harvesting rather than being trucked in from thousands of miles away. Even if the supermarket is your main source of produce, it's possible to shop seasonally if you know what to look for. Take a look at the Produce Guide that starts on page 328, then get cooking with the freshest and best of the season.

Omelet with Wilted Greens, *recipe page 28*

breakfast & brunch

START THE DAY WITH A SMILE It's easy to do when something fresh and fabulous crosses your lips. Good mornings come in many forms. Tuck into delicate crepes stuffed with strawberries and lemon cream, gingery waffles topped with fresh peaches—or an omelet filled with sautéed winter greens, feta cheese, and smoky bacon.

Crepes with Strawberries and Lemony Crème Fraîche

Browned butter—what the French call *beurre noisette* for the light hazelnut (*noisette*) color to which the butter is cooked before using—infuses the batter for these crepes with a nutty flavor that is sublime with perfectly ripe strawberries. Red all of the way through, the berries drip with juice and flavor.

PREP 15 minutes
CHILL 30 minutes
COOK 1 minute per batch
MAKES 8 (2-crepe) servings

3   tablespoons butter
1¼ cups milk
⅔   cup all-purpose flour
⅓   cup cornmeal
2   eggs
¼   teaspoon salt
1   8-ounce container crème fraîche
3   tablespoons purchased or homemade lemon curd
1   tablespoon butter, melted
2   tablespoons honey
2   tablespoons lemon juice
4   cups sliced fresh strawberries
¼   cup coarsely chopped fresh mint leaves

1. In a medium skillet heat 3 tablespoons butter over medium-high heat; cook about 3 minutes or until melted and golden brown. Set butter aside. In a blender combine milk, flour, cornmeal, eggs, and salt; cover and blend until combined, scraping down sides as necessary. Add browned butter and blend until smooth. Chill covered blender at least 30 minutes.

2. Meanwhile, in a small bowl whisk together crème fraîche and lemon curd until smooth. Cover and chill until ready to serve.

3. Heat the medium skillet over medium-high heat; brush lightly with some of the 1 tablespoon melted butter. Add 2 tablespoons of the batter to the skillet and swirl to create a thin crepe. Cook about 1 minute or until golden brown. Invert skillet over paper towels and remove crepe. Repeat with remaining batter, brushing skillet with remaining butter as needed.

4. Add honey and lemon juice to skillet; cook and stir until honey is melted. Place strawberries and mint in a large bowl. Drizzle berries with honey mixture; toss to coat.

5. To assemble, place a crepe, browned side down, on a platter. Spread half of the crepe with 1 tablespoon of the crème fraîche mixture. Top with a rounded tablespoon of strawberry mixture. Fold crepe in half over filling and then in half again. Repeat with remaining crepes, crème fraîche mixture, and strawberry mixture. Serve with remaining crème fraîche mixture and remaining strawberry mixture.

EACH SERVING *313 cal, 20 g fat, 111 mg chol, 177 mg sodium, 30 g carb, 3 g fiber, 5 g pro.*

Lemon-Ricotta Blueberry Pancakes with Black and Blue Sauce

These lemony pancakes offer a double dose of blueberries—in the griddle cakes themselves and the glossy sauce that goes on top. (The "black" in the sauce is blackberry jam.) Ricotta cheese gives the pancakes texture and moistness, while a little bit of cornmeal gives them a pleasant crunch. Use any kind of ricotta that suits your taste—whole milk, part skim, or fat free.

PREP 40 minutes
COOK 4 minutes per batch
MAKES 8 servings

1½   cups all-purpose flour
½   cup cornmeal
2   tablespoons sugar
1   teaspoon baking powder
¾   teaspoon salt
½   teaspoon baking soda
2   eggs, lightly beaten
1¼   cups milk
½   cup ricotta cheese
2   tablespoons butter, melted
1   tablespoon honey
1   teaspoon finely shredded lemon peel
1   cup fresh blueberries
1   recipe Black and Blue Sauce
      Fresh blueberries (optional)

1. In a large bowl stir together flour, cornmeal, sugar, baking powder, salt, and baking soda. In another large bowl combine eggs, milk, ricotta cheese, melted butter, honey, and lemon peel. Add egg mixture all at once to flour mixture. Stir just until moistened (batter should be lumpy). Stir in the 1 cup blueberries.
2. For each pancake, pour about ¼ cup batter onto a hot, lightly buttered griddle or heavy skillet, spreading batter in an even layer if necessary. Cook over medium heat for 2 to 3 minutes on each side or until pancakes are golden brown, turning to second side when surfaces are bubbly and edges slightly dry.
3. Serve pancakes with warm Black and Blue Sauce. If desired, top with additional blueberries.

Black and Blue Sauce In a medium saucepan combine 1½ cups fresh blueberries, ¾ cup seedless blackberry jam, ⅓ cup pure maple syrup, 1½ teaspoons finely shredded lemon peel, ¼ cup lemon juice, and 1½ teaspoons grated fresh ginger. Bring to boiling; reduce heat. Gently simmer, uncovered, for 18 to 20 minutes or until desired consistency.

EACH 2 PANCAKES + 2 TABLESPOONS SAUCE *373 cal, 7 g fat, 65 mg chol, 445 mg sodium, 69 g carb, 2 g fiber, 8 g pro.*

Puffed Apple Pancake

For maximum "oohs" and "ahhs," seat everyone at the breakfast table before you take this gorgeous fruit-filled pancake out of the oven. It rises to fabulous heights as it bakes but begins to collapse immediately upon cooling. Good apple varieties for the filling include Granny Smith, Jonathan, McIntosh, Pippin, and Rome Beauty.

PREP **15 minutes**
BAKE **18 minutes**
OVEN **450°F**
MAKES **6 servings**

3   eggs
½   cup all-purpose flour
½   cup milk
2   tablespoons butter, melted
¼   teaspoon salt
2   tablespoons butter
⅓   cup packed brown sugar
2   cooking apples, peeled, cored, and sliced (2 cups)
¼   teaspoon ground cinnamon
¼   teaspoon ground nutmeg
     Sifted powdered sugar

1. In a medium bowl beat eggs with a wire whisk until frothy. Add flour, milk, 1 tablespoon of the melted butter, and the salt; beat until smooth.

2. Heat an 8½-inch round baking pan or medium ovenproof skillet in a 450°F oven for 2 minutes. Add the remaining 1 tablespoon melted butter; swirl to coat pan. Pour batter into the hot pan. Bake pancake for 18 to 20 minutes or until puffed and golden.

3. Meanwhile, for filling, in a medium skillet melt 2 tablespoons butter over medium heat. Stir in brown sugar until combined. Stir in apple slices, cinnamon, and nutmeg. Cook, uncovered, for 3 to 5 minutes or until apples are crisp-tender, stirring occasionally.

4. To serve, remove pancake from oven. Spoon some of the filling into center of pancake. Sprinkle with powdered sugar. Cut into wedges. Pass the remaining filling. (Pancake will collapse as it cools.)

EACH SERVING *239 cal, 11 g fat, 115 mg chol, 214 mg sodium, 32 g carb, 2 g fiber, 5 g pro.*

Blueberry Cream Biscuits with Blueberry Sauce

These biscuits don't contain any butter, so there's no cutting in to be done—just some very gentle stirring and folding of the dough. Gentle handling ensures that the biscuits will be meltingly tender and protects the ripe blueberries from getting crushed. Tossing the berries in the flour mixture helps prevent them from bleeding color into the dough.

PREP **20 minutes**
BAKE **17 minutes**
OVEN **425°F**
MAKES **12 to 16 (1-biscuit) servings**

2   cups all-purpose flour
2   tablespoons sugar
2   teaspoons baking powder
½   teaspoon salt
¼   teaspoon grated whole nutmeg
1   cup fresh blueberries
1½   cups whipping cream
1   recipe Blueberry Sauce

1. Preheat oven to 425°F. In a large bowl whisk flour, sugar, baking powder, salt, and nutmeg. Add blueberries to flour mixture; toss to mix. Stir in whipping cream just until flour mixture is moistened.
2. Turn dough out onto a floured work surface. Gently lift and fold dough four or five times until dough holds together, making a quarter turn between each fold. Place dough on a parchment-lined baking sheet. Pat dough into a 7- to 8-inch square, approximately 1 inch thick. Using a floured pizza cutter or knife, cut into 12 or 16 squares, but do not separate.
3. Bake for 17 to 20 minutes or until golden brown. Cut through or pull apart biscuits. Serve warm with Blueberry Sauce.

Blueberry Sauce In a medium saucepan combine 1 cup blueberries, ⅓ cup sugar, and 2 tablespoons water. Bring to simmering; cook and stir until blueberries pop and sauce has thickened. Remove from heat. Stir in 1 cup blueberries and 1 teaspoon vanilla. Serve warm or at room temperature.
EACH SERVING *231 cal, 11 g fat, 41 mg chol, 191 mg sodium, 30 g carb, 1 g fiber, 3 g pro.*

Ginger-Green Tea Waffles with Summer Peach Sauce

This recipe makes crisp, light Belgian-style waffles but also works fine in a regular waffle baker. All-butter waffles are the richest and all-shortening waffles are the most crisp. If you use half melted butter and half melted shortening, you will get a perfect blend of buttery flavor and airy, melt-in-your-mouth texture.

PREP 20 minutes
BAKE per waffle baker directions
MAKES 12 to 16 (4-inch) waffles or 6 large Belgian waffles

¾   cup milk
1½   teaspoons loose green tea
1½   cups all-purpose flour
2   tablespoons sugar
2   teaspoons baking powder
¼   teaspoon baking soda
½   teaspoon salt (reduce to ¼ teaspoon if using all or part butter)
3   eggs, separated
1   6-ounce container plain yogurt, ¾ cup sour cream, or ¾ cup buttermilk
½   cup shortening and/or butter, melted and cooled
1   tablespoon finely grated fresh ginger
1   recipe Summer Peach Sauce
     Chopped fresh peaches (optional)
     Vanilla yogurt, crème fraîche, or whipped cream (optional)
     Chopped candied ginger and/or freshly grated nutmeg (optional)

1. In a small saucepan heat milk over medium heat just until simmering (small bubbles on the surface); remove from heat. Place green tea in an infuser (or place on a 4-inch square of 100%-cotton cheesecloth and tie with 100%-cotton string). Add tea to hot milk and steep for 5 minutes; remove tea and discard. Set milk aside to cool slightly.

2. In a large bowl combine flour, sugar, baking powder, baking soda, and salt; set aside. In a medium bowl lightly beat egg yolks with a whisk. Whisk in the warm milk, yogurt, shortening, and fresh ginger. Add yolk mixture all at once to flour mixture. Stir just until moistened (batter should be slightly lumpy).

3. In a clean large mixing bowl beat egg whites with an electric mixer on medium to high until stiff peaks form (tips stand straight). Stir a spoonful of whites into batter to lighten. Gently fold in the remaining whites.

4. Add batter to a preheated, lightly greased regular or Belgian waffle baker according to manufacturer's directions. Close lid quickly; do not open until done. Bake according to manufacturer's directions. When done, use a fork to lift waffle off the grid. Repeat with the remaining batter. Serve warm with Summer Peach Sauce. If desired, garnish with chopped peaches, yogurt, and/or candied ginger.

Summer Peach Sauce Peel and chop 4 ripe medium peaches; set aside ¾ cup of the chopped peaches. Place the remaining chopped peaches in a small saucepan. Using a potato masher, mash peaches in saucepan. Stir in 3 tablespoons lemon juice, 2 tablespoons cornstarch, 1 tablespoon crystallized ginger or ¼ teaspoon ground ginger, and ⅛ teaspoon grated whole nutmeg. Bring to boiling over medium-high heat, stirring constantly. Reduce heat to medium; cook and stir for 2 minutes. Remove from heat. Stir in the reserved ¾ cup chopped peaches and 2 tablespoons honey. Serve warm or at room temperature. Makes about 2½ cups sauce.

EACH 1 WAFFLE +
3 TABLESPOONS SAUCE *216 cal, 11 g fat, 49 mg chol, 217 mg sodium, 26 g carb, 1 g fiber, 5 g pro.*

Cranberry-Buttermilk Muffins

For an interesting presentation, line the muffin cups with squares of natural brown parchment instead of paper bake cups—and serve the warm muffins in the parchment cups. Be sure the parchment sits as smoothly as possible in the bottom of the muffin cups before filling.

PREP **20 minutes**
BAKE **15 minutes**
COOL **10 minutes**
OVEN **400°F**
MAKES **12 to 14 muffins**

1   cup fresh cranberries
2   tablespoons sugar
2   cups all-purpose flour
⅓   to ½ cup sugar
4   teaspoons baking powder
1   teaspoon finely shredded orange peel
½   teaspoon salt
1   egg, lightly beaten
¾   cup buttermilk
¼   cup butter, melted
     Coarse sugar

1. Preheat oven to 400°F. Grease twelve to fourteen 2½-inch muffin cups or line with paper bake cups or parchment paper squares. In a medium bowl toss cranberries with 2 tablespoons sugar; set aside.
2. In a large bowl combine flour, ⅓ to ½ cup sugar, the baking powder, orange peel, and salt; stir well. In a small bowl combine egg, buttermilk, and butter. Make a well in center of flour mixture; add egg mixture and cranberries. Stir just until moistened. Spoon into prepared muffin cups. Sprinkle with coarse sugar.

3. Bake about 15 minutes or until golden and a toothpick inserted in center comes out clean. Cool on a wire rack. Serve warm.
EACH MUFFIN *163 cal, 5 g fat, 29 mg chol, 306 mg sodium, 27 g carb, 1 g fiber, 3 g pro.*

Melon Ribbons and Raspberries with Anise Syrup *pictured page 22*

Anise seeds give this honeyed syrup a hint of licorice, while crushed pink or green peppercorns give it just a little bit of bite. The savory flavors are a wonderful complement to the sweetness of the melon. You can make the syrup up to 24 hours ahead of serving and keep in a covered container in the refrigerator.

PREP **40 minutes**
CHILL **30 minutes to 24 hours**
MAKES **8 servings**

2   cups orange juice
¼   cup honey
1   teaspoon anise seeds
¼   to ½ teaspoon cracked pink or green peppercorns
1   ripe cantaloupe and/or honeydew melon, halved, seeded, and peeled
2   teaspoons snipped fresh mint
1½ cups fresh red raspberries
1   recipe Poppy Seed Yogurt (optional)
1   cup purchased granola (optional)
8   mint sprigs

1. For anise syrup, in a medium saucepan combine orange juice, honey, anise seeds, and peppercorns. Bring to boiling; reduce heat. Simmer, uncovered, for 10 to 15 minutes or until slightly syrupy. Remove from heat; let cool. Cover and chill for at least 30 minutes or up to 24 hours.

2. For melon ribbons, draw a vegetable peeler across each melon half to cut melon ribbons.* Place melon in a large bowl. Stir the 2 teaspoons mint into anise syrup. Add anise syrup to melon ribbons; gently toss to coat. Cover and chill for at least 30 minutes or up to 24 hours.

3. To serve, using a slotted spoon, divide melon among 8 dessert dishes. Sprinkle with raspberries. Drizzle with some of the anise syrup remaining in bowl. If desired, top with Poppy Seed Yogurt and sprinkle with granola. Garnish with mint sprigs.

*Tip If you have a mandoline, use it to make the melon ribbons. It's easier and makes more uniform slices. Or use a melon baller to make melon balls.

EACH SERVING *92 cal, 0 g fat, 0 mg chol, 12 mg sodium, 23 g carb, 2 g fiber, 1 g pro.*

Poppy Seed Yogurt In a small bowl stir together one 7-ounce container plain Greek yogurt, ½ teaspoon finely shredded orange peel, and ½ teaspoon poppy seeds. Cover and chill for up to 4 hours.

Melon Ribbons and Raspberries
with Anise Syrup, *recipe page 21*

6 Fresh Ideas for Cantaloupe

Some people like a little salt on their cantaloupe—Italians like to wrap it with salty prosciutto. The intense sweetness of a perfectly ripe melon makes it a good candidate for salty or sweet embellishments.

1 Creamy Melon Cooler

In a blender combine 2 cups cubed ripe cantaloupe, ¾ cup vanilla-flavored Greek yogurt, 1 tablespoon frozen orange juice concentrate, ¼ teaspoon chopped fresh mint, and 4 ice cubes. Blend until smooth. Makes 2 servings.

2 Melon in Balsamic Vinegar

Divide 4 cups chilled, cubed cantaloupe (or use half cantaloupe and half honeydew) among 4 dessert dishes or salad plates. Stir 1 teaspoon sugar into ¼ cup balsamic vinegar until dissolved. Drizzle some of the balsamic vinegar mixture over each serving. Sprinkle each serving with some fresh-ground black pepper if desired. Makes 4 servings.

3 Melon-Radish Salad with Creamy Watercress Dressing

In a large bowl combine 4 cups cubed ripe cantaloupe (or use half cantaloupe and half honeydew) and 1 cup thinly sliced red radishes or French breakfast radishes. In a blender combine ¼ cup fresh watercress leaves, 1 tablespoon honey, and ½ cup sour cream or Greek yogurt. Cover and blend until smooth. Transfer to a small bowl and season with salt and freshly ground pepper to taste. Divide melon mixture among salad plates. Drizzle with watercress dressing. Makes 4 servings.

4 Melon with Smoked Salmon

Wrap thin wedges of chilled ripe cantaloupe with thin slices of smoked lox-style salmon. Drizzle with extra virgin olive oil and squeeze a lemon wedge over. Grind some black pepper over the top.

5 Chilled Melon Soup with Grilled Shrimp

In a food processor or blender combine 6 cups peeled, seeded, and cubed ripe cantaloupe, ½ cup sour cream or plain Greek yogurt, and 1 tablespoon grated fresh ginger. Cover and process until smooth. (Do this in two batches if necessary.) Transfer to a large bowl. Cover and chill until serving time, 2 to 24 hours. Divide among serving bowls and top with grilled shrimp. Makes 4 servings.

6 Melon and Champagne Slush

Place 3 cups cubed cantaloupe in a single layer on a baking sheet. Cover and freeze for at least 6 hours. Place ⅓ cup sugar in a blender; cover and blend about 2 minutes. Add ¼ cup mint leaves; blend until finely chopped. In a very large pitcher combine sugar mixture, frozen melon, 2 cups ice cubes, 1 cup chilled champagne, ¾ cup orange juice, and 2 tablespoons lime juice. Return to blender, in batches if necessary. Blend until smooth. Return to pitcher for serving. Makes 4 servings.

Melon with Smoked Salmon

Polenta with Eggs and Zucchini

If you have a little trouble making perfectly poached eggs, here's a trick: After you've cracked the eggs into the ramekins or custard cups, set the cup in the bubbling water for about 30 seconds—just long enough so that the egg white firms up enough around the edges to stay tidy when the egg is slipped into the water to finish cooking.

START TO FINISH 40 minutes
MAKES 4 servings

½   cup snipped dried tomatoes (not oil-packed)
2¼ cups milk
1   14.5-ounce can reduced-sodium chicken broth
1   cup yellow cornmeal
⅓   cup grated Parmesan cheese
1   tablespoon olive oil
1   medium onion, thinly sliced
2   medium zucchini and/or yellow summer squash, thinly sliced lengthwise
1   medium yellow or green sweet pepper, stemmed, seeded, and cut into bite-size strips
1   lemon, halved
8   eggs
    Fresh Italian (flat-leaf) parsley, shaved Parmesan cheese, and/or dried Italian seasoning (optional)

1. In a small bowl cover dried tomatoes with enough boiling water to cover; set aside. For polenta, in a large saucepan combine milk and broth; heat over high heat just until boiling. Gradually whisk in cornmeal. Reduce heat to medium-low. Cook for 12 to 15 minutes or until thick and creamy, stirring frequently. Stir in grated Parmesan cheese. Reduce heat to low; cover and keep warm.

2. Meanwhile, drain tomatoes. In a large skillet heat oil over medium heat. Add onion, zucchini and/or summer squash, sweet pepper, and tomatoes; cook for 3 to 5 minutes or until tender. Remove from heat; cover to keep warm.

3. Fill another deep large skillet halfway with water. Squeeze half of the lemon into water in skillet. Cut the remaining lemon half into wedges; set aside. Bring water mixture to simmering (bubbles should begin to break the surface of the water). Crack 1 of the eggs into a cup and slip egg into the simmering water. Repeat with 3 more of the eggs, allowing each egg an equal amount of space in the water-juice mixture. Simmer eggs for 3 to 5 minutes or until whites are completely set and yolks begin to thicken but are not hard. Use a slotted spoon to remove eggs; drain on a paper towel-lined plate. Repeat with the remaining 4 eggs.

4. To serve, divide polenta among 4 bowls; top with zucchini mixture and 2 poached eggs. If desired, sprinkle with parsley, shaved Parmesan cheese, and/or Italian seasoning. Serve with the lemon wedges.

EACH SERVING 465 cal, 21 g fat, 445 mg chol, 953 mg sodium, 44 g carb, 6 g fiber, 29 g pro.

Kale-Goat Cheese Frittata

From kale chips to kale salad, this dark leafy green is everywhere these days thanks to delicious new ways to enjoy it. It can't hurt that it's loaded with immune system- and vision-boosting vitamin A either. Be sure to remove the center rib from the kale leaves before tearing them into pieces—it's fibrous and not particularly pleasant to eat.

START TO FINISH 25 minutes
MAKES 6 servings

2   teaspoons olive oil
2   cups coarsely torn fresh kale
1   medium onion, halved and thinly sliced
6   eggs
4   egg whites
¼   teaspoon salt
⅛   teaspoon ground black pepper
¼   cup oil-packed dried tomatoes, thinly sliced
¼   cup crumbled goat cheese (chèvre) (1 ounce)

1. Preheat broiler. In a large nonstick broilerproof skillet heat oil over medium heat. Add kale and onion; cook and stir over medium heat about 10 minutes or until onion is tender.
2. Meanwhile, in a medium bowl beat together eggs, egg whites, salt, and pepper. Pour egg mixture over kale mixture in skillet. Cook over medium-low heat. As mixture sets, run a spatula around edge of skillet, lifting egg mixture so uncooked portion flows underneath. Continue cooking and lifting edge until egg mixture is nearly set (surface will be moist).
3. Arrange dried tomatoes on top of egg mixture; sprinkle with cheese. Broil 4 to 5 inches from the heat for 1 to 2 minutes or just until top is set. Cut into wedges to serve.

EACH SERVING *145 cal, 9 g fat, 216 mg chol, 242 mg sodium, 6 g carb, 1 g fiber, 11 g pro.*

Good Eggs

Farm-fresh or pastured eggs are the best choice for quality and animal health. (Pastured eggs are produced by chickens who roam and forage for their natural diet of seeds and insects.) Find them at farmers' markets, co-ops, natural-food stores, or from the producer. If you can't, make the best choice possible at the supermarket.

Here's how to decipher the language on egg cartons:

Certified Organic Typically, thousands of birds are very tightly packed but uncaged in warehouses. They have some outdoor access, but there are no USDA rules governing size, time, or quality of it. They are fed an all-vegetarian diet free of antibiotics and pesticides.

Natural The USDA stipulates only that the eggs have no artificial ingredients or added color and are minimally processed. Because this applies to most eggs, the term is meaningless.

Cage-Free The hens are uncaged and very tightly packed inside warehouses but generally don't have access outside. There are no restrictions on diet.

Free Range The hens are uncaged and very tightly packed in warehouses. They have some outdoor access, but there are no USDA rules governing size, time, or quality of it. There are no restrictions on diet.

Omelet with Wilted Greens *also pictured page 10*

This recipe calls for a mix of red kale, beet leaves or Swiss chard, and sorrel or fresh spinach to make a total of 1½ cups of greens per omelet. The blend of greens lends the filling an interesting and varied flavor and texture, but you can substitute equal amounts of any combination of the greens—or all of one kind, depending on what is available. It's a good way to take advantage of the last-of-the-season tomatoes.

START TO FINISH **25 minutes**
MAKES **1 serving**

2   slices bacon, chopped
1   teaspoon white wine vinegar
½   teaspoon sugar
½   cup torn sorrel or fresh spinach leaves
½   cup torn red kale leaves or baby kale leaves (stems removed)
½   cup torn beet leaves or Swiss chard (stems removed)
1   teaspoon snipped fresh golden leaf oregano or oregano
2   eggs
2   tablespoons water
⅛   teaspoon salt
     Dash ground black pepper
1   tablespoon butter
¼   cup quartered cherry tomatoes
1   tablespoon crumbled feta cheese
     Golden leaf oregano sprig or oregano sprig (optional)

1. For wilted greens, in a medium nonstick skillet or omelet pan cook the bacon until crisp. Remove bacon from skillet, reserving 1 tablespoon of the drippings in the pan. Drain bacon on paper towels; set aside. Carefully stir vinegar and sugar into drippings in skillet. Add sorrel, kale, beet leaves, and the 1 teaspoon oregano. Using tongs, toss until greens are wilted, 30 seconds to 1 minute. Remove greens and liquid from skillet; set aside.

2. In a small bowl combine eggs, the water, salt, and pepper. Beat with a fork until combined but not frothy. Heat the same skillet over medium-high heat until hot. Add butter to skillet. When butter has melted, add egg mixture to skillet. Reduce heat to medium. Immediately begin stirring egg mixture gently but continuously with a spatula until mixture resembles small pieces of cooked egg surrounded by liquid egg. Stop stirring. Cook for 30 to 60 seconds more or until egg mixture is set but shiny.

3. Spoon wilted greens onto one side of the omelet. Top with half the bacon. Fold the omelet over filling. Transfer to a warm plate. Top with remaining bacon, the tomatoes, and feta cheese. If desired, garnish with oregano sprig.

EACH SERVING *527 cal, 43 g fat, 441 mg chol, 1,090 mg sodium, 12 g carb, 4 g fiber, 23 g pro.*

English Muffin and Asparagus Bake

The proteins in eggs bond with the cooking surface, making it notoriously difficult to scrub the pan clean. A nonstick skillet with flared sides is best for sliding this dish onto a platter for serving. If your nonstick skillet isn't ovenproof, use a regular skillet and serve straight from the pan.

PREP **25 minutes**
BAKE **12 minutes**
BROIL **2 minutes**
OVEN **375°F**
MAKES **6 servings**

1   orange, yellow, or red sweet pepper
10 eggs
½   cup half-and-half or milk
2   teaspoons Dijon mustard
1   teaspoon lemon-pepper seasoning
1   teaspoon curry powder
¼   teaspoon salt
1   tablespoon olive oil
6   to 8 ounces thin asparagus spears, trimmed
1   cup fresh sugar snap pea pods, trimmed
1   cup red or yellow cherry tomatoes
2   English muffins, split and halved
4   ounces fresh mozzarella cheese, thinly sliced, or 1 cup shredded mozzarella
¼   cup small fresh basil leaves

1. Preheat oven to 375°F. Slice bottom half of the sweet pepper into thin rings; seed and chop remaining pepper. Set aside.

2. In large bowl whisk together eggs, half-and-half, mustard, lemon-pepper seasoning, curry powder, and salt; set aside.

3. In a very large nonstick ovengoing skillet heat oil over medium heat. Add asparagus spears; cook for 1 to 2 minutes or until bright green. Remove asparagus with tongs; set aside. Add chopped sweet pepper and pea pods; cook for 2 minutes. Stir in tomatoes. Cook until tomato skins begin to split. Arrange muffin pieces on top of vegetables. Slowly pour egg mixture over all, making sure to saturate muffin pieces. Top with asparagus spears, pressing lightly with the back of spoon.

4. Transfer to oven. Bake, uncovered, for 12 minutes. Top with pepper rings and cheese. Turn oven to broil. Broil for 2 to 3 minutes or until top is golden brown, cheese is melted, and eggs are set.

5. Loosen the edges and carefully slide onto serving platter. Top with fresh basil leaves. Cut into wedges to serve.

EACH SERVING *293 cal, 18 g fat, 375 mg chol, 525 mg sodium, 16 g carb, 2 g fiber, 18 g pro.*

Ham-Asparagus and Cheese Strata

Ham, asparagus, and nutty-flavor Swiss cheese are very happy together in this elegant strata that is perfect for a celebration brunch—or even a simple supper. Assemble it the night before you plan to serve. Cover with plastic wrap and refrigerate overnight. Let the dish sit on the counter for about 30 minutes before baking.

PREP 30 minutes
CHILL 2 to 24 hours
BAKE 50 minutes
STAND 15 minutes
OVEN 325°F
MAKES 6 to 8 servings

8   ounces asparagus spears, trimmed and cut into 2-inch pieces
5   cups French bread cubes
2   cups shredded Gruyère, Swiss, or white cheddar cheese (8 ounces)
½   cup chopped onion (1 medium)
¼   cup chopped chives, green onions, or scallions
1½   cups finely chopped cooked ham (8 ounces)
10   eggs
1½   cups milk
     Olive oil, salt, and cracked black pepper (optional)

1. Bring a large pot of salted water to boiling. Add asparagus; cook about 5 minutes or until bright green. Drain; pat dry with paper towels.

2. In a greased 3-quart rectangular baking dish spread half the bread cubes. Top with cheese, onion, chives, and half of the ham and half of the asparagus. Top with remaining bread.

3. In a large bowl whisk together 4 of the eggs and the milk. Evenly pour over layers in dish. Press down bread pieces into the egg mixture with the back of a spoon. Top with the remaining ham and asparagus. Cover; chill until ready to bake.

4. To bake, preheat oven to 325°F. Bake, uncovered, for 30 minutes. With the back of a wooden spoon, press 6 indentations in top of strata. Pour a whole egg into each indentation. Bake for 20 to 25 minutes more or until an instant-read thermometer inserted in center of strata registers 170°F and eggs are set. Let stand for 15 minutes.

5. Cut into squares to serve. If desired, drizzle lightly with olive oil and sprinkle with salt and cracked black pepper.

EACH SERVING *454 cal, 26 g fat, 421 mg chol, 936 mg sodium, 22 g carb, 2 g fiber, 34 g pro.*

Spicy Poached Eggs in Tomato Sauce

Eggs bubble in a bath of fresh tomato sauce in this gorgeous dish. The rich flavor of the soft egg yolks and the piquant sauce make terrific breakfast companions. Serve with focaccia or thick slices of toasted country bread to soak up every last juicy drop.

PREP **15 minutes**
COOK **17 minutes**
MAKES **4 servings**

2   tablespoons olive oil
3   cloves garlic, minced
6   ripe medium tomatoes (about 2 pounds), peeled and coarsely chopped
½   teaspoon salt
¼   teaspoon crushed red pepper
¼   teaspoon ground black pepper
4   eggs
2   tablespoons snipped fresh basil or oregano
4   wedges Italian flatbread (focaccia)

1. For tomato sauce, in a large skillet heat 1 tablespoon of the olive oil over medium heat. Add garlic and cook for 1 minute. Stir in tomatoes, salt, crushed red pepper, and black pepper. Bring to boiling; reduce heat. Boil gently, uncovered, for 12 to 15 minutes or until tomatoes juices begin to thicken, stirring and crushing tomatoes occasionally with the back of a spoon.

2. Crack 1 egg into a small bowl or cup. Slip the egg into the tomato mixture. Repeat with remaining eggs, allowing each egg an equal amount of space in the tomato mixture. Reduce heat to medium-low. Simmer, covered, for 5 minutes or until egg whites are set and yolks are thickened.

3. Drizzle eggs with the remaining 1 tablespoon olive oil before serving. Sprinkle with fresh basil and serve with focaccia.

EACH SERVING *310 cal, 16 g fat, 186 mg chol, 691 mg sodium, 29 g carb, 3 g fiber, 13 g pro.*

Herbed Spinach Torte in Potato Crust

This spectacular dish is a bit fussy to assemble, but you do have a whole hour to clean up after it goes in the oven—and the end result is truly worth the time spent putting it together. Crispy potatoes create a crownlike crust filled with a creamy mixture of spinach, artichokes, mushrooms, eggs, and cheese. Make it for a very special brunch.

PREP **1 hour**
BAKE **1 hour**
STAND **15 minutes**
OVEN **375°F**
MAKES **12 servings**

3   large russet potatoes, peeled
5   tablespoons olive oil
8   ounces fresh cremini mushrooms, sliced
½   cup chopped red onion (1 medium)
1   tablespoon snipped fresh dill
10   ounces fresh spinach, chopped (about 10 cups)
1   9-ounce package frozen artichoke hearts, thawed, drained, and chopped
½   teaspoon salt
¼   teaspoon ground black pepper
5   eggs, lightly beaten
½   of a 15-ounce container ricotta cheese (¾ cup)
6   ounces light garlic and herb individually foil-wrapped spreadable cheese
1   teaspoon finely shredded lemon peel
     Nonstick cooking spray
     Halved grape tomatoes (optional)

1. Slice the potatoes crosswise ⅛ inch thick. In a large nonstick skillet heat 1 tablespoon of the olive oil. Cook one-fourth of the potato slices over medium-high heat about 4 to 5 minutes or until potatoes are tender, turning once. Transfer potatoes to paper towels to drain; set aside cooked.

2. For spinach filling, in a large skillet heat the remaining 1 tablespoon of olive oil over medium-high heat. Add mushrooms and onion; cook and stir for 6 to 8 minutes or until tender. Stir in dill. Add spinach, artichokes, salt, and pepper; cook and stir over medium heat for 3 to 4 minutes or until spinach wilts. Using a fine-mesh strainer, drain spinach mixture, pressing down with the back of a wooden spoon to release any liquid. In a large bowl combine eggs, ricotta cheese, spreadable cheese, and lemon peel. Stir in spinach mixture. Set aside.

3. Preheat oven to 375°F. Generously coat a 9-inch springform pan with cooking spray. Place the springform pan in a foil-lined 15×10×1-inch baking pan. Cover the bottom of the springform pan with potato rounds, overlapping as necessary and making sure that there are no empty spaces. Arrange some of the potato rounds around the sides of the pan. Pour spinach filling into the pan.

4. Bake about 1 hour or until filling is set. Remove pan from oven; transfer to a wire rack. Let stand for 15 minutes. Working quickly, gently run a sharp knife between the pan and the potatoes. Release the sides of pan and carefully lift.

5. Cut torte into wedges. If desired, garnish with halved grape tomatoes.

EACH SERVING *195 cal, 11 g fat, 93 mg chol, 318 mg sodium, 15 g carb, 3 g fiber, 9 g pro.*

Grilled Arugula Bruschetta, *recipe page 43;* **Cucumber Sangria***, recipe page 65*

appetizers, snacks & drinks

NIBBLE, NOSH, SIP Enjoy the fruits of the garden in party fare that's perfectly suited to seasonal entertaining. In spring, crunch on sweet-spicy radishes on toasts spread with herbed butter. In summer, sip a spirited and minty lemonade on the porch. Whatever the season, savor it with friends.

Toasted Baguette with Herbed Butter and Radish

This extrapolation on the classic French hors d'oeuvre of radishes, butter, and salt gives the humble original a little more flair without losing the essence of its simplicity. Here an herbed butter spread on toasted bread serves as the vehicle for crisp spring radishes sprinkled with smoked sea salt.

START TO FINISH 30 minutes
OVEN 425°F
MAKES 8 to 10 servings

½   cup unsalted butter, softened
2   tablespoons finely chopped green onion or scallion (1)
1   tablespoon snipped fresh basil
2   teaspoons snipped fresh Italian (flat-leaf) parsley
1   teaspoon snipped fresh thyme
1   teaspoon finely shredded lemon peel
⅛   teaspoon freshly ground black pepper
8   ounces baguette-style French bread, diagonally sliced ¼ inch thick
2   bunches assorted radishes with stems
2   teaspoons smoked coarse sea salt or plain coarse sea salt
     Coarse smoked sea salt or plain sea salt (optional)

1. Preheat oven to 425°F. In a medium bowl stir together butter, green onion, basil, parsley, thyme, lemon peel, and pepper. Set aside.
2. Arrange bread slices on a baking sheet. Bake for 4 to 5 minutes or until lightly toasted, turning once. Allow bread to cool. Spread cooled toasts with butter mixture. Arrange bread slices on a platter. Set aside.
3. Stem and thinly slice about 5 of the radishes (¾ cup). Just before serving, top bread slices with sliced radishes. Add the remaining radishes to the platter. Sprinkle toasts with salt. If desired, serve with a small bowl of sea salt for dipping whole radishes.
EACH SERVING *180 cal, 12 g fat, 31 mg chol, 591 mg sodium, 16 g carb, 1 g fiber, 3 g pro.*

What Does Organic Mean?

Sales of organic food have experienced double-digit growth nearly every year in the last decade. A significant segment of the population is willing to pay for the higher prices of organic food in return for knowing that it was grown and processed according to certain noninterventionist methods. Stated simply, organic produce is grown without the use of pesticides, synthetic fertilizers, sewage sludge, genetically modified organisms, or irradiation. Animals that produce meat, poultry, eggs, and dairy products are not given antibiotics or growth hormones and are fed an organic diet.

According to the USDA, these are definitions for the various degrees of organic food:

100% Organic Every ingredient is certified organic.

Organic At least 95% of the ingredients are organic.

Made with Organic Ingredients A minimum of 70% of the ingredients are organic with strict restrictions on the remaining 30% not including any GMOs (genetically modified organisms).

USDA Organic Seal This seal on a product means that the producers are inspected annually and are in compliance with the USDA National Organic Program (NOP).

Roasted Cherry Tomato Pizza Poppers

These tasty little two-bite appetizer pizzas have a crisp texture when grilled and are chewy-crisp when baked. Look for frozen pizza dough among frozen breakfast pastries and baked goods.

PREP **1 hour**
GRILL **8 minutes + 4 minutes per batch**
STAND **10 minutes**
MAKES **56 to 60 appetizers**

2	pints red and/or yellow cherry or grape tomatoes, halved
1	tablespoon extra virgin olive oil
2	to 4 cloves garlic, minced
2	teaspoons balsamic vinegar
1	teaspoon snipped fresh oregano or ½ teaspoon dried oregano, crushed
2	1-pound loaves frozen pizza dough, thawed
¼	cup extra virgin olive oil
1	teaspoon dried oregano
1	teaspoon dried basil
12	to 14 ounces deli-sliced mozzarella or provolone cheese, cut into 2-inch pieces Small fresh basil leaves (optional)

1. For roasted tomatoes, in a 13×9×2-inch disposable foil pan combine tomatoes, the 1 tablespoon olive oil, the garlic, vinegar, and the 1 teaspoon fresh oregano. For a charcoal or gas grill, place pan on the rack of a covered grill directly over medium heat. Grill for 8 to 9 minutes or until tomatoes are wilted, stirring occasionally. Remove from grill.

2. Meanwhile, on a lightly floured surface roll pizza dough, 1 loaf at a time, into a 15×12-inch rectangle (if dough becomes difficult to roll, cover and let rest a few minutes). Cover dough loosely and let rest for 10 minutes. Using a 2- to 2½-inch round cutter (depending on your grill grate, the larger size may be easier to work with), cut out dough rounds. Discard trimmings. Place dough rounds on lightly greased baking sheets. Combine the ¼ cup olive oil, the dried oregano, and the dried basil in a bowl; brush over both sides of dough rounds. Prick dough rounds all over with a fork.

3. For a charcoal or gas grill, using tongs place about 12 dough rounds directly onto well-oiled grill rack directly over medium heat. Cover and grill for 2 minutes. Carefully flip the rounds and press down lightly to flatten. Top each with a piece of cheese. Cover grill and cook until cheese melts and dough is cooked

through, about 2 minutes more. Remove rounds; transfer to a baking sheet. Repeat with remaining dough rounds and cheese. Keep warm in a 250°F oven until ready to serve. Top each round with a spoonful of roasted cherry tomatoes and, if desired, basil leaves. Serve warm or at room temperature.

EACH (4-APPETIZER) SERVING *64 cal, 2 g fat, 3 mg chol, 104 mg sodium, 8 g carb, 0 g fiber, 2 g pro.*

Oven Method Preheat oven to 450°F. Cook tomatoes in oven for 10 to 12 minutes, stirring occasionally. Bake dough rounds on baking sheets for 7 minutes; turn and top with cheese. Return to oven and bake 2 minutes more. Top with tomatoes as above.

Make-Ahead Directions Grill or bake dough rounds but do not top with cheese. Store up to 3 days at room temperature. Just before serving, top with cheese and return to grill (about 12 at a time) over medium-low heat for 2 minutes. Or bake in a 350°F oven for 2 minutes or until cheese melts. Top with roasted cherry tomatoes and, if desired, basil leaves.

Mixed Peppers in a Gougère Crust

A gougère is a savory French cheese pastry made with egg-rich *choux* (cream puff pastry) pastry dough. The dough is piped from a pastry bag onto a baking sheet and put into the oven, where it puffs up into ethereal balls. Gougères are generally served warm with wine. The gougère-style crust for this sweet pepper-topped tart contains tangy blue cheese.

PREP **35 minutes**
COOK **10 minutes**
BAKE **50 minutes**
OVEN **375°F**
MAKES **8 servings**

2 tablespoons olive oil
3 medium red, yellow, and/or green sweet peppers, seeded and sliced into rings
½ of a red onion, sliced
1 clove garlic, minced
¼ cup snipped fresh basil
1 tablespoon snipped fresh rosemary
   Salt and ground black pepper
¾ cup milk
5 tablespoons butter, cut up
½ teaspoon salt
½ teaspoon ground black pepper
1 cup all-purpose flour
4 ounces blue cheese, crumbled
4 eggs
¼ cup blue cheese, crumbled (1 ounce)
   Fresh basil leaves (optional)

1. Preheat oven to 375°F. Grease an 11-inch tart pan with a removable bottom; set aside. In a large skillet heat oil over medium heat. Add sweet peppers, onion, and garlic; cook until tender, stirring occasionally. Stir in the snipped basil and rosemary. Season with salt and black pepper; set aside.

2. In a small saucepan combine milk, butter, ½ teaspoon salt, and ½ teaspoon black pepper. Bring to boiling. Remove from heat. Using a wooden spoon, vigorously beat in flour. Reduce heat and return saucepan to heat. Stir for 2 minutes. Transfer dough mixture to a large bowl. Add the 4 ounces blue cheese. Using a handheld electric mixer, beat on high for 2 minutes. Add eggs, 1 at a time, beating on medium after each addition, until each egg is fully incorporated.

3. Spread dough evenly in the prepared pan. Bake for 10 minutes. Spread sweet pepper mixture over dough. Bake about 40 minutes more or until puffed and golden brown. Sprinkle the ¼ cup blue cheese over tart before serving. If desired, top with basil leaves.

EACH SERVING *278 cal, 19 g fat, 140 mg chol, 345 mg sodium, 17 g carb, 2 g fiber, 10 g pro.*

Grilled Arugula Bruschetta *pictured page 36*

Arugula is a cool-weather green of many names and uses. It's known variously as rocket, roquette, rugula, Italian cress, and rucola. It adds a burst of peppery flavor to salad mixes, soups, and pasta.

PREP **15 minutes**
GRILL **10 minutes**
MAKES **20 appetizers**

1   12-ounce loaf Italian bread, cut diagonally into 1-inch slices
1   garlic clove, halved lengthwise
1   tablespoon olive oil
1¼ cups shredded fresh mozzarella cheese (5 ounces)
1¼ cups chopped arugula
7   tablespoons Basil Pesto (see recipe, right)

1. For a charcoal or gas grill, place bread on grill rack directly over medium heat. Grill for 2 to 3 minutes per side or until lightly toasted. Remove bread from grill.
2. Rub one side of each toast with garlic; brush with olive oil. On each slice of toast layer ½ tablespoon cheese, 1 tablespoon arugula, and another ½ tablespoon cheese.
3. Return bruschetta to grill; grill for 6 to 7 minutes more or until cheese is melted. Top each bruschetta with 1 teaspoon pesto; serve immediately.

EACH APPETIZER *99 cal, 5 g fat, 7 mg chol, 168 mg sodium, 9 g carb, 1 g fiber, 3 g pro.*

Pesto Love

The Italian sauce of basil, garlic, Parmesan cheese, pine nuts, and olive oil originated in the port city of Genoa. It's said to have sated the cravings of sailors longing for something fresh and green after months at sea. Its intoxicating flavor and aroma have timeless appeal, but that hasn't stopped cooks from coming up with twists on the original (see Dried Tomato Pesto, page 224, or Fire-Roasted Jalapeño Pesto, page 194).

Try the classic, then one of the variations:

Basil Pesto In a food processor combine 2 cups packed basil leaves, 2 large cloves of garlic, and 3 tablespoons pine nuts. Process until finely chopped. With machine running, slowly add ¼ cup olive oil; process for 1 minute. Transfer to a storage container and stir in ⅓ cup grated Parmesan cheese and ¾ teaspoon salt. Makes ¾ cup.

Arugula Pesto In a food processor combine ½ cup toasted walnuts, ¼ cup finely shredded Parmesan cheese, and 4 cloves garlic. Process with on/off turns until walnuts are coarsely chopped. Add 2 cups packed baby arugula leaves. Cover and process with on/off turns until leaves are coarsely chopped. With machine running, slowly add ¼ cup olive oil. Transfer to a storage container and season to taste with salt. Makes 1 cup.

Butternut-Sage Crostini with Ricotta and Hazelnuts

These crostini are the essence of fall eating. Roasted butternut squash is pureed with fresh sage and toasted hazelnuts to a creamy texture, then spread on toasted bread and topped with a spoonful of ricotta cheese. Serve with a chilled dry Riesling or sparkling apple cider.

PREP 40 minutes
BAKE 44 minutes
OVEN 375°F/400°F
MAKES 30 appetizers

1   2-pound butternut squash
¾   cup whole-milk ricotta cheese
1   teaspoon finely shredded lemon peel
½   teaspoon cracked black pepper
¼   teaspoon salt
     Dash cayenne pepper
1   tablespoon slivered fresh sage leaves
⅔   cup hazelnuts, toasted and chopped
2   tablespoons lemon juice
1   1-pound loaf baguette-style French bread
¼   cup extra virgin oilve oil
     Fresh sage leaves (optional)

1. Preheat oven to 375°F. Line a baking sheet with parchment paper. Cut squash in half lengthwise; scoop out seeds. Place halves, cut sides down, on prepared baking sheet. Roast squash for 35 to 40 minutes or until tender. Set aside to cool slightly. Increase oven temperature to 400°F.

2. Meanwhile, in a medium bowl combine ricotta cheese, lemon peel, black pepper, salt, and cayenne pepper; set aside.

3. Scoop flesh from squash halves and transfer to the bowl of a food processor. Add the 1 tablespoon slivered sage, ⅓ cup of the hazelnuts, and the lemon juice. Cover and process until smooth; set aside.

4. Slice baguette diagonally into ½-inch slices. On a very large baking sheet arrange baguette slices in a single layer. Brush slices lightly with half of the olive oil. Bake for 5 to 6 minutes or until slices begin to brown. Turn the baguette slices over; brush lightly with the remaining olive oil. Bake for 4 to 5 minutes more or until second sides begin to brown.

5. Thickly spread the butternut squash mixture over baguette slices. Top with ricotta mixture. Sprinkle with the remaining ⅓ cup chopped hazelnuts. Serve warm or at room temperature. If desired, garnish with whole sage leaves.

EACH APPETIZER *108 cal, 4 g fat, 3 mg chol, 139 mg sodium, 15 g carb, 1 g fiber, 4 g pro.*

Eggplant Rolls

Salting eggplant before cooking is a common step in recipes featuring this glossy-skinned vegetable. The salt helps draw some of the water out of the eggplant so that its retains its shape and doesn't disintegrate during cooking. Be sure to thoroughly rinse the salt off before proceeding with the next step in the recipe.

PREP **25 minutes**
STAND **15 minutes**
BAKE **25 minutes**
OVEN **400°F**
MAKES **12 servings**

1   medium eggplant
1   teaspoon salt
2   medium red and/or yellow tomatoes, sliced
½   cup coarse bread crumbs (torn from focaccia)
2   tablespoons olive oil
¼   teaspoon freshly ground black pepper
¼   cup purchased basil pesto or dried tomato pesto
4   ounces fresh mozzarella cheese, cut into 12 pieces
1½ cups arugula or baby spinach
    Fresh basil leaves (optional)

1. Trim sides from eggplant, removing most of the skin and forming a rectangular block. Using a sharp knife or mandoline, cut eggplant into 12 lengthwise slices (⅛ to ¼ inch thick). Line a very large baking sheet with paper towels. Arrange eggplant slices in a single layer on the prepared baking sheet. Sprinkle both sides of eggplant slices with salt; let stand for 15 minutes. Rinse eggplant; drain well.

2. Meanwhile, in a 3-quart square baking dish arrange tomato slices in a single layer; set aside. In a small bowl combine bread crumbs, olive oil, and pepper; set aside.

3. Preheat oven to 400°F. Spread about 1 teaspoon pesto over each eggplant slice. Top with cheese and arugula. Roll up slices; secure with wooden toothpicks. Place eggplant rolls, seam sides down, in baking dish on top of tomato slices. Cover with foil.

4. Bake for 20 minutes. Remove foil; sprinkle with bread crumb mixture. Bake, uncovered, for 5 to 10 minutes more or until bread crumbs are crisp and eggplant is tender. To serve, use a small spatula to lift tomato slices topped with eggplant rolls from dish. If desired, garnish with basil.

EACH SERVING *93 cal, 7 g fat, 8 mg chol, 90 mg sodium, 5 g carb, 2 g fiber, 3 g pro.*

Stuffed Endive with Pear, Walnut, and Goat Cheese

The sweetness of the ripe pear and a drizzle of honey balance out the pleasant bitterness of the endive. You can also slice endive thinly into strips and toss it with a mix of other greens and viniagrette to make a delicious salad.

START TO FINISH 25 minutes
MAKES 6 (2-appetizer) servings

1   tablespoon olive oil
2   teaspoons lemon juice
      Salt and ground black pepper
1   firm medium pear, such as
      Bartlett, cored and thinly
      sliced lengthwise
¼   cup coarsely chopped walnuts
      (toasted if desired)
¼   cup loosely packed fresh
      parsley leaves
4   ounces goat cheese, crumbled
12   Belgian endive leaves
      (1 large head)
      Honey (optional)

1. In a medium bowl whisk together olive oil and lemon juice. Season with salt and pepper. Add pear, walnuts, parsley, and goat cheese. Toss to coat.
2. Spoon pear mixture into endive leaves. Arrange stuffed endive on a serving platter. If desired, drizzle with honey.
EACH SERVING *140 cal, 11 g fat, 15 mg chol, 197 mg sodium, 6 g carb, 1 g fiber, 5 g pro.*

Here's the Scoop

The shape of Belgian endive leaves makes them ideal for holding all sorts of fillings— sweet or savory, hot or cold, creamy or crunchy.

Try one of these additional ideas for stuffing the leaves of Belgian endive:

Asian Peanut Slaw In a small bowl whisk together 2 tablespoons hoisin sauce, 2 teaspoons creamy peanut butter, 1 teaspoon water, ½ teaspoon cider vinegar, and ⅛ teaspoon crushed red pepper. Stir in 2 cups shredded cabbage with carrot (coleslaw mix) and ¼ cup chopped roasted peanuts. Divide among 16 endive leaves.

Apple-Pancetta In a medium skillet cook 2 ounces chopped pancetta, 3 tablespoons chopped celery, and 3 tablespoons chopped shallot over medium heat for 5 minutes. Add ⅓ cup chopped cooking apple. Cook 3 to 4 minutes more or until apple is just tender and pancetta is browned and crisp. Divide mixture among 12 endive leaves. Sprinkle with crumbled goat cheese. Serve warm.

Blue Cheese, Bacon, and Cranberry In a medium bowl combine 8 ounces softened cream cheese, ½ cup crumbled blue cheese, ½ cup chopped walnuts, ½ cup chopped dried cranberries, ¼ cup crumbled cooked bacon, and 2 tablespoons milk. Divide among 12 endive leaves.

Stuffed Mushrooms with Lemon-Pea Hummus, *recipe page 52*

Stuffed Mushrooms with Lemon-Pea Hummus *pictured page 51*

Spring garlic—also called green garlic—is simply the immature garlic plant, harvested before the bulb has fully developed. It looks like a small leek or scallion and has a milder flavor than mature garlic. The same principle applies to pea shoots, which are the first viney greens to appear when a pea is planted in the soil. Their delicate leaves and tendrils have a concentrated fresh pea taste.

PREP **25 minutes**
BAKE **13 minutes**
OVEN **425°F**
MAKES **12 appetizers**

12   large fresh mushrooms
    (1½ to 2 inches in diameter)
    Nonstick cooking spray
1   cup shelled fresh English peas
    (1 pound in pods)
2   tablespoons olive oil
½   teaspoon finely shredded
    lemon peel
1   tablespoon lemon juice
1   to 2 teaspoons snipped fresh
    mint
1   tablespoon chopped fresh
    spring garlic*
    Salt and ground black pepper
2   tablespoons grated
    Parmigiano-Reggiano or Grana
    Padana cheese
    Pea shoots or small fresh mint
    leaves (optional)

1. Preheat oven to 425°F. Clean mushrooms. Remove stems from mushrooms; discard stems or save for another use. Place mushroom caps, stem sides down, in a 15×10×1-inch baking pan. Lightly coat the rounded side of each mushroom cap with cooking spray. Bake for 5 minutes. Carefully place mushroom caps, stem sides down, on a double thickness of paper towels to drain while preparing filling. Set pan aside.

2. For hummus, fill a medium saucepan half full of water. Bring to boiling. Add peas and cook for 2 to 3 minutes or just until tender. Drain and quickly add to a large bowl of ice water to cool quickly. Drain peas well. Place ¾ cup of the peas in a blender or food processor. Add olive oil, lemon peel, lemon juice, and 1 to 2 teaspoons mint. Cover and blend or process until almost smooth. Transfer pea mixture to a medium bowl. Stir in the remaining peas and the spring garlic. Season with salt and pepper.

3. Spoon hummus into mushroom caps. Arrange the stuffed mushroom caps in the baking pan. Sprinkle with cheese. Bake about 8 minutes more or until heated through and cheese melts. Serve warm or at room temperature. If desired, garnish with pea shoots or mint leaves.

***Tip** If spring garlic is not available, substitute 1 tablespoon chopped green onion or scallion and 1 clove minced garlic.

EACH APPETIZER *40 cal, 3 g fat, 1 mg chol, 39 mg sodium, 3 g carb, 1 g fiber, 2 g pro.*

Wasabi-Vinegar Kale Chips

If you think you can't convince the kids to toss aside the potato chip bag, try these tasty, perfectly seasoned kale chips. Roasting torn kale leaves with just a smidgen of oil transforms them into crisp, delicate chips that have a satisfying crunch and a delightful texture. You don't have to mention that they're packed with vitamins and minerals.

PREP **15 minutes**
BAKE **8 minutes**
OVEN **375°F**
MAKES **6 servings**

1   large bunch kale, preferably Dinosaur kale leaves
2   tablespoons seasoned rice vinegar
1   to 2 tablespoons peanut oil, canola oil, or olive oil
½   to 1 teaspoon wasabi paste*
¼   teaspoon toasted sesame oil (optional)
¼   teaspoon sea salt

1. Preheat oven to 375°F. Line two baking sheets with parchment paper. Thoroughly rinse kale under cool running water; pat dry with paper towels or dry in a salad spinner. Remove and discard stems. Tear or chop kale into pieces, about 2 inches each.

2. Place kale in a very large bowl. In a small screw-top jar combine vinegar, peanut oil, wasabi paste, and, if desired, sesame oil. Cover and shake well. Pour the oil mixture over the kale pieces; toss to coat. Spread kale evenly in the prepared baking sheets. Sprinkle with salt.

3. Bake for 8 to 10 minutes or until dark green and crisp, rotating pans and switching pans in oven halfway through baking.

4. Carefully lift the parchment paper with kale onto wire racks, keeping kale intact. Cool completely. To store, place kale chips in a covered container for up to 3 days.

*Tip Most of the wasabi purchased in the U.S. is really horseradish that has been colored green. Real wasabi can be purchased as a root and grated to make a paste or as wasabi paste in a tube or wasabi powder (reconstitute the powder by adding an equal amount of water). A range amount is given for wasabi because the strength and flavor will vary depending on what kind of wasabi you use and the amount of heat you prefer.

EACH SERVING *51 cal, 3 g fat, 0 mg chol, 140 mg sodium, 6 g carb, 1 g fiber, 2 g pro.*

Cheese and Almond Guacamole

Toasted almonds add a delightful crunch to this creamy, luxurious guacamole, while feta or goat cheese adds a salty tanginess. Serrano peppers are slightly smaller and hotter than jalapeños. If you like your guacamole spicy, add the peppers, seeds and all, or remove them to reduce the heat.

START TO FINISH **20 minutes**
MAKES **10 (¼-cup) servings**

4   medium avocados, halved, seeded, peeled, and coarsely chopped
½   cup chopped red onion (1 medium)
2   fresh serrano peppers, halved, seeded (if desired), and finely chopped*
¾   cup crumbled feta cheese or goat cheese
½   cup sliced almonds, toasted and coarsely chopped
⅓   cup chopped fresh cilantro
2   tablespoons lime juice
¾   teaspoon salt
     Carrots, jicama strips, flatbread, and/or lime wedges
     Cilantro sprig (optional)

1. In a large bowl combine the avocados, onion, and serrano peppers; mash slightly with a fork. Fold in the cheese, almonds, cilantro, lime juice, and salt. Spoon into serving bowl. Serve at once or cover surface with plastic wrap and chill for up to 6 hours.
2. Serve with carrots, jicama, flatbread, and/or lime wedges. If desired, garnish guacamole with a cilantro sprig.
***Tip** Because hot chile peppers, such as serranos, contain volatile oils that can burn your skin and eyes, avoid direct contact with chiles as much as possible. When working with chile peppers, wear plastic or rubber gloves. If your bare hands do touch the chile peppers, wash your hands well with soap and water.
EACH SERVING *183 cal, 16 g fat, 13 mg chol, 268 mg sodium, 8 g carb, 5 g fiber, 6 g pro.*

How Hot Is Your Pepper?

The heat level of different chile peppers varies widely—even among fruit of the same variety, depending on growing conditions. The color of a chile pepper has nothing to do with how hot it is but rather its maturity. Immature fruit is usually green. When left on the vine, it turns various shades of red, yellow, brown, or orange. However, its size is a signal to how much burn it has. In general, the smaller the pepper, the hotter it is. Chile heat is measured in Scoville Heat Units. For comparison, sweet peppers have 0 Scoville Units—and pepper spray has between 2 million and 5.3 million.

Take a look at what's hot, hotter, and hottest in the world of chiles—and use according to your tolerance:

Anaheim 500 to 1,000 units. Good for adding mild flavor to soups, sauces, and casseroles.

Poblano 1,000 to 2,000 units. The chile of choice for chiles rellenos.

Jalapeño 2,500 to 8,000 units. There is a wide range for this most commonly used chile, which may explain why one time your jalapeños really bring the heat and another, they're almost mild enough to munch on.

Serrano 8,000 to 23,000 units. Often used alternately with jalapeños to flavor salsa and guacamole, these are never mild enough to munch on.

Cayenne 30,000 to 50,000 units. The most common form of this pepper is dried and ground.

Habañero 200,000 to 300,00 units. Although you might find hotter at a farmer's market, this is likely the hottest pepper you'll find at a grocery store.

6 Fresh Ideas for Avocado

In some parts of the world, avocado—the fruit of a tree native to Central Mexico—is called butterfruit. One bite of a perfectly ripe avocado and you can see why. At its best, it needs no other embellishment other than a sprinkling of salt. But it also adds creaminess (and healthful fat) to soups, dips, and sauces.

1 Chilled Avocado Soup

Place 3 halved, seeded, and peeled avocados and 1 trimmed scallion (white and green parts) in a blender or food processor. Add 1 cup chicken broth and ¼ cup water. Cover and blend until smooth. Add 1 cup half-and-half, ¼ teaspoon salt, and a dash ground white pepper. Cover and blend until smooth. Transfer mixture to a glass bowl. Stir in 1 tablespoon lemon juice. Cover and chill for 3 to 24 hours. Stir before serving. Makes 6 servings.

2 Avocado Grapefruit Salad

On a large serving platter or 6 individual plates arrange 8 cups of mixed salad green or baby spinach, the sections of 2 grapefruits, and 1 seeded, peeled, and sliced avocado. In a small bowl whisk together 3 tablespoons raspberry vinegar, 3 tablespoons avocado oil or olive oil, 1 tablespoon water, 1½ teaspoons sugar, and ¼ teaspoon salt. Drizzle over avocado-greens mixture. Makes 6 servings.

3 Lemon-Avocado Dip

In a medium bowl use a fork to mash 1 halved, seeded, and peeled avocado with 1 tablespoon fresh lemon juice. Stir in ½ cup sour cream, 1 clove minced garlic, and ¼ teaspoon salt. Serve with assorted dippers such as fresh vegetables, pita chips, or tortilla chips. Makes 1 cup.

4 Avocado BLT Sandwiches

Halve, seed, and peel a ripe avocado. Transfer one half to a small bowl; mash with a potato masher or fork. Stir in 2 tablespoons mayonnaise, 1 teaspoon lemon juice, 1 clove minced garlic, and ⅛ teaspoon salt. Thinly slice remaining half. Arrange slices on 4 thin slices of toasted bread. To each sandwich half, add 1 slice of crisp-cooked and halved bacon, 1 slice ripe tomato, and 1 leaf romaine lettuce. Spread mashed avocado on 4 additional thin slices toasted bread; place on filled bread slices. Makes 4 servings.

5 Avocado-Cilantro Cream

In a blender or food processor combine half of a peeled, seeded, and cubed avocado; ½ cup sour cream; 2 teaspoons fresh lime juice; 1 tablespoon chopped cilantro; ¼ teaspoon salt; and 6 drops hot red pepper sauce. Blend until smooth. Serve over poached or grilled salmon, chicken, or shrimp. Makes about ⅔ cup.

6 Ancho-Avocado Butter

In a small saucepan stir together 1 small ancho pepper, 2 tablespoons lime juice, and 2 tablespoons water. Cook over low heat, covered, for 10 minutes or until pepper is soft. Drain and cool. Remove stem and seeds from pepper (see tip, page 55). Finely chop pepper. Stir into 3 tablespoons softened butter. Gently mash half of a seeded, peeled, and chopped avocado into the butter mixture, along with ⅛ teaspoon salt. Refrigerate the butter mixture for up to 1 week. Serve on grilled steak or salmon. Makes about ⅓ cup.

Avocado BLT Sandwiches, *recipe page 66*

Zucchini Fritters with Caper Mayonnaise

Smart gardeners who grow zucchini have devised all kinds of ways to deal with this mild-mannered and prolific summer squash—one of which is to leave bags of them on their neighbors' doorsteps. And then there are the zucchini-infused soups, sautés, salads, breads, and brownies. Add these crispy fritters to the list.

PREP **35 minutes**
COOK **8 minutes per batch**
MAKES **5 to 6 (3-fritter) servings**

8	ounces zucchini, coarsely shredded
½	teaspoon salt
⅓	cup mayonnaise
1	teaspoon finely shredded lemon peel (set aside)
2	teaspoons lemon juice
1	tablespoon capers, drained and coarsely chopped
1	teaspoon snipped fresh lemon thyme or thyme
⅛	teaspoon ground black pepper
8	ounces russet potatoes
½	cup all-purpose flour
½	teaspoon baking powder
⅛	teaspoon cayenne pepper
1	egg, lightly beaten
2	tablespoons olive oil

1. Line a 15×10×1-inch baking pan with several layers of paper towels. Spread zucchini on paper towels; sprinkle with salt. Top with another layer of paper towels. Let stand for 15 minutes, pressing occasionally to release liquid.

2. Meanwhile, for caper mayonnaise, in a small bowl stir together mayonnaise, lemon juice, capers, lemon thyme, and black pepper; set aside.

3. Transfer zucchini to a large bowl. Peel and finely shred the potatoes;* add to the zucchini. Add the lemon peel, flour, baking powder, and cayenne pepper; toss to mix well. Add egg, stirring until combined.

4. In a large nonstick skillet heat 2 teaspoons of the olive oil over medium-high heat. Working in batches, drop batter by slightly rounded tablespoons into the hot skillet. Use a spatula to flatten into patties. Cook for 4 to 5 minutes per side or until golden brown, decreasing heat to medium if necessary. (Keep fritters warm in 200°F oven while cooking additional batches.) Repeat with remaining batter, adding more oil as needed. Serve fritters with caper mayonnaise.

***Tip** Don't shred the potatoes ahead of time or they will darken.

EACH SERVING *249 cal, 18 g fat, 43 mg chol, 436 mg sodium, 18 g carb, 1 g fiber, 4 g pro.*

Crispy Fried Okra with Creole Remoulade

If you think you don't like okra because you associate it with the slimy version that appears in overcooked gumbo, think again. Very fresh okra has a crisp texture and mild flavor. This preparation—quick frying in a cornmeal coating—only enhances that crispness. Serve the slices hot with this spicy mayo, and they will disappear in a flash.

START TO FINISH **25 minutes**
MAKES **16 servings**

⅔ cup mayonnaise
⅓ cup finely chopped cooked shrimp and/or andouille sausage
1 tablespoon Creole mustard
1 teaspoon prepared horseradish
¼ teaspoon paprika
⅛ teaspoon bottled hot pepper sauce
16 whole fresh okra, stemmed and diagonally sliced ½ inch thick
¼ cup all-purpose flour
1 egg
1 tablespoon water
⅔ cup yellow cornmeal
1 teaspoon Old Bay seasoning or celery salt
2 cups peanut oil or other vegetable oil

1. For dipping sauce, in a medium bowl combine mayonnaise, shrimp and/or sausage, mustard, horseradish, paprika, and hot pepper sauce; cover and chill.
2. Pat okra dry with paper towels.
3. Place flour in a shallow dish. In another shallow dish lightly beat egg and the water until combined. In a third shallow dish combine cornmeal and Old Bay seasoning. Dip okra slices in flour, then egg mixture. Roll in cornmeal mixture to coat.

4. In a heavy medium saucepan heat oil over medium-high heat. Using a spoon, carefully add okra, a few at a time, to hot oil. Fry about 4 minutes or until crisp and golden brown, turning once. Drain on paper towels. Repeat with remaining okra, adding more oil if necessary.
5. Serve warm okra slices with dipping sauce.
EACH 4 SLICES + 1 TABLESPOON DIPPING SAUCE *164 cal, 14 g fat, 35 mg chol, 275 mg sodium, 6 g carb, 1 g fiber, 3 g pro.*

Ginger Peach Margaritas

Peach season is fleeting but intense. Although you might be tempted by piles of the blushing fruit in the market in early summer, wait until late summer—and then eat your fill. Other than eating it out of hand, there may be no better way to enjoy a perfectly ripe peach than in this lovely cocktail.

START TO FINISH **15 minutes**
FREEZE **3 to 4 hours**
MAKES **5 to 6 (6-ounce) servings**

1	tablespoon coarse sugar
1	tablespoon crystalized sugar, very finely chopped
1	lime
2	medium peaches (6 to 8 ounces each), unpeeled, pitted, and cut up
1	recipe Ginger Syrup
½	cup tequila
⅓	cup Cointreau or Triple Sec
⅓	cup lime juice
2½	cups ice cubes

1. In a shallow dish combine sugar and crystalized ginger; set aside. Cut a thick lime slice; cut slice in half. Rub halves around rims of 5 or 6 glasses. Dip rims into the sugar mixture to coat; set glasses aside. Slice remaining lime into 5 or 6 slices; set aside for garnish.

2. In a blender combine peaches, Ginger Syrup, tequila, Cointreau, and lime juice. Cover and blend until smooth. Gradually add ice cubes, blending until smooth (blender will be full). Pour into glasses. Garnish with the reserved lime slices.

Ginger Syrup In a small saucepan combine ¼ cup sugar, ¼ cup water, and one 1-inch piece fresh ginger. Bring to boiling, stirring to dissolve the sugar. Boil gently, uncovered, for 4 minutes or until thickened. Remove from heat; let cool. Remove and discard the ginger.

EACH SERVING *188 cal, 0 g fat, 0 mg chol, 2 mg sodium, 29 g carb, 1 g fiber, 1 g pro.*

Cucumber Sangria   *also pictured page 36*

The crisp texture and mild, slightly floral flavor of cucumber are naturally refreshing. Combined with the sweetness of honeydew melon, lime, and mint, the fruit shines in this light and effervescent wine-based summer drink.

PREP **20 minutes**
CHILL **2 hours**
MAKES **8 servings**

1   small honeydew melon
1   seedless cucumber, thinly sliced
1   lime, thinly sliced
12 fresh mint leaves
¼   cup lime juice
¼   cup honey
1   750-milliliter bottle Sauvignon Blanc or other semidry white wine, chilled
1   1-liter bottle carbonated water, chilled
    Fresh mint sprigs and/or leaves (optional)

1. Cut the melon in half; remove and discard seeds and rind. Cut melon into thin slices. In a large pitcher* combine melon, cucumber, lime slices, and the 12 mint leaves. In a small bowl stir together lime juice and honey until combined; pour over melon mixture. Add wine, stirring gently. Cover and chill for at least 2 hours.

2. To serve, stir in carbonated water. Ladle or pour into glasses. If desired, garnish with additional mint.

*Tip If a large pitcher will not fit into your refrigerator, divide the mixture in half and place in 2 smaller pitchers or covered containers.

EACH SERVING *147 cal, 0 g fat, 0 mg chol, 18 mg sodium, 21 g carb, 1 g fiber, 1 g pro.*

Watermelon Martinis

This pink-flesh (sometimes yellow) fruit is made up of 92 percent water—hence its name. There is no other fruit that can quench the thirst and bring a smile to the lips as easily as watermelon. It is the quintessential fruit of summer. Of course, it is most often enjoyed in wedges—preferably outside, where the juice can drip on the ground. But its slushy sweetness is only enhanced in this grown-up drink.

START TO FINISH **20 minutes**
MAKES **6 servings**

5   cups watermelon cubes (rind and seeds removed)
¾   cup lemon vodka
6   tablespoons lime juice
3   tablespoons Cointreau or Triple Sec
3   tablespoons sugar
      Ice cubes

1. Place watermelon in blender. Cover and blend until smooth. Pour puree into a pitcher. Chill or freeze until very cold.

2. For 2 martinis, in the blender combine 1 cup watermelon puree, ¼ cup lemon vodka, 2 tablespoons lime juice, 1 tablespoon Cointreau, and 1 tablespoon sugar. Add 3 to 6 ice cubes. Cover and blend until slushy. Repeat two more times to make 6 martinis.

EACH SERVING *150 cal, 0 g fat, 0 mg chol, 2 mg sodium, 20 g carb, 1 g fiber, 1 g pro.*

Electric Lemonade

You will find the best and most inexpensive lemons when they are at peak season—during the winter months—but you will crave this sparkling and spirited lemonade in the summer, when the weather is hot and you need a slowdown and cooldown. In any season look for lemons that are firm, smooth, and heavy for their size—an indication that they contain a lot of juice. Avoid those that have any green mottling, which is a sign of underripeness.

START TO FINISH **25 minutes**
MAKES **4 servings**

1   cup fresh-squeezed lemon juice
1   cup sparkling mineral water
½   cup fresh mint leaves
¼   to ½ cup sugar
     Dash ginger ale
2   to 3 cups ice
1   cup vodka
     Mint sprigs and lemon slices (optional)

1. Chill 4 serving glasses in the freezer. In a blender combine lemon juice, sparkling water, the ½ cup mint, the sugar, and ginger ale. Add ice. Cover and slowly blend until thick.

2. Remove the 4 glasses from the freezer and pour a jigger (¼ cup) vodka into each. Top with frozen lemonade mixture.

3. If desired, add a straw and garnish each glass with a fresh mint sprig and a slice of lemon.

EACH SERVING *210 cal, 0 g fat, 0 mg chol, 8 mg sodium, 21 g carb, 2 g fiber, 1 g pro.*

Bartending Basics

Most cocktails consist of three basic parts: a base (the spirit); a mixer (vermouth, seltzer, juices, etc.); and an accent (citrus juice, olives, bitters, liqueurs). Having a selection of these three parts of the equation on hand means you can mix almost anything.

Try one of these classics at your next gathering:

Dry Martini In a cocktail shaker combine 2 ounces gin or vodka and ¼ ounce dry vermouth. Add ice cubes. Cover and shake until very cold. Strain into a chilled martini glass. Garnish with a lemon twist or olives on a cocktail pick.

Tom Collins In a cocktail shaker combine 2 ounces gin, 1½ ounces lemon juice, and 1½ teaspoons sugar. Add ice cubes. Cover and shake until sugar dissolves and drink is very cold. Strain into a glass filled with crushed ice and 1 or 2 lemon slices. Add a splash of sparkling water; stir.

Margarita Cut a slice and a wedge from a lime half; set aside. Rub rim of a margarita glass with wedge; dip rim in coarse salt. Juice 1½ limes to get 1 ounce juice. In a cocktail shaker combine lime juice, 2 ounces tequila, and 1 ounce orange liqueur. Add ice cubes. Cover and shake until very cold. Strain into prepared glass with additional ice. Garnish with lime slice.

Pork Roast with Baby Artichokes, *recipe page 79*

main dishes

WHOLE FOODS, WHOLE MEALS Fresh produce plays a more-than-major role in these innovative recipes. Herbed beets hold their own with perfectly poached salmon; butter beans, fresh peas, and scallions "green up" a juicy pork chop; and a chunky sauce of just-warmed peppered citrus fruits enlivens sautéed shrimp.

Soy-Glazed Flank Steak with Blistered Green Beans

This Asian-style dish is for those who like that little edge of burnt toast, the charring on a pizza crust, the slightly incinerated spot on a french fry—anything served "blackened." After a spin in hot oil, these blistered green beans have spots that are "overcaramelized" just enough to be pleasantly flavorful.

PREP **20 minutes**
COOK **15 minutes**
MAKES **4 servings**

1   pound fresh green beans
1   pound beef flank steak
6   cloves garlic, minced
      (1 tablespoon)
1   tablespoon finely chopped
      fresh ginger
2   tablespoons soy sauce
1   teaspoon packed brown sugar
2   to 3 tablespoons peanut oil
1   cup cherry or grape tomatoes
      (optional)
4   green onions or scallions,
      white parts only, thinly sliced
2   tablespoons sweet rice wine
      (mirin)
1   teaspoon red chile paste
      (sambal oelek)
      Sesame seeds, toasted
      (optional)
      Hot cooked jasmine rice
      (optional)

1. Trim and halve green beans on the diagonal; set aside. Cut flank steak across the grain into thin slices; set aside. In a small bowl combine garlic and ginger; set aside. In another small bowl combine soy sauce and brown sugar; set aside.
2. In a very large skillet or wok heat 2 tablespoons oil over medium-high heat. Add green beans; cook and stir for 7 to 8 minutes or until beans are blistered and brown in spots. Add cherry tomatoes, if using. Cook and stir until wilted and slightly softened, 1 to 2 minutes. Transfer bean mixture to paper towels to drain. If necessary, add the remaining tablespoon of oil to skillet.

3. Add garlic-ginger mixture to the skillet; cook and stir for 30 seconds. Add half of the beef strips to the skillet. Cook and stir about 3 minutes or until beef browns. Transfer to bowl with a slotted spoon; repeat with the remaining beef. Return all beef to skillet. Stir in green onions, rice wine, chile paste, and the soy sauce-sugar mixture. Cook and stir for 1 minute; add green beans. Cook and stir until beans are heated through, about 2 minutes more.
4. If desired, sprinkle with toasted sesame seeds and serve with hot cooked rice.

EACH SERVING *312 cal, 16 g fat, 53 mg chol, 672 mg sodium, 15 g carb, 4 g fiber, 28 g pro.*

Quick Paprika Steaks with Tomato Gravy

This dish features a gravy in the sense that it's a liquid thickened with flour. Try to get the ripest, juiciest tomatoes you can. The more juice the tomatoes give off, the saucier the gravy. Earthy and flavored with paprika, garlic, and sage, this is the perfect dish for those early fall days when the weather cools and the last tomatoes of the season are coming off the vines.

START TO FINISH 25 minutes
MAKES 4 servings

¼ cup all-purpose flour
1   teaspoon paprika
½   teaspoon salt
¼   to ½ teaspoon ground black pepper
4   4-ounce beef breakfast or skillet steaks, about ½ inch thick
3   tablespoons olive oil
2   ounces queso fresco or Monterey Jack cheese, thinly sliced
6   medium tomatoes, seeded and cut up
6   cloves garlic, chopped
1   to 2 tablespoons snipped fresh sage
¼   teaspoon salt
½   teaspoon ground black pepper
    Arugula (optional)

1. For steaks, in a shallow dish combine flour, paprika, ½ teaspoon salt, and ¼ to ½ teaspoon pepper. Dredge steaks in flour mixture (reserve any remaining flour mixture). In a very large skillet heat 1 tablespoon of the oil over medium-high heat. Reduce heat to medium. Cook steaks, uncovered, in hot oil for 4 to 5 minutes per side or until medium (160°F); top with cheese the last 2 minutes of cooking. Remove steaks from skillet; keep warm.

2. While steaks are cooking, place tomatoes in a food processor. Cover and pulse with several on-off turns until tomatoes are coarsely chopped.

3. For tomato gravy, in the same skillet heat the remaining 2 tablespoons olive oil over medium heat. Add garlic; cook and stir about 1 minute or until garlic is golden. Stir in the tomatoes, sage, ¼ teaspoon salt, ½ teaspoon pepper, and any remaining flour mixture. Bring to boiling; reduce heat. Simmer, uncovered, about 5 minutes or until desired consistency. If desired, place a small handful of arugula on each plate. Place steaks on plates. Spoon some of the tomato gravy over steaks; pass remaining gravy.

EACH SERVING *310 cal, 16 g fat, 67 mg chol, 551 mg sodium, 16 g carb, 3 g fiber, 26 g pro.*

Aromatic Beef Stew with Butternut Squash

As hot as it is in North Africa year-round, Moroccan cooks sure know a thing or two about making tasty and warming stews. A *tagine* refers to both the slow-braised melanges of meats, vegetables, and spices—and to the cone-shape pot in which they are cooked. Serve this Moroccan-spiced stew with couscous (another North African specialty) to soak up the delicious sauce.

PREP **40 minutes**
COOK **35 minutes**
MAKES **6 servings**

2   teaspoons olive oil
1   pound beef stew meat (round or chuck), cut into 1-inch cubes
1   cup chopped onion (1 large)
1   tablespoon minced fresh ginger
2   cloves garlic, minced
1   pound butternut squash, peeled and cut into 1½-inch cubes (about 2½ cups)
1   14.5-ounce can no-salt-added diced tomatoes, undrained
1   8-ounce can no-salt-added tomato sauce
1½ cups lower-sodium beef broth
1½ teaspoons ground cumin
1   teaspoon ground cinnamon
½   teaspoon crushed red pepper
    Salt (optional)
3   cups cooked whole wheat couscous
¼   cup sliced almonds, toasted*
1   to 2 tablespoons coarsely chopped fresh parsley

1. In 4-quart Dutch oven heat oil over medium-high heat. Add beef. Cook about 5 minutes or until browned on all sides. Remove beef. Add onion to drippings in Dutch oven. Cook about 6 minutes or until tender and translucent, stirring often. Add ginger and garlic. Cook and stir for 1 minute more.

2. Return beef to pan. Stir in squash, undrained tomatoes, tomato sauce, beef broth, cumin, cinnamon, and crushed red pepper. Bring to boiling; reduce heat. Cover and simmer for 35 to 40 minutes or until beef is tender. If desired, season with salt.

3. Serve stew in bowls with couscous. Sprinkle with almonds and parsley.

*Tip Toast almonds in a dry skillet over medium-high heat about 2 minutes or until golden brown, stirring frequently.

EACH SERVING *421 cal, 11 g fat, 29 mg chol, 206 mg sodium, 57 g carb, 10 g fiber, 25 g pro.*

Short Ribs with Port Wine, Apples, Figs, and Onions

This braised dish combines ingredients that straddle the seasons. In late summer and early fall, figs are at their succulent best—and in early fall the first at-peak apples and onions are coming into the markets. Make this on a leisurely weekend, when you can putter around the house and take in the delicious aromas emanating from your oven. Serve with hot cooked polenta or spaetzle.

PREP **20 minutes**
COOK **23 minutes**
BROIL **15 minutes**
BAKE **2 hours 35 minutes**
STAND **10 minutes**
OVEN **350°F**
MAKES **10 servings**

1   tablespoon olive oil
1   medium sweet Vidalia onion or other sweet onion, thinly sliced
1   medium red onion, thinly sliced
1   cup port
¼   cup tomato paste
2   sprigs fresh thyme
1   teaspoon salt
½   cup water
5   pounds meaty beef short ribs
2   tablespoons Worcestershire sauce
1½   teaspoons freshly ground black pepper
5   small apples, halved and, if desired, cored
5   fresh figs, halved or quartered

1. In a large skillet heat olive oil over medium-low heat; add Vidalia and red onions. Cover and cook about 15 minutes or until onions are very tender, stirring occasionally. Whisk in port, tomato paste, thyme sprigs, and ½ teaspoon of the salt. Simmer, uncovered, for 8 to 10 minutes more or until liquid is reduced by about half. Stir in the water.
2. Meanwhile, preheat broiler. Place ribs on a broiler pan, bone sides down. Brush ribs with Worcestershire sauce; sprinkle with the pepper and the remaining ½ teaspoon salt. Broil about 4 inches from the heat for 15 to 20 minutes or until well browned, turning to brown all sides evenly. Preheat oven to 350°F.

3. Transfer ribs to a 5- to 6-quart Dutch oven. Pour onion mixture over ribs.
4. Cover and bake for 2¼ hours. Add apples. Bake, covered, for 20 to 25 minutes or just until apples are tender and meat pulls easily from the bone. Stir in figs. Let stand for 10 minutes before serving. Skim fat from cooking juices and serve with meat and fruit.

EACH SERVING *676 cal, 51 g fat, 114 mg chol, 402 mg sodium, 24 g carb, 4 g fiber, 25 g pro.*

Caramelized Pork with Melon

This is your go-to recipe for those times when you have a melon so ripe that it can't wait a minute longer to be eaten—and a schedule that requires that dinner can't wait another minute to be made. The sweet-spicy sauce of pureed melon and hoisin sauce pairs perfectly with the pork chops and crunchy cabbage.

START TO FINISH **25 minutes**
MAKES **4 servings**

1   small cantaloupe
¼   cup orange juice
3   tablespoons hoisin sauce
4   pork loin rib chops, cut ½ inch thick
     Salt and ground black pepper
1   tablespoon vegetable oil
3   green onions or scallions, thinly sliced
     Shredded napa cabbage (optional)

1. Remove rind and seeds from cantaloupe; chop. In a food processor or blender combine 2 cups of the chopped melon and orange juice. Cover and process or blend until smooth. Transfer ½ cup of the pureed melon to a small bowl; stir in hoisin sauce. Strain remaining puree and reserve the juice; discard solids.
2. Sprinkle chops lightly with salt and pepper; brush generously with some of the hoisin mixture. In a very large skillet heat oil over medium-high heat. Add chops to skillet; cook for 6 to 8 minutes or until well browned and only a trace of pink remains (160°F), turning once. Remove chops from skillet.
3. Meanwhile, combine the remaining chopped melon, the strained juice, and the green onions; set aside.

4. For sauce, add the remaining hoisin mixture to skillet; cook and stir until heated through. Spoon sauce onto serving plates. Top each with a chop. Add chopped melon mixture to skillet to warm slightly; spoon over chops. If desired, serve with shredded napa cabbage.
EACH SERVING *327 cal, 10 g fat, 117 mg chol, 452 mg sodium, 19 g carb, 2 g fiber, 39 g pro.*

Pork Roast with Baby Artichokes *also pictured page 68*

Three types of artichokes appear in spring: large globe artichokes, small artichokes, and baby artichokes. It is difficult to tell the difference between the latter two. Baby artichokes have no fuzzy "choke" inside, which makes them a breeze to prepare. Small artichokes could have a choke. If so, dig it out with a spoon after you cut it in half.

PREP **20 minutes**
ROAST **1 hour 5 minutes**
STAND **15 minutes**
OVEN **350°F**
MAKES **8 to 10 servings**

¼   cup snipped fresh rosemary
¼   cup olive oil
6   cloves garlic, minced
½   teaspoon salt
½   teaspoon ground black pepper
1½ pounds tiny new potatoes, halved
1   3- to 4-pound boneless single loin pork roast
6   to 8 baby artichokes
1   tablespoon lemon juice
2   cups baby carrots with tops

1. Preheat oven to 350°F. In a small bowl combine rosemary, olive oil, garlic, salt, and pepper. In a large bowl toss together the potatoes and half of the olive oil mixture; set aside.
2. Place the pork roast on a rack in a shallow roasting pan. Spread the remaining olive oil mixture over the roast. Arrange the potato mixture around the roast. Insert an oven-going meat thermometer into center of roast.
3. Roast, uncovered, for 45 minutes. Meanwhile, wash artichokes; trim stems and remove loose outer leaves. Cut off ½ inch from top of each artichoke. Cut each artichoke into quarters lengthwise. Place the artichoke quarters in a medium bowl; toss with lemon juice. In a covered large saucepan cook artichokes and carrots in lightly salted boiling water for 10 minutes; drain.
4. Add artichokes and carrots to the roasting pan, stirring to combine with potatoes. Roast for 20 to 40 minutes more or until meat thermometer registers 145°F and vegetables are tender, stirring vegetables occasionally. Remove roasting pan from oven. Cover roast and vegetables with foil; let stand for 15 minutes before slicing roast.
EACH SERVING *385 cal, 15 g fat, 93 mg chol, 239 mg sodium, 20 g carb, 4 g fiber, 40 g pro.*

Mustard-Rubbed Pork Loin with Rhubarb Sauce

More than any other meat, pork pairs most successfully with fruit— peaches, pineapple, and apples are among the choices. Pork also takes kindly to the sweet-tart flavor of rhubarb. Although rhubarb is botanically a vegetable, it is really only eaten as a fruit. This rhubarb-based sauce is delicious with the savory, crisp-skinned roasted pork—and pretty in pink too.

PREP **30 minutes**
ROAST **45 minutes**
OVEN **325°F**
MAKES **8 to 10 servings**

1   2- to 2½-pound boneless pork top loin roast (single loin)
¼   cup Dijon mustard
1   tablespoon snipped fresh rosemary
6   to 12 cloves garlic, minced
½   teaspoon salt
¼   teaspoon ground black pepper
3   cups sliced rhubarb (about 1 pound)
⅓   cup orange juice
1   tablespoon cider vinegar
⅓   to ½ cup sugar

1. Preheat oven to 350°F. Trim fat from meat. Score top and bottom of meat in a diamond pattern by making shallow diagonal cuts at 1-inch intervals. For rub, in a small bowl combine mustard, rosemary, garlic, salt, and pepper. Spread mixture evenly over all sides of meat; rub in with your fingers.

2. Roast for 45 to 60 minutes or until the thermometer registers 145°F. Remove roast to a platter and cover with foil. Let stand while preparing rhubarb sauce.

3. For rhubarb sauce, in a medium saucepan stir rhubarb, orange juice, vinegar, and sugar. Bring to boiling; reduce heat. Cover and simmer about 15 minutes or until rhubarb is very tender.

4. To serve, slice the roast and serve with warm rhubarb sauce.

Grilling Directions For a charcoal grill, arrange medium coals around a drip pan. Test for medium-low heat above pan. Place meat on grill rack over drip pan. Cover and grill for 45 minutes to 1 hour or until an instant-read thermometer inserted in center of meat registers 145°F. (For a gas grill, preheat grill. Reduce heat to medium-low. Adjust for indirect cooking. Grill as above, except place meat on a rack in a roasting pan; place pan on grill rack.) Remove meat from grill. Cover with foil; let stand while preparing rhubarb sauce.

EACH SERVING *195 cal, 8 g fat, 73 mg chol, 364 mg sodium, 13 g carb, 1 g fiber, 17 g pro.*

Roast Pork Loin with Pears, Thyme, and Shallots

Ingredients are added to the roasting pan sequentially in order to ensure that each one is perfectly cooked. The shallots and pork cook for nearly an hour, then the pears are added. And a combination of mustard, honey, apple juice, and fresh thyme coats and glazes the shallots and pears as they finish cooking.

PREP **25 minutes**
ROAST **1 hour 20 minutes**
STAND **15 minutes**
OVEN **325°F**
MAKES **6 to 8 servings**

1	2- to 2½-pound boneless pork top loin roast (single loin) Salt and ground black pepper
4	shallots, halved
3	firm ripe red pears, such as red Anjou
1	tablespoon olive oil
¼	cup stone-ground mustard
¼	cup honey
2	tablespoons apple juice
2	tablespoons snipped fresh thyme

1. Preheat oven to 325°F. Trim fat from roast. Generously sprinkle meat with salt and pepper. Place roast in a shallow roasting pan. Arrange the shallots around the meat. Roast, uncovered, for 50 minutes.

2. Meanwhile, halve, core, and slice pears lengthwise into ½-inch slices. In a large bowl toss pears with olive oil. If desired, sprinkle with salt and pepper. Arrange pears in a single layer around meat in roasting pan. Roast for 10 minutes more.

3. In a small bowl combine mustard, honey, apple juice, and 1 tablespoon of the thyme. Pour mixture over pears and shallots in roasting pan; toss to coat. Roast for 20 minutes more or until an instant-read meat thermometer inserted in center of meat registers 145°F, stirring pear mixture once. Let meat stand for 15 minutes before slicing. Serve with pear mixture. Sprinkle with the remaining 1 tablespoon thyme.

EACH SERVING *329 cal, 12 g fat, 81 mg chol, 375 mg sodium, 27 g carb, 3 g fiber, 28 g pro.*

Pulled Pork with Rhubarb Barbecue Sauce and Kohlrabi Slaw

The homemade Rhubarb Barbecue Sauce takes a few minutes to make—and so does the slaw—but the pork shoulder can cook unattended and fuss-free for up to 10 hours in the slow cooker. If you like, make the barbecue sauce up to 3 days ahead.

PREP **30 minutes**
COOK **20 minutes**
SLOW COOK **9 to 10 hours (low) or 4½ to 5 hours (high) + 1 hour (low)**
MAKES **8 to 10 sandwiches**

1   2½- to 3-pound pork shoulder roast
1   teaspoon dried thyme, crushed
1   teaspoon paprika
½   teaspoon garlic-pepper seasoning
1   large onion, sliced
½   cup reduced-sodium beef or chicken broth
1   recipe Rhubarb Barbecue Sauce
2   cups shredded, peeled kohlrabi (2 small)
1   cup shredded carrots (2 medium)
1½ tablespoons cider vinegar or seasoned rice wine vinegar
1   tablespoon vegetable oil
1½ teaspoons sugar
    Salt and ground black pepper
8   to 10 whole grain hamburger buns or kaiser rolls, split

1. Trim fat from meat. In a small bowl combine thyme, paprika, and garlic-pepper seasoning; rub mixture all over meat. Place onion in a 3½- or 4-quart slow cooker. If necessary, cut meat to fit in the cooker. Place meat in cooker. Pour broth over meat. Cover and cook on low-heat setting for 9 to 10 hours or high-heat setting for 4½ to 5 hours.
2. Transfer meat to a cutting board. Using two forks, pull meat apart into shreds. Remove cooking liquid and onion from slow cooker. Skim fat from cooking liquid. Discard onion. Measure ¼ cup of the liquid. Return meat and the ¼ cup liquid to slow cooker. Measure ½ cup Rhubarb Barbecue Sauce and set aside. Stir the remaining barbecue sauce into the meat. If using high-heat setting, turn to low-heat setting. Cover and cook for 1 hour.
3. Meanwhile, for kohlrabi-carrot slaw, in a medium bowl combine kohlrabi and carrots. For dressing, in a small screw-top jar combine vinegar, oil, and sugar. Cover and shake to combine. Drizzle dressing over kohlrabi mixture; toss to combine. Season with salt and pepper. Serve immediately or cover and chill for up to 24 hours.

4. To serve, spoon meat mixture onto bun bottoms. Top each with some of the reserved ½ cup Rhubarb Barbecue Sauce and kohlrabi-carrot slaw. Add bun tops.

Rhubarb Barbecue Sauce In a medium saucepan combine 3 cups sliced rhubarb, 1 cup ketchup, ½ cup apple-cranberry juice, ⅓ to ½ cup packed brown sugar, 2 tablespoons cider vinegar, 1 tablespoon coarse-ground mustard, and ¼ teaspoon crushed red pepper. Bring to boiling; reduce heat. Simmer, uncovered, about 20 minutes or until rhubarb is very tender and sauce is slightly thickened, stirring occasionally. Mash rhubarb slightly with a potato masher or back of a wooden spoon. (Sauce can be cooled and stored in a covered container in the refrigerator for up to 3 days.)

EACH SANDWICH *340 cal, 6 g fat, 60 mg chol, 775 mg sodium, 46 g carb, 5 g fiber, 26 g pro.*

Skillet Pork Chops with Butter Beans, Peas, and Charred Scallions

This dish features simple ingredients and the fresh flavors of lemon and herbs that are given a boost by the cooking method. The chops are seared in a skillet to create a beautiful crust, then finished in the oven. As the meat roasts, the pan juices mingle with the scallions and help flavor the butter beans, baby spinach, and peas when they are added right before serving.

PREP **25 minutes**
ROAST **10 minutes**
OVEN **400°F**
MAKES **4 servings**

2   tablespoons snipped fresh Italian (flat-leaf) parsley
2   tablespoons snipped fresh tarragon
2   teaspoons finely shredded lemon peel
¼   teaspoon salt
¼   teaspoon ground black pepper
1   tablespoon olive oil
4   pork loin rib chops, cut 1¼ inches thick
6   scallions or green onions, cut into 2- inch pieces
1   15.5- to 16-ounce can butter beans, rinsed and drained
1   5-ounce package fresh baby spinach
1   cup shelled fresh English peas or frozen peas, thawed
1   tablespoon lemon juice
1   lemon, cut into wedges

1. Preheat oven to 400°F. In a small bowl combine parsley, tarragon, lemon peel, salt, and pepper. In a very large ovenproof skillet heat oil over medium-high heat. Rub chops with herb mixture. Add chops to skillet; cook about 6 minutes or until browned, turning once. Stir scallions into skillet around chops. Transfer skillet to oven. Roast, uncovered, for 10 to 12 minutes or until an instant-read thermometer inserted into chops registers 145°F.

2. Remove chops from skillet; cover to keep warm. Stir butter beans, baby spinach, peas, and lemon juice into scallions in skillet. Cook and stir until heated through and peas are tender. Serve vegetable mixture with chops and lemon wedges.

EACH CHOP + ¾ CUP VEGETABLES *467 cal, 22 g fat, 99 mg chol, 603 mg sodium, 27 g carb, 8 g fiber, 43 g pro.*

Stuffed Poblano Chiles with Chorizo Gravy

This fresh twist on chiles rellenos—the classic Mexican dish of poblano peppers stuffed with cheese, then batter-dipped and fried—features a grilled-vegetable and Mexican cheese filling. The peppers are grilled and served with a kicky chorizo gravy. Oaxaca (wuh-HAH-kuh) cheese is a mild melting cheese similar to Monterey Jack. Look for it at Mexican markets.

PREP **20 minutes**
COOK **21 minutes**
GRILL **15 minutes**
STAND **10 minutes**
MAKES **4 servings**

1 pound tomatoes, coarsely chopped
½ cup chopped onion (1 medium)
½ cup water
2 cloves garlic, minced
6 ounces uncooked bulk chorizo sausage
2 tablespoons all-purpose flour
¼ cup whipping cream
2 ears fresh sweet corn
4 fresh poblano peppers (see tip, page 55)
1 small zucchini, quartered lengthwise
1 cup shredded Oaxaca cheese or Monterey Jack cheese (4 ounces)
1 teaspoon ground cumin
¼ teaspoon salt
  Nonstick cooking spray
  Sour cream (optional)

1. For tomato sauce, in a large skillet combine tomatoes, onion, the water, and garlic. Bring to boiling; reduce heat. Cover and simmer about 10 minutes or until onions are tender. Remove skillet from heat; cool slightly. Transfer half of the mixture to a food processor or blender. Cover and process or blend until nearly smooth; pour into a bowl. Repeat with remaining tomato mixture. Press through a fine-mesh sieve. Discard seeds and solids. Set tomato sauce aside.

2. For chorizo gravy, in the same skillet cook chorizo over medium heat for 5 to 7 minutes or until browned, stirring to break up meat as it cooks. Drain off fat. Stir flour into sausage. Add whipping cream and the tomato sauce. Cook and stir until thickened and bubbly. Cook for 1 minute more. Remove skillet from heat.

3. Remove husks from the ears of corn. Scrub with a stiff brush to remove silks; rinse.

4. For a charcoal or gas grill, place corn, peppers, and zucchini on the rack of a covered grill directly over medium heat. Grill for 10 minutes or until peppers are charred and corn and zucchini are tender,

turning occasionally. Place peppers in a bowl; cover and let stand for 10 minutes.

5. For stuffing, cut corn kernels from cobs; place kernels in a large bowl. Cut zucchini into pieces the size of corn kernels. Add zucchini to corn. Stir in half the cheese, the cumin, and salt; set aside.

6. Peel skins away from peppers. Discard skins. Cut a lengthwise slit in each pepper. Remove ribs and seeds, leaving stems intact. Spoon stuffing into peppers. Coat a 9×9×2-inch disposable foil pan with cooking spray. Place peppers in pan; sprinkle with the remaining cheese. Place pan on grill rack over medium heat. Cover and grill for 5 to 10 minutes or until filling is heated through and cheese is melted.

7. To serve, divide chorizo gravy among 4 plates. Place a stuffed poblano pepper on each. If desired, top with sour cream.

EACH SERVING *472 cal, 30 g fat, 82 mg chol, 700 mg sodium, 30 g carb, 3 g fiber, 24 g pro.*

Bourbon-Soaked Pork Chops with Squash Hash

The sweetness of the maple syrup and squash, the spiciness of the hot chiles, and the smoky, woodsy flavor of the bourbon add up to a flavor combination that is the essence of fall. Be sure the marinade boils for a good 5 minutes before drizzling it over the chops and hash to ensure that it is safe to eat.

PREP **40 minutes**
ROAST **35 minutes**
STAND **5 minutes**
OVEN **400°F**
MAKES **4 servings**

4 pork loin chops (bone-in), cut 1 inch thick (about 3 pounds)
⅓ cup bourbon or beef broth
¼ cup pure maple syrup
2 tablespoons soy sauce
2 tablespoons tomato paste
1 tablespoon lime juice
1 serrano pepper, seeded and finely chopped*
1 small butternut squash, peeled and cut into ¾-inch pieces (3 cups)
¾ cup chopped red or green sweet pepper (1 medium)
⅔ cup sliced leeks
4 tablespoons olive oil
1 jalapeño pepper, seeded and finely chopped*
¼ teaspoon salt
¼ teaspoon ground black pepper

1. Preheat oven to 400°F. Trim fat from chops. Place chops in a large resealable plastic bag set in a shallow dish. For marinade, in a small bowl whisk together bourbon, maple syrup, soy sauce, tomato paste, lime juice, and serrano pepper. Pour marinade over chops in bag, turning bag to coat evenly. Marinate in the refrigerator while preparing squash hash, turning bag occasionally.

2. For squash hash, in a large bowl combine the squash, sweet pepper, leeks, 3 tablespoons of the olive oil, the jalapeño pepper, salt, and black pepper. Spread the squash mixture in a 15×10×1-inch baking pan. Roast, uncovered, for 25 to 30 minutes or until vegetables are tender and browned, stirring twice.

3. Meanwhile, drain chops, reserving marinade. In a very large skillet heat the remaining 1 tablespoon oil over medium-high heat. Add chops to hot oil; cook for 6 to 8 minutes or until browned, turning once. Place chops in a shallow baking pan. Place chops in oven on the rack below squash.

Roast for 10 to 12 minutes or until an instant-read thermometer inserted in chops registers 145°F. Let chops stand for 5 minutes before serving.

4. For sauce, place the marinade in a small saucepan. Bring to boiling; reduce heat. Simmer, uncovered, about 5 minutes or until reduced by half (⅓ cup). Transfer chops and squash mixture to serving plates. Drizzle chops with sauce.

*Tip Because hot chile peppers contain volatile oils that can burn your skin and eyes, avoid contact with chiles as much as possible. When working with chile peppers, wear plastic or rubber gloves. If your bare hands do touch the chile peppers, wash your hands well with soap and water.

EACH CHOP + ¾ CUP HASH
565 cal, 23 g fat, 114 mg chol, 834 mg sodium, 32 g carb, 3 g fiber, 47 g pro.

Aromatic Pork with Baby Zucchini and Figs

Fresh figs are so delicate and juicy that when they are being eaten as part of a cooked dish, they require only the slightest bit of warming through to heighten their flavor. More than a very brief exposure to heat causes them to break down and disappear.

PREP **20 minutes**
COOK **15 minutes**
MAKES **4 servings**

¾ teaspoon ground cumin
¾ teaspoon paprika
½ teaspoon whole black peppercorns, crushed
2 cloves garlic, minced
¼ teaspoon salt
12 ounces pork tenderloin
6 ounces pearl onions, peeled and halved (about 12)
½ teaspoon cardamom seeds (without pods), crushed
1 bay leaf
½ teaspoon salt
½ cup water
12 ounces baby zucchini, ends trimmed (about 24)
1 tablespoon olive oil
8 fresh figs, halved

1. In a small bowl combine cumin, paprika, crushed peppercorns, garlic, and the ¼ teaspoon salt. Trim fat from pork. Cut pork crosswise into ¾-inch slices. Rub spice mixture over both sides of pork slices; set aside.

2. In a large nonstick skillet combine onions, crushed cardamom seeds, bay leaf, and the ½ teaspoon salt. Add the water. Bring to boiling; reduce heat. Cover and simmer for 5 minutes. Add zucchini. Simmer, covered, for 3 to 4 minutes or just until zucchini and onions are tender. Discard bay leaf. Transfer mixture to a bowl; keep warm. Carefully wipe skillet with paper towels.

3. In the dry skillet heat oil over medium-high heat. Add pork slices. Cook about 6 minutes or just until pork is slightly pink in center, turning once. Remove pork from skillet; keep warm. Add figs to the skillet. Cook about 1 minute or until heated through.

4. To serve, divide pork among 4 plates. Serve with zucchini mixture and figs.

EACH SERVING *247 cal, 6 g fat, 50 mg chol, 475 mg sodium, 27 g carb, 5 g fiber, 24 g pro.*

Braised Collards and Black-Eyed Peas with Andouille Sausage and Couscous

Two pounds of collard greens makes a very large pile—but don't be intimidated. The high water content of collards means they will shrink down considerably as they are cooked. This spin on a traditional Southern dish includes a handful of golden raisins for a bit of sweetness to complement the spiciness of the sausage and cayenne pepper.

START TO FINISH 45 minutes
MAKES 6 servings

1   14-ounce package fully cooked andouille sausage, cut into 1-inch pieces
½   cup water
2   tablespoons olive oil
1   cup chopped onion (1 large)
6   cloves garlic, minced
1   cup chicken broth
2   pounds collard greens, cut into 1-inch strips
1   11-ounce container fresh black-eyed peas or one 11-ounce package frozen black-eyed peas (2 cups), thawed
½   cup golden raisins
2   tablespoons snipped fresh mint
2   tablespoons snipped fresh cilantro
1   tablespoon lemon juice
¼   teaspoon cayenne pepper
¼   teaspoon ground cumin
¼   teaspoon ground cinnamon
1   10-ounce package couscous

1. In a very large skillet combine sausage and the water. Cook over medium-high heat about 8 minutes or until sausage is browned and the water evaporates. Remove sausage from skillet; set aside.

2. In the same skillet heat oil over medium-high heat. Add onion; cook for 4 to 5 minutes or until tender. Add garlic; cook and stir for 1 minute. Carefully add broth to the hot skillet. Add collard greens in small batches, cooking and stirring just until greens are wilted.

3. Add black-eyed peas, raisins, mint, cilantro, lemon juice, cayenne pepper, cumin, and cinnamon to greens in skillet; mix well. Cover and cook over medium heat for 10 minutes, stirring occasionally. Return sausage to skillet and heat through.

4. Meanwhile, cook couscous according to package directions. Serve collard greens mixture over couscous.

EACH SERVING *619 cal, 23 g fat, 41 mg chol, 832 mg sodium, 78 g carb, 12 g fiber, 26 g pro.*

Moroccan Lamb Chops with Couscous and Minted Kumquats

Tiny kumquats stand alone among citrus fruits because the whole thing is edible—skin and all (though you might want to put the seeds to the side as you eat). Their sweet-tart flavor is a lovely complement to the intense spices in this aromatic dish. Use lamb loin chops (shown here) or rib chops, which have the shapely Frenched bone attached.

START TO FINISH **35 minutes**
MAKES **4 servings**

1½   cups water
1   cup tricolor or plain Israeli (large pearl) couscous
1   cup raisins
4   tablespoons thinly sliced green onions or scallions (2)
1½   teaspoons salt
3   tablespoons snipped fresh mint
1   tablespoon ground coriander
2   teaspoons ground cumin
1½   teaspoons ground cinnamon
8   lamb rib or loin chops, cut 1 inch thick (about 1½ to 2 pounds)
2   teaspoons olive oil
1½   cups kumquats, halved
½   cup orange juice
3   tablespoons sugar

1. In a medium saucepan bring water to boiling. Stir in couscous, raisins, 2 tablespoons of the green onions, and ½ teaspoon of the salt. Return to boiling; reduce heat. Cover and simmer for 8 to 10 minutes, stirring occasionally. Remove from heat.
2. Meanwhile, in a small bowl combine 1 tablespoon of the mint, the coriander, cumin, cinnamon, and the remaining 1 teaspoon salt. Sprinkle spice mixture on both sides of lamb chops; rub in with your fingers. In a very large skillet heat olive oil over medium-high heat. Add chops to skillet. Reduce heat to medium and cook for 10 to 12 minutes or until desired doneness, turning once.

3. For sauce, in a medium saucepan combine kumquats, orange juice, sugar, and the remaining 2 tablespoons green onions. Bring to boiling; reduce heat. Simmer, uncovered, until liquid is reduced and almost syrupy, about 10 minutes. Remove from heat. Cool slightly. Stir in the remaining 2 tablespoons mint.
4. Serve lamb chops over couscous. Spoon sauce over all.

EACH SERVING *592 cal, 13 g fat, 83 mg chol, 956 mg sodium, 89 g carb, 11 g fiber, 33 g pro.*

Shepherd's Pie with Root Vegetable Mash

On a cold fall or winter night, this hearty casserole is pure comfort. A savory filling of lamb and beef simmered in red wine and seasonings is crowned with a creamy, crispy breadcrumb-topped mash of celery root, sweet potato, and parsnips spiked with horseradish.

PREP **45 minutes**
BAKE **30 minutes**
STAND **10 minutes**
OVEN **375°F**
MAKES **8 servings**

1   large celery root (celeriac), peeled and cut into 1-inch pieces
2   parsnips, peeled and cut into 1-inch pieces
1   large sweet potato, peeled and cut into 1-inch pieces
½   cup milk
3   tablespoons butter
1   tablespoon prepared horseradish
½   teaspoon salt
1   pound lean ground lamb
8   ounces lean ground beef
½   cup chopped onion (1 medium)
2   cloves garlic, minced
⅔   cup shredded carrot (1 large)
½   cup dry red wine
¼   cup tomato paste
2   teaspoons Worcestershire sauce
1   teaspoon ground black pepper
3   teaspoons snipped fresh thyme
½   teaspoon freshly grated nutmeg or ¼ teaspoon ground nutmeg
½   cup fresh bread crumbs
2   teaspoons olive oil

1. Preheat oven to 375°F. For the vegetable mash, in a covered medium saucepan cook celery root in enough lightly salted boiling water to cover for 5 minutes. Add parsnips and sweet potato. Cook, covered, about 20 minutes more or until tender; drain. Mash with a potato masher or beat with an electric mixer on low. Add milk, butter, horseradish, and salt. Mash or beat until light and fluffy. Cover to keep warm.

2. Meanwhile, for the filling, in a large skillet cook the lamb, beef, onion, and garlic over medium heat until meat is browned, stirring to break up meat as it cooks. Drain if necessary. Stir in carrot, wine, tomato paste, Worcestershire sauce, pepper, 1 teaspoon of the thyme, and the nutmeg. Bring to boiling; reduce heat. Simmer, uncovered, for 5 minutes.

3. Transfer filling to a 2-quart square baking dish, spreading evenly. Spread vegetable mash over filling in an even layer. In a small bowl toss together the bread crumbs, the remaining 2 teaspoons thyme, and the olive oil. Sprinkle over vegetable mash.

4. Bake, uncovered, for 30 to 35 minutes or until heated through and bread crumbs are toasted. Let stand for 10 minutes before serving.

EACH SERVING *394 cal, 22 g fat, 72 mg chol, 459 mg sodium, 28 g carb, 5 g fiber, 19 g pro.*

Ham and Asparagus-Stuffed Chicken

The savory filling in this chicken dish is a homemade deviled ham—finely chopped ham with mayo, onion, tarragon, Worcestershire, vinegar, mustard, cayenne, and a little black pepper. It's good enough to eat spread on crackers—but even better stuffed into meaty chicken breasts along with tender spring asparagus.

PREP **30 minutes**
COOK **20 minutes**
MAKES **4 servings**

1   cup diced cooked ham, rind removed
2   tablespoons mayonnaise
1   tablespoon finely chopped onion
1   tablespoon snipped fresh tarragon or parsley
1   teaspoon Worcestershire sauce
1   teaspoon cider vinegar
1   teaspoon Dijon or whole-grain mustard
⅛   teaspoon cayenne pepper
      Freshly ground black pepper
4   large skinless, boneless chicken breast halves (about 2 pounds)
8   ounces green, white, and/or purple asparagus, trimmed
      Salt and ground black pepper
1   tablespoon olive oil

1. For deviled ham, in a food processor combine ham, mayonnaise, onion, tarragon, Worcestershire, vinegar, mustard, cayenne pepper, and a few grinds of black pepper. Cover and process until ham is very finely chopped and almost smooth, scraping processor bowl as needed. Set aside while butterflying chicken breasts (see Step 2) or cover and chill for up to 2 days.

2. To butterfly chicken breasts, place each breast half on a flat surface or cutting board. With palm on chicken and fingers away from blade, cut through one side of the chicken breast to within ¾ inch of the opposite side. Open to lie flat. Pound chicken with flat side of meat mallet to ¼-inch thickness.

3. To stuff chicken breasts, spread ¼ cup of the deviled ham on half of each chicken piece. Top with 3 to 5 asparagus spears. Fold unstuffed half over stuffing. Tie closed with 100%-cotton kitchen string. Sprinkle chicken with salt and black pepper.

4. In a very large skillet heat oil over medium heat. Cook chicken in hot oil for 10 to 12 minutes per side or until browned and no longer pink (170°F).

EACH SERVING *399 cal, 17 g fat, 167 mg chol, 929 mg sodium, 3 g carb, 1 g fiber, 54 g pro.*

Chicken Sausage, Fingerling Potato, and Leek Packets

These sausage-and-potato packets are perfect for camping or tailgating. Make them at home, then keep them cold in a refrigerator or cooler until it's time to grill. Leave the packets intact when you serve them so that each diner can enjoy the wonderful smell that wafts out when they're opened.

PREP **25 minutes**
GRILL **30 minutes**
MAKES **4 servings**

½   teaspoon fennel seeds, crushed
½   teaspoon sea salt
½   teaspoon paprika
½   teaspoon garlic-pepper seasoning
1   12-ounce package fully cooked poultry sausage (chicken and apple, spinach and feta, or Italian-style)
2   leeks
1   pound fingerling potatoes, quartered lengthwise
2   tablespoons olive oil
1   tablespoon snipped fresh sage or thyme or 1 teaspoon dried sage or thyme, crushed

1. For seasoning mixture, in a small bowl stir together crushed fennel seeds, sea salt, paprika, and garlic-pepper seasoning; set aside.

2. For a charcoal or a gas grill, place the poultry sausage on the rack of a covered grill directly over medium heat. Grill for 5 to 7 minutes or until sausages are browned and heated through, turning once halfway through grilling. Transfer sausages to a cutting board and cool slightly. Cut into ½-inch slices; set aside.

3. Meanwhile, fold four 24×12-inch pieces of foil in half to make a double thickness of foil so each measures 12×12 inches. Cut leeks in half lengthwise and wash thoroughly in cool running water; slice white and green parts of each leek crosswise into ¼-inch pieces. Divide potato wedges and leeks among the pieces of foil, placing vegetables in the center. Drizzle with olive oil and sprinkle with seasoning mixture. Top with sausage slices. For each packet, bring up opposite edges of foil and seal with a double fold. Fold remaining edges to completely enclose the vegetables, leaving space for steam to build.

4. Grill on the rack of the covered grill directly over medium heat about 25 minutes or until potatoes and leeks are tender, turning packets over once halfway through grilling. Carefully open packets and sprinkle with the fresh sage.

EACH SERVING *336 cal, 14 g fat, 60 mg chol, 789 mg sodium, 37 g carb, 4 g fiber, 17 g pro.*

Lime and Tangerine Chicken Breasts

Even the depth of winter has a bright spot. It's found in the produce section in the form of citrus fruits—oranges, grapefruits, lemons, limes, and tangerines—which are at peak during the winter months. This refreshing, quick-to-fix chicken dish will bring a splash of sunshine to your dinner table.

PREP 25 minutes
COOK 13 minutes
MAKES 6 servings

1   lime
2   tangerines
     Nonstick cooking spray
6   skinless, boneless chicken
     breast halves
     Ground black pepper
⅓   cup chicken broth
¼   cup sliced green onions or
     scallions (2)
1   teaspoon snipped fresh
     rosemary or basil or
     ¼ teaspoon dried rosemary
     or basil, crushed
1   tablespoon water
½   teaspoon cornstarch
3   cups hot cooked couscous
     or rice

1. Finely shred ½ teaspoon lime peel and 1 teaspoon tangerine peel; set aside. Halve lime and squeeze 1 tablespoon juice; set aside. Peel and section tangerines over a bowl to catch any juice; set aside.

2. Lightly coat a large skillet with cooking spray. Sprinkle chicken breasts lightly with pepper. Cook chicken in skillet over medium heat about 5 minutes or until browned, turning once. Add broth, green onions, rosemary, reserved lime and tangerine peels, and the 1 tablespoon lime juice. Bring to boiling; reduce heat. Cover and simmer about 8 minutes or until chicken is tender. Remove chicken from skillet; keep warm.

3. In a small bowl stir together the water and cornstarch. Add to juices in skillet. Cook and stir until thickened and bubbly. Cook and stir for 2 minutes more. Add tangerine sections and any juice; heat through. Pour sauce over chicken. Serve with couscous. If desired, garnish with lime wedges.

EACH SERVING *241 cal, 4 g fat, 60 mg chol, 98 mg sodium, 26 g carb, 1 g fiber, 24 g pro.*

Roast Chicken with Fiery Lemon Glaze

Honey balances the pucker from the lemon and the heat from cayenne in the glaze for this fabulous roast chicken. It's the main dish to make for a wintry Sunday supper when everyone is hanging around the house and can take in the wonderful aroma coming from the oven. Serve it with buttered green beans and sour cream mashed potatoes.

PREP 30 minutes
MARINATE 8 to 12 hours
ROAST 1 hour 30 minutes
STAND 15 minutes
OVEN 375°F
MAKES 8 servings

1   4- to 5-pound whole roasting chicken
4   to 6 small lemons
¼   cup olive oil
2   tablespoons snipped fresh parsley
4   cloves garlic, minced
1   teaspoon cayenne pepper
½   teaspoon salt
½   teaspoon ground black pepper
2   to 3 small lemons, halved or quartered (optional)
½   cup honey

1. Remove giblets from chicken if present. Place chicken in a resealable plastic bag set in a shallow dish. Slice 2 of the lemons; add to bag. Finely shred 2 teaspoons peel from the remaining lemons; set aside. Squeeze lemons to make ½ cup plus 2 tablespoons juice.
2. For marinade, in a small bowl combine the ½ cup lemon juice, the olive oil, parsley, garlic, ½ teaspoon of the cayenne pepper, the salt, and black pepper. Pour marinade over chicken; turn to coat. Seal bag. Marinate in the refrigerator for 8 to 12 hours, turning bag occasionally.
3. Adjust oven rack to lowest position. Preheat oven to 375°F. Let chicken stand at room temperature for 15 minutes. Drain chicken and set aside lemon slices; discard marinade. Pull neck skin to back and fasten with a skewer. Tie drumsticks to tail. Twist wing tips under back.
4. Place chicken, breast side up, on a rack in a shallow roasting pan. Cover with the reserved lemon slices. If desired, arrange lemon halves or quarters on rack around chicken. Roast on lowest rack, uncovered, for 1 hour.
5. Meanwhile, in small saucepan combine honey, the shredded lemon peel, the 2 tablespoons lemon juice, and the remaining ½ teaspoon cayenne pepper. Bring to boiling over medium heat, stirring occasionally. Remove from heat and set aside.
6. Cut string between drumsticks and reposition any lemon slices that have slid off of chicken. Continue roasting for 30 to 60 minutes more or until drumsticks move easily in their sockets and chicken is no longer pink (180°F), occasionally brushing with some of the honey mixture during the last 20 minutes of roasting. If lemons begin to darken, tent loosely with foil. Remove chicken from oven. Let stand for 15 minutes before slicing. Pass remaining honey glaze.
EACH SERVING *469 cal, 30 g fat, 116 mg chol, 257 mg sodium, 23 g carb, 2 g fiber, 29 g pro.*

Warm Glass Noodles with Edamame, Basil, and Chicken

Bean thread noodles are an Asian-style noodle most commonly made from mung bean starch. They are sometimes called cellophane or glass noodles because they have a translucent appearance when cooked. They come in dry form and require boiling to reconstitute before using in soups or stir-fries. They have a delightfully chewy consistency.

PREP 10 minutes
COOK 15 minutes
MAKES 4 servings

1	3.75-ounce package bean thread noodles
1½	cups frozen sweet soybeans (edamame)
½	cup soy sauce
⅓	cup thinly sliced green onions or scallions (3)
¼	cup chicken broth
2	tablespoons packed brown sugar
2	tablespoons toasted sesame oil
4	teaspoons grated fresh ginger
4	teaspoons sesame seeds, toasted*
2	cloves garlic, minced
3	cups shredded cooked chicken (about 1 pound)
½	cup small fresh basil leaves
	Carrot ribbons, for garnish (optional)
	Asian chili sauce (Sriracha sauce) (optional)

1. Cook noodles according to package directions, adding edamame during the last 1 minute of cooking. Drain and set aside.
2. Meanwhile, for sauce, in a medium bowl stir together soy sauce, green onions, chicken broth, brown sugar, sesame oil, ginger, sesame seeds, and garlic. Set aside.
3. Transfer noodles and edamame to a large serving bowl. Using clean kitchen shears, snip noodles into short lengths. Add chicken and basil; toss to mix. Pour sauce over the noodle mixture; toss to coat. If desired, garnish with carrot ribbons and serve with Asian chili sauce.

*Tip To toast sesame seeds, place seeds in a small skillet. Cook over medium heat about 2 minutes or until golden, stirring often so they don't burn.

EACH SERVING *327 cal, 13 g fat, 63 mg chol, 872 mg sodium, 26 g carb, 3 g fiber, 26 g pro.*

Chicken and Lentils in Apple-Curry Sauce

Garam masala—which translates from Hindi to mean "hot mixture"—is a blend of spices used extensively in North Indian cooking. Despite its name, it is not really hot at all. The heat refers to the sense of warmth it adds to the flavor of the dish and to the spirit of the person eating it. There are many variations of blends, but a typical garam masala might include black pepper, cinnamon, cloves, coriander, cumin, cardamom, chiles, fennel, mace, and nutmeg.

PREP 25 minutes
COOK 40 minutes
MAKES 6 servings

2   tablespoons olive oil
6   skinless, boneless chicken thighs
1   large onion, peeled, halved, and thinly sliced
4   cloves garlic, minced
1   tablespoon finely shredded fresh ginger
2   tablespoons tomato paste
1   tablespoon mild curry powder
1   teaspoon salt
1   teaspoon garam masala
3   cups reduced-sodium chicken broth
1½   cups lentils, rinsed and drained
3   red and/or green cooking apples, cored and cut into 1-inch pieces
2   5-ounce packages baby spinach
     Plain yogurt (optional)

1. In a very large skillet with a tight-fitting lid heat olive oil over medium-high heat. Add chicken thighs; cook for 4 to 6 minutes or until golden brown, turning once. Transfer chicken to a plate and set aside.

2. Add onion to skillet; cook and stir over medium heat for 3 minutes. Stir in garlic and ginger; cook for 1 minute more. Stir in tomato paste, curry powder, salt, and garam masala. Mix well. Add chicken broth and lentils; return chicken to skillet. Bring to boiling; reduce heat. Cover and simmer for 30 minutes.

3. Add apples to skillet. Cover and simmer about 10 minutes or until lentils are tender. Gradually stir in about 3 cups of the spinach. Divide remaining spinach among 4 shallow serving bowls. Add 1 chicken thigh to each bowl. Top with lentil mixture and, if desired, yogurt.

EACH SERVING *383 cal, 8 g fat, 66 mg chol, 812 mg sodium, 49 g carb, 19 g fiber, 30 g pro.*

Chicken with Melted Tomatoes

The tomatoes in this dish are cooked at a relatively low temperature—300°F—for 1½ to 2 hours. The low-and-slow cooking process causes most of the water in the tomatoes to evaporate, concentrating their natural flavors and sugars. It's a great way to rescue tomatoes that come off the vine a little under- or overripe.

PREP **15 minutes**
MARINATE **8 to 24 hours**
BAKE **1 hour 30 minutes**
GRILL **55 minutes**
OVEN **300°F**
MAKES **4 to 6 servings**

4   whole chicken legs (drumstick and thigh)
½   cup chopped scallions or green onions, white and green portions (about 4)
¼   cup olive oil
       Salt and ground black pepper
2   pounds medium tomatoes, cut up (about 7 cups)
3   tablespoons olive oil
¼   cup snipped fresh basil
¼   teaspoon salt
¼   teaspoon ground black pepper
       Lemon wedges (optional)
       Fresh basil (optional)

1. Skin chicken if desired. In a resealable plastic bag set in a shallow dish place chicken, scallions, and the ¼ cup olive oil. Sprinkle with salt and pepper. Turn chicken to coat in scallions. Cover and chill for at least 8 hours or overnight.

2. For melted tomatoes, preheat oven to 300°F. Place tomatoes in an even layer in a 3-quart baking dish. Drizzle with the 3 tablespoons olive oil. Sprinkle with basil, salt, and pepper. Bake, uncovered, for 1½ to 2 hours or until tomatoes are slightly dried and soft. Cool about 15 minutes.

3. For charcoal grill, arrange medium-hot coals around drip pan. Test for medium heat above the pan. Place chicken, bone sides down, on grill rack over drip pan. Cover and grill for 30 minutes. Turn chicken over; grill for 25 to 30 minutes more or until chicken is no longer pink (180°F). (For gas grill, preheat grill. Reduce heat to medium; adjust for indirect cooking. Grill as above.)

4. To serve, transfer melted tomatoes to a serving platter. Top with chicken. If desired, garnish with lemon wedges and sprinkle with small basil leaves.

Oven Method If desired, place the chicken in a 15×10×1-inch baking pan and bake in a 300°F oven with the melted tomatoes. (Bake the melted tomatoes on a lower oven rack.) Bake 1 hour 15 minutes to 1 hour 20 minutes or until chicken is no longer pink (180°F).

EACH SERVING *436 cal, 34 g fat, 139 mg chol, 280 mg sodium, 1 g carb, 0 g fiber, 31 g pro.*

Pan-Seared Chicken with Cherry-Tarragon Sauce

The intense licorice flavor of tarragon is often paired with chicken. Tarragon is also one of those ingredients that many people feel strongly about—one way or another. If not everyone at your table is a fan of tarragon, you can substitute fresh basil.

START TO FINISH **30 minutes**
MAKES **4 servings**

¼   cup all-purpose flour
2   teaspoons smoked paprika
1   teaspoon dry mustard
¼   teaspoon salt
¼   teaspoon ground black pepper
8   skinless, boneless chicken thighs
2   tablespoons olive oil
2   cups dark sweet cherries
2   tablespoons snipped fresh tarragon
3   cloves garlic, minced
1   cup dry red wine or cherry juice
½   cup chicken broth
2   tablespoons butter
    Salt and ground black pepper
2   cups hot cooked couscous, rice, or pasta
    Snipped fresh tarragon (optional)

1. In a shallow dish combine flour, paprika, mustard, salt, and pepper. Coat chicken with flour mixture. In a very large skillet heat oil over medium-high heat. Add chicken; cook for 8 to 10 minutes or until chicken is no longer pink, turning once. Remove from pan. Cover; keep warm.

2. For cherry-tarragon sauce, add cherries, the 2 tablespoons tarragon, and the garlic to the same skillet. Cook and stir over medium heat for 1 minute. Stir in wine and broth. Simmer, uncovered, for 3 to 5 minutes or until sauce is reduced to about 2 cups. Stir in butter until melted. Season with salt and pepper.

3. To serve, spoon sauce over chicken and serve with couscous. If desired, sprinkle with additional tarragon.

EACH SERVING *573 cal, 21 g fat, 180 mg chol, 631 mg sodium, 40 g carb, 3 g fiber, 44 g pro.*

Honey Roast Chicken with Spring Peas and Shallots

The sauce for roast chicken often contains white wine for flavor. In this case—for something a little different—it's champagne or sparkling wine. Be sure to use a flameproof roasting pan so you can set it over the burner to make the shallot-champagne sauce. If you like, use a cut-up whole chicken for the Pan Stew Chicken variation below.

PREP 15 minutes
COOK 13 minutes
ROAST 1 hour 20 minutes
OVEN 375°F
MAKES 6 servings

1	3½- to 4-pound whole broiler-fryer chicken
2	tablespoons butter, melted
½	teaspoon salt
½	teaspoon freshly ground black pepper
¾	cup honey
2	tablespoons fresh tarragon
1	cup peeled and sliced shallots
1	cup champagne, sparkling wine, or reduced-sodium chicken broth
½	cup chicken broth
1½	cups fresh or frozen peas
1	small lemon, thinly sliced

1. Preheat oven to 375°F. Rinse chicken cavity; pat chicken dry with paper towels. Skewer neck skin to back; tie legs to tail. Place chicken in a shallow roasting pan. Brush with butter; sprinkle with salt and pepper.

2. Roast, uncovered, for 1¼ to 1¾ hours or until drumsticks move easily in sockets and chicken is no longer pink (180°F). Brush with half the honey and sprinkle with half the tarragon. Roast 5 minutes longer or until the chicken has a golden brown glaze.

3. Remove chicken from pan and tent with foil. Transfer roasting pan to stove top. Add shallots, champagne, broth, remaining honey, and fresh peas (if using). Simmer, uncovered, about 10 minutes, until juices thicken slightly and shallots are tender. Add frozen peas (if using) and lemon slices to pan. Simmer 3 to 5 minutes

or until heated through. To serve, return chicken to pan, sprinkle with remaining tarragon, and, if desired, top with additional honey.

EACH SERVING *811 cal, 44 g fat, 209 mg chol, 461 mg sodium, 47 g carb, 3 g fiber, 52 g pro.*

Pan Stew Chicken Arrange chicken, skin sides up, in a shallow baking pan. Brush with butter, then sprinkle with salt and pepper. Roast, uncovered, for 35 minutes. Brush with half the honey and sprinkle with half the tarragon. Roast about 5 minutes more or until honey forms a golden-brown glaze. Continue as directed in Step 3.

Roast Chicken with Roasted Treviso, Potatoes, Rosemary, and Oranges

Treviso radicchio is a milder variety of radicchio. It has long, dainty magenta leaves; white veins; and a delicately crinkled texture. When roasted or grilled, its slightly bitter, nutty flavor mellows considerably. If you can't find it, regular radicchio works well. The sweetness of the oranges balances out the pleasant bitterness of the radicchio.

PREP **20 minutes**
ROAST **50 minutes**
OVEN **425°F**
MAKES **4 to 6 servings**

3   to 3½ pounds meaty chicken pieces (breast halves, thighs, and drumsticks)
    Salt and ground black pepper
3   tablespoons olive oil
3   medium Yukon gold potatoes, cut lengthwise into 4 wedges each
4   sprigs fresh rosemary
2   tablespoons honey
1   orange, quartered
1   tablespoon sherry vinegar
2   teaspoons finely shredded orange peel
2   heads Treviso radicchio or radicchio, halved and thinly sliced
    Snipped fresh parsley

1. Preheat oven to 425°F. Season chicken with salt and pepper. In a large skillet heat 1 tablespoon of the oil over medium-high heat. Add the chicken; cook about 8 minutes or until browned on all sides, about 8 minutes. Transfer chicken to a large roasting pan.

2. In a large bowl combine potato wedges, rosemary sprigs, 1 tablespoon of the oil, and 1 tablespoon of the honey. Toss to coat.

3. Arrange the chicken and potato mixture in the roasting pan in a single layer. Add orange quarters to the pan. Roast for 50 to 60 minutes or until chicken is tender and no longer pink (170°F for breasts; 180°F for thighs and drumsticks). Transfer chicken to a serving platter; cover to keep warm.

4. Meanwhile, in a large bowl whisk together the remaining 1 tablespoon oil, the remaining 1 tablespoon honey, the vinegar, and the orange peel. Add the radicchio and gently stir until coated. Add radicchio to potatoes in pan; toss until wilted. Add potatoes and radicchio to serving platter. Sprinkle with snipped fresh parsley.

EACH SERVING *719 cal, 44 g fat, 172 mg chol, 451 mg sodium, 34 g carb, 4 g fiber, 47 g pro.*

Lime-Marinated Chicken and Tomatillo-Corn Salsa

Tomatillos are sometimes referred to in their native Mexico as "*tomate verde*," or green tomato. They look like green tomatoes covered in a papery husk and have a flavor similar to green tomatoes as well—with hints of tart citrus and apple.

PREP **40 minutes**
MARINATE **1 to 2 hours**
GRILL **19 minutes**
STAND **10 minutes**
MAKES **6 servings**

6   boneless, skinless chicken breasts
¼   cup olive oil
1½   teaspoons finely shredded lime peel (set aside)
3   tablespoons lime juice
6   cloves garlic, minced (about 1 tablespoon)
1½   teaspoons kosher salt
½   teaspoon ground black pepper
2   slices yellow onion, cut ½ inch thick
5   tomatillos (about 8 ounces), papery skins removed, rinsed
1   ear fresh sweet corn, husked
1   medium poblano chile, 3 to 4 inches long*
¼   cup tightly packed fresh cilantro leaves
½   teaspoon brown sugar
¼   teaspoon salt
½   cup sour cream
1   tablespoon olive oil
     Fresh lime wedges
     Sliced jalapeño peppers*
     Cilantro sprigs

1. Remove tenders from underside of each breast if present (save for another use). Place each breast, smooth side down, between two sheets of plastic wrap. Pound to even ½ inch thickness.
2. In large resealable plastic bag combine the ¼ cup olive oil, lime juice, garlic, the 1½ teaspoons kosher salt, and the black pepper. Add chicken to marinade in bag. Seal bag; turn to coat. Marinate in the refrigerator for 1 to 2 hours.
3. Meanwhile, for salsa, brush onion, tomatillos, corn, and chile with olive oil. For a charcoal or gas grill, place vegetables on grill rack over heat. Cover and grill until onions are lightly charred, tomatillos soften and begin to collapse, corn is tender, and chile is softened and lightly charred, turning as needed (about 10 minutes for onion; 12 to 15 minutes for tomatillos and chile). Place chile in bowl. Cover with plastic; let steam for 10 minutes.
4. Peel off skin from chile; discard. Remove stem and seeds. Place vegetables (except corn), cilantro, brown sugar, and ¼ teaspoon salt in food processor or blender. Cover and process or blend until pureed; stir in corn. Add more brown sugar or salt to taste.

5. For a gas grill, increase grill temperature to high (about 500°F); for charcoal grill, add additional coals and heat until high heat is reached. Remove chicken from bag; discard liquid. Cover and grill chicken, smooth sides down, directly over high heat for 3 to 4 minutes. Turn; grill just until cooked all the way through, 1 to 2 minutes more. Transfer to a serving platter.
6. For lime sour cream, in a small bowl whisk together sour cream, the 1 tablespoon olive oil, the lime peel, ¼ teaspoon salt, and ¼ teaspoon pepper. Stir in enough of the remaining 1 tablespoon lime juice to make desired consistency. To serve, spoon salsa over chicken. Pass lime sour cream, lime wedges, sliced jalapeños, and cilantro.

*Tip Because hot chile peppers contain volatile oils that can burn your skin and eyes, avoid contact with chiles as much as possible. When working with chile peppers, wear plastic or rubber gloves. If your bare hands do touch the chile peppers, wash your hands well with soap and water.

EACH SERVING *328 cal, 16 g fat, 96 mg chol, 579 mg sodium, 10 g carb, 1 g fiber, 37 g pro.*

Golden Grilled Chicken Thighs with Apricots

Chicken thighs are an economical buy—and when they're boneless and skinless, they're actually fairly healthful too. In this dish, the flavors of mint, curry, and garlic infuse the chicken with great flavor—then the chicken and apricots are grilled with an apricot-pistachio glaze.

PREP 25 minutes
MARINATE 2 to 4 hours
GRILL 12 minutes
MAKES 4 servings

1   pound skinless, boneless chicken thighs
     Salt and ground black pepper
½   cup apricot nectar
6   tablespoons apricot preserves
4   tablespoons snipped fresh mint
1   tablespoon olive oil
1   tablespoon sherry vinegar
½   teaspoon curry powder
1   clove garlic, minced
4   medium apricots, halved and pitted
¼   cup chopped green onions or scallions (2)
¼   cup chopped pistachios
1   tablespoon Dijon mustard
1   teaspoon olive oil
½   teaspoon mustard seeds
¼   teaspoon salt

1. Sprinkle chicken with salt and pepper. Place in a large resealable plastic bag set in a shallow dish. For marinade, in a small bowl combine ¼ cup of the nectar, 2 tablespoons of the preserves, 2 tablespoons of the mint, the 1 tablespoon olive oil, the vinegar, curry powder, and garlic. Pour over chicken. Seal bag; turn to coat. Marinate in the refrigerator for 2 to 4 hours.

2. Remove chicken from marinade; discard marinade. For a charcoal or gas grill, place chicken on the rack of a covered grill directly over medium heat. Grill for 12 to 15 minutes or until chicken is no longer pink (180°F), turning once halfway through. Add apricots to grill, cut sides down, for the last 5 minutes of grilling or until lightly browned.

3. For sauce, in a small bowl combine the remaining ¼ cup apricot nectar, 3 tablespoons preserves, 2 tablespoons of the mint, the chopped green onions, 3 tablespoons of the pistachios, the mustard, the 1 teaspoon olive oil, the mustard seeds, and ¼ teaspoon salt. Serve chicken with sauce and apricots; sprinkle with the remaining 1 tablespoon pistachios.

EACH SERVING *348 cal, 13 g fat, 94 mg chol, 504 mg sodium, 33 g carb, 2 g fiber, 25 g pro.*

6 Fresh Ideas for Basil

It could be argued that basil is the most popular herb. It has a heavenly fragrance and enticing flavor with hints of anise, clove, and pepper. Planted in a sunny spot, it produces generously. Got a bounty of basil?

1 Basil Lemonade

In a small saucepan bring 1½ cups cold water and 1 cup sugar to a simmer over medium heat. Cook, without stirring, until sugar dissolves and mixture thickens slightly, about 5 minutes. Remove from heat. Add 1 cup fresh basil leaves; cool. Strain the syrup into a resealable container; discard solids. Pour 2 to 3 teaspoons of the basil syrup into an ice-filled glass, then fill with lemonade. Garnish with an additional sprig of basil. (Cover and refrigerate the remaining syrup for up to 2 weeks.) Makes enough syrup for 16 servings.

2 Basil-Infused Olive Oil

Bring a large saucepan of water to boiling. Add 2 cups tightly packed basil leaves, making sure that leaves are submerged, and blanch for 5 seconds. Drain and immediately plunge basil into bowl of ice water. Drain well and squeeze out all liquid. Puree in a blender with 1 cup extra virgin olive oil. Strain puree through a fine-mesh strainer. Strain again through four layers of cheesecloth. Store, tightly covered, in the refrigerator up to 1 week. Drizzle oil over salad greens or over roasted or grilled chicken. Stir into mashed potatoes or use as a dipping sauce for bread. Makes 1 cup.

3 Creamy Basil-Scrambled Eggs

In a medium bowl whisk 4 eggs and 3 tablespoons sour cream. Stir in ½ cup shredded mozzarella cheese. Season with salt and freshly ground black pepper. Melt 2 teaspoons butter in a nonstick skillet over medium heat. Pour in egg mixture and cook, stirring occasionally, until eggs are almost to the desired consistency. Stir in 1 tablespoon minced fresh basil. Serve immediately. Makes 2 servings.

4 Pesto Vinaigrette

In a food processor or blender puree 1 clove peeled garlic and ½ teaspoon salt until a paste forms. Add ¼ cup toasted pine nuts and 2 cups fresh basil (stems removed) and process until a fine paste forms. With the motor running, add 4 tablespoons red wine vinegar. Slowly add ¾ cup extra virgin olive oil in a thin stream until the mixture is emulsified. Transfer to a small bowl. Whisk in ¼ teaspoon cracked black pepper. Taste and adjust seasoning. Makes 1½ cups.

5 Basil-Tomato Grilled Cheese

On a slice of Italian country bread, layer slices of Havarti or Muenster cheese. Sprinkle with finely chopped basil. Add slices of ripe tomato, sliced ham, and another slice of Italian country bread. Brush the outsides of both slices of bread with olive oil. Grill sandwich on the cool side of a grill or in a skillet over medium heat until golden brown and cheese is melted. Makes 1 sandwich.

6 Basil Mayonnaise

In a food processor or blender combine 1 cup fresh basil leaves (stems removed), 1 cup mayonnaise, and 1 clove minced garlic. Process until blended. Add 1 teaspoon lemon juice and process until creamy and smooth. Use on sandwiches, in potato salad, or as a dipping sauce for oven fries or roasted Brussels sprouts, cauliflower, or broccoli. Makes about 1¼ cups.

Basil Lemonade

Grilled Bacon-Wrapped Turkey Tenderloins with Glazed Plums

Didn't know you could cook bacon ahead? Here's how: After frying, drain well on paper towels. Wrap the cooked bacon in clean paper towels and refrigerate in a sealed plastic bag for later use. To reheat it, simply heat it in the microwave—wrapped in a paper towel—for 20 seconds.

PREP **20 minutes**
COOK **10 minutes**
GRILL **12 minutes**
MAKES **6 (2-piece) servings**

1   teaspoon ground black pepper
1   teaspoon ground coriander
1   teaspoon ground cumin
½   teaspoon salt
3   turkey breast tenderloins (2 to 2½ pounds)
12   slices packaged ready-to-serve cooked bacon
3   medium plums, pitted and sliced
¼   cup plum jelly
1   tablespoon cider vinegar
     Grilled asparagus* (optional)

1. In a small bowl stir together pepper, coriander, cumin, and salt; sprinkle mixture evenly on both sides of turkey tenderloins. Cut each tenderloin crosswise into quarters to make 12 total pieces. Wrap each turkey piece with a slice of bacon; secure with a wooden toothpick.
2. For a charcoal or gas grill, place turkey on the rack of a covered grill directly over medium heat. Grill for 12 to 15 minutes or until turkey is no longer pink (170°F), turning once halfway through grilling.
3. Meanwhile, in a medium saucepan stir together plum slices, jelly, and vinegar. Bring to boiling over medium heat, stirring frequently; reduce heat. Simmer, uncovered, for 4 to 6 minutes or until plums are tender. Serve over turkey. If desired, serve with grilled asparagus.

*Tip For grilled asparagus, place trimmed asparagus spears on the rack of a covered grill directly over medium heat for 3 to 5 minutes or until asparagus is tender and starting to brown, turning once halfway through grilling.
EACH SERVING *270 cal, 5 g fat, 104 mg chol, 453 mg sodium, 14 g carb, 1 g fiber, 40 g pro.*

Turkey Lettuce Wraps with Spicy Peanut Sauce

Boston or Bibb lettuce is a type of lettuce known as butterhead. Butterhead lettuces grow in rosettes of soft, buttery-textured leaves that are perfect for serving as a bed for other foods or, because they roll easily, as a wrap for savory fillings such as this ground turkey and broccoli mixture served with peanut sauce. Add as much or as little Asian chili sauce as you like, depending on how much you love the heat.

PREP 15 minutes
COOK 20 minutes
MAKES 8 wraps

1   pound ground turkey
3   cloves garlic, minced
1   tablespoon grated fresh ginger
1   teaspoon Chinese five-spice powder or curry powder
2   cups coarsely shredded broccoli* (1 small bunch)
1   small red onion, thinly sliced
     Salt and ground black pepper
1   recipe Spicy Peanut Sauce or ½ cup hoisin sauce
8   large Boston (Bibb) lettuce leaves (about 2 heads)
8   lime wedges
     Snipped fresh cilantro (optional)

1. In a large nonstick skillet cook turkey over medium-high heat for 5 minutes, breaking up turkey with a wooden spoon. Stir in garlic, ginger, and ½ teaspoon of the five-spice powder; cook about 5 minutes more or until turkey is no longer pink. Using a slotted spoon, transfer turkey mixture to a bowl; set aside.
2. In the same skillet cook the broccoli, onion, and the remaining ½ teaspoon five-spice powder about 4 minutes or just until broccoli and onion are tender. Stir in the turkey mixture; heat through. Season with salt and pepper.
3. To serve, spoon 1 tablespoon Spicy Peanut Sauce on each lettuce leaf. Divide turkey-broccoli mixture among lettuce leaves. Squeeze a lime wedge over the filling on each wrap. If desired, top with cilantro. Fold in the two opposite sides of the lettuce leaf; fold one of the remaining sides over the filling and tuck it under the other side. Serve immediately.

Spicy Peanut Sauce In a small saucepan combine ¼ cup sugar, ¼ cup crunchy peanut butter, 2 tablespoons water, and 1 teaspoon vegetable oil. Cook over medium-low heat just until bubbly and smooth (it looks a little curdled before this stage), stirring frequently. Season to taste with Asian chili sauce.
*Tip Before shredding the broccoli, consider peeling the stalks, especially if they seem tough. Shred broccoli in a food processor fitted with a coarse shredding blade or use a manual shredder. Or use purchased shredded broccoli.
EACH WRAP *210 cal, 13 g fat, 44 mg chol, 160 mg sodium, 12 g carb, 2 g fiber, 13 g pro.*

Roast Duck with Blackberry-Orange Sauce

Duck is a special-occasion dish—the preparation is often a bit fussy. This recipe is no exception, although it is well worth the puttering. This duck is double-roasted—the first time to render the fat and partially cook the meat. In the second roasting—after it is cut in pieces—a sweet and spicy blackberry sauce glazes the duck.

PREP **45 minutes**
ROAST **2 hours**
STAND **15 minutes**
OVEN **500°F/350°F**
MAKES **4 servings**

1   4- to 6-pound domestic duck
1   teaspoon sea salt
1   teaspoon cracked black pepper
1   small orange, quartered
1   stalk celery, cut up
1   small onion, quartered
2   sprigs fresh thyme
2   tablespoons orange liqueur
1   cup hot water
1   tablespoon finely shredded orange peel
½   cup orange juice
¼   cup packed brown sugar
¼   cup orange liqueur
¼   cup mild-flavor molasses
1   teaspoon grated fresh ginger
2   cloves garlic, minced
½   teaspoon sea salt
½   teaspoon cracked black pepper
2   cups blackberries
     Blackberries (optional)

1. Adjust oven rack to lower third of the oven. Preheat oven to 500°F. Rinse duck body cavity; pat dry. Rub cavity with the 1 teaspoon salt and 1 teaspoon pepper. Place orange, celery, onion, and thyme in cavity. Skewer neck skin to back; tie legs to tail. Twist wing tips under back. Brush duck with the 2 tablespoons orange liqueur.

2. Place duck, breast side down, on rack in a shallow roasting pan. Add the hot water to the roasting pan. Place in lower third of oven. Reduce oven temperature to 350°F. Roast, uncovered, for 45 minutes.

3. Carefully remove roasting pan from oven; drain fat.* Turn duck, breast side up. Roast for 45 to 60 minutes more or until drumsticks move easily in their sockets (165°F). Juices may still appear pink.

4. Meanwhile, for sauce, in a small saucepan whisk together orange peel, orange juice, brown sugar, the ¼ cup orange liqueur, the molasses, ginger, garlic, ½ teaspoon salt, and ½ teaspoon pepper. Bring to boiling; reduce heat. Simmer, uncovered, for 10 to 12 minutes or until thickened and syrupy. Stir in 2 cups blackberries. Use a potato masher or fork to coarsely mash berries. Cover and set aside.

5. Transfer duck to a cutting board; let stand for 15 minutes. Discard stuffing mixture. Using kitchen shears, cut duck in half lengthwise. Cut each half between the breast and the thigh into two pieces. Drain fat from roasting pan. Arrange duck quarters in pan. Pour blackberry sauce over the duck. Return to oven. Roast in the 350°F oven for 30 minutes.

6. Transfer duck pieces to a serving platter. Pour any juices in roasting pan over duck pieces. If desired, serve with additional blackberries.

*Tip If you like, reserve the fat and toss a few tablespoons with potatoes or other root vegetables. Roast at 400°F for 35 to 40 minutes or until light brown and tender.

EACH SERVING *302 cal, 8 g fat, 14 mg chol, 902 mg sodium, 49 g carb, 5 g fiber, 4 g pro.*

Pepper-Poached Salmon and Herbed Beets, *recipe page 118*

Pepper-Poached Salmon and Herbed Beets *pictured page 117*

Poaching—simmering in liquid such as water, wine, broth, or some combination—is one of the best ways to cook fish because it doesn't dry out. The liquid is usually flavored. Here it's infused with the flavors of watercress, tarragon, lemon, peppercorn, and bay leaves in a bouquet garni—traditionally a bunch of herbs tied together with string or wrapped in a cheesecloth.

PREP **45 minutes**
COOK **24 minutes**
STAND **10 minutes**
MAKES **4 servings**

1   to 1½ pounds fresh or frozen salmon fillets
1   cup loosely packed watercress leaves
2   tablespoons snipped fresh tarragon
½   of a lemon, cut into thick slices
2   teaspoons whole peppercorns
3   bay leaves
½   cup sour cream
1   teaspoon snipped fresh tarragon
½   teaspoon ground black pepper
¼   teaspoon salt
1   tablespoon snipped fresh chives
1   recipe Herbed Beets
    Watercress and fresh tarragon sprigs (optional)

1. Thaw fish, if frozen. Measure thickness of fish. Cut fish into 4 serving-size pieces if necessary. In a large skillet combine 1 cup water and ½ teaspoon salt.

2. For the bouquet garni, place ½ cup of the watercress, the 2 tablespoons tarragon, lemon slices, peppercorns, and bay leaves in the center of a double-thick, 9-inch-square of 100%-cotton cheesecloth. Bring the corners of the cheesecloth together and tie with clean 100%-cotton string. Place the bouquet garni in the skillet. Bring water to boiling; reduce heat. With a slotted spatula, gently lower the fillets into water. Cover and simmer for 4 to 6 minutes for each ½ inch of thickness or just until fish flakes when tested with a fork. Using a slotted spoon, carefully remove the fish fillets to a platter. Cover fish; keep warm while preparing sauce.

3. For sauce, in a blender or food processor combine sour cream, the remaining ½ cup watercress, the 1 teaspoon tarragon, the black pepper, and salt. Cover and blend or process until smooth. Stir in chives.

Spoon sauce onto plates and top with fish. Serve with Herbed Beets. If desired, garnish with additional watercress and tarragon.

Herbed Beets Cut green tops from 1 pound fresh baby beets (about 12) or small beets. Discard tops. Cut beets into quarters. Wash beets; do not peel. In a small saucepan bring a small amount of lightly salted water to boiling. Add the beets. Cover and cook over medium heat about 20 minutes or until crisp-tender. Drain. Allow beets to stand at room temperature until cool enough to handle (about 10 minutes). Holding beets under running water, slip skins off beets. Place beets in a serving bowl. Add 1 tablespoon olive oil, 1 tablespoon red wine vinegar, and ⅛ teaspoon salt. Toss to mix. Sprinkle with 2 tablespoons snipped fresh watercress and 1 tablespoon snipped fresh tarragon.

EACH SERVING *289 cal, 16 g fat, 75 mg chol, 379 mg sodium, 12 g carb, 3 g fiber, 25 g pro.*

Grilled Salmon and Oyster Mushrooms

Oyster mushrooms grow in the wild and in cultivated situations in tight clusters—often on decaying tree trunks. They have a rich, slightly peppery flavor that mellows when they're cooked. Look for young oyster mushrooms—1½ inches or under in diameter—to get the best-tasting, most-tender textured mushrooms.

PREP **25 minutes**
GRILL **8 minutes**
MAKES **4 servings**

4   6- to 8-ounce fresh or frozen salmon fillets
5   tablespoons peanut oil
¼   cup chopped fresh cilantro
3   tablespoons chopped fresh parsley
3   tablespoons rice vinegar
1   tablespoon miso paste
1   pound oyster mushrooms, trimmed
3   cups trimmed watercress or baby mustard greens

1. Thaw salmon, if frozen. Rinse salmon; pat dry with paper towels. Brush salmon on all sides with 2 tablespoons of the oil. Place salmon, skin sides down, on a plate or in a shallow dish.
2. In a large bowl combine cilantro and parsley. Sprinkle about 1 teaspoon herb mixture on each of the salmon fillets.
3. In a small bowl combine the remaining herb mixture, the remaining 3 tablespoons oil, the vinegar, and miso paste; stir until miso is blended into mixture. Set aside 2 tablespoons of the herb mixture for dressing. Place mushrooms in a bowl. Add the remaining herb mixture; toss to coat.
4. For a charcoal or gas grill, place salmon fillets, skin sides down, on the rack of a covered grill directly over medium heat. Grill for 8 to 10 minutes or just until fish flakes when tested with a fork. Using tongs, remove mushrooms from marinade, discarding any remaining marinade. Place mushrooms in a grill wok or basket. Grill about 5 minutes or until tender and edges begin to brown, stirring 3 or 4 times during grilling.
5. Meanwhile, arrange watercress on 4 plates or a platter. Transfer salmon* and mushrooms to plates with watercress. Drizzle with the reserved herb mixture.
*Tip To remove skin from salmon, carefully slide a spatula between skin and fish when removing from the grill.
EACH SERVING *446 cal, 28 g fat, 94 mg chol, 268 mg sodium, 9 g carb, 3 g fiber, 39 g pro.*

Rosemary Salmon over Roasted Root Vegetables and Lentils

Refrigerated steamed lentils are convenient but pricey. If you have the time and inclination, cook your own. Rinse 8 ounces of dry lentils under cool running water in a sieve or colander. Place the lentils in a large saucepan with 2½ cups water. Bring to boiling. Cook, covered, for about 25 minutes or until tender. Do not overcook or the lentils will get mushy. Drain any excess water. You should have about 3½ cups cooked lentils. Store the cooked lentils in a tightly sealed container in the refrigerator for up to 3 days.

PREP **25 minutes**
ROAST **50 minutes**
OVEN **400°F**
MAKES **6 servings**

1   1¼-pound fresh or frozen salmon fillet
1½ pounds root vegetables such as carrots, parsnips, sweet potatoes, rutabagas, and/or beets
4   tablespoons olive oil
1   teaspoon cumin seeds, crushed
½   teaspoon sea salt
2   cloves garlic, minced
¼   teaspoon freshly ground black pepper
    Pinch sea salt
1   17.6-ounce package refrigerated steamed lentils (3 cups)
1   lemon, thinly sliced

1. Thaw salmon, if frozen. Preheat oven to 400°F. Peel root vegetables and cut into ½-inch pieces. In a large bowl toss together root vegetables, 3 tablespoons of the olive oil, the cumin seeds, the ½ teaspoon salt, and the garlic. Transfer vegetables mixture to a large shallow roasting pan.
2. Roast vegetable mixture, uncovered, for 30 minutes, stirring occasionally. Push vegetables to one side of the pan to make room for the salmon.
3. Rinse salmon; pat dry with paper towels. In a small bowl combine the remaining 1 tablespoon olive oil, the pepper, and the pinch salt. Brush salmon with the oil mixture. Place salmon, skin side down, in the roasting pan; top with lemon slices. Roast, uncovered, for 15 to 18 minutes or just until fish flakes when tested with a fork. Remove salmon; cover with foil to keep warm. Stir lentils into roasted vegetables. Roast for 5 minutes.
4. To serve, divide lentil-vegetable mixture among 6 dinner plates. Break salmon into large chunks and add to plates. Garnish with fresh lemon slices.

EACH SERVING *378 cal, 16 g fat, 52 mg chol, 503 mg sodium, 34 g carb, 11 g fiber, 28 g pro.*

Grilled Halibut and Leeks with Mustard Vinaigrette

Leeks are most often used as a flavoring for the main ingredient in a dish, but here they get equal billing. Related to both onion and garlic, they have flavor qualities of each—but in a milder form. Grilled and dressed with a mustard-balsamic vinaigrette, they make a lovely side dish. For a little extra green, serve with mâche (also called lamb's lettuce) or baby spinach if you like.

PREP **20 minutes**
GRILL **8 minutes**
MAKES **4 servings**

1¼	pounds fresh or frozen halibut steaks, cut 1 inch thick
2	tablespoons white balsamic vinegar
2	tablespoons coarse-grain mustard
1	tablespoon water
4	teaspoons olive oil
1	clove garlic, minced
4	small leeks
3	cloves garlic, minced
¼	teaspoon salt
¼	teaspoon ground black pepper
1	to 2 cups mâche or baby spinach (optional)
	Fresh chives (optional)

1. Thaw fish, if frozen. Rinse fish; pat dry with paper towels. Cut into 4 serving-size pieces. Chill fish until needed. In a small bowl whisk together vinegar, mustard, the water, 2 teaspoons of the olive oil, and the 1 clove garlic. Set aside.
2. Trim roots and cut off green tops of leeks; remove 1 or 2 outer white layers. Wash well (if necessary, cut a 1-inch slit from bottom end to help separate layers for easier washing). Drain. In a medium saucepan combine leeks and a small amount of water. Bring to boiling; reduce heat. Cover and simmer for 3 minutes. Drain. Pat dry. Brush with 1 teaspoon of the remaining olive oil.
3. In a small bowl stir together the remaining 1 teaspoon olive oil, the 3 cloves garlic, the salt, and pepper. Spread evenly over fish; rub in with your fingers.

4. For a charcoal or gas grill, place fish and leeks on the greased rack of an covered grill directly over medium heat. Grill for 8 to 12 minutes or just until fish flakes when tested with a fork, gently turning fish and leeks once. Cut leeks into ½-inch pieces. Divide fish and leeks among 4 shallow bowls. Drizzle with vinegar mixture. If desired, serve with greens and sprinkle with chives.

EACH SERVING *231 cal, 8 g fat, 45 mg chol, 331 mg sodium, 7 g carb, 1 g fiber, 30 g pro.*

Parchment-Baked Halibut with Asian Vegetables

Cooking "en papillote," which means "in parchment," is a fabulous way to cook fish and vegetables simply, healthfully, and with outstanding results. The flavors mingle together as the packets bake and the fish gently steams, so it stays moist and tender. Let diners open their own packets to experience the tantalizing aromas that waft out.

PREP **30 minutes**
BAKE **15 minutes**
OVEN **400°F**
MAKES **4 servings**

4   6-ounce fresh or frozen halibut fillets
1   red sweet pepper, cut into thin strips
1   yellow sweet pepper, cut into thin strips
6   bunches baby bok choy, ends trimmed and leaves separated
¼   cup soy sauce
1   tablespoon grated fresh ginger
2   teaspoons rice vinegar
2   teaspoons toasted sesame oil
¼   teaspoon Asian chili sauce (Sriracha)
½   cup thinly bias-sliced green onions or scallions (4)
2   tablespoons slivered tangerine peel
¼   teaspoon freshly ground black pepper
4   15-inch squares parchment paper
    Bias-sliced green onions or scallions (optional)

1. Thaw fish, if frozen. Rinse fish; pat dry with paper towels. Set fish aside. Preheat oven to 400°F.
2. Divide red pepper, yellow pepper, and bok choy among the parchment squares. Spread the vegetables in an even layer in the middle of the squares. Top vegetables with fish fillets.
3. For sauce, in a small bowl combine soy sauce, ginger, rice vinegar, sesame oil, and Asian chili sauce. Whisk to combine. Spoon sauce over fillets. Top each fillet with 2 tablespoons green onions. Sprinkle with tangerine peel and black pepper.

4. Bring up two opposite sides of parchment and fold several times over fish. Fold ends of parchment. Repeat to make 3 more packets. Place packets in a shallow baking pan.
5. Bake for 15 to 20 minutes or until packets puff slightly (carefully open a packet to check fish doneness; fish should flake with a fork). If desired, sprinkle fish with additional sliced green onions.
EACH SERVING *228 cal, 5 g fat, 83 mg chol, 1,209 mg sodium, 10 g carb, 3 g fiber, 35 g pro.*

Seared Halibut with Fennel Puree and Olive, Hazelnut, and Parsley Gremolata

Cerignola olives, from Southern Italy, are the largest olives in the world—about the size of a large pecan in a shell. They have a meaty, rich texture and mild, fruity flavor. The simplest way to pit them is with a cherry pitter. If you don't have one, you can lightly crush them with the flat side of a large knife and slip the pit out. Because they are chopped for this recipe, they don't have to stay intact.

PREP **20 minutes**
COOK **22 minutes**
MAKES **4 servings**

4   6-ounce fresh or frozen halibut fillets
¼   teaspoon salt
⅛   teaspoon ground black pepper
1   large fennel bulb
1   medium Yukon gold potato, peeled and cut into 2-inch pieces
2   tablespoons butter
1   teaspoon finely shredded lemon peel
¼   cup green olives (such as Cerignola), pitted and chopped
2   tablespoons chopped hazelnuts, toasted
2   tablespoons snipped fresh parsley
3   tablespoons olive oil
1   tablespoon lemon juice

1. Thaw fish, if frozen. Rinse fish; pat dry with paper towels. Season both sides with salt and pepper; set fish aside.

2. For fennel puree, cut off and discard fennel stalks, reserving fronds. Remove any wilted outer layers from the fennel bulb. Cut a thin slice from base. Cut the bulb lengthwise into quarters. Cut cores from quarters and discard; cut fennel quarters into 2-inch pieces. Place a steamer basket in a medium saucepan. Add water to just below the bottom of the steamer. Bring water to boiling. Place fennel and potato pieces in the steamer basket. Cover and reduce heat. Steam about 15 minutes or until potato is tender. Transfer fennel and potato to a food processor or blender. Add butter and lemon peel. Cover and process or blend until smooth.

3. Meanwhile, for gremolata, in a small bowl stir together olives, hazelnuts, parsley, 2 tablespoons of the olive oil, and the lemon juice. Chop enough of the reserved fronds to make 2 tablespoons. Stir the chopped fennel fronds into the gremolata.

4. In a very large nonstick skillet heat the remaining 1 tablespoon olive oil over medium-high heat. Cook fish in the hot oil for 4 minutes. Gently turn fish over. Cook about 3 minutes more or just until fish flakes when tested with a fork.

5. To serve, spoon fennel puree onto plates. Top with fish and gremolata.

EACH SERVING *392 cal, 22 g fat, 99 mg chol, 479 mg sodium, 16 g carb, 4 g fiber, 34 g pro.*

Fish Tacos with Cabbage and Chile Pepper Slaw

Crunchy, slightly spicy, and sweet slaw gives a pleasing crunch to these fish tacos. The fish is gently cooked in a foil pack in the oven with tomatillos, garlic, and citrus zest—so it stays moist and flavorful.

PREP 40 minutes
BAKE 10 minutes
OVEN 400°F
MAKES 6 (2-taco) servings

1½ pounds fresh or frozen cod or halibut fillets, thawed and cut into 1-inch pieces
2   tomatillos, cut into ½-inch pieces (2 cups)
2   teaspoons olive oil
1   clove garlic, minced
½   teaspoon finely shredded orange peel
½   teaspoon finely shredded lime peel
    Salt and ground black pepper
12 6-inch corn tortillas
1   recipe Cabbage and Green Chile Pepper Slaw

1. Thaw fish, if frozen. Rinse fish; pat dry with paper towels. Preheat oven to 400°F. In large bowl toss together fish, tomatillos, oil, garlic, orange peel, and lime peel. Season with salt and black pepper; set aside.
2. Cut six 12-inch-square sheets of foil. Place one-sixth (about ⅔ cup) fish mixture in center of each square. Fold diagonally in half in a triangle. Fold edges two or three times to make a packet. Place packets in single layer on a large baking sheet.
3. Bake for 10 to 12 minutes or until packets puff slightly (carefully open a packet to check fish doneness; fish should flake with a fork). Meanwhile, in a dry skillet warm tortillas over medium-high heat until soft, about 15 seconds per side.
4. To serve, divide fish mixture among tortillas. Top with Cabbage and Chile Pepper Slaw. Serve immediately.

Cabbage and Chile Pepper Slaw
Cut 1 poblano or pasilla pepper in half crosswise; remove seeds and thinly slice.* In a medium bowl combine the poblano pepper, 1¼ cups thinly shredded green cabbage, ½ cup thinly sliced red onion, ½ cup shredded carrot, and ¼ cup chopped cilantro. For dressing, in a small bowl combine 3 tablespoons olive oil, 2 tablespoons lime juice, and 1 tablespoon orange juice. Season with salt. Pour dressing over cabbage mixture; toss to coat.

*Tip Because hot chile peppers contain volatile oils that can burn your skin and eyes, avoid contact with chiles as much as possible. When working with chile peppers, wear plastic or rubber gloves. If your bare hands do touch the chile peppers, wash your hands well with soap and water.

EACH SERVING *341 cal, 13 g fat, 36 mg chol, 293 mg sodium, 30 g carb, 5 g fiber, 28 g pro.*

Swordfish with Pickled Onion, Olive, and Orange Salsa

This lovely dish brightens up the dreariest winter day. The salty, rich taste of the olives and the sweet, acidic flavor of the oranges and red onion pickle balance one another perfectly—as does the buttery texture of the fish and the chewy, earthy flavor of the wild rice pilaf. Make the Pickled Onions up to 3 days ahead.

PREP **25 minutes**
MARINATE **30 minutes**
GRILL **4 to 6 minutes per ½-inch thickness of fish**
MAKES **4 servings**

4	5- to 6-ounce fresh or frozen swordfish or tuna steaks
2	oranges
3	tablespoons olive oil
¼	teaspoon salt
⅛	teaspoon ground black pepper
1	recipe Pickled Onions
¼	cup chopped, pitted kalamata olives
2	tablespoons snipped fresh Italian (flat-leaf) parsley, thyme, oregano, basil, and/or tarragon
1	recipe Herbed Wild Rice or hot cooked rice (optional)

1. Thaw fish, if frozen. Rinse fish; pat dry with paper towels. Measure thickness of fish. Section orange over a medium bowl to catch juice. Reserve orange sections. Add 2 tablespoons of the oil, the salt, and pepper to the orange juice. Whisk to combine. Place swordfish in a large resealable plastic bag set in a shallow dish. Pour orange juice mixture over fish in the bag; seal bag. Turn to coat fish. Marinate in the refrigerator for 30 minutes to 1 hour, turning bag occasionally.

2. Meanwhile, for salsa, chop the reserved orange sections and place in a medium bowl. Drain Pickled Onions, discarding the liquid. Add onions to the bowl with the oranges. Add the olives, fresh herbs, and the remaining 1 tablespoon olive oil. Toss to combine; set aside.

3. For a charcoal or gas grill, place fish on the greased rack of a covered grill directly over medium heat. Grill for 4 to 6 minutes per ½-inch thickness of fish or just until fish begins to flake when tested with a fork, turning once halfway through grilling. Remove from grill. Serve fish over Herbed Wild Rice and top with orange salsa.

Pickled Onions In a medium screw-top jar combine ⅔ cup very thinly sliced red onion cut into 1-inch pieces, ⅔ cup sherry vinegar or cider vinegar, 2 tablespoons sugar, and ¼ teaspoon salt. Cover and shake to combine. Chill for at least 30 minutes or up to 3 days.

Herbed Wild Rice Rinse ⅔ cup uncooked wild rice in a strainer under cold running water about 1 minute. In a medium saucepan combine the wild rice, one 14.5-ounce can chicken broth, 1 cup water, 1 bay leaf, and ⅛ teaspoon ground black pepper. Bring to boiling; reduce heat. Cover and simmer for 20 minutes. Stir in ⅔ cup uncooked long grain white rice. Return to boiling; reduce heat. Cover and simmer about 20 minutes more or until rices are tender and liquid is absorbed. Discard bay leaf. Stir in 1 tablespoon snipped fresh Italian (flat-leaf) parsley, thyme, oregano, basil, and/or tarragon.

EACH SERVING *586 cal, 21 g fat, 94 mg chol, 744 mg sodium, 62 g carb, 4 g fiber, 36 g pro.*

Grilled Trout with Fennel and Citrus

Fennel and lemon slices are stuffed inside the trout to flavor it as it cooks—and slices of fresh, crunchy fennel are tossed with orange sections and peppery watercress to create a crisp and refreshing salad to go with the fish after it's cooked. To buy the best trout, look for fish that is glistening, flawless, and clean smelling. The flesh should be firm to the touch and spring back when lightly pressed.

PREP **20 minutes**
GRILL **10 minutes**
MAKES **4 servings**

2   **8- to 10-ounce fresh or frozen whole dressed trout**
¼   **teaspoon salt**
¼   **teaspoon cracked black pepper**
1   **small lemon, thinly sliced**
1   **small bulb fennel, cored and thinly sliced**
4   **cups watercress, tough stems removed**
1   **tablespoon snipped fresh dillweed**
1   **small orange, peeled and sectioned**
1   **tablespoon olive oil**
2   **teaspoons white wine vinegar**
1   **teaspoon snipped fresh dillweed**

1. Thaw fish, if frozen. Rinse fish; pat dry with paper towels.
2. Sprinkle inside of fish with ⅛ teaspoon of the salt and ⅛ teaspoon of the pepper. Arrange the lemon slices on the inside of fish. Top with half of the sliced fennel, a few of the watercress leaves, and the 1 tablespoon dill. Fold fish to enclose.
3. Place fish in a well-greased grill basket. For a charcoal or gas grill, place the grill basket on the rack of a covered grill directly over medium heat. Grill for 10 to 12 minutes or just until fish flakes when tested with a fork, turning basket once halfway through grilling.

4. Meanwhile, for salad, in a serving bowl combine the remaining fennel, the remaining watercress, and the orange sections. For dressing, in a screw-top jar combine oil, white wine vinegar, the 1 teaspoon dillweed, the remaining ⅛ teaspoon salt, and ⅛ teaspoon pepper. Cover and shake well to combine. Drizzle dressing over salad; toss to mix. Serve with fish.

EACH SERVING *241 cal, 11 g fat, 66 mg chol, 249 mg sodium, 10 g carb, 3 g fiber, 26 g pro.*

Seared Tuna with Grapefruit-Orange Relish

Tuna is a very lean fish and tends to dry out very quickly if overcooked. Pan-searing over high heat is ideal—it seals the juices on the inside and gives the outside an irresistible caramel-color crust.

PREP **20 minutes**
COOK **6 minutes**
MAKES **4 servings**

4   4-ounce fresh or frozen tuna steaks, cut ¾ inch thick
2   teaspoons sherry vinegar or white wine vinegar
2   teaspoons soy sauce
½   teaspoon grated fresh ginger
1   tablespoon olive oil
1   medium grapefruit, peeled and sectioned
1   medium orange, peeled and sectioned
2   tablespoons finely chopped red onion
2   tablespoons snipped fresh cilantro
2   teaspoons olive oil
     Salt and ground black pepper
     Fresh cilantro sprigs (optional)

1. Thaw fish, if frozen. Rinse fish; pat dry with paper towels. Set aside.
2. For grapefruit-orange relish, in a small bowl combine vinegar, soy sauce, and ginger. Whisk in the 1 tablespoon olive oil. Cut grapefruit sections into thirds and orange sections in half. Stir fruit pieces, red onion, and the 2 tablespoons cilantro into vinegar mixture. Set aside.
3. In a large skillet heat the 2 teaspoons olive oil over medium-high heat. Add fish; cook for 6 to 9 minutes or just until fish flakes when tested with a fork, turning once. Sprinkle with salt and pepper. Serve the fish with citrus relish. If desired, garnish with cilantro sprigs.
EACH SERVING *256 cal, 12 g fat, 47 mg chol, 287 mg sodium, 7 g carb, 1 g fiber, 29 g pro.*

Fish Smarts

Fish is among the higher-priced sources of protein. Its somewhat delicate nature also requires some gentle handling. The trick to cooking great fish is to buy the best-quality and freshest you can afford and avoid overcooking it.

For best results when choosing and preparing fish, follow these guidelines:

Selecting Look for fresh fish that has clear, bright, bulging eyes with black pupils; shiny, taught bright skin; and red gills that are not slippery. The flesh should feel firm, elastic, and tight to the bone and should have a fresh, briny "sea" smell (if that is its source; freshwater fish should just smell fresh). Steaks and fillets should be moist and cleanly cut. Avoid fish that has a strong "fishy" odor; dull, bloody, or sunken eyes; and fading skin with bruises, red spots, or browning or yellowing flesh.

Storing Plan to cook fresh fish the same day you buy it. If that's not possible, wrap it loosely in plastic wrap and store it in the coldest part of your refrigerator; use within 2 days.

Testing for Doneness The delicate texture of fish makes it easy to overcook. To test for doneness, insert a fork into the fish and gently twist. The fish is done as soon as it begins to flake. Be sure to check for doneness at the minimum cooking time.

Quinoa and Caraway-Crusted Tuna Steaks with
Wilted Red Cabbage Slaw, *recipe page 134*

Quinoa and Caraway-Crusted Tuna Steaks with Wilted Red Cabbage Slaw *pictured page 133*

Quinoa is something of a miracle food. Although it's eaten as a grain, it's actually an edible seed. It is lower in carbohydrates than most of the grains with which it keeps company—and highest in protein of all of them. It has become popular for use in pilafs and is made into flour to make gluten-free pasta that has a toothsome, chewy bite. Here it creates a crunchy crust for succulent tuna steaks.

START TO FINISH **20 minutes**
MAKES **4 servings**

4	5- to 6-ounce fresh or frozen tuna steaks
3	tablespoons olive oil
1	small red onion, thinly sliced
¼	cup dry red wine
3	cups shredded red cabbage
2	tablespoons clementine juice (from 1 clementine) or orange juice
	Salt and ground black pepper
¾	cup cooked quinoa
1½	teaspoons caraway seeds, lightly crushed
¼	cup all-purpose flour
¼	teaspoon salt
¼	teaspoon ground black pepper
1	egg
1	tablespoon water
1	lemon, cut into wedges

1. Thaw tuna steaks, if frozen.

2. For slaw, in a large skillet heat 1 tablespoon of the oil over medium heat. Add onion; reduce heat to low. Cook, uncovered, for 10 minutes, stirring occasionally. Remove skillet from heat; add red wine. Return to heat; cook until most of the liquid has evaporated. Stir in cabbage. Add clementine juice; toss to mix. Cook about 1 minute more or until cabbage starts to wilt. Remove from heat. Season with salt and pepper. Cover; set aside until serving time.

3. Rinse fish; pat dry with paper towels. In a shallow dish combine quinoa and caraway seeds. In another shallow dish combine flour, the ¼ teaspoon salt, and the ¼ teaspoon pepper. In a third shallow dish lightly beat egg and water. Dust tops and bottoms of tuna steaks with flour mixture (but don't coat the sides). Dip tops and bottoms of steaks in egg mixture. Press tops and bottoms of steaks into quinoa mixture.

4. In another large skillet heat the remaining 2 tablespoons oil over medium-high heat. Add tuna steaks; cook for 4 to 6 minutes per ½-inch thickness of fish or until coating is golden and tuna is slightly pink inside, turning once halfway through cooking. Serve tuna with slaw and lemon wedges.

EACH TUNA STEAK + 3/4 CUP SLAW *377 cal, 13 g fat, 102 mg chol, 241 mg sodium, 23 g carb, 4 g fiber, 40 g pro.*

Shrimp with Peppered Citrus Fruits

Fresh, coarsely crushed black pepper lends the most flavor—and in a dish in which pepper is one of the star flavors, it's important to be sure the pepper is as fresh as possible. To crush whole peppercorns, place them in a clean kitchen towel and fold the towel over them. Roll over the towel with a rolling pin until they are the consistency you want.

START TO FINISH **30 minutes**
MAKES **4 servings**

- 1   pound fresh or frozen large shrimp in shells
- 3   medium clementines or seedless tangerines
- ¾   cup water
- ⅓   cup sugar
- 1   teaspoon whole black peppercorns, coarsely crushed
- 1   small pink grapefruit
- ½   teaspoon salt
- ½   teaspoon freshly ground black pepper
- ¼   teaspoon cumin
- 1   tablespoon canola oil

1. Thaw shrimp, if frozen. For pepper-citrus sauce, use a vegetable peeler to remove 2 to 3 strips of the thin outer peel of one of the clementines, taking care not to remove the bitter white pith. Place peel in small saucepan; add the water, sugar, and peppercorns. Bring to boiling, stirring to dissolve sugar. Boil gently, uncovered, for 15 to 20 minutes or until mixture is reduced to ⅓ cup, stirring occasionally.

2. Meanwhile, peel and devein shrimp, leaving tails intact. Rinse shrimp; pat dry with paper towels.

3. Peel and remove white pith from the remaining clementines and the grapefruit. If desired, leave one clementine whole; break remaining clementines into segments. Cut grapefruit crosswise into ½-inch slices. Remove seeds and set slices aside.

4. For shrimp, in a medium bowl combine salt, freshly ground pepper, and cumin. Add shrimp; toss to coat. In large skillet heat oil over medium heat. Add shrimp; cook for 3 to 4 minutes or until opaque, turning occasionally. Add clementines and grapefruit to shrimp. Cover and cook over medium heat for 1 minute, turning fruit once. Transfer to serving bowl. Pour pepper-citrus sauce over shrimp mixture; toss gently to coat.

EACH SERVING *260 cal, 6 g fat, 172 mg chol, 461 mg sodium, 29 g carb, 2 g fiber, 24 g pro.*

Seared Scallops with Meyer Lemon Beurre Blanc and Warm Savoy-Citrus Slaw

Meyer lemons are thought to be a cross between a lemon and either a common or Mandarin orange. They have thinner skin than standard lemons and sweeter, less lip-puckering flesh. Here they infuse a classic French beurre blanc—a white wine-butter sauce—with their wonderful flavor. The sauce is conveniently kept warm in an insulated container while you finish the rest of this company-worthy dish.

PREP **20 minutes**
COOK **30 minutes**
MAKES **5 servings**

20 fresh or frozen large sea scallops, adductor muscles removed
1 cup Sauvignon Blanc
¼ cup Meyer lemon juice
¼ cup finely chopped shallots (2 medium)
1 tablespoon whipping cream
12 tablespoons cold butter, cubed
¼ teaspoon salt
2 tablespoons olive oil
2 ounces pancetta, cut into ¼-inch cubes
½ cup thinly sliced scallions or green onions
¼ cup white wine vinegar
4 cups tightly packed savoy cabbage, thinly sliced
1 large orange, peeled and sectioned
1 small red grapefruit, peeled and sectioned
¼ cup snipped fresh chives or sliced scallions or green onions

1. Thaw scallops, if frozen. Rinse scallops; pat dry with paper towels. Set scallops aside.
2. To prepare Meyer lemon beurre blanc, in a medium saucepan combine wine, lemon juice, and shallots. Bring to boiling; reduce heat. Simmer, uncovered, until mixture is reduced to 2 tablespoons. Add whipping cream to saucepan. Return to simmering, then reduce heat to low. Add butter, 1 cube at a time, whisking between additions, until a rich sauce forms. Whisk in salt. Ladle sauce into a wide mouth thermos; close tightly and set aside.
3. In a large skillet heat oil over medium-high heat. Working in batches, add scallops and sear about 1 minute on each side or until golden brown. Transfer scallops to a platter; keep warm in a 200°F oven while you prepare the slaw.
4. For warm savoy-citrus slaw, in a large skillet cook and stir pancetta cubes over medium heat for 6 to 8 minutes or until crisp. Using a slotted spoon, transfer pancetta cubes to paper towels to drain. Add scallions to the drippings in the skillet; cook for 1 to 2 minutes or until tender. Stir in vinegar. Cook and sir, scraping up any browned bits from bottom of skillet. Bring to boiling. Add cabbage; cook and stir for 2 to 3 minutes or until cabbage is lightly wilted. Add orange and grapefruit sections; toss gently to combine.
5. To serve, divide slaw among serving plates; top with scallops. Spoon Meyer lemon beurre blanc over scallops. Garnish with pancetta cubes and chives.
EACH SERVING *502 cal, 38 g fat, 103 mg chol, 803 mg sodium, 18 g carb, 4 g fiber, 16 g pro.*

Green Curry-Style Vegetables with Sizzled Tofu and Rice

It's important to thoroughly dry the tofu with clean paper towels before frying to avoid splattering. If you'd like it to have an even firmer texture, press more of the liquid out of it: Set the block of tofu on a plate lined with several layers of clean paper towels. Lay several more clean paper towels on top of the block, then set a plate on top of the towels. Place something weighty—a can of tomatoes or broth, for instance—on top to press the water out. Let stand for 10 minutes.

START TO FINISH **45 minutes**
MAKES **6 to 8 servings**

2   4-ounce cans fire-roasted diced green chiles
⅓   cup coarsely chopped fresh cilantro leaves and stems
⅓   cup fresh mint leaves
⅓   cup Thai or sweet basil leaves
1   to 2 Thai, serrano, or jalapeño chile peppers*
5   cloves garlic, smashed
2   tablespoons lime juice
1   tablespoon minced fresh lemongrass
1   tablespoon grated fresh ginger
1   teaspoon ground cumin
1   teaspoon ground coriander
½   teaspoon sea salt or salt
10   ounces firm silken-style tofu (fresh bean curd)
2   tablespoons olive oil
1   peeled, cored fresh pineapple
6   cups fresh vegetables, such as 1-inch pieces eggplant, 2-inch pieces green beans, sliced carrots, sweet pepper strips, and/or summer squash, halved lengthwise and sliced
2   tablespoons sour cream
1½   cups uncooked jasmine rice

1. For green curry sauce, in a blender combine canned chiles, cilantro, mint, basil, Thai chiles, garlic, lime juice, lemongrass, ginger, cumin, coriander, and sea salt. Cover and blend until smooth; set aside.

2. Slice tofu; pat dry with paper towels. In a very large skillet heat 1 tablespoon of the oil over medium-high heat. Cook tofu in hot oil until golden and beginning to crisp, turning to brown evenly. Remove tofu from skillet.

3. Measure ¼ cup juice from the pineapple container (or use ¼ cup canned pineapple juice); set aside. Chop enough pineapple to make 1 cup (reserve remaining pineapple for another use). Add remaining 1 tablespoon oil to skillet. Add chopped pineapple and the vegetables to skillet. Cook and stir over medium-high heat for 10 minutes or until vegetables are crisp-tender. Stir in ¾ cup of the green curry sauce, sour cream, and ¼ cup reserved pineapple juice just until combined. Bring to boiling; reduce heat. Cover and simmer about 5 minutes or until vegetables

are tender. Add tofu to vegetable mixture; gently stir to combine.

4. Meanwhile, in a medium saucepan cook rice according to package directions. Serve vegetable mixture over rice. Drizzle some of the remaining green curry sauce over each serving.

*Tip Because hot chile peppers contain volatile oils that can burn your skin and eyes, avoid contact with chiles as much as possible. When working with chile peppers, wear plastic or rubber gloves. If your bare hands do touch the chile peppers, wash your hands well with soap and water.

EACH SERVING *327 cal, 7 g fat, 2 mg chol, 294 mg sodium, 60 g carb, 5 g fiber, 8 g pro.*

Rustic Swiss Chard and Mozzarella Tart

Swiss chard is a member of the beet family and has an earthy flavor similar to its bulbous cousin's. Among its many names, it is called "perpetual spinach," perhaps because when the spinach is wilting in the heat or the lettuce is zapped by frost, this hardy leafy green just keeps on going. It is positively packed with nutrients and is thought to have cancer-fighting properties.

PREP **30 minutes**
BAKE **30 minutes**
OVEN **400°F**
MAKES **4 servings**

1   recipe Savory Tart Pastry
1   tablespoon olive oil
5   cups chopped Swiss chard
    (1 bunch)
1   cup chopped leeks
4   cloves garlic, minced
1   teaspoon fresh thyme
¼   teaspoon salt
¼   teaspoon ground black pepper
¾   cup shredded mozzarella
    cheese (3 ounces)
    Fresh Italian (flat-leaf) parsley
    (optional)

1. Prepare Savory Tart Pastry. Wrap dough in plastic wrap and chill while preparing filling.
2. Preheat oven to 400°F. For filling, in a large skillet heat oil over medium heat. Add chard, leeks, garlic, thyme, salt, and pepper. Cook about 4 minutes or until chard wilts and leeks are tender. Cool slightly. Stir in cheese; set filling aside.
3. On a lightly floured surface roll pastry to a 12-inch circle. Transfer to a parchment-lined greased baking sheet. Spoon filling into center of the pastry circle, leaving a 2-inch border. Fold dough over filling, leaving center open and pleating edges of dough.

4. Bake for 30 to 40 minutes or until golden. Serve warm. If desired, sprinkle with parsley.
Savory Tart Pastry In a large bowl combine 1¼ cups all-purpose flour and ¼ teaspoon salt. Cut up ½ cup cold butter; cut into flour mixture until mixture resembles coarse crumbs. In a small bowl stir together ¼ cup cold water, ¼ cup sour cream, and 2 teaspoons lemon juice. Add half of the sour cream mixture to flour mixture; toss with a fork. Add the remaining sour cream mixture; toss with a fork until moistened. Form into a ball.
EACH SERVING *487 cal, 34 g fat, 79 mg chol, 709 mg sodium, 37 g carb, 2 g fiber, 11 g pro.*

Rustic Phyllo Pie with Mustard Greens and Fresh Goat Cheese

A crisp topping of phyllo ribbons gives way to a creamy filling in this twist on Greek spanakopita. Peppery mustard greens stand in for the usual spinach; goat cheese and yogurt take the place of traditional feta cheese—and instead of the time-intensive layering and brushing of phyllo with olive oil or butter, pastry sheets are simply cut into strips and lightly sprayed with olive oil cooking spray before baking.

PREP **20 minutes**
COOK **11 minutes**
BAKE **30 minutes**
OVEN **375°F**
MAKES **6 servings**

1	tablespoon olive oil
½	cup chopped onion (1 medium)
2	cloves garlic, minced
¼	teaspoon mustard seeds
10	cups torn mustard greens (1½ bunches)
10	cups torn Swiss chard (2 bunches)
1½	cups plain Greek yogurt
1½	cups crumbled goat cheese (6 ounces)
2	egg yolks, lightly beaten
¼	teaspoon freshly grated nutmeg
¼	teaspoon cayenne pepper
	Salt and ground black pepper
10	sheets frozen phyllo dough (14×9-inch sheets), thawed and thinly sliced crosswise (4 ounces)
	Nonstick olive oil cooking spray

1. Preheat oven to 375°F. In a very large skillet heat oil over medium heat. Add onion, garlic, and mustard seeds. Cook about 6 minutes or until onion is tender.

2. Working in batches, stir in handfuls of mustard greens and chard (adding more greens as there becomes room in the pan). Cook until greens are wilted and tender (about 5 minutes). Transfer greens mixture to a colander. Press greens with a wooden spoon to remove excess liquid.

3. Transfer greens to a large bowl. Stir in yogurt, goat cheese, egg yolks, nutmeg, and cayenne pepper. Season with salt and pepper. Transfer greens mixture to a 2-quart square baking dish.

4. On a large sheet of waxed paper spread the phyllo strips in a single layer. Coat with cooking spray; toss to coat evenly. Pile phyllo strips on top of mustard greens mixture. Bake for 30 to 35 minutes or until topping is golden brown.

EACH SERVING *314 cal, 16 g fat, 95 mg chol, 396 mg sodium, 24 g carb, 5 g fiber, 21 g pro.*

Farro-Stuffed Peppers

Farro is an ancient Roman grain that has a chewy texture and a nutty taste with hints of oats and barley. Because it contains a starch similar to that of arborio rice—the rice used in risotto—it takes on a creamy texture when cooked. Long lauded for its health benefits, it is high in fiber and very low in gluten. Mixed with fresh summer vegetables, cheese, curry, and fresh basil, farro is the base of a hearty and fragrant filling for juicy sweet peppers.

PREP 20 minutes
COOK 35 minutes
BAKE 45 minutes
OVEN 400°F
MAKES 4 servings

1   14.5-ounce can reduced-sodium vegetable or reduced-sodium chicken broth
1   cup farro
1   cup water
2   ears fresh sweet corn
2   tablespoons butter or olive oil
1   teaspoon curry powder
½   cup sliced green onions or scallions (4)
1   cup chopped yellow summer squash and/or zucchini
¼   teaspoon salt
¼   teaspoon ground black pepper
2   cups shredded fontina cheese (8 ounces)
½   cup snipped fresh basil
4   large red sweet peppers

1. In a medium saucepan combine broth, farro, and the water. Bring to boiling; reduce heat. Cover and simmer about 30 minutes or until farro is tender. Drain farro, reserving ½ cup of the cooking liquid; set farro and the cooking liquid aside.

2. Preheat oven to 400°F. Remove husks from the ears of corn. Scrub with a stiff brush to remove silks; rinse. Cut corn from cobs; discard cobs. Set corn aside.

3. In a large skillet melt the butter over medium heat. Stir in curry powder. Add the corn and green onions. Cook for 2 minutes, stirring occasionally. Stir in squash; cook for 2 minutes more. Stir in cooked farro, salt, and black pepper. Remove from heat; cool slightly. Stir in 1 cup of the cheese and ¼ cup of the basil.

4. Cut sweet peppers in half lengthwise. Remove and discard seeds and membranes. Spoon farro mixture into pepper halves. Place stuffed peppers in a 3-quart rectangular baking dish. Pour the reserved cooking liquid into dish around the peppers. Cover with foil.

5. Bake for 30 minutes. Remove foil. Sprinkle with the remaining 1 cup cheese. Bake, uncovered, about 15 minutes more or until peppers are crisp-tender. Sprinkle with the remaining ¼ cup basil.

EACH SERVING *536 cal, 25 g fat, 81 mg chol, 943 mg sodium, 53 g carb, 7 g fiber, 25 g pro.*

Wild Rice-Stuffed Acorn Squash with Cranberries, Pecans, and Pancetta

When the leaves turn colors and the weather turns cool, this sweet and savory stuffed squash hits the spot. Pancetta is a cured but unsmoked Italian bacon that usually comes in thin, round spiraled slices. If you can't find it, you can certainly use smoky American bacon. You will likely not get any complaints.

PREP **30 minutes**
BAKE **1 hour 10 minutes**
OVEN **400°F**
MAKES **6 servings**

3   1½-pound acorn squash, halved lengthwise and seeds removed
¼   cup butter, melted
¼   cup packed brown sugar
½   teaspoon salt
¼   teaspoon freshly ground black pepper
4   ounces pancetta, chopped
½   cup chopped onion (1 medium)
2   cups lightly packed baby spinach
1   tablespoon snipped fresh sage
2   cups cooked brown and/or wild rice
⅔   cup pecans, toasted and chopped
½   cup dried cranberries

1. Preheat oven to 400°F. Add ½-inch water to the bottom of a large roasting pan. Arrange the squash halves, cut sides down, in the roasting pan. Bake, uncovered, for 30 minutes. Turn squash halves cut sides up. Brush cut sides of squash with 2 tablespoons of the melted butter. Sprinkle with brown sugar, salt, and pepper. Bake, uncovered, for 20 to 25 minutes more or just until tender.

2. Meanwhile, in a large skillet cook and stir pancetta over medium heat for 5 to 6 minutes or until crisp. Using a slotted spoon, remove pancetta from skillet. Drain on paper towels.

3. Add onion to drippings in skillet; cook and stir for 4 to 5 minutes or until onion is tender. Add spinach, sage, and the crisped pancetta. Cook and stir for 2 minutes or until spinach wilts. Remove skillet from heat. Stir in the cooked rice, pecans, and cranberries. Mix well.

4. Divide rice mixture among squash halves, filling each cavity with about ⅔ cup rice mixture. Drizzle with remaining melted butter. Bake, uncovered, for 20 to 25 minutes more or until heated through.

EACH SERVING *462 cal, 23 g fat, 27 mg chol, 391 mg sodium, 63 g carb, 7 g fiber, 9 g pro.*

Spinach-Tarragon Supper Soufflé

A soufflé brings to mind a time-consuming, temperamental, intimidating dish—not something easily whipped up for a weeknight supper. But soufflés are very simple. They involve very few (and basic) ingredients, a short prep time, and a good 30-minutes in the oven that allows you to do other things. (The 30 minutes standing time in this recipe allows the eggs come to room temperature.) Serve this airy, cheese-and-spinach dish with a green salad and crusty bread.

PREP 30 minutes
STAND 30 minutes
BAKE 35 minutes
OVEN 375°F
MAKES 4 servings

4   eggs
1½   cups lightly packed chopped spinach
3   tablespoons butter
3   tablespoons all-purpose flour
¼   teaspoon salt
¼   teaspoon dry mustard
        Pinch cayenne pepper
1   cup milk
1   tablespoon snipped fresh tarragon
½   cup finely shredded Swiss or Gruyère cheese (2 ounces)

1. Separate eggs. Allow egg yolks and whites to stand at room temperature for 30 minutes. Position oven rack so it is in the bottom third of the oven. Preheat oven to 375°F. Grease bottom and sides of a 1-quart soufflé dish with a 6-inch diameter. To make a collar for the soufflé dish, measure enough foil to wrap around the top of the soufflé dish and add 3 inches. Fold the foil in thirds lengthwise. Lightly grease 1 side of the foil. Attach the foil with greased side toward center, around the outside of the dish so the foil extends 2 inches above the dish. Tape or pin the ends of the foil together; set aside.

2. In a medium saucepan cook spinach in a small amount of boiling water about 3 minutes or just until wilted. Drain in a colander, pressing most of the liquid from the spinach. Pat dry with paper towels. You should have about ¼ cup cooked spinach; set aside.

3. For sauce, in a medium saucepan melt butter over medium heat. Stir in flour, salt, mustard, and cayenne pepper. Cook and stir over medium heat about 2 minutes or until mixture starts to turn golden. Carefully add milk whisking constantly until combined. Cook and stir until thickened and bubbly, about 3 minutes. Remove from heat. Whisk in egg yolks, one at a time. Stir in cooked spinach and the tarragon.

4. In a large mixing bowl beat egg whites with an electric mixer on medium to high until stiff peaks form (tips stand straight). Fold about 1 cup of the egg whites into the sauce to lighten. Fold the sauce and the cheese into the remaining egg whites in bowl. Pour mixture into the prepared soufflé dish.

5. Bake in the lower third of the oven about 35 minutes or until a wooden skewer inserted near the center comes out clean and top is golden brown. Carefully remove the foil collar. Serve immediately. To serve, insert two forks into the center to gently tear the soufflé into four pieces.

EACH SERVING *257 cal, 19 g fat, 227 mg chol, 358 mg sodium, 9 g carb, 0 g fiber, 13 g pro.*

Brussels Sprouts, Walnuts, Fennel, and Pearl Onions over Bacon-Swiss Polenta

This dish relies on a melange of filling fall and winter vegetables for its heartiness. The only meat called for is a little bit of bacon to add some smoky flavor to the creamy, cheesy polenta. Substitute a nice sharp Cheddar or even smoked Gouda for the Swiss cheese if you like.

PREP 25 minutes
ROAST 30 minutes
COOK 25 minutes
OVEN 400°F
MAKES 6 servings

1   pound fresh Brussels sprouts
2   tablespoons olive oil
½   teaspoon coarse salt
¼   teaspoon coarsely ground black pepper
2   tablespoons butter
1   16-ounce package frozen pearl onions, thawed and patted dry
1   teaspoon sugar
2   large fennel bulbs, trimmed, cored, and thinly sliced
2   cups chicken or vegetable broth
2   bay leaves
3   tablespoons snipped fresh Italian (flat-leaf) parsley
2   teaspoons snipped fresh thyme
½   cup chopped walnuts, toasted*
2   tablespoons walnut oil
1   recipe Bacon-Swiss Polenta Chopped fennel fronds (optional)

1. Preheat oven to 400°F. Trim Brussels sprouts. In a large bowl combine Brussels sprouts and olive oil; toss to coat sprouts with oil. Transfer sprouts to a 15×10×1-inch baking pan. Sprinkle with salt and pepper. Roast, uncovered, for 30 to 35 minutes or until tender and browned, stirring once.

2. Meanwhile, in a large skillet melt butter over medium heat. Add onions; sprinkle with sugar. Cook and stir just until onions begin to brown. Cover skillet and cook for 5 to 10 minutes more or until onions are almost tender. Add fennel; cover skillet and cook for 8 to 10 minutes or until fennel is tender, stirring occasionally. Remove lid; add broth, bay leaves, parsley, and thyme. Cook, uncovered, over medium heat until liquid is reduced to 2 to 3 tablespoons. Discard bay leaves. Stir in roasted Brussels sprouts, walnuts, and walnut oil.

3. Serve vegetable mixture over Bacon-Swiss Polenta. If desired, garnish with fennel fronds.

Bacon-Swiss Polenta In a medium saucepan over medium-high heat bring 3¾ cups milk to boiling. Stir in ¾ cup quick-cooking polenta or cornmeal; 3 tablespoons butter, softened; ½ teaspoon salt; and ¼ teaspoon ground black pepper. Cook over medium heat for 5 to 8 minutes or until mixture thickens, whisking constantly. Stir in ½ cup shredded Swiss cheese (2 ounces) and 3 slices crumbled, crisp-cooked bacon; serve immediately.

*Tip Toast walnuts in a dry skillet over medium-high heat about 2 minutes or until golden brown, stirring frequently.

EACH SERVING *580 cal, 33 g fat, 52 mg chol, 978 mg sodium, 57 g carb, 11 g fiber, 18 g pro.*

Smoky Grilled Vegetable Torte

This gorgeous vegetarian torte makes an impressive company dish for a casual, late-summer dinner party. Serve it with a big platter of arugula drizzled with olive oil, lemon juice, sea salt and black pepper—and sprinkled with a few shards of Parmesan cheese.

PREP **45 minutes**
GRILL **40 minutes**
STAND **15 minutes**
MAKES **8 servings**

½   cup olive oil
4   cloves garlic, minced
1   16-ounce tube refrigerated cooked polenta, sliced ½ inch thick
2   medium red, green, and/or yellow sweet peppers, quartered and seeded
2   fresh portobello mushrooms, stems removed
1   large eggplant, bias-sliced ¼ inch thick
1   medium zucchini, bias-sliced ¼ inch thick
1   medium yellow summer squash, bias-sliced ¼ inch thick
    Salt and ground black pepper
1½ cups shredded smoked Gouda cheese (6 ounces)
½   cup lightly packed fresh basil leaves
1   cup halved pear, grape, or cherry tomatoes
    Basil leaves (optional)

1. In a small saucepan heat olive oil and garlic over medium heat until fragrant and garlic is translucent but not browned; remove from heat and set aside.

2. Place polenta, sweet peppers, mushrooms, eggplant, zucchini, and summer squash on large baking sheets. Brush polenta and vegetables generously with the garlic oil. Season with salt and pepper. For a charcoal or gas grill, place polenta slices on the rack of a covered grill directly over medium heat. Grill for 4 to 5 minutes on each side or until polenta is lightly browned and heated through, using a metal spatula to carefully turn slices. Grill vegetables directly over medium heat for 4 to 6 minutes or until tender, turning once. (Grill in batches, if necessary.) Remove from heat and let cool slightly. When cool enough to handle, slice mushrooms.

3. In a 9-inch springform pan layer grilled vegetables and polenta, starting with eggplant. Sprinkle some of the cheese and a few basil leaves over each layer. Press to compact the layers. Top with tomatoes, more basil leaves, and the remaining cheese. Place torte in a foil pan or wrap the outside of the pan with a double layer of foil. Grill torte over medium-low heat for 15 to 20 minutes or until heated through.

4. Cool on a wire rack for at least 15 minutes. Remove outer ring of springform pan. Use a sharp serrated knife to cut into wedges. If desired, garnish slices with additional basil leaves.

EACH SERVING *283 cal, 20 g fat, 24 mg chol, 476 mg sodium, 19 g carb, 5 g fiber, 9 g pro.*

Herbed Chanterelle Risotto with Thyme Browned Butter

Mushroom hunters call the golden, lily-shape chanterelle the "queen of the forest" for its earthy but mild flavor. It is an elegant mushroom—perfect for flavoring this creamy risotto made with nutty-tasting browned butter. If you can't find chanterelles, cremini mushrooms make a fine substitute.

START TO FINISH 50 minutes
MAKES 4 (1⅓-cup) servings

1	pound chanterelle or cremini mushrooms
6	tablespoons butter
	Salt and ground black pepper
4	to 4½ cups reduced-sodium chicken broth
¼	cup finely chopped shallots (2 medium)
1¼	cups uncooked arborio rice
2	teaspoons snipped fresh thyme
½	cup dry white wine
⅓	cup grated Pecorino Romano cheese
1	tablespoon snipped fresh chives
1	tablespoon snipped fresh Italian (flat-leaf) parsley
	Grated Pecorino Romano cheese and/or snipped fresh chives (optional)

1. Halve any large mushrooms. In a very large skillet melt 4 tablespoons of the butter over medium-high heat. Add mushrooms; cook for 4 to 6 minutes or until tender and beginning to brown, stirring occasionally. Season with salt and pepper. Set mushrooms aside.

2. In a medium saucepan bring broth to boiling; reduce heat to maintain simmer.

3. Meanwhile, in a large heavy saucepan melt the remaining 2 tablespoons butter over medium-low heat. Add shallots; cook and stir for 4 to 5 minutes or until tender. Add rice and thyme; increase heat to medium. Cook and stir for 2 minutes. Add wine; cook and stir about 1 minute or until liquid is absorbed. Add about 1 cup broth; stir until almost all of the broth is absorbed. Continue cooking and adding broth, 1 cup at a time, stirring until almost all the broth is absorbed before adding more, until the rice is halfway cooked, about 10 minutes. Measure ½ cup of the mushrooms and set aside; stir the remaining mushrooms into the rice mixture. Continue adding broth and cooking until rice is tender but still firm to the bite and risotto is creamy, 10 to 12 minutes more. Stir in the ⅓ cup Pecorino Romano cheese, the 1 tablespoon chives, and the parsley. If desired, season with additional salt and pepper.

4. Divide risotto among 4 serving bowls. Top with the reserved mushrooms. If desired, sprinkle with additional Pecorino Romano cheese and/or chives.

EACH SERVING *459 cal, 20 g fat, 53 mg chol, 945 mg sodium, 55 g carb, 5 g fiber, 11 g pro.*

Pumpkin Parmesan Risotto

The flavor of fresh pumpkin puree is worth the effort to make it. It can be made when pumpkins are plentiful and stored in the freezer to use in risotto, pie, breads, and pancakes. To make Parmesan shavings for garnishing the finished risotto, draw a vegetable peeler across a wedge of cheese. The cheese will be easier to work with if you bring it to room temperature before shaving.

PREP **20 minutes**
COOK **45 minutes**
MAKES **4 to 6 servings**

2   to 2½ cups water
1¾ cups chicken broth
3   tablespoons unsalted butter
1   cup finely chopped onion
     (1 large)
1   clove garlic, minced
2   cups uncooked arborio rice
1   cup dry white wine
1½ tablespoons snipped fresh
     sage
1   cup Pumpkin Puree or canned
     pureed pumpkin
½   cup finely shredded
     Parmigiano-Reggiano cheese
     Shaved Parmigiano-Reggiano
     cheese (optional)
     Sage leaves (optional)

1. In a large saucepan bring the water and broth to boiling; reduce heat to maintain simmer.
2. In a heavy 4-quart saucepan melt butter over medium heat. Add onion and garlic; cook about 3 minutes or until tender, stirring occasionally. Add rice; cook and stir for 2 minutes. Add wine; cook and stir until liquid is absorbed. Stir in the snipped sage and about 1 cup of the broth mixture; stir until almost all of the liquid is absorbed. Continue cooking and adding broth, 1 cup at a time, stirring until almost all of the liquid is absorbed before adding more. Continue cooking and adding broth until rice is tender but still firm to the bite and risotto is creamy.
3. Stir Pumpkin Puree and the ½ cup cheese into risotto. Cook until heated through, about 1 minute. Serve in bowls. If desired, top with shaved cheese and sage leaves.

Pumpkin Puree Preheat oven to 375°F. Cut 2½ pounds pie pumpkins into 5×5-inch pieces. Remove and discard seeds and strings. Arrange pieces in a single layer, skin sides up, in a foil-lined baking pan. Cover with foil. Bake about 1 hour or until tender. When cool enough to handle, scoop pulp from rind. Place pulp in food processor or blender. Cover and process or blend until smooth. Measure 1 cup puree to use in risotto. Transfer remaining puree to an airtight container. Store for up to 3 days in the refrigerator or freeze for up to 6 months. Thaw frozen puree in the refrigerator. Makes 1¾ cups.
EACH SERVING *385 cal, 12 g fat, 26 mg chol, 547 mg sodium, 61 g carb, 6 g fiber, 10 g pro.*

Brussels Sprouts and Noodle Stir-Fry with Cilantro and Almonds

Brussels sprouts are a bit small to shred on a box grater—your knuckles and fingertips are in too close a proximity to the grating blades. If you have a shredding disk on your food processor, simply fill up the feed tube with sprouts and push them down with the pusher tool provided. It's a safe and fast way to shred.

START TO FINISH **30 minutes**
MAKES **4 (1½-cup) servings**

3	ounces dried whole wheat thin spaghetti
2	tablespoons olive oil
1	large red onion, thinly sliced
3	cloves garlic, minced
12	ounces Brussels sprouts, thinly sliced or shredded
1	tablespoon grated fresh ginger
¼	to ½ teaspoon crushed red pepper
½	cup reduced-sodium chicken broth
2	tablespoons reduced-sodium soy sauce
½	cup finely shredded carrot (1 medium)
⅓	cup snipped fresh cilantro
3	tablespoons slivered almonds, toasted*

1. Break pasta into 1-inch pieces. Cook pasta according to package black directions; drain and set aside.
2. Heat a 4-quart Dutch oven over high heat. When hot, carefully add oil, onion, and garlic all at once, stirring vigorously for 1 minute. Stir in Brussels sprouts, ginger, and crushed red pepper; cook for 1 minute, stirring constantly. Add chicken broth and soy sauce; cook until nearly dry, 2 minutes.
3. Remove from heat; stir in the cooked pasta, carrot, and cilantro. Sprinkle servings with almonds.
*Tip Toast almonds in a dry skillet over medium-high heat about 2 minutes or until golden brown, stirring frequently.
EACH SERVING *230 cal, 10 g fat, 0 mg chol, 393 mg sodium, 31 g carb, 6 g fiber, 9 g pro.*

Green Power

Cilantro inspires strong feelings. There are those who absolutely love it—and those who have yet to be converted by its culinary wiles. Used widely in Mexican and Asian cooking, it is best uncooked—as in guacamole and salsa—or stirred into hot food right before serving. Cilantro is actually the leaf of the coriander plant. Ground coriander seeds are prevalent in Indian cooking.

Here are some ideas for working more cilantro and coriander into your cooking:

Crab Cakes Try cilantro in crab cakes or cold shrimp salad in place of parsley.

Salad Dressing For a creamy low-fat dressing, mix equal parts Greek yogurt and buttermilk with salt, pepper, and finely chopped cilantro.

Cilantro Mayonnaise Stir chopped cilantro into prepared mayonnaise, along with finely chopped jalapeño, minced garlic, lemon juice, salt, and black pepper. Spread on wraps or slices of ripe tomato.

Grilled Meats Make a dry rub for grilled meats with freshly ground coriander. Toast the seeds in a skillet over medium heat until fragrant. Cool, then grind in a spice grinder. Stir together with kosher salt, ground cumin, and chili powder.

6 Fresh Ideas for Garlic

Garlic is a beloved flavor all over the world, whether it's pungent and aromatic garlic quick-cooked in hot oil or sweet, nutty, and mellow garlic slow-roasted in the oven. Try a new way to enjoy an old favorite.

1 White Bean Dip with Garlic and Cilantro

In a medium skillet over medium heat cook 2 cloves minced garlic and ¼ teaspoon crushed red pepper in 2 tablespoons olive oil for 30 seconds or until fragrant. Remove from heat. In a food processor combine two 15-ounce cans cannellini beans, rinsed and drained; ⅓ cup packed fresh cilantro; 3 tablespoons lime juice; ¾ teaspoon salt; and garlic mixture. Process until smooth. Serve with pita chips and fresh vegetables for dipping. Makes about 2 cups.

2 Garlic Soup

Crush 10 cloves of unpeeled garlic with the flat side of a large knife. Heat 3 tablespoons olive oil in a skillet over medium-high heat. Cook garlic in hot oil until browned, 2 to 3 minutes. In a large saucepan bring 6 cups of chicken broth and browned garlic to a simmer. Remove from heat; let steep for 10 minutes. Toast 4 thick slices of hearty country bread in oil in skillet. Remove garlic from broth; discard. Bring broth to boiling; poach 4 eggs in broth. Place one piece of toast in each of 4 bowls. Divide broth among bowls. Place 1 egg in each bowl. Season to taste with salt and pepper. Makes 4 servings.

3 Real Garlic Bread

In a small bowl combine ¼ cup softened unsalted butter, 2 tablespoons olive oil, 2 cloves minced garlic, and ¼ teaspoon salt. Slice a 1-pound loaf of hearty country bread into 18 pieces without cutting through the bottom crust, so slices stay attached. Spread butter mixture evenly between slices, about 1 teaspoon each. Wrap bread tightly in foil and bake in a 350°F oven for 15 to 20 minutes or until butter is melted and bread is hot. Carefully unwrap and serve hot. Makes 18 servings.

4 Lemon-Garlic Olives

In a medium bowl whisk ¼ cup extra virgin olive oil, 1½ tablespoons red wine vinegar, ½ teaspoon crushed red pepper, ½ teaspoon finely grated lemon peel, and 2 cloves of peeled, crushed garlic. Stir in 3 cups of mixed olives. Cover and refrigerate for at least 4 hours before serving. Makes 3 cups.

5 Roasted Garlic-Parmesan Polenta

Slice ½ inch off the top of a head of garlic. Drizzle with olive oil and wrap in foil. Bake in a 400°F oven until tender, about 45 minutes. Cool slightly. Unwrap and squeeze out the cloves. Set aside, discarding skins. In a medium saucepan bring 4 cups water to a boil. Slowly whisk in 1 cup yellow cornmeal. Stir until it begins to thicken, about 1 minute. Reduce heat; cover and simmer for 5 minutes. Add garlic, ¼ cup grated Parmesan cheese, and 1 tablespoon butter. Season to taste with salt and pepper. Makes 6 servings.

6 Cheesy Roasted Garlic-Topped Flatbread

Cut ½ inch off top of a garlic bulb. Place garlic, cut side up, in a custard cup. Drizzle with olive oil; cover with foil. Roast in a 425°F oven for 30 to 35 minutes or until soft. Cool; squeeze pulp from cloves. Lightly grill the top of a flatbread, such as focaccia. Spread pulp on grilled side. Drizzle with olive oil and sprinkle with ¾ cup shredded provolone cheese. Return flatbread to grill just until cheese melts. Sprinkle with flat-leaf parsley. Cut into wedges. Makes 8 servings.

Cheesy Roasted Garlic-Topped Flatbread

Penne with Five Herbs and Ricotta Salata

This is summer in a bowl. Hot cooked pasta is tossed with a little olive oil and five varieties of fresh herbs—basil, oregano, thyme, parsley, and chives—then tomatoes that have been gently sautéed until they begin to caramelize and release their juice. It's all topped with salty, tangy ricotta salata—a Sicilian sheep's milk cheese.

PREP 20 minutes
COOK 13 minutes
MAKES 6 servings

8   ounces dried penne pasta
2   tablespoons extra virgin
     olive oil
⅓   cup snipped fresh basil
1   teaspoon snipped fresh
     oregano
1   teaspoon fresh thyme leaves
½   teaspoon cracked black pepper
4   cups grape tomatoes
2   cloves garlic, minced
½   cup vegetable broth
¼   cup snipped fresh Italian
     (flat-leaf) parsley
2   tablespoons snipped
     fresh chives
1½   cups crumbled ricotta salata

1. Cook pasta according to package directions; drain well. Transfer drained pasta to a large bowl. Add 1 tablespoon of the olive oil, the basil, oregano, thyme, and black pepper. Toss to combine; cover to keep warm.

2. In a very large skillet heat the remaining 1 tablespoon of olive oil. Add tomatoes and garlic; cook and stir over medium-high heat for 5 to 6 minutes or until tomatoes caramelize, skins burst, and tomatoes begin to break down. Stir in broth; bring to boiling.

3. Add tomato mixture, parsley, and chives to pasta mixture; toss gently to combine. Divide pasta mixture among serving plates. Top with ricotta salata.

EACH SERVING *287 cal, 11 g fat, 25 mg chol, 569 mg sodium, 34 g carb, 3 g fiber, 11 g pro.*

Choosing Cheese

A cheese-loving wit once quipped that cheese was "milk's leap toward immortality." For something of such basic ingredients—milk, salt, rennet (an enzyme), and time—cheese is a wildly varied and complex food. First, there is the type of milk it's made from—cow, goat, sheep, or buffalo—and then how that milk is processed. Finally, the length of time a cheese is aged largely determines its taste and texture.

Most cheese falls into one of the following categories:

Fresh These mild cheeses, including cottage cheese, cream cheese, fresh mozzarella, and ricotta, are not aged at all.

Soft Aged for 60 days or less, these can easily be cut with a fork. Havarti and most types of feta are considered soft cheeses.

Semisoft These are often "young" versions of cheeses such as Gouda, Manchego, and cheddar that are aged 90 days or less. They can be aged much longer to achieve a semifirm or even hard texture.

Hard These cheeses are cooked, pressed, and aged for long periods of time—at least 2 years—until they have a hard, dry texture and intense, complex flavor. They are also called grating cheeses and include the likes of Parmesan and Pecorino.

Blue Spores of *Penicillium roqueforti* or *Penicillium glaucum* molds are sprayed or injected into these cheeses during the aging process, which creates the characteristic blue marbling and tangy flavor. Roquefort, Stilton, Gorgonzola, Cabrales, and Maytag all fall into this category.

Orecchiette in Creamed Corn with Wilted Tomatoes and Arugula

Fresh corn infuses this pasta dish with a distinctive sweetness that's complemented by the addition of peppery arugula. Reserving a bit of the pasta cooking water and using it in the sauce is a neat trick to remember any time you are making pasta. The starch that leaches out into the water from the pasta during cooking helps bind the sauce and give it a creamier texture—as well as flavor—than plain water does.

PREP **20 minutes**
COOK **15 minutes**
MAKES **4 servings**

4	ears fresh sweet corn
8	ounces dried orecchiette pasta
¼	cup pine nuts
1	tablespoon olive oil
1	cup grape tomatoes
1	medium shallot, thinly sliced
1½	cups half-and-half or light cream
½	teaspoon sea salt or kosher salt
½	teaspoon freshly cracked black pepper
½	teaspoon freshly grated nutmeg or ¼ teaspoon ground nutmeg
2	cups torn arugula
	Sea salt and freshly cracked black pepper
2	ounces Pecorino Romano or Parmesan cheese, shaved

1. Remove husks from ears of corn. Scrub with a stiff brush to remove silks; rinse. Cut kernels from cobs; set kernels aside. Discard cobs. In a 5- to 6-quart Dutch oven cook pasta in lightly salted boiling water for 12 to 15 minutes or until al dente. Remove ½ cup of the pasta water; set aside. Drain pasta; return pasta to the Dutch oven.

2. Meanwhile, in a very large skillet cook pine nuts over medium heat for 2 to 3 minutes or just until toasted. Remove pine nuts from skillet; set aside.

3. For sauce, heat the olive oil in the skillet over medium heat. Add corn kernels, tomatoes, and shallot. Cook for 5 to 7 minutes or until corn begins to brown and shallot is tender, stirring occasionally. Stir in half-and-half and the reserved pasta water. Bring to boiling. Boil gently, uncovered, for 5 minutes, stirring occasionally. Stir in ½ teaspoon sea salt, ½ teaspoon pepper, and the nutmeg. Pour sauce over pasta in pot. Add arugula and toss until well combined. Season with additional sea salt and cracked black pepper.

4. To serve, divide pasta mixture among bowls. Top with cheese and toasted pine nuts.

EACH SERVING *564 cal, 26 g fat, 48 mg chol, 669 mg sodium, 68 g carb, 5 g fiber, 20 g pro.*

Pappardelle with Spring Vegetables and Hazelnuts

Pappardelle—which means "gulp down" in Italian—are long, elegant ribbons of pasta that intertwine with sugar snap peas, broccoli, carrots, grape tomatoes, and a white browned-butter sauce in this colorful meatless dish. Serve it with a crisp white wine, such as Pinot Grigio or Sauvignon Blanc.

PREP 20 minutes
COOK 20 minutes
MAKES 4 to 6 (1½- to 2¼-cup) servings

1   8.8-ounce package dried pappardelle pasta
1   cup sliced leeks
2   cups broccoli florets
1   cup bias-sliced carrots (2 medium)
2   cups sugar snap pea pods, trimmed
1   cup halved grape tomatoes
¼   cup butter
2   cloves garlic, minced
½   cup dry white wine
1   to 2 teaspoons snipped fresh thyme
¼   cup coarsely chopped hazelnuts, toasted
¼   teaspoon salt
⅛   teaspoon ground black pepper
¼   cup finely shredded Parmigiano-Reggiano or Parmesan cheese

1. In a large pot cook pasta according to package directions; drain. Return pasta to pot. Cover and set aside.

2. Place a steamer basket in a large saucepan. Add water to just below the bottom of the basket. Bring water to boiling. Add leeks. Cover and steam for 2 minutes. Add broccoli and carrots; cover and steam for 3 minutes or until vegetables are crisp-tender. Add pea pods. Cover and steam for 1 minute or just until crisp-tender. Add vegetables to pasta in pot. Stir in tomatoes. Cover to keep warm.

3. Meanwhile, for sauce, in a medium saucepan combine butter and garlic. Cook and stir over medium heat until butter is melted. Cook about 5 minutes more or until butter is lightly browned, stirring occasionally. Remove from heat. Stir in wine and thyme. Return to heat; heat through.

4. Add the sauce and nuts to pasta and vegetables Toss to mix. Season with salt and pepper. Top with cheese.

EACH SERVING *489 cal, 19 g fat, 34 mg chol, 381 mg sodium, 63 g carb, 7 g fiber, 15 g pro.*

Flank Steak and Plum Salad with Creamy Chimichurri Dressing, *recipe page 167*

big
salads

A MEAL IN ONE Whether tossed in a big bowl or artfully arranged on a platter, these salads of fresh greens, grains, fruits, vegetables, legumes, and cheeses are all substantial enough to be a full meal. Add a little bread (maybe) and dinner is done.

Flank Steak and Plum Salad with Creamy Chimichurri Dressing

Chimichurri is a thick and flavor-packed herb sauce that is as commonly served with steak in Argentina as ketchup is served with french fries in North America. The traditional version is oil-and-vinegar-based—this inspired take incorporates some creaminess in the form of light mayo and yogurt.

PREP **10 minutes**
GRILL **10 minutes**
STAND **5 minutes**
MAKES **4 servings**

8   ounces beef flank steak
1   teaspoon ground cumin
¼   teaspoon salt
1   medium sweet onion, sliced horizontally into ½-inch slices
2   teaspoons olive oil
¼   teaspoon freshly ground black pepper
6   cups mâche (lamb's lettuce) or baby greens
4   ripe plums, pitted and cut into thin wedges
1   recipe Creamy Chimichurri Dressing

1. Trim fat from meat. Sprinkle meat with cumin and salt. Brush onion slices on both sides with oil; sprinkle with pepper. For a charcoal or gas grill, place meat and onion slices on the rack of a covered grill directly over medium-high heat. Grill meat for 10 to 14 minutes for medium-rare to medium (145°F to 160°F) and onion slices for 10 minutes or until tender, turning meat and onion slices once halfway through grilling. Let meat stand for 5 minutes. Thinly slice meat. Coarsely chop onion.

2. Place mâche in a large salad bowl or arrange on a large platter. Top with meat, onion, and plums. Drizzle with half of the Creamy Chimichurri Dressing. If desired, pass remaining dressing.

Creamy Chimichurri Dressing In a small bowl stir together ¾ cup light mayonnaise, ¼ cup plain Greek yogurt, 1 tablespoon white vinegar, and 3 cloves garlic, minced. Stir in 3 tablespoons snipped fresh Italian (flat-leaf) parsley, ½ teaspoon crushed red pepper, and ⅛ teaspoon salt. Serve immediately or cover and chill for up to 1 week. Before serving, stir in enough milk if necessary to reach desired consistency.

EACH SERVING *336 cal, 22 g fat, 53 mg chol, 546 mg sodium, 19 g carb, 2 g fiber, 16 g pro.*

Market-Stand Pasta Salad with Garlic and Shallot Dressing

This truly is a farmer's market feast. You can use any kind of vegetables that look beautiful at the Saturday-morning market, whatever arrives in your CSA box—or what's ripe and ready in your own garden. The freeform nature of this salad extends to the pasta. It calls for lasagna noodles broken into imperfect pieces for a perfectly gorgeous result.

PREP **25 minutes**
COOK **20 minutes**
CHILL **1 hour**
MAKES **4 servings**

6	cloves garlic
¼	cup olive oil
2	tablespoons chopped shallot (1 medium)
½	teaspoon salt
¼	teaspoon ground black pepper
2	teaspoons finely shredded lemon peel
¼	cup lemon juice
2	tablespoons agave syrup or honey
8	ounces lasagna noodles, broken into 3-inch pieces
3	cups assorted fresh vegetables, such as carrots, wax or green beans, pattypan squash, and/or sugar snap pea pods, cut into bite-size pieces
2	cups baby kale, arugula, or spinach
1	cup grape or cherry tomatoes, halved
6	ounces hard salami, cut into thin slices and halved
½	cup fresh basil leaves, slivered

1. For dressing, on a work surface lightly smash garlic cloves; remove and discard skins. In a small saucepan combine the garlic, olive oil, shallot, salt, and pepper. Cook over medium-low heat about 15 minutes or until garlic and shallot are very tender and caramelized. Let cool. Scrape garlic mixture into a blender. Add lemon peel, lemon juice, and agave syrup. Cover and blend until almost smooth. Set dressing aside.

2. In a large pot cook lasagna noodles in boiling salted water according to package directions, adding the 3 cups garden vegetables for the last 5 to 7 minutes. Drain; rinse with cold water. Drain again. Lightly pat noodle mixture with paper towels to remove excess moisture.

3. In a large bowl combine the noodle mixture, baby kale, tomatoes, salami, and basil. Lightly toss to mix. Pour dressing over salad; toss to coat. Cover and chill for 1 hour before serving.

EACH SERVING *595 cal, 28 g fat, 43 mg chol, 1,056 mg sodium, 68 g carb, 6 g fiber, 21 g pro.*

Watercress and Radish Salad on Smoky White Bean-Bacon Croutons

This is actually a hybrid between an open-face, knife-and-fork sandwich and a salad. Toasted slices of hearty country bread spread with a garlicky bean spread are vehicles for a spring salad featuring the peppery flavors and crisp textures of radishes and watercress.

PREP 25 minutes
BAKE 8 minutes
OVEN 400°F
MAKES 4 (2-slice) servings

8   ½-inch slices Italian bread
1   15-ounce can cannellini beans (white kidney beans), rinsed and drained
3   tablespoons almond butter or tahini (sesame seed paste)
1   teaspoon finely shredded lemon peel (set aside)
2   teaspoons lemon juice
2   cloves garlic, minced
½   to 1 teaspoon smoked paprika
5   tablespoons olive oil
     Sea salt and freshly ground black pepper
4   cups lightly packed fresh watercress
2   cups thinly biased-sliced radishes (8 ounces)
4   thick slices applewood bacon, crisp-cooked and crumbled
2   tablespoons lemon juice

1. Preheat oven to 400°F. Place bread slices on a baking sheet. Place in oven on the lowest rack. Bake for 8 to 10 minutes or until bread is toasted, turning bread over halfway through baking. Place bread on a wire rack.

2. In a food processor combine beans, almond butter, the 2 teaspoons lemon juice, garlic, and smoked paprika. Cover and process until almost smooth. With processor running, add 2 tablespoons of the olive oil through the top. Process until smooth. Season with salt and pepper.* Spread bean mixture over the bread slices. Place 2 slices on each of 4 plates.

3. In a large bowl combine the watercress, radishes, the crumbled bacon, the remaining 3 tablespoons olive oil, and the 2 tablespoons lemon juice. Toss to mix. Season with additional salt and pepper.

4. Using salad tongs, place watercress mixture on top of the croutons on each plate. Sprinkle with the reserved 1 teaspoon lemon peel.

*Make-Ahead Tip The white bean mixture can be made ahead and stored in a covered container in the refrigerator for up to 3 days.

EACH SERVING *519 cal, 30 g fat, 8 mg chol, 930 mg sodium, 51 g carb, 9 g fiber, 18 g pro.*

Warm Salad with Lamb Chops and Mediterranean Dressing

The contrast between the warm, smoky lamb and the crisp salad greens makes for a thoroughly satisfying eating experience. A savory blend of olive oil, red wine vinegar, scallion, marjoram, and thyme does double duty as both a marinade for the lamb and a vinaigrette that is drizzled over all before serving.

PREP 30 minutes
MARINATE 1 to 2 hours
GRILL 8 minutes
MAKES 4 servings

⅓   cup olive oil
3   tablespoons red wine vinegar
2   tablespoons finely chopped scallion or green onion (1)
1   tablespoon snipped fresh marjoram
2   teaspoons snipped fresh thyme
½   teaspoon salt
¼   teaspoon freshly ground black pepper
8   lamb rib chops, cut 1 inch thick
2   small heads radicchio
1   cup small red and/or yellow cherry or grape tomatoes
6   cups torn romaine, arugula, and/or spinach
4   radishes, coarsely chopped

1. For dressing, in a medium bowl combine oil, vinegar, scallion, marjoram, thyme, salt, and pepper.
2. Place lamb chops in a shallow dish. Spoon about ¼ cup of the dressing over lamb. Turn chops to coat with dressing. Cover dish and marinate in the refrigerator for 1 to 2 hours. Cover and set aside remaining dressing.
3. Meanwhile, cut each head of radicchio through the core into 6 wedges; brush lightly with some of the remaining dressing. Thread tomatoes onto 4 wooden skewers.* Thread radicchio wedges onto additional skewers, leaving a ¼-inch space between pieces.
4. For a charcoal or gas grill, place chops on rack of a covered grill directly over medium heat. Grill to desired doneness, turning once. Allow 12 to 14 minutes for medium-rare (145°F) and 15 to 17 minutes for medium (160°F). Add radicchio and tomatoes to grill. Grill for 2 to 3 minutes or until radicchio is slightly wilted and tomatoes are beginning to blister, turning once.

5. Divide greens among 4 plates. Remove radicchio and tomatoes from skewers. Arrange lamb chops, radicchio, and tomatoes on greens. Drizzle with remaining dressing; top with radishes.
*Tip Soak wooden skewers in water 30 minutes before using.
EACH SERVING *264 cal, 22 g fat 28 mg chol, 338 mg sodium, 7 g carb, 3 g fiber, 11 g pro.*

Smoked Chicken Salad with Broken Raspberry Vinaigrette

The sum of this salad is greater than its parts. The elements are simple, but each one is so flavorful—smoked chicken, fresh greens, sweet-tart summer raspberries—that it doesn't take a long ingredients list or one filled with exotic items to make a memorable meal. The "broken" vinaigrette refers to the breaking up of a portion of the raspberries into a mustard-shallot vinaigrette before tossing it with the chicken.

START TO FINISH **20 minutes**
MAKES **4 servings**

⅓   cup red wine vinegar
¼   cup canola or vegetable oil
1   tablespoon minced shallots
1   teaspoon honey
½   teaspoon Dijon mustard
      Dash salt
3   cups fresh raspberries
12   ounces smoked chicken or turkey breast,* sliced
8   cups mixed salad greens
¼   cup sliced almonds, toasted** (optional)

1. For raspberry vinaigrette, in a bowl combine vinegar, oil, shallots, honey, mustard, and salt. Whisk until mixture is well combined. Add 1 cup raspberries and whisk until raspberries are thoroughly broken up in the vinaigrette.

2. In a large bowl toss chicken with half of the dressing. Line a large platter with greens. Top with chicken mixture, the remaining 2 cups raspberries, and, if desired, almonds. Pass remaining dressing.

*Tip To smoke your own chicken or turkey, soak 3 cups of wood chips in enough water to cover for at least 1 hour. Brush 1 pound skinless, boneless chicken breast halves or turkey tenderloin lightly with olive oil and sprinkle with salt and pepper. Arrange medium-hot coals around a drip pan. Test for medium heat above drip pan. Add 1 inch of water to drip pan. Drain wood chips. Sprinkle wood chips over hot coals. Place chicken on grill rack over the drip pan. Close grill hood. Grill chicken for 15 to 18 minutes (allow 25 to 30 minutes for turkey) or until tender and no longer pink (170°F). (For a gas grill, preheat grill. Reduce heat to medium. Adjust for indirect cooking. Add wood chips according to manufacturer's directions. Place chicken on grill rack over burner that is turned off. Grill as directed.)

**Tip Toast almonds in a dry skillet over medium-high heat about 2 minutes or until golden brown, stirring frequently.

EACH SERVING *457 cal, 30 g fat, 62 mg chol, 558 mg sodium, 31 g carb, 4 g fiber, 18 g pro.*

Anaheim Chicken and Mango Salad

Long, slender, light green Anaheim chiles—also called California green chiles—have a sweet pepper flavor with just enough heat to be interesting. Grilling gives them a nice smoky flavor that pairs beautifully with the sweetness of the mangoes.

PREP **25 minutes**
GRILL **8 minutes**

3   tablespoons vegetable oil
3   6-inch corn tortillas
½   teaspoon ground cumin
1   pound skinless, boneless chicken breast halves
3   Anaheim peppers*
2   tablespoons extra virgin olive oil
3   large or 4 small mangoes, seeded, peeled, and cubed (1½ cups)**
1   tablespoon lime juice
1   tablespoon honey
1   teaspoon salt
½   teaspoon freshly ground black pepper
8   ounces romaine lettuce, chopped

1. For tortilla crisps, in a medium skillet heat the vegetable oil over medium-high heat. Stack tortillas; cut into thin wedges or strips. Fry tortilla pieces in hot oil for 1 to 2 minutes or until crisp. Using a slotted spoon, remove tortilla pieces from skillet; drain on paper towels. Sprinkle with cumin; set aside.

2. Using the flat side of a meat mallet, pound chicken breast halves to ¼-inch thickness. Using a small paring knife, remove stems from peppers. Use the knife to scrape seeds from inside of peppers, leaving peppers whole. Brush chicken and peppers with 1 tablespoon of the olive oil.

3. For a charcoal or gas grill, place chicken and peppers on the rack of a covered grill directly over medium heat. Grill for 8 to 10 minutes or until chicken is no longer pink and peppers are charred and blistered, turning once.

4. For dressing, in a blender or food processor combine ½ cup of the mangoes, the lime juice, honey, salt, black pepper, the remaining 1 tablespoon olive oil, and 1 of the grilled peppers. Cover and blend or process until smooth.

5. Chop chicken and the remaining 2 peppers. Place romaine in a large bowl. Add chicken, peppers, and the remaining mango. Toss to mix. Drizzle with dressing; toss to coat. Sprinkle with tortilla crisps.

*Tip Because hot chile peppers contain volatile oils that can burn your skin and eyes, avoid contact with chiles as much as possible. When working with chile peppers, wear plastic or rubber gloves. If your bare hands do touch the chile peppers, wash your hands well with soap and water.

**Tip If fresh mangoes are not available, substitute one 20-ounce jar refrigerated mango slices.

EACH SERVING *441 cal, 21 g fat, 73 mg chol, 723 mg sodium, 39 g carb, 6 g fiber, 27 g pro.*

Succotash Salad with Buttermilk Avocado Dressing

There are many versions of succotash—that most Southern of summer side dishes. Some are simply lima beans and corn and others include chopped sweet pepper as well. This hearty salad expands on that theme with butterhead lettuce, blue cheese, chicken, and bacon. Lima beans have a very short growing season and are very seldom available fresh. If you can find them, by all means use them. Otherwise, frozen lima beans—like frozen peas—are very high quality.

PREP 25 minutes
COOK 20 minutes
MAKES 4 servings

2   ears fresh sweet corn
½   cup fresh or frozen lima beans
¾   cup buttermilk
½   of an avocado, halved, seeded, and peeled
1   tablespoon snipped fresh Italian (flat-leaf) parsley
¼   teaspoon salt
¼   teaspoon onion powder
¼   teaspoon dry mustard
¼   teaspoon ground black pepper
1   clove garlic, minced
1   large head butterhead (Boston) lettuce, torn
2   cups sliced grilled chicken breast* (8 ounces)
6   slices bacon, crisp-cooked, drained, and crumbled
½   cup finely chopped red onion
½   cup crumbled blue or feta cheese (2 ounces)

1. Cut corn kernels from cobs; set kernels aside. In a small saucepan bring 1 cup of lightly salted water to boiling. Add lima beans; simmer about 15 minutes or until tender. Remove with a slotted spoon; set aside. Add corn to saucepan. Simmer for 3 minutes or until tender; drain and set aside.
2. For dressing, in a blender combine buttermilk, avocado, parsley, salt, onion powder, dry mustard, pepper, and garlic. Cover and blend until smooth. Pour into a small pitcher.

3. Line a large platter or 4 serving plates with the lettuce. Arrange chicken, crumbled bacon, corn, lima beans, onion, and cheese in rows on lettuce. Serve with dressing.
*Tip For grilled chicken, lightly season 12 ounces skinless, boneless chicken breast halves with salt and ground black pepper. For a charcoal or gas grill, place chicken on the rack of a covered grill directly over medium heat. Grill for 12 to 15 minutes or until chicken is no longer pink (170°F), turning once halfway through grilling.
EACH SERVING *375 cal, 15 g fat, 87 mg chol, 692 mg sodium, 24 g carb, 5 g fiber, 36 g pro.*

Lemony Grilled Chicken with Green Bean-Potato Salad

Fingerling potatoes are heirloom varieties of potatoes that grow in small, knobby fingerlike shapes. They come in a variety of colors—from creamy white and yellow to red and purple. They are prized for their tender texture and naturally buttery flavor.

PREP **30 minutes**
COOK **10 minutes**
GRILL **12 minutes**
MAKES **4 servings**

1   pound fingerling potatoes, halved lengthwise if large
8   ounces tender young green beans, trimmed
3   tablespoons sherry vinegar
2   teaspoons finely shredded lemon peel
3   tablespoons lemon juice
2   teaspoons Dijon mustard
2   teaspoons honey
1½ teaspoons snipped fresh thyme
½   teaspoon salt
¼   teaspoon ground black pepper
½   cup olive oil
4   skinless, boneless chicken breast halves
½   cup sliced green onions or scallions (4)
8   to 12 romaine heart leaves
1   cup crumbled goat cheese (8 ounces)
¼   cup slivered pitted kalamata olives

1. In a large pot of boiling salted water cook potatoes for 8 to 10 minutes or just until tender. Add green beans; cook for 2 minutes more or until beans are crisp-tender. Drain; spread potatoes and beans in a single layer in a shallow pan to cool.

2. For dressing, in a large bowl combine vinegar, lemon peel, lemon juice, mustard, honey, thyme, salt, and pepper. Add oil in a steady drizzle while whisking constantly. Place chicken in a resealable plastic bag set in a shallow dish. Add ¼ cup of the dressing to bag. Seal bag; turn to coat chicken. Marinate in the refrigerator until ready to grill or up to 1½ hours. Add potatoes, beans, and green onions to remaining dressing in bowl; toss to combine. Cover and chill until ready to serve.

3. Drain chicken, discarding marinade. For a charcoal or gas grill, place chicken on the rack of a covered grill directly over medium heat. Grill for 12 to 15 minutes or until chicken is no longer pink (170°F), turning once. Cool slightly.

4. To serve, arrange romaine leaves on a serving platter or divide among 4 dinner plates. Top with potato mixture. Slice chicken; add to potato mixture. Sprinkle with goat cheese and olives.

EACH SERVING *643 cal, 39 g fat, 105 mg chol, 698 mg sodium, 32 g carb, 6 g fiber, 43 g pro.*

Heirloom Tomato Salad with Grilled Tuna and Cannellini *pictured page 180*

Tomato salads that feature big, meaty slices of succulent, multicolor heirloom tomatoes are a classic way to enjoy what is perhaps the most popular type of all summer produce. The addition of grilled tuna and white beans dressed with an aromatic citrus-anise dressing turns a side salad into a main-dish salad that's elegant enough to serve to company.

PREP **25 minutes**
CHILL **up to 4 hours**
GRILL **6 minutes**
MAKES **4 servings**

2   15-ounce cans cannellini beans (white kidney beans), rinsed and drained
¼   cup snipped fresh basil
¼   cup white balsamic vinegar
2   teaspoons Dijon mustard
2   cloves garlic, minced
1   teaspoon finely shredded orange peel
¼   teaspoon anise seeds, crushed
2   6-ounce fresh or frozen yellowfin tuna steaks, 1 inch thick
2   tablespoons snipped fresh rosemary
2   tablespoons orange juice
1   tablespoon finely shredded lemon peel
3   cloves garlic, minced
2   teaspoons olive oil
3   large heirloom tomatoes, cut into wedges
    Flaked sea salt and freshly ground black pepper
    Fresh basil sprigs (optional)

1. In a large bowl combine cannellini beans, snipped basil, balsamic vinegar, mustard, the 2 cloves garlic, the orange peel, and anise seeds. Cover and chill for up to 4 hours.
2. Thaw fish, if frozen; pat dry with paper towels. In a small bowl combine rosemary, orange juice, lemon peel, and the 3 cloves garlic. Brush tuna with olive oil. Spread rosemary mixture over both sides of tuna, pressing to adhere.
3. For a charcoal or gas grill, place fish on the greased rack of a covered grill directly over medium heat. Grill for 6 to 8 minutes or just until fish flakes easily when tested with a fork, gently turning fish halfway through grilling. Thinly slice tuna steaks.

4. To serve, divide tomatoes and bean mixture among serving plates. Place tuna slices on top of beans. Sprinkle with salt and pepper. If desired, garnish with fresh basil sprigs. Serve immediately.
EACH SERVING *351 cal, 4 g fat, 33 mg chol, 651 mg sodium, 42 g carb, 11 g fiber, 34 g pro.*

Heirloom Tomato Salad with Grilled Tuna and Cannellini, *recipe page 179*

Spinach Salad with Indian-Spiced Chickpeas, Apricots, and Onions

Pappadams are a delightfully crunchy, wafer-thin Indian cracker made from lentil flour. They come unseasoned or with a variety of seasonings such as garlic, black pepper, cumin seed, or hot chile. You can broil them—as is done here—or toast them over an open flame using a gas burner and tongs, in which case they take on a wonderfully smoky flavor. Indian cooks sometimes deep-fry them to make them puff up to almost double their original size. Look for them at Indian markets.

START TO FINISH **20 minutes**
MAKES **6 (2-cup) servings**

¼ extra virgin olive oil
2 cloves garlic, minced
2 15-ounce cans chickpeas (garbanzo beans), rinsed and drained
3 tablespoons lemon juice
2 teaspoons packed brown sugar
2 teaspoons ground cumin
1½ teaspoons garam masala
1 teaspoon ground coriander
¼ teaspoon ground cinnamon
¼ teaspoon cayenne pepper
2 5-ounce packages fresh baby spinach
¾ cup dried apricots, cut into thin slices
½ of a small red onion, thinly sliced
    Toasted Pappadams (optional)

1. In a large skillet heat olive oil over medium heat. Add garlic; cook for 1 minute. Remove skillet from heat. Add garbanzo beans, lemon juice, brown sugar, cumin, garam masala, coriander, cinnamon, and cayenne pepper. Bring mixture just to a simmer. Cover skillet and set aside.

2. In a large bowl combine spinach, apricots, and red onion. Toss well. Add warm chickpea mixture; toss well to combine.

3. Divide mixture among serving plates. If desired, garnish with broken pieces of Toasted Pappadams. Serve immediately.

EACH SERVING *339 cal, 11 g fat, 0 mg chol, 325 mg sodium, 53 g carb, 9 g fiber, 9 g pro.*

Toasted Pappadams Preheat broiler. Arrange four 7-inch plain pappadams in a single layer on an ungreased baking sheet. Broil pappadams 6 inches from heat for 15 to 30 seconds or until bubbly and golden. Using tongs, gently turn pappadams; broil about 5 seconds or until bubbly and golden on the other side. Remove pappadams from oven and let cool. Break each pappadam into 5 or 6 pieces.

Honey-Soaked Quinoa Salad with Cherries and Cashews

You can serve this satisfying fruit, nut, and grain salad to mixed company that includes dedicated carnivores and vegans alike and everyone will be happy. There's not a single animal product in it— just fresh, juicy sweet cherries, protein-packed quinoa, chewy dried apricots, buttery lettuce, and crunchy cashews.

PREP **30 minutes**
COOK **10 minutes**
STAND **10 minutes**

¼ cup honey
2 tablespoons grated fresh ginger
2 tablespoons white wine vinegar
2 tablespoons lime juice
1 small clove garlic, minced
¼ teaspoon salt
¼ teaspoon freshly ground black pepper
¼ cup extra virgin olive oil
1 cup water
⅔ cup uncooked quinoa (rinsed)*
¼ teaspoon salt
1 cup fresh dark sweet cherries, pitted and halved, or red seedless grapes, halved
½ cup whole cashews, coarsely chopped
½ cup dried apricots, cut into thin slivers
¼ cup thinly sliced red onion
1 small head butter lettuce, torn (4 cups)

1. For honey vinaigrette, in a small bowl whisk together honey, ginger, vinegar, lime juice, garlic, ¼ teaspoon salt, and pepper. Drizzle in olive oil, whisking constantly, until well combined. Set aside.
2. In a medium saucepan combine the water, quinoa, and ¼ teaspoon salt. Bring to boiling; reduce heat. Simmer, covered, about 10 minutes or until liquid is absorbed. Remove from heat; let stand for 10 minutes.

3. Fluff quinoa with a fork. In a large bowl combine quinoa, cherries, cashews, apricots, and onion; toss to mix. Add lettuce; drizzle with ½ cup of the honey vinaigrette. If desired, season with salt and pepper. Toss again. Pass remaining vinaigrette. Store any remaining vinaigrette in the refrigerator for up to 5 days.
*Tip Place the quinoa in a fine-mesh strainer and hold under running water to remove any saponin, the natural coating on the grain, which may taste bitter.
EACH SERVING *372 cal, 17 g fat, 0 mg chol, 230 mg sodium, 52 g carb, 5 g fiber, 9 g pro.*

Barley-Sweet Corn Chopped Salad with Lime-Cumin Vinaigrette

The corn in this salad is grilled until lightly charred, which gives it a delicious caramelly flavor. It's then tossed with black beans, barley, grape tomatoes, chopped lettuce, and a slightly spicy Mexican-inspired vinaigrette. Serve with additional fresh lime wedges for squeezing.

PREP 25 minutes
GRILL 15 minutes
CHILL 1 hour
MAKES 12 to 14 (1- to 1¼-cup) servings

6   ears fresh sweet corn, husked
1   cup regular pearled barley
6   cups chopped iceberg and/or romaine lettuce
1   15-ounce can black beans, rinsed and drained
1   cup grape tomatoes, quartered
⅓   cup snipped fresh cilantro
½   cup apple juice
1   teaspoon finely shredded lime peel
⅓   cup lime juice
¼   cup extra virgin olive oil
2   tablespoons snipped fresh cilantro
1½ teaspoons ground cumin
1½ teaspoons finely chopped chipotle chile in adobo sauce
1   teaspoon sugar
¼   teaspoon salt
    Salt and ground black pepper
    Lime wedges (optional)

1. For a charcoal or gas grill, place corn on the rack of a covered grill directly over medium heat. Cover and grill about 15 minutes or until corn is tender and lightly charred, turning occasionally. When cool enough to handle, cut kernels from ears and transfer to a large bowl.
2. Cook barley according to package directions. Spread cooked barley on a piece of foil; cool to room temperature. Add barley to the bowl with corn. Cover and chill for at least 1 hour.
3. Add lettuce, black beans, grape tomatoes, and the ⅓ cup cilantro to the bowl with corn and barley. Toss well to combine.

4. For vinaigrette, in a screw-top jar combine apple juice, lime peel, lime juice, olive oil, the 2 tablespoons cilantro, the cumin, chipotle, sugar, and the ¼ teaspoon salt. Cover and shake well to combine.
5. Pour vinaigrette over salad; toss to combine. Season with additional salt and pepper. If desired, serve with lime wedges.

EACH SERVING *179 cal, 6 g fat, 0 mg chol, 201 mg sodium, 31 g carb, 6 g fiber, 6 g pro.*

Avocado and Blood Orange Salad with Almonds and Chili Oil

Blood oranges—also called Moro oranges—are among the juiciest, best-tasting of all the orange varieties. Cut one open and you will find gorgeous ruby-color flesh that has an intense orange flavor laced with raspberry. If you can't find them, Cara Cara oranges—in season at the same time—work equally well in this salad. Their pinkish-red flesh is very sweet with a cranberry-like tang.

PREP 20 minutes
MAKES 4 servings

2   tablespoons olive oil
¼   to ½ teaspoon crushed
    red pepper
4   blood oranges or Cara Cara
    oranges
2   ripe avocados, halved, seeded,
    peeled, and cut into wedges
1½ cups torn baby arugula
⅓   cup coarsely chopped
    almonds, toasted*
1   tablespoon lemon juice

1. For chile oil, in a small skillet heat oil over medium heat. Add crushed red pepper; cook about 1 minute or until fragrant. Let cool.
2. Meanwhile, using a paring knife, cut a thin slice from both ends of one of the oranges. Place a flat end on a cutting board and cut away the peel and the white part of rind. Working over a bowl to catch juices, hold the orange on its side and cut between one section and membrane. Cut along the other side of the section next to the membrane to release the section into the bowl. Repeat with the remaining 3 oranges.
3. Place the orange sections and juices on a serving platter. Add avocado wedges, arugula, and almonds to serving platter. Drizzle with chile oil and the lemon juice.
*Tip To toast nuts, spread them in a shallow baking pan. Bake in 350°F oven for 5 to 10 minutes or until light brown, shaking pan once or twice. Watch carefully so the nuts don't burn.
EACH SERVING *287 cal, 22 g fat, 0 mg chol, 8 mg sodium, 24 g carb, 9 g fiber, 5 g pro.*

Sparkling Salads

Many varieties of flavored oils and vinegars on the market can be used to handily dress up fresh produce with zero effort—just a splash, a sprinkle of salt, and a grind of fresh pepper. You don't have to use flavored products though. Just having a selection of basic, good-quality oils and vinegars on hand gives you lots of options for simply drizzling or whipping up a quick vinaigrette.

Stock your pantry with these oils and vinegars and you're prepared for nearly any kind of produce:

Olive oil For the fruitiest flavor, choose extra virgin olive oil. For a milder flavor, choose pure olive oil.

Vegetable oil Canola, safflower, and sunflower oils all have very neutral flavors, so the flavors of the salad ingredients or other flavors in the dressing come through.

Nut oils Almond, hazelnut, and walnut oils add rich flavor to a salad. They're highly perishable and need to be stored in the refrigerator.

Cider vinegar Tartly acidic, this is most often used for dressing hearty vegetables.

Flavored vinegars Infused with herbs, nuts, or fruits, these bring a subtle taste of the flavoring ingredient to foods.

Rice vinegar Mild in flavor, this vinegar made from fermented rice has a subtle sweetness.

Wine vinegars This type includes red wine vinegar, white wine vinegar, Champagne vinegar, sherry vinegar, and balsamic vinegar.

Grilled Zucchini Salad with Mozzarella and Dill

This rustic salad couldn't be any simpler. Slices of grilled zucchini are arranged on a serving platter with torn-up fresh mozzarella, then sprinkled with aromatic fresh dill and crushed red pepper and drizzled with lemon juice and olive oil. Just season to taste with salt and black pepper, if you like, and serve with slices of toasted bread.

PREP **10 minutes**
GRILL **8 minutes**
MAKES **4 servings**

3   medium zucchini, sliced lengthwise into ¼-inch planks
3   tablespoons extra virgin olive oil
    Salt and ground black pepper
1   8-ounce fresh mozzarella ball, pulled into large pieces
2   tablespoons coarsely snipped fresh dill
¼   teaspoon crushed red pepper
1   tablespoon lemon juice

1. On a baking sheet arrange zucchini in a single layer. Drizzle with 1 tablespoon of the olive oil; sprinkle with salt and black pepper.
2. For a charcoal or gas grill, place zucchini on the rack of a covered grill directly over medium heat. Grill about 8 minutes or until tender, turning once.
3. On a serving platter arrange warm zucchini and mozzarella. Sprinkle with dill and crushed red pepper. Drizzle with lemon juice and the remaining 2 tablespoons olive oil.

Stove Top Method To cook zucchini indoors, prepare zucchini as directed in Step 1. Preheat a grill pan over medium heat. Add zucchini to grill pan. Cook for 6 to 8 minutes or until tender, turning once. Continue as directed.
EACH SERVING *265 cal, 22 g fat, 40 mg chol, 323 mg sodium, 3 g carb, 1 g fiber, 11 g pro.*

Frizzled Egg Spinach Salad

A frizzled egg is created by cracking an egg into a pan that has hot fat in it at fairly high temperature—in this case, it's bacon drippings—so that the edge of the egg white immediately turns crisp, then turning the temperature down so that the rest of the egg doesn't get overcooked. The result is an egg with a crispy edge and a yolk that runs over the vegetables when a fork is stuck into it. Perfect.

START TO FINISH **45 minutes**
MAKES **4 servings**

2   large round red potatoes
6   ounces fresh green beans
    (2 cups)
8   slices bacon
8   ounces cremini or button
    mushrooms, halved (3 cups)
2   cloves garlic, minced
4   eggs
    Salt and ground black pepper
5   to 6 ounces baby spinach
1   recipe Raspberry Dressing

1. Cut each potato into 8 wedges. Place in a very large skillet. Add water to cover. Bring to boiling; reduce heat. Simmer, covered, for 5 minutes. Add green beans; return to boiling. Reduce heat and simmer, covered, for 5 minutes more. Drain; rinse in cold water.

2. Wipe out skillet to dry. Cook bacon in the skillet over medium heat until crisp. Drain on paper towels. Reserve 2 tablespoons drippings in skillet. Set aside the additional drippings for cooking the potatoes and the eggs.

3. Add mushrooms and garlic to the skillet. Cook over medium-high heat for 4 minutes. Remove from skillet; keep warm.

4. Add potato wedges to skillet; cook over medium heat for 8 to 10 minutes, turning to brown on both sides and adding reserved drippings as needed. Remove from skillet.

5. Break eggs into skillet; sprinkle with salt and pepper. Reduce heat to low; cook eggs for 4 to 5 minutes or until whites are completely set and yolks start to thicken. For more doneness on top, cover during the last 2 minutes of cooking.

6. Line 4 plates with spinach. Top with beans, bacon, mushrooms, potatoes, and eggs. Add Raspberry Dressing to skillet to warm. Drizzle salads with some of the dressing; pass remaining dressing.

Raspberry Dressing In a bowl whisk together ⅓ cup canola oil, ⅓ cup raspberry vinegar, 2 tablespoons honey, 2 teaspoons bottled chipotle pepper sauce, 1 teaspoon Dijon mustard, ¼ teaspoon ground cinnamon, and ¼ teaspoon ground cumin.

EACH SERVING *523 cal, 37 g fat, 232 mg chol, 662 mg sodium, 33 g carb, 5 g fiber, 17 g pro.*

Grilled Panzanella

Panzanella—Italian bread salad—is one of the many creative ways frugal cooks have devised for using up less-than-fresh bread (see sidebar, right). This version of panzanella incorporates grilled sweet peppers and crunchy cucumbers into the usual mix of bread and ripe summer tomatoes.

PREP **20 minutes**
GRILL **20 minutes**
STAND **30 minutes**
MAKES **12 servings**

8   ounces crusty country bread, sliced 1 inch thick
2   medium yellow, red, and/or green sweet peppers, seeded and quartered lengthwise
1   medium red onion, sliced ½ inch thick
4   tablespoons olive oil
3   large tomatoes, cut up
1   medium cucumber, coarsely chopped
3   tablespoons drained capers (optional)
1   tablespoon red wine vinegar
¼   teaspoon salt
¼   teaspoon ground black pepper

1. Brush bread slices, sweet peppers, and onion with 2 tablespoons of the olive oil. For a charcoal or gas grill, place bread and vegetables on the rack of a covered grill directly over medium heat. Grill bread slices for 2 to 4 minutes or until browned, turning once. Grill sweet peppers for 20 minutes, turning once. Grill onion for 10 to 15 minutes or until crisp-tender, turning once.

2. Cut bread and sweet peppers into 1-inch pieces. Coarsely chop onion. In a large serving bowl combine bread, sweet peppers, onion, tomatoes, cucumber, and, if desired, capers. Gently toss to mix.

3. For dressing, in a small bowl whisk together the remaining 2 tablespoons olive oil, the vinegar, salt, and black pepper. Drizzle over vegetable mixture; toss gently to coat. Let stand at room temperature for 30 minutes before serving.

EACH SERVING *113 cal, 5 g fat, 0 mg chol, 175 mg sodium, 15 g carb, 2 g fiber, 5 g pro.*

New Life for Old Bread

Because they don't contain preservatives or dough conditioners—and usually no fats—European- and artisan-style breads get stale and dried out quickly after they are baked. Italian cooks make bread salad and bread soup to put stale loaves to good use, but there are simpler ways as well.

Have some old bread lying around? Give it a purpose with one of these great ideas:

Homemade Croutons In a small saucepan melt ¼ cup butter. Stir in 3 tablespoons finely grated Parmesan cheese and 2 cloves finely minced garlic. In a large bowl toss flavored butter with 3½ cups of 1-inch cubes of stale bread. Spread in a single layer in a shallow baking pan and bake at 300°F for 10 minutes; stir. Bake 10 minutes more or until cubes are crisp and golden. Cool completely.

Savory French Toast In a medium bowl beat 2 eggs and ⅓ cup milk. Stir in 3 tablespoons finely grated Parmesan, a dash of salt and pepper, 1 tablespoon finely chopped parsley, and 2 teaspoons snipped fresh chives. Melt 1 tablespoon butter in a frying pan over medium heat. Soak 4 to 6 slices stale bread in egg mixture. Cook bread in hot butter 2 to 3 minutes per side until golden brown. Serve immediately. Makes 3 servings.

Grilled Romaine Salad with Tomato and Corn Tumble

Hearts of romaine are the inner leaves of the elongated head of lettuce. They are smaller, sweeter, and a lighter green—tending to yellow—than the outer leaves. Despite their more delicate nature, they're still sturdy enough to stand up to a grilling. Grilled lettuce is surprisingly good, too—held over the coals just until it's slightly charred and wilted.

PREP **20 minutes**
SOAK **1 hour**
GRILL **27 minutes**
MAKES **4 servings**

2   to 3 ears fresh sweet corn
4   tablespoons extra virgin olive oil
2   tablespoons sherry vinegar or red wine vinegar
1   tablespoon Dijon mustard
1   tablespoon snipped garlic chives*
2   hearts of romaine lettuce, halved lengthwise
1   cup grape and/or pear tomatoes (red, yellow, and/or green), quartered
    Sea salt and freshly ground black pepper
¼   cup crumbled ricotta salata or feta cheese (1 ounce)

1. Place corn with husks and silks intact in a large bowl. Add enough cold water to cover. Let soak for 1 hour.
2. Meanwhile, for garlic-chive vinaigrette, in a screw-top jar combine 3 tablespoons of the olive oil, the vinegar, mustard, and garlic chives. Cover and shake well; set aside.
3. Brush the romaine with the remaining 1 tablespoon olive oil; set aside. For a charcoal or gas grill, place corn on the rack of a covered grill directly over medium heat. Grill for 25 to 30 minutes or until kernels are tender, turning once and rearranging ears occasionally. Grill romaine, cut sides down, directly over medium heat for 2 to 3 minutes or until slightly charred and wilted.
4. Place a romaine heart half on each of 4 salad plates. Remove corn husks and silks from ears. Cut kernels from cobs. In a medium bowl combine corn kernels and tomatoes. Drizzle with some of the vinaigrette; toss to coat. Drizzle romaine with the remaining vinaigrette. Spoon the corn and tomato mixture over romaine halves. Season with salt and pepper. Top with cheese.

*Tip For the garlic chives, you can substitute 1 tablespoon snipped fresh chives and 1 clove garlic, minced.

EACH SERVING *200 cal, 16 g fat, 6 mg chol, 255 mg sodium, 13 g carb, 3 g fiber, 4 g pro.*

6 Fresh Ideas for Jalapeños

Jalapeños serve as the entry-level hot pepper for many. Without seeds, they provide a comfortable amount of heat to start building up a tolerance. Learn to love them even more with these ideas.

1 Fire-Roasted Jalapeño Pesto

Roast 12 jalapeño peppers over the open flame of a gas burner (pierce wide ends of peppers with a long-handle fork and hold over the flame until skin is lightly charred and bubbly). Wrap peppers in foil and let stand for 20 minutes or until cool enough to handle. Peel and seed peppers.* In a food processor or blender combine roasted jalapeños, ½ cup freshly grated Parmesan or Romano cheese, 4 tablespoons olive oil, and ½ teaspoon salt. Process or blend until smooth. Toss with cooked pasta or vegetables. Makes ¾ cup.

2 Jalapeño Marinade

In a screw-top jar combine ¼ cup vegetable oil, 3 tablespoons white wine vinegar, 2 tablespoons lime juice, 1 tablespoon honey, 2 teaspoons Jamaican jerk seasoning, and 1 jalapeño, seeded and finely chopped.* Cover and shake well. Pour over pork, poultry, fish, or shellfish in a resealable plastic bag. Refrigerate for 1 hour, turning bag occasionally. Drain, discarding the marinade; grill as desired. Makes ⅔ cup.

3 Baked Poppers

Cut 12 jalapeño peppers in half lengthwise.* Remove seeds and membranes. Combine 5 ounces cream cheese, ¼ cup sliced scallions, and ¼ cup finely shredded cheddar cheese. In another bowl combine ¾ cup panko bread crumbs, ⅛ teaspoon each of paprika, garlic powder, and chili powder, salt, and black pepper. Fill pepper halves with cheese mixture. Drizzle with 1 beaten egg and sprinkle with panko mixture. Arrange on oiled baking sheet and coat lightly with olive oil spray. Bake in a 350°F oven for 20 to 25 minutes or until cheese begins to ooze out. Makes 24 appetizers.

4 Hot Chile Mayonnaise

In a small bowl combine ⅓ cup mayonnaise; 1 fresh jalapeño, finely chopped;* 1 tablespoon Dijon mustard; and 1 teaspoon lemon juice. Serve with grilled fish. Makes about ½ cup.
*Tip Because hot chile peppers contain volatile oils that can burn your skin and eyes, avoid contact with chiles as much as possible. When working with chile peppers, wear plastic or rubber gloves. If your bare hands do touch the chile peppers, wash your hands well with soap and water.

5 Grilled Bacon, Cheddar, and Hot Pepper Jelly Sandwich

Spread one side of 4 slices of toasted whole-grain or sourdough bread with 2 tablespoons each of Hot Pepper Jelly (see recipe, right). Layer with sliced sharp cheddar cheese and strips of cooked bacon. Broil on a cookie sheet just until cheese melts. Cut slices in half and serve warm. Makes 4 servings.

6 Hot Pepper Jelly

Process 4 seeded sweet peppers and 6 seeded jalapeños* in a food processor until very finely chopped. In a Dutch oven combine peppers, 1½ cups cider vinegar, and 6 cups sugar. Bring to boiling, stirring. Remove from heat. In a small saucepan stir one 2¾-ounce package fruit pectin into ¾ cup cold water. Bring to boiling, stirring constantly. Boil 1 minute, stirring constantly. Stir into pepper mixture. Pour into plastic freezer containers, leaving ½-inch headspace. Cover; let stand for 24 hours. Chill until set. Chill up to 3 weeks or freeze up to 1 year. Makes 2½ pints.

Baked Poppers, *page 194*

MAIN INGREDIENT Beets BEST IN Midsummer to midfall

Roasted Beet Salad with Shredded Greens, Golden Raisins, and Pine Nuts

This autumnal salad uses the whole beet—the sweet and earthy bulb roasted with rosemary—and the mild, supernutritious greens. Manchego, a sheep's milk cheese from Spain, contributes a buttery texture and tanginess to the mix. Serve with some hearty multigrain country bread to round out the meal.

PREP 25 minutes
ROAST 55 minutes
OVEN 450°F
MAKES 4 (1½-cup) servings

- 2 pounds fresh beets with tops
- 2 sprigs fresh rosemary
- 3 tablespoons olive oil
- Salt and ground black pepper
- ½ cup golden raisins
- 2 tablespoons pine nuts, toasted
- 4 ounces Manchego cheese or ricotta salata, sliced
- Balsamic vinegar (optional)

1. Preheat oven to 450°F. Cut tops from beets; set tops aside. Place beets and rosemary on a piece of heavy foil. Drizzle with 1 tablespoon of the oil. Bring up two opposite edges of foil; seal with a double fold. Fold in remaining edges to completely enclose. Roast beets in packet about 55 minutes or until tender when pierced with a knife. Carefully open packet to release steam. Set aside until cool enough to handle. Peel skins from beets and cut into wedges. Discard rosemary.
2. Meanwhile, thoroughly wash and dry beet greens. Thinly slice beet greens, discarding stalks.
3. In a large bowl gently toss together warm beets, shredded beet greens, and the remaining 2 tablespoons oil until greens are slightly wilted. Season with salt and pepper.
4. On a large platter or 4 salad plates arrange beet mixture. Sprinkle with raisins and nuts. Top with cheese. If desired, drizzle with balsamic vinegar.

EACH SERVING *353 cal, 22 g fat, 25 mg chol, 419 mg sodium, 32 g carb, 5 g fiber, 11 g pro.*

Fresh Tomato Pizza with Oregano
and Mozzarella, *recipe page 239*

soups, sandwiches & pizzas

KNIFE-AND-FORK-FREE ZONE There's something casual and comfortable about food you can sip with a spoon or eat with your hands. These beautiful bowls of soup (both hot and cold), hearty sandwiches, and fresh and innovative pizzas are perfect for fun, relaxed meals.

French Garden Soup with Cheese Croutons

Late spring and early summer is the prime time to make this light and lovely soup. It is a take on *soupe au pistou*—the broth-based Provençal soup that is loaded with fresh vegetables and finished with a spoonful of basil pesto. Instead of the pesto, this version is topped with toasty cheese croutons made with a breaded cheese firm enough to stand up to broiling without melting.

PREP 30 minutes
COOK 36 minutes
MAKES 6 servings

2   tablespoons butter
1   small fennel bulb, trimmed, cored, and finely chopped
1   cup pearl onions, peeled and halved
1   cup fresh baby green beans, trimmed and cut into 1-inch pieces
1   cup baby or small carrots, trimmed and thinly sliced
3   cups homemade vegetable broth or two 14.5-ounce cans vegetable or chicken broth
1   14.5-ounce can petite diced tomatoes, undrained
1   cup dry white wine or homemade or canned vegetable or chicken broth
2   teaspoons herbes de Provence, crushed
1   cup shelled peas or frozen peas
     Salt and ground black pepper
1   recipe Cheese Croutons

1. In a Dutch oven melt butter over medium heat. Add fennel and pearl onions; cook for 3 to 4 minutes or until fragrant and translucent. Add green beans and carrots; cook for 3 minutes, stirring frequently. Add broth, undrained tomatoes, wine, and herbes de Provence. Bring to boiling; reduce heat. Simmer, covered, for 25 to 30 minutes.
2. Add peas to soup and simmer about 5 minutes more or until vegetables are tender. Season with salt and pepper.
3. To serve, ladle soup into bowls. Top with Cheese Croutons.

Cheese Croutons Preheat broiler. Cut 4 ounces firm feta or Halloumi cheese (not crumbled) into ½-inch pieces. In a shallow dish whisk together 1 egg white, 2 tablespoons water, and 1 tablespoon Dijon mustard. Place ½ cup fine dry bread crumbs in another shallow dish. Dip cheese pieces into egg white mixture, coating all sides. Toss cheese with bread crumbs until coated on all sides. Place coated cheese pieces on a baking sheet. Lightly coat with nonstick olive oil cooking spray. Broil 4 to 5 inches from the heat for 2 to 3 minutes or just until coating is crisp and golden but cheese is not melted.
EACH SERVING *241 cal, 9 g fat, 27 mg chol, 1,014 mg sodium, 27 g carb, 5 g fiber, 8 g pro.*

Fresh Sweet Corn Soup with Toasted Corn Guacamole

Boiling the corn cobs in the chicken broth might seem like a strange thing to do, but it accomplishes two things: It adds fresh sweet corn flavor to the soup, and the starch that cooks out of the cobs into the broth as they boil helps thicken the soup and give it body.

START TO FINISH **75 minutes**
MAKES **4 to 6 servings**

8	ears fresh sweet corn
2	tablespoons olive oil
¼	cup chopped shallots (2 medium)
1	fresh poblano pepper, roasted* and chopped
2	cloves garlic, minced
3½ to 4	cups reduced-sodium chicken broth
2	tablespoons snipped fresh cilantro
1	teaspoon finely shredded lime peel
2	tablespoons lime juice
½	teaspoon coarse salt
¼	teaspoon freshly ground coarse black pepper
1	large avocado, halved, seeded, peeled, and coarsely chopped
½	cup crumbled queso fresco cheese

1. Using a sharp knife, cut the corn kernels off the cobs (you should have about 4 cups). Set aside ¾ cup of the corn for the guacamole.

2. In a large skillet heat 1 tablespoon of the olive oil over medium heat. Add 2 tablespoons of the shallots, half of the roasted pepper, and half of the garlic. Cook and stir for 4 to 5 minutes or until shallots are tender. Remove from skillet and set aside.

3. Add 1½ cups of the chicken broth and reserved corn cobs to the skillet. Bring to boiling; reduce heat. Cover and simmer for 5 minutes. Using tongs, remove corn cobs and discard; reserve broth in skillet.

4. Add the 3¼ cups corn kernels to the broth in the skillet. Bring to boiling; reduce heat. Cover and simmer for 4 to 5 minutes or until corn is tender. Cool slightly. In a blender or food processor combine corn and shallot mixture. Cover and blend or process until almost smooth. Return corn mixture to the skillet. Slowly whisk in enough remaining broth to reach desired consistency; heat through. Keep soup warm while preparing guacamole.

5. For guacamole, in a large skillet heat the remaining 1 tablespoon oil over medium-high heat. Add the ¾ cup reserved corn kernels. Cook for 8 to 10 minutes or until kernels are tender and lightly browned, stirring occasionally. Remove from heat and cool slightly.

6. In a medium bowl combine toasted corn, the remaining garlic, the remaining shallot, the remaining chopped roasted pepper, the cilantro, lime peel, lime juice, salt, and black pepper. Add the avocado. Lightly toss to combine.

7. Ladle soup into serving bowls; top with guacamole. Sprinkle with crumbled queso fresco cheese.

***Tip** To roast the poblano pepper, cut the pepper lengthwise in half. Wearing plastic gloves, remove seeds and membranes. Place pepper halves, cut sides down, on foil-lined baking sheet. Roast in a preheated 425°F oven about 20 minutes or until skins are charred. Wrap pepper in foil. Let stand for 20 to 30 minutes or until cool enough to handle. Peel off skin.

EACH SERVING *372 cal, 19 g fat, 10 mg chol, 806 mg sodium, 45 g carb, 7 g fiber, 14 g pro.*

Spring Greens Soup

When winter brown turns to spring green, this is the ideal soup to make as a first course for a celebratory supper. Cooked potatoes give the verdant puree made from fresh spinach and arugula creaminess without a touch of cream. Each serving is topped with sautéed mushrooms and additional arugula if you like.

PREP 20 minutes
COOK 16 minutes
MAKES 6 servings

1   tablespoon vegetable oil
1   medium onion, halved and
     sliced
3   cups reduced-sodium chicken
     broth or vegetable broth
¼   to ½ teaspoon freshly ground
     black pepper
12   ounces Yukon gold potatoes,
     quartered
2   tablespoons butter
3   cups sliced fresh mushrooms
3   cups spinach leaves
3   cups arugula leaves
2   cups fresh Italian (flat-leaf)
     parsley leaves and tender
     stems
     Salt
     Fresh arugula (optional)

1. In a 3-quart saucepan heat oil over medium heat. Add onion; cook for 5 minutes. Add broth and pepper. Bring to boiling. Add potatoes and return to boiling; reduce heat. Simmer, covered, for 10 minutes.

2. Meanwhile, in large skillet melt butter over medium heat. Add mushrooms; cook for 6 to 8 minutes or until tender and liquid has evaporated. Set mushrooms aside.

3. Remove saucepan from heat. Using an immersion blender, blend onion-potato mixture until almost smooth. Add spinach, arugula, and parsley. Return to heat. Bring to boiling; remove from heat. Using immersion blender, puree soup again until nearly smooth and flecks of green remain. Season to taste with salt. Ladle soup into bowls. Top with sautéed mushrooms and, if desired, additional arugula.

EACH SERVING *92 cal, 3 g fat, 0 mg chol, 412 mg sodium, 14 g carb, 3 g fiber, 4 g pro.*

White Bean and Roasted Garlic Soup with Escarole

Escarole—a sturdy salad green that belongs to the endive family—has a milder flavor than its chicory and Belgian endive relatives. Tuscans use it as the green element in white bean soup, though in a different form than appears here. Instead of being stirred into the soup, it is used as a topping. It wilts just slightly and stays bright green and fresh.

PREP **20 minutes**
ROAST **20 minutes**
COOK **30 minutes**
OVEN **400°F**
MAKES **6 servings**

2   bulbs garlic
1   teaspoon olive oil
1   cup chopped fennel (1 bulb)
⅔   cup chopped leeks
⅓   cup chopped onion (1 small)
3   tablespoons olive oil
3   cups vegetable broth or
      chicken broth
2   15-ounce cans cannellini beans
      (white kidney beans), rinsed
      and drained
1   cup half-and-half or light
      cream
3   tablespoons lemon juice
      Salt and ground black pepper
6   ½-inch slices baguette-style
      French bread
6   slices Swiss cheese (about
      3 ounces)
4   cups lightly packed torn
      escarole or spinach

1. Preheat oven to 400°F. Cut off the top ½ inch of the garlic bulbs to expose ends of individual cloves. Leaving bulbs whole, remove any loose papery outer layers. Place bulbs, cut ends up, on a double thickness of foil. Drizzle bulbs with the 1 teaspoon olive oil. Bring foil edges up around bulbs to loosely enclose. Roast for 20 to 25 minutes or until garlic feels soft when squeezed. Let cool. Squeeze garlic from skins into a small bowl; mash with a fork.

2. In a large saucepan cook fennel, leeks, and onion in 1 tablespoon of the olive oil over medium heat for 15 to 20 minutes or until tender and caramelized, stirring occasionally. Add half of the roasted garlic, the broth, and 1½ cans (2⅔ cups) of the beans. Bring to boiling; reduce heat. Cover and simmer for 15 minutes. Remove from heat; cool slightly. Place mixture in a food processor or blender. Cover and process or blend until smooth. Return mixture to the saucepan.

3. Add the remaining beans, half-and-half, and 2 tablespoons of the lemon juice to pureed mixture in saucepan. Cook over low heat until heated through. Season with salt and pepper.

4. Meanwhile, preheat broiler. Place baguette slices on a baking sheet. Broil 1 to 2 minutes or until lightly toasted, turning once. Spread toast with the remaining roasted garlic. Place a cheese slice on each toast slice. Broil until cheese melts and begins to brown.

5. In a large bowl whisk together the remaining 2 tablespoons olive oil and remaining 1 tablespoon lemon juice. Season with salt and pepper. Add escarole; toss to coat.

6. To serve, divide soup among 6 soup bowls. Top with baguette toasts and escarole.

EACH SERVING *387 cal, 17 g fat, 28 mg chol, 990 mg sodium, 42 g carb, 9 g fiber, 16 g pro.*

Celery Root Soup with Parsley Oil

It may be knobby and ugly on the outside, but when celery root is cooked, its inner beauty is revealed. This creamy soup has an almost gossamer texture and the delicate flavor of celery root, which has hints of celery and parsley. The parsley oil—made by pureeing the herb with olive oil and then straining it—underscores that flavor and adds a beautiful swath of green to the pale yellow soup.

PREP **25 minutes**
COOK **25 minutes**
MAKES **4 servings**

4   cups chicken broth
½   of a medium celery root (about 10 ounces), peeled and cut into 1-inch pieces
2   medium russet baking potatoes (about 12 ounces), peeled and cut into 1-inch pieces
½   cup lightly packed fresh parsley
¼   cup olive oil
     Pinch salt
1   teaspoon lemon juice
     Salt and ground black pepper
     Fresh parsley (optional)

1. In a large saucepan combine chicken broth, celery root, and potatoes. Bring to boiling; reduce heat. Cover and simmer for 25 to 30 minutes or until vegetables are very tender. Remove saucepan from heat; cool slightly.

2. Meanwhile, for parsley oil, in a food processor or blender combine the ½ cup parsley, the olive oil, and the pinch of salt. Cover and process or blend until well combined (parsley will still be in small pieces). Press mixture firmly through a strainer into a small bowl; discard parsley in strainer. Set parsley oil aside.

3. Transfer half of the celery root mixture to the food processor or blender. Cover and process or blend until smooth. Repeat with remaining celery root mixture. Return all the soup to the saucepan. Stir in lemon juice; heat through. Season with salt and pepper. Ladle soup into bowls. Drizzle with parsley oil. If desired, garnish with additional parsley.

EACH SERVING *228 cal, 14 g fat, 5 mg chol, 1,123 mg sodium, 23 g carb, 3 g fiber, 4 g pro.*

Chilled Cucumber-Chickpea Soup

The main ingredients of hummus—chickpeas, tahini, lemon juice, and garlic—come together in this soup that's lightened up by pureeing crisp cucumbers with those ingredients. It can be made several hours ahead of serving time. Right before you ladle it into the bowls and top it with spiced cocktail shrimp, sliced cucumber, tomatoes, and scallions, the soup is pureed with ice cubes to make it refreshingly cold.

START TO FINISH 25 minutes
MAKES 4 to 6 servings

1   recipe Coriander-Paprika Spice Rub
8   ounces peeled and deveined cooked cocktail shrimp, chopped
2   medium cucumbers
1   15-ounce can chickpeas (garbanzo beans), rinsed and drained
¼   cup tahini (sesame seed paste)
¼   cup lightly packed fresh mint leaves
2   tablespoons lemon juice
1   tablespoon olive oil
1   tablespoon honey
2   cloves garlic, smashed
1½ teaspoons ground coriander
¼   teaspoon salt
¼   teaspoon cayenne pepper
¼   teaspoon ground black pepper
3   cups ice cubes
½   cup cherry tomatoes, halved
4   scallions or green onions, cut into 1-inch slivers

1. Prepare Coriander-Paprika Spice Rub. In a medium bowl toss shrimp with Coriander-Paprika Spice Rub; set aside. Thinly slice enough cucumber to measure ⅓ cup; set aside. Peel, seed, and cut up remaining cucumbers.

2. In a blender combine cut-up cucumbers, chickpeas, tahini, mint, lemon juice, olive oil, honey, garlic, coriander, salt, cayenne pepper, and black pepper. Cover and blend until smooth, scraping sides as needed.

3. Just before serving, with motor running, add ice cubes, a few at a time, through lid opening until smooth and thickened (blender will be full). Pour into bowls. Top soup with shrimp, sliced cucumber, tomatoes, and scallions.

Coriander-Paprika Spice Rub In a small bowl combine 1 teaspoon ground coriander, ½ teaspoon paprika, ¼ teaspoon salt, and ¼ teaspoon ground black pepper.

EACH SERVING *357 cal, 14 g fat, 111 mg chol, 752 mg sodium, 41 g carb, 7 g fiber, 22 g pro.*

Butternut Squash Soup with Thai Gremolata

Put everything in the slow cooker and turn it on, then run errands for a few hours and come home to the exotic aroma of butternut squash cooking in coconut milk, onions, and spicy chili sauce. After being pureed, the soup is topped with a fresh blend of snipped basil, chopped peanut, and shredded lime peel—and a squeeze of fresh lime.

PREP 25 minutes
SLOW COOK 4 hours (low) or 2 hours (high)
MAKES 4 to 6 servings

2   pounds butternut squash, peeled and cut into 1-inch pieces
2   cups chicken broth
1   14-ounce can unsweetened coconut milk
¼   cup finely chopped onion
1   tablespoon packed brown sugar
1   tablespoon fish sauce or soy sauce
½   to 1 teaspoon Asian chili sauce (Sriracha) sauce or crushed red pepper
2   tablespoons lime juice
1   recipe Thai Gremolata
       Lime wedges (optional)

1. In a 3½- or 4-quart slow cooker stir together squash, broth, coconut milk, onion, brown sugar, fish sauce, and Asian chili sauce.
2. Cover and cook on low-heat setting for 4 to 5 hours or on high-heat setting for 2 to 2½ hours.
3. Using an immersion blender, carefully blend soup until completely smooth. (Or transfer the mixture in batches to a food processor or blender; process or blend until completely smooth.) Stir in lime juice. Ladle soup into bowls; sprinkle with Thai Gremolata. If desired, serve with lime wedges.

Thai Gremolata In a small bowl stir together ½ cup snipped fresh basil or cilantro, ½ cup chopped peanuts, and 1 tablespoon finely shredded lime peel.

EACH SERVING *189 cal, 10 g fat, 1 mg chol, 581 mg sodium, 24 g carb, 4 g fiber, 5 g pro.*

A Garnish of Gremolata

Traditional Italian gremolata—a combination of minced parsley, garlic, and lemon peel—is the classic garnish for osso bucco, the Milanese dish of veal shanks braised in olive oil, white wine, stock, onions, tomatoes, garlic, anchovies, carrots, celery, and lemon peel. It adds a bright, fresh flavor to this rich, hearty dish.

Here are two fun twists on traditional gremolata. Sprinkle on soups and stews, cooked vegetables or rice, or roasted or grilled meats.

Bacon Gremolata In a small bowl stir together 16 slices bacon, crisp-cooked, drained, and finely crumbled; 1 cup finely shredded Parmesan cheese; ¼ cup snipped fresh basil; ¼ cup finely chopped pepperoncini or fresh jalapeño chile pepper; 4 teaspoons finely shredded lemon peel; 2 cloves garlic, minced; and ½ teaspoon ground black pepper.

Citrus-Hazelnut Gremolata In a small bowl stir together 2 tablespoons finely chopped toasted hazelnuts; 2 tablespoons snipped Italian (flat-leaf) parsley; 1½ teaspooons finely shredded orange peel; 1 teaspoon finely shredded lemon peel; ½ teaspoon finely shredded lime peel; 2 cloves minced garlic; ¼ teaspoon salt; and ⅛ teaspoon ground black pepper.

Quinoa-Nectarine Gazpacho with Crispy-Spice Tortilla Strips, *recipe page 212*

Quinoa-Nectarine Gazpacho with Crispy-Spice Tortilla Strips *pictured page 211*

This cold soup is an amazing blend of textures and flavors. It is sweet from the nectarines, a little bit spicy from the jalapeño, creamy from the avocado, and crunchy from crisp cucumbers. It makes a very light and fresh first course for a summer barbecue.

PREP **30 minutes**
CHILL **30 minutes to 6 hours**
MAKES **8 (¾-cup) servings**

⅓ cup quinoa
⅔ cup water
¼ teaspoon salt
3 cups coarsely chopped nectarines or peeled peaches (about 4 medium)
1 small ripe avocado, halved, seeded, peeled, and chopped
½ cup coarsely chopped cucumber*
¼ cup lime juice
2 tablespoons chopped red onion or green onion
2 tablespoons snipped fresh mint and/or cilantro
1 fresh jalapeño pepper,** seeded and finely chopped
1 12-ounce bottle ginger beer
1 cup pineapple juice
Mexican crema or sour cream (optional)
1 recipe Crispy-Spice Tortilla Strips

1. In a colander rinse quinoa well; drain. In a small saucepan bring the water and salt to boiling. Stir in quinoa. Reduce heat. Simmer, covered, about 15 minutes or until tender. Drain and discard any excess water; set quinoa aside to cool.
2. Place nectarines in a large bowl. If desired, mash some of the pieces slightly with a potato masher. Gently stir in cooled quinoa, avocado, cucumber, lime juice, onion, mint and/or cilantro, and jalapeño. Cover and chill for 30 minutes to 6 hours.
3. To serve, stir ginger beer and pineapple juice into nectarine mixture. Ladle into bowls. If desired, top with crema. Garnish with Crispy-Spice Tortilla Strips.
Crispy-Spice Tortilla Strips
Preheat oven to 350°F. In a small bowl combine 1 tablespoon vegetable oil, ½ teaspoon chili powder, and ¼ teaspoon ground cinnamon. Brush three 7- to 8-inch flour tortillas with the oil mixture. Sprinkle tortillas with salt. Roll up each tortilla and slice crosswise

into long thin strips. If desired, cut strips in half. Spread strips on a baking sheet. Bake about 12 to 15 minutes or until golden. Cool on a wire rack. Use immediately or store in a covered container at room temperature for up to 3 days.
*Tip If desired, peel cucumber before chopping.
**Tip Because hot chile peppers contain volatile oils that can burn your skin and eyes, avoid contact with chiles as much as possible. When working with chile peppers, wear plastic or rubber gloves. If your bare hands do touch the chile peppers, wash your hands well with soap and water.
EACH SERVING *168 cal, 5 g fat, 0 mg chol, 241 mg sodium, 29 g carb, 4 g fiber, 3 g pro.*

Grilled Asparagus Soup with Chili Croutons

Grilling the asparagus before pureeing it gives the finished soup a subtle smoky flavor and heightens the natural sweetness of the vegetable. The chili croutons are simple—they're slices of baguette that are brushed with a mixture of melted butter and Asian chili sauce before grilling.

PREP **10 minutes**
GRILL **4 minutes**
COOK **15 minutes**
MAKES **4 servings**

¼   cup butter, melted
1½ to 2 tablespoons Asian chili sauce (Sriracha sauce)
1   small baguette, sliced diagonally
2   pounds green, white, and/or purple asparagus, trimmed
2   tablespoons butter
⅓   cup finely chopped onion (1 small)
¼   teaspoon salt
3   tablespoons all-purpose flour
½   teaspoon ground coriander
2   14.5-ounce cans reduced-sodium chicken broth
½   cup milk
1   tablespoon lemon juice
    Olive oil (optional)

1. For chili croutons, in a large bowl stir together the ¼ cup melted butter and chili sauce; brush one side of each baguette slice with some of the butter mixture. For a charcoal or gas grill, grill bread over medium heat about 2 minutes or until toasted and crisp, turning once. Set croutons aside.

2. Add asparagus to the remaining butter mixture; toss to coat. Grill asparagus over medium heat for 2 to 4 minutes or until crisp-tender, turning once. Remove from grill.

3. Set aside one-fourth of the spears. Slice the remaining spears ½ inch thick; set aside.

4. For soup, in a large saucepan melt the 2 tablespoons butter over medium heat. Cook onion in the hot butter about 5 minutes or until tender. Add salt. Sprinkle flour over onions; cook and stir for 1 minute. Stir in the coriander. Slowly whisk in chicken broth. Add sliced asparagus. Bring soup to simmering. Simmer, uncovered, about 10 minutes or until thickened, stirring occasionally. Cool slightly.

5. Transfer soup to a food processor or blender, in batches if necessary. Cover and process or blend soup until smooth. Return pureed soup to saucepan. Stir in milk and heat through. Cut the reserved asparagus spears into 2-inch lengths. Add asparagus pieces and lemon juice to soup. Ladle soup into bowls. If desired, drizzle with a little olive oil. Serve with chili croutons.

Tip No time to grill? Toast baguette slices under the broiler for 1 to 2 minutes each side. To quickly blanch the asparagus, place spears in a single layer in a shallow baking pan. Cover with about 2 cups boiling salted water. Let stand for 10 to 12 minutes, until bright green and crisp-tender. Drain. Continue with Step 3.

EACH SERVING *310 cal, 13 g fat, 33 mg chol, 1,029 mg sodium, 38 g carb, 4 g fiber, 11 g pro.*

6 Fresh Ideas for Lemon

The sunny, bright flavor of lemon perks up so many foods with just the tiniest bit of its aromatic peel or juice. Bring some sunshine into your kitchen on a winter day with one of these ideas. Or in the case of the Preserved Lemons, put some up in a jar for a rainy day. Chop and add to soups, sauces, and cooked vegetables for a hit of lemon flavor.

1 Lemon-Lime Mint Iced Tea

Shred peel from 1 lemon and 1 lime. In a large teapot combine citrus peels, 3 tablespoons loose-leaf black tea, ½ cup fresh mint leaves, and 4 cups hot water. Let steep for 8 minutes. Strain into a pitcher through a fine-mesh sieve. Add 3 cups cold water. Chill. Serve over ice. Garnish with sliced lemon if desired. Makes 6 servings.

2 Quick Lemon Aïoli

In a small bowl stir together ¼ cup mayonnaise, 2 to 3 tablespoons milk, ½ teaspoon finely shredded lemon peel, 2 teaspoons lemon juice, and 1 to 2 minced garlic cloves. Use as a sandwich spread or as a dipping sauce for meats, fish, or vegetables. Makes ⅓ cup.

3 Lemon Milkshake

In a blender combine ¼ cup whole milk, 1¾ cups good-quality vanilla ice cream, and 1 tablespoon lemon peel. Cover and blend until smooth. Add 3 tablespoons lemon juice; pulse to combine. Pour into 2 serving glasses. Top with whipped cream and lemon slices or additional lemon peel. Makes 2 servings.

4 Lemon Vinaigrette

In a screw-top jar combine ¼ cup olive oil, ½ teaspoon finely shredded lemon peel, 3 tablespoons lemon juice, 1 tablespoon snipped fresh oregano, and 2 cloves minced garlic. Cover and shake well. Season to taste with salt and freshly ground black pepper. Use on salads and steamed vegetables. Makes ½ cup.

5 Limoncello

Scrub 10 large lemons. Using a vegetable peeler, cut enough of the yellow peel away to make 2 cups peel. In a large glass pitcher combine peel and one 750-milliliter bottle of vodka. Cover and let stand in a cool, dry place for 10 days, gently swirling pitcher each day. Strain through a fine-mesh sieve; discard peel. Return vodka to pitcher. In a saucepan combine 3 cups sugar and 2½ cups water. Bring to boiling, stirring to dissolve sugar. Cool. Pour syrup into lemon vodka and stir. Cover and chill overnight. Funnel into clean bottles; secure lids. Store in refrigerator. Makes 7 cups.

6 Preserved Lemons

Cut 4 Meyer lemons into quarters from tips to within ½ inch of stem ends. Combine ½ cup kosher salt and ½ teaspoon each crushed fennel seeds and crushed coriander seeds. Toss lemons with salt mixture, packing salt into cut edges. Re-form and pack into a sterilized quart-size canning jar along with any remaining salt mixture, 2 whole cloves, 1 bay leaf, and a 2-inch piece cinnamon stick. Pour in juice of 2 lemons; seal. Store in cool place for 1 week, tipping jar once a day. Refrigerate for 3 more weeks. Rinse lemons before using. Makes 4 cups.

Burger with Pickled Beets and Fried Egg

This burger has an Australian accent: Pickled beets and a fried egg are a classic Aussie way to top a burger. You pickle the beets yourself—it only takes 30 minutes of standing time. Be sure that the yolk is still runny. The richness of the egg with the sweetness and acidity of the pickled beets is fabulous!

PREP **30 minutes**
COOK **30 minutes**
STAND **30 minutes**
GRILL **11 minutes**
MAKES **4 burgers**

2   medium beets
½   cup sugar
½   cup water
½   cup white wine vinegar
3   strips orange peel
2½   teaspoons salt
½   teaspoon cracked black pepper
1   pound ground beef chuck
8   ounces ground beef sirloin
¼   teaspoon ground black pepper
4   kaiser rolls, split
2   teaspoons olive oil
4   eggs
2   ounces soft goat cheese (chèvre)
4   Bibb lettuce leaves

1. In a large saucepan combine the beets and enough water to cover. Bring to boiling; reduce heat. Cook, covered, about 30 minutes or until tender. Drain and let cool slightly. Under running water, rub off the peels. Slice the beets thinly; set aside. In a medium saucepan bring sugar, the ½ cup water, vinegar, orange peel, 2 teaspoons salt, and the cracked black pepper to a simmer, stirring to dissolve the sugar. Add the beets, remove from the heat. Let stand for 30 minutes; drain, discarding vinegar mixture.
2. Meanwhile, for burgers, in a medium bowl combine beef chuck and sirloin. Sprinkle with the remaining ½ teaspoon salt and the ¼ teaspoon ground black pepper; mix well. Shape into 4 patties, about ¾ inch thick.
3. For a charcoal or gas grill, place patties on the rack of a covered grill directly over medium heat. Grill for 10 to 12 minutes or until done (160°F), turning once halfway through grilling. Remove patties

from grill. Let stand for 5 minutes. Place rolls, cut sides down, on grill rack for 1 to 2 minutes or until lightly toasted.
4. In a large nonstick skillet heat the olive oil over medium heat. Break eggs into skillet; cook for 2 minutes. Cover skillet; remove from heat. Let eggs stand about 2 minutes or until whites are set and yolks begin to thicken.
5. Spread chèvre on the cut side of each roll bottom. Top with lettuce, burgers, beets, and eggs. Add roll tops to burgers.
Tip Store any remaining pickled beets in an airtight container in the refrigerator for 1 week. Use them in salads or as a sandwich relish.
EACH BURGER *671 cal, 36 g fat, 310 mg chol, 777 mg sodium, 36 g carb, 2 g fiber, 48 g pro.*

Lamb Meatballs on Flatbread with Quick Pickled Cucumber Salad

Harissa paste is a North African chili sauce whose main ingredients are piri piri and serrano chiles, garlic, coriander, cumin, and caraway. It spices up the sweetly flavored lamb meatballs in these hearty sandwiches. It is sold in jars, cans, bottles, and tubes. Look for it in specialty food markets or online.

PREP 35 minutes
COOK 12 minutes
CHILL 1 to 6 hours
MAKES 4 sandwiches

3   tablespoons vegetable oil
½   cup chopped pitted dates (6 to 8 whole)
¼   cup finely chopped onion
4   cloves garlic, minced
1   pound ground lamb
½   cup chopped fresh cilantro leaves and stems
3   tablespoons snipped fresh mint
3   teaspoons harissa paste or Asian chili sauce
½   teaspoon salt
1   teaspoon ground coriander
½   teaspoon ground cumin
¼   teaspoon ground cinnamon
1   5- to 6-ounce container honey-flavor Greek yogurt
4   flatbreads or naan, warmed
1   recipe Quick Pickled Cucumber Salad

1. In a very large skillet heat 1 tablespoon of the oil over medium heat. Add dates, onion, and garlic. Cook and stir for 4 to 5 minutes or until onion is tender. Remove from skillet; cool slightly.

2. For meatballs, in a large bowl combine lamb, cilantro, 2 tablespoons of the mint, 2 teaspoons of the harissa paste, the salt, coriander, cumin, cinnamon, and the cooled date mixture. Mix well. Shape mixture into twenty 1-inch meatballs. Heat the remaining 2 tablespoons oil in the same skillet. Add meatballs; cook for 12 to 15 minutes or until browned and cooked through (160°F), turning frequently. Remove with a slotted spoon and drain on paper towels.

3. For yogurt sauce, in a small bowl stir together yogurt, the remaining 1 tablespoon mint, and the remaining 1 teaspoon harissa paste. Divide meatballs among flatbreads. Top with Quick Pickled Cucumber Salad and the yogurt sauce.

Quick Pickled Cucumber Salad Thinly slice 1 small seedless cucumber and place in a medium bowl. Cut 1 small white onion lengthwise into quarters; thinly slice each quarter. Add onion to bowl with cucumber. In a small bowl combine ½ cup cider vinegar, 1 tablespoon snipped fresh cilantro, 2 teaspoons sugar, and ½ teaspoon salt. Stir vinegar mixture into cucumber mixture. Cover and chill for 1 to 6 hours.

EACH SANDWICH *757 cal, 36 g fat, 85 mg chol, 848 mg sodium, 76 g carb, 4 g fiber, 31 g pro.*

Muenster, Cabbage, and Apple Sandwiches

These toasty sandwiches make a quick and satisfying weeknight supper. Onions, apples, and shredded cabbage are briefly cooked in a mixture of vinegar and water—just until tender—then seasoned with coarse mustard before being grilled with Muenster cheese on caraway rye.

START TO FINISH 25 minutes
MAKES 4 sandwiches

1	medium onion, halved lengthwise and thinly sliced
¼	cup cider vinegar
¼	cup water
1	cup coarsely shredded green cabbage
1	large cooking apple, such as Granny Smith, Rome Beauty, or Jonathan, thinly sliced
1	tablespoon stone-ground mustard
8	slices caraway rye bread
1	cup shredded Muenster cheese (4 ounces)
	Nonstick cooking spray

1. In a medium skillet combine onion, vinegar, and the water. Bring just to boiling; reduce heat. Simmer, covered, for 3 minutes. Stir in cabbage; simmer, covered, for 3 minutes. Stir in apple slices. Simmer, covered, about 3 minutes more or just until vegetables and apple are tender; drain. Stir in mustard.

2. Layer 4 of the bread slices with cabbage mixture and cheese. Top with the remaining 4 bread slices. Lightly coat outsides of sandwiches with cooking spray.

3. Preheat a large nonstick skillet over medium heat. Place sandwiches, half at a time if necessary, in skillet. Weight down with a heavy skillet and cook for 1 to 2 minutes or until bread is toasted. Turn sandwiches, weight down again, and cook for 1 to 2 minutes more or until bread is toasted and filling is heated through.

EACH SANDWICH *296 cal, 11 g fat, 27 mg chol, 606 mg sodium, 39 g carb, 5 g fiber, 12 g pro.*

Peachy Po-Boy

Sweet, spicy, and salty come together in these hearty Southern-style sandwiches. A grill wok or tray makes it easy to grill the shrimp. The shrimp can also be cooked in a skillet over medium heat for 2 to 4 minutes or until opaque.

PREP **35 minutes**
GRILL **10 minutes**
MAKES **6 sandwiches**

⅓   cup fresh or frozen medium shrimp (36 to 40)
⅓   cup butter, melted
1   tablespoon lemon juice
1   clove garlic, minced
¼   teaspoon salt
¼   teaspoon ground black pepper
6   miniature baguettes or two 8-ounce baguettes, cut into thirds and split lengthwise
1½ teaspoons Cajun seasoning
1   large jalapeño pepper, thinly sliced*
3   peaches, halved and sliced
½   cup light mayonnaise
1   teaspoon coarsely ground black pepper
6   slices bacon, crisp-cooked and broken into small pieces
     Snipped fresh cilantro
     Lemon wedges (optional)

1. Thaw shrimp, if frozen. Peel and devein shrimp. Rinse shrimp; pat dry with paper towels. Set aside.
2. In a medium bowl stir together butter, lemon juice, garlic, salt, and ¼ teaspoon pepper. Lightly brush some of the butter mixture on cut sides of bread; set bread aside. Stir 1 teaspoon of the Cajun seasoning into the remaining butter mixture. Add shrimp and jalapeño; toss to coat. Place shrimp mixture in a large grill tray or grill wok.
3. For a charcoal or gas grill, place a grill tray on rack of a covered grill directly over medium heat. Grill for 10 to 14 minutes or until shrimp are opaque, turning occasionally. Add baguettes to grill rack, cut sides down, in batches and grill about 2 minutes or until toasted.
4. Sprinkle sliced peaches with the remaining ½ teaspoon Cajun seasoning. Gently fold peaches into hot shrimp mixture. In a small bowl stir together mayonnaise and 1 teaspoon coarsely ground pepper. Spread mayonnaise mixture on top halves of baguettes. Pile shrimp mixture on bottom halves. Top with crumbled bacon and cilantro. If desired, serve with lemon wedges.
*Tip Because hot chile peppers contain volatile oils that can burn your skin and eyes, avoid contact with chiles as much as possible. When working with chile peppers, wear plastic or rubber gloves. If your bare hands do touch the chile peppers, wash your hands well with soap and water.

EACH SANDWICH *554 cal, 23 g fat, 186 mg chol, 1,167 mg sodium, 55 g carb, 4 g fiber, 32 g pro.*

Avocado, Prosciutto, and Egg Sandwiches

A sweet and spicy wasabi mayonnaise gives these luxurious sandwiches a bit of a kick. The poached eggs and crispy prosciutto make them just as appropriate for a hearty breakfast as they are for lunch or dinner. For even more of a bite, use spicy sprouts—usually a blend of radish, clover, and alfalfa.

PREP **30 minutes**
COOK **3 minutes**
MAKES **4 sandwiches**

1   tablespoon vinegar
4   eggs
     Salt and ground black pepper
¼   cup mayonnaise
2   teaspoons wasabi paste
1   teaspoon packed brown sugar
4   ounces very thinly sliced prosciutto
1   avocado, halved, seeded, peeled, and sliced
1   cup sunflower seed sprouts,* alfalfa sprouts,* or packaged baby salad greens
8   slices hearty whole grain bread, toasted

1. For poached eggs, fill a large skillet with water to a depth of ½ inch. Add 1 tablespoon vinegar. Bring to boiling; reduce heat to simmering. Crack eggs, one at a time, into a shallow bowl. Carefully slide eggs into simmering water. Sprinkle eggs with salt and pepper. Cover and cook for 3 to 4 minutes or until whites are completely set and yolks begin to thicken. Using the edge of a metal spatula, separate the eggs. Use a slotted spoon to remove the eggs; set eggs aside. Discard liquid and dry skillet.
2. In a small bowl stir together mayonnaise, wasabi paste, and brown sugar. Set aside.
3. Cook the prosciutto in the clean, dry skillet over medium-high heat until crisp. Remove prosciutto from skillet.

4. To assemble sandwiches, layer avocado, prosciutto, poached eggs, and sprouts on 4 of the toasted bread slices. Spread about 1 tablespoon of the wasabi mayonnaise on one side of the remaining 4 bread slices; add to sandwiches, mayonnaise sides down.
*Tip Because sprouts are grown in warm, humid conditions where bacteria can quickly multiply, sprouts have the potential of causing illness when eaten raw.
EACH SANDWICH *433 cal, 26 g fat, 221 mg chol, 1,093 mg sodium, 29 g carb, 6 g fiber, 21 g pro.*

Roasted Vegetable and Fresh Mozzarella Panini

The bread in this sandwich is hollowed out slightly to make more room for the fabulous filling. Vegetables are roasted, then layered on the bread with fresh mozzarella and Dried Tomato Pesto and grilled until the cheese is melty and the bread toasted and crisp. It's special enough to serve to company—perfect for a late-summer supper on the porch with a glass of chilled white wine.

PREP **30 minutes**
ROAST **30 minutes**
GRILL **6 minutes**
OVEN **400°F**
MAKES **6 panini**

1   large Vidalia onion, peeled, halved, and sliced ¼ inch thick
¼   cup garlic-flavor olive oil
1   red sweet pepper, seeded and cut into quarters
1   large zucchini, trimmed and sliced ¼ inch thick
1   medium eggplant, peeled and sliced ¼ inch thick
1   1-pound baguette
1   recipe Dried Tomato Pesto
½   cup fresh basil leaves
8   ounces fresh mozzarella cheese, sliced

1. Preheat oven to 400°F. Line 2 large baking sheets with parchment paper; set aside.

2. In a medium bowl toss onion with 1 tablespoon of the oil to coat each piece with olive oil. Transfer onion to one of the baking sheets. In same bowl toss sweet pepper with 1 tablespoon of the oil and place on same baking sheet. Roast onion and pepper on the upper rack for 15 minutes.

2. Meanwhile, coat zucchini and eggplant with the remaining 2 tablespoons oil; arrange on the second baking sheet. Place in oven with first baking sheet. Roast all the vegetables for 15 to 20 minutes or until tender, turning vegetables every 5 minutes. Cool slightly.

3. Preheat an electric sandwich press or covered indoor grill. (Or heat a nonstick grill pan or large skillet over medium heat.) Slice the baguette in half lengthwise. Hollow out the soft centers of both halves. Spread cut sides of the baguette evenly with Dried Tomato Pesto. Carefully arrange zucchini in the bottom half. Add layers of sweet pepper, eggplant, basil leaves, and onion. Arrange mozzarella evenly over the vegetables.

4. Add baguette top. Reposition vegetables back into the loaf if necessary. Cut in half crosswise.

5. Place loaf halves (1 at a time if necessary) in the sandwich press or indoor grill; cover and cook about 6 minutes or until cheese melts and bread is toasted. (Or place sandwiches on grill pan or skillet. Weight sandwiches with another skillet. Grill about 3 minutes or until bread is toasted. Turn sandwiches over, weight them down, and grill until second side is toasted, 2 to 3 minutes.) Using a serrated knife, carefully cut each loaf half crosswise into 2 to 3 sandwiches.

Dried Tomato Pesto In a food processor or blender combine ½ cup oil-packed dried tomatoes; 3 tablespoons extra virgin olive oil; 2 tablespoons coarsely chopped fresh Italian (flat-leaf) parsley; 2 tablespoons coarsely chopped fresh basil; 2 cloves garlic, coarsely chopped; 2 teaspoons lemon juice; ¼ teaspoon salt; and ⅛ teaspoon coarsely ground black pepper. Cover and process or blend until mixture is smooth. Transfer pesto to a small bowl. Stir in ⅓ cup finely shredded Parmesan cheese.

EACH PANINI *510 cal, 27 g fat, 30 mg chol, 718 mg sodium, 49g carb, 5 g fiber, 15 g pro.*

Prosciutto-Wrapped Asparagus Panini

This sandwich is very interesting and pretty when cut in half. Four prosciutto-wrapped spears of asparagus are layered with cheese and arugula between two slices of marble rye bread and then grilled. When the sandwich is cut, the row of cut spears is visible.

PREP **25 minutes**
COOK **5 minutes**
MAKES **4 sandwiches**

16   asparagus spears (12 ounces)
8   very thin prosciutto slices
    (5 ounces)
8   slices marble rye bread
1   tablespoon coarse ground
    mustard
1   cup lightly packed arugula
    (optional)
8   thin slices provolone cheese
1   tablespoon bottled balsamic
    vinaigrette (or 2 teaspoons
    olive oil combined with
    1 teaspoon balsamic vinegar)

1. Snap off and discard woody bases from asparagus. Trim stalks barely longer than the bread slices. Place a steamer rack in the bottom of a large saucepan and add water to just below the basket. Bring to boiling. Add asparagus. Cover and reduce heat. Steam for 3 to 5 minutes or until crisp-tender. Transfer asparagus to a bowl of ice water for 30 seconds to cool; drain.
2. Using kitchen scissors, cut each piece of prosciutto in half lengthwise. Starting at the base of an asparagus spear, wrap a prosciutto piece around the asparagus spear diagonally to the top of the spear. Repeat with remaining asparagus and prosciutto.
3. Spread 4 slices of the bread with mustard. Place 4 prosciutto-wrapped asparagus spears horizontally on each mustard-topped bread slice. If desired, top with arugula. Add 2 slices of cheese to each sandwich, arranging slices to completely cover bread. Brush the remaining

4 bread slices lightly with balsamic vinaigrette. Place bread, vinaigrette sides down, on top of cheese.
4. Preheat a panini press; place sandwiches (half at a time if necessary) in grill. Cover and cook for 4 to 5 minutes or until cheese melts. (Or place sandwiches in preheated grill pan or skillet. Weight sandwiches down with another skillet. Grill about 3 minutes or until bread is toasted. Turn sandwiches over, weight them down, and grill until second side is toasted, 2 to 3 minutes.)

EACH SANDWICH *402 cal, 15 g fat, 54 mg chol, 1,713 mg sodium, 39 g carb, 4 g fiber, 29 g pro.*

Caramelized Onion, Thyme, and Winter Squash Pizza

Pizza is casual food, but this autumnal pie has a kind of rustic elegance. The combination of sweet roasted butternut squash with tangy blue cheese is divine. A sprinkling of pecans on top adds an irresistible crunch. Baking it on a pizza stone or an inverted baking sheet that has been heated in a 500°F oven will make the crust crisper.

PREP 1 hour
BAKE 30 minutes
OVEN 425°F/500°F
MAKES 4 servings

1   small butternut squash (1 to 1½ pounds)
2   teaspoons olive oil
      Kosher salt and freshly ground black pepper
2   tablespoons butter
2   large sweet onions (such as Vidalia or Walla Walla), halved and thinly sliced
2   large cloves garlic, peeled and thinly sliced
1   tablespoon balsamic vinegar
1   crust (half recipe) Pizza Dough (see page 237)
      Cornmeal
¼   to ½ cup crumbled Gorgonzola, blue cheese, or goat cheese (2 to 4 ounces)
2   to 3 tablespoons pecan pieces (optional)
1   teaspoon snipped fresh thyme

1. Preheat oven to 425°F. Peel squash and halve lengthwise. Remove and discard seeds. Cut squash into ½-inch pieces. Arrange in a single layer on a 15×10×1-inch pan. Drizzle with the 2 teaspoons olive oil and sprinkle with salt and pepper. Bake about 20 minutes or until tender and starting to brown on edges, stirring once. Remove from oven; set aside. Increase oven temperature to 500°F. Place a baking stone or greased inverted baking sheet in the oven.

2. To caramelize onions, in a large skillet melt butter over medium-low heat. Add onions. Cook, covered, about 12 minutes or just until tender, stirring occasionally. Uncover; cook and stir over medium-high heat for 3 to 5 minutes more or until golden. Remove from heat; stir in vinegar.

3. On a lightly floured surface roll or stretch Pizza Dough into a 13-inch circle, about ¼ inch thick. Place the dough on a pizza peel or inverted baking sheet that has been sprinkled with cornmeal.

4. Spread the caramelized onion mixture over pizza crust on pizza peel. Top with squash, cheese, nuts (if desired), and thyme. If desired, sprinkle with additional pepper.

5. Transfer pizza to the pizza stone or inverted baking sheet. Bake for 10 to 12 minutes or until crust is golden brown and toppings are heated through.

EACH SERVING *544 cal, 19 g fat, 25 mg chol, 849 mg sodium, 84 g carb, 7 g fiber, 13 g pro.*

Caramelized Onion, Thyme, Winter Squash, and Pesto Pizza: Spread the pizza dough with ⅓ to ½ cup homemade or purchased pesto before adding the caramelized onion mixture. Continue as directed.

Chorizo, Kale, and Sweet Potato Galette

A galette is a type of crusty tart that can have either a sweet or savory filling. The Olive Oil Galette Dough in this recipe creates a crust that is crisp on the outside but soft and tender on the inside. If you like things spicy, you could substitute the mild chorizo for one with more heat.

PREP **40 minutes**
RISE **1 hour**
BAKE **25 minutes**
COOL **5 minutes**
OVEN **425°F**
MAKES **8 servings**

1   recipe Olive Oil Galette Dough
2   medium sweet potatoes, peeled and sliced into ¼-inch rounds
2   tablespoons olive oil
¼   teaspoon salt
¼   teaspoon ground black pepper
8   ounces bulk mild chorizo
½   of a medium red onion, thinly sliced
2   cloves garlic, minced
2   cups shredded Manchego cheese (8 ounces)
2   cups lightly packed coarsely chopped kale
1½ tablespoons sherry vinegar
1   egg white, lightly beaten
1   tablespoon cornmeal

1. Prepare Olive Oil Galette Dough.
2. Preheat oven to 425°F. In a large bowl combine sweet potato slices and olive oil. Toss to coat. On a baking sheet arrange sweet potatoes in a single layer. Sprinkle with salt and pepper. Bake about 10 minutes or until tender. Set aside.
3. Meanwhile, in a large skillet cook chorizo, onion, and garlic over medium-high heat for 6 to 8 minutes or until meat is browned, stirring to break up chorizo. Drain fat from skillet. Set chorizo mixture aside.
4. On a large sheet of parchment paper roll Olive Oil Galette Dough from center to edges into a 17×12-inch rectangle. Place dough and paper on a large baking sheet. (Dough may beyond edges of baking sheet slightly.)
5. Sprinkle galette dough evenly with chorizo mixture, leaving a 2-inch border around the edges. Sprinkle with cheese; arrange sweet potato slices on top.
6. In a medium bowl combine kale and sherry vinegar. Toss well, coating kale evenly with vinegar. Sprinkle kale mixture evenly over galette. Fold dough border over filling, pleating dough as needed. Brush egg white over dough border; sprinkle lightly with cornmeal.

7. Bake for 15 to 20 minutes or until crust is golden and cheese is melted. Cool galette for 5 minutes before serving.

Olive Oil Galette Dough In a small bowl combine ¾ cup warm water (105°F to 115°F), 1 package active dry yeast, and 1 teaspoon sugar. Let stand for 5 to 7 minutes or until foamy. Meanwhile, in a large bowl whisk together 1 egg and 1 egg yolk. Whisk in 2 tablespoons olive oil, 1 teaspoon salt, and the yeast mixture. Stir in enough bread flour (2 to 2½ cups) to form a dough. Turn out dough onto a lightly floured surface. Knead in enough bread flour (about ½ cup) to make a soft dough that is smooth and elastic (3 to 5 minutes total). Place dough in a greased large bowl, turning once to grease the surface. Cover; let rise in a warm place until nearly double (about 1 hour). Punch down dough.

EACH SERVING *540 cal, 31 g fat, 101 mg chol, 1,079 mg sodium, 42 g carb, 3 g fiber, 22 g pro.*

Char-Grilled Spring Onion, Pineapple, and Shrimp Pizzas

Spring or green onions are simply regular onions that have been harvested before they fully mature. They are similar to scallions but have a bigger bulb. Their flavor is not as potent as a fully mature onion but is stronger than that of a scallion. They only make an appearance in late spring and early summer. If they are not in season or you can't find them, scallions make a perfectly good substitute on this pizza.

PREP 25 minutes
GRILL 9 minutes
MAKES 4 individual pizzas

12 ounces fresh or frozen large shrimp in shells
2   tablespoons olive oil
½   teaspoon salt
½   teaspoon crushed red pepper
½   of a peeled, cored pineapple, cut into wedges
6   to 8 ounces red and/or green spring onions or scallions, trimmed
4   3- to 4-ounce pieces garlic-flavor naan or flatbread
1½ cups shredded Manchego cheese (6 ounces)
¼   cup crumbled blue cheese (1 ounce)
8   large basil leaves, thinly sliced
1   tablespoon honey
    Fresh basil laves (optional)

1. Thaw shrimp, if frozen. Peel and devein shrimp. Rinse shrimp; pat dry with paper towels. Thread shrimp on 4 long metal skewers, leaving a ¼-inch space between shrimp. In a small bowl combine olive oil, salt, and crushed red pepper. Brush oil mixture over shrimp, pineapple, and onions.

2. For a charcoal or gas grill, place shrimp, pineapple, and onions on the rack of a covered grill directly over medium-high heat. Grill for 5 to 8 minutes or until shrimp are opaque and pineapple and onions are nicely charred, turning occasionally. Coarsely chop shrimp, pineapple, and onions.

3. Place naan on the grill rack. Grill for 1 minute or until lightly toasted. Turn and sprinkle with Manchego cheese and blue cheese. Top with shrimp, pineapple, and onions. Cover and grill for 3 to 4 minutes or until cheese is melted and bottom crusts are toasted. Remove pizzas from grill. Sprinkle with thinly sliced basil and drizzle with honey. If desired, top with basil leaves.

EACH PIZZA *609 cal, 24 g fat, 151 mg chol, 1,415 mg sodium, 65 g carb, 4 g fiber, 33 g pro.*

Brussels Sprouts and Spicy Fennel Sausage Pizza

Gone are the days when Brussels sprouts were spoken of disparagingly. It wasn't so surprising, really, when the most common way to prepare them was to steam or boil them to mush. The recent popularity of crisp and caramelized oven- or pan-roasted Brussels sprouts has caused this humble vegetable to undergo a renaissance. Even kids will eat Brussels sprouts when they top a cheese-and-sausage pizza.

PREP **40 minutes**
RISE **1 to 2 hours**
BAKE **20 minutes**
OVEN **500°F**
MAKES **8 servings**

1 cup warm water (105°F to 115°F)
1 teaspoon active dry yeast
2½ to 3 cups bread flour
3 tablespoons olive oil
1½ teaspoons salt
12 ounces ground pork
1 teaspoon fennel seeds
½ teaspoon salt
½ teaspoon crushed red pepper
1 pound fresh Brussels sprouts
2 cups shredded Gruyère cheese (8 ounces)
1 small red onion, thinly sliced and separated into rings
4 cloves garlic, minced
1 tablespoon olive oil

1. For crust, in a small bowl stir together the water and yeast. In a large mixing bowl combine 2 cups of the flour, the 3 tablespoons olive oil, the 1½ teaspoons salt, and the yeast mixture. Beat with an electric mixer on low until combined. Turn dough out onto a lightly floured surface. Knead in enough of the remaining flour to make a moderately stiff dough that is smooth and elastic (6 to 8 minutes total). Shape dough into a ball. Place in a lightly greased bowl, turning once to grease surface of dough. Cover; let rise in a warm place until double in size (1 to 2 hours).

2. Meanwhile, for sausage, in a large bowl combine pork, fennel seeds, the ½ teaspoon salt, and crushed red pepper. Preheat a large nonstick skillet over medium-high heat. Drop ½-inch pieces of meat mixture into the hot skillet. Cook until meat is no longer pink, stirring occasionally. Remove skillet from heat; drain off fat. Set sausage aside.

3. Punch dough down; let rest for 10 minutes. Preheat oven to 500°F. Adjust oven rack to lowest position.

Meanwhile, trim bottoms from Brussels sprouts and remove any browned outer leaves. Thinly slice Brussels sprouts; set aside.

4. Place dough on a well-oiled 17×13-inch baking pan or a 14-inch pizza pan. Press and stretch the dough to the edges of the pan. Let dough rest for 5 minutes. If necessary, stretch dough again to cover pan.

5. Bake on lowest oven rack for 10 minutes. Remove crust from oven. Top with cheese, sausage, Brussels sprouts, onion, and garlic. Drizzle with 1 tablespoon oil. Bake for 10 to 12 minutes more or until edges are crisp and toppings are browned, turning pan once to ensure even browning.

Make-Ahead Tip Sausage can be made ahead and stored in a covered container in the refrigerator for up to 3 days.

EACH SERVING *500 cal, 29 g fat, 64 mg chol, 722 mg sodium, 38 g carb, 3 g fiber, 22 g pro.*

Zucchini, Cheddar, and Sage Crust Pizza with Chicken and Apples

This unusual pizza falls perfectly in the seasonal space between late summer and early fall, when the last zucchini is coming off the vine and the first apples are coming off the tree. Prebaking the zucchini crust makes it surprisingly crisp—a delicious vehicle for chicken, green olives, sweet pepper, and apple.

PREP **25 minutes**
BAKE **30 minutes**
OVEN **425°F/400°F**
MAKES **4 servings**

2   tablespoons olive oil
1   tablespoon coarse cornmeal
2½ cups packed shredded
     zucchini (2 small)
1   egg, lightly beaten
1½ cups shredded cheddar cheese
     (6 ounces)
¼   cup all-purpose flour
¼   cup coarse cornmeal
1   tablespoon snipped fresh sage
1   tablespoon minced garlic
¼   cup purchased dried tomato
     pesto
1   cup shredded cooked chicken
     (5 ounces)
½   cup chopped pimiento-stuffed
     green olives
½   cup finely chopped yellow
     sweet pepper
½   cup finely chopped apple

1. Preheat oven to 425°F. Brush a 12-inch pizza pan with the olive oil. Sprinkle with 1 tablespoon cornmeal.

2. Place shredded zucchini in a colander. Press zucchini several times with paper towels to remove excess moisture (should have 2 cups after pressing and draining).

3. In a large bowl combine egg, 1 cup of the cheese, the flour, ¼ cup cornmeal, the sage, garlic, and the drained zucchini. Transfer zucchini mixture to the prepared pan. Press into an even thickness to form a crust.

4. Bake, uncovered, about 20 minutes or until golden. Cool slightly. Using a spatula, loosen crust from pan. (Don't skip this step; it keeps the crust from sticking at the end of baking.)

5. Spread pesto on crust; top with chicken. Top with olives, sweet pepper, and apple. Sprinkle with the remaining ½ cup cheese.

6. Reduce oven temperature to 400°F. Bake, uncovered, for 10 minutes more. Cut into wedges to serve.

EACH SERVING *460 cal, 29 g fat, 123 mg chol, 829 mg sodium, 24 g carb, 4 g fiber, 26 g pro.*

Morel and Asparagus Crispy Pizzas

Morel mushroom hunters are protective of their hunting grounds—and it's no wonder. This highly prized wild mushroom has a unique, buttery flavor and tender texture. It shows up in Midwestern woods in spring—the peak is usually May. If you don't happen to have a secret spot in the woods—or a really good friend who does—you can sometimes buy fresh morels in your local supermarket.

PREP **30 minutes**
RISE **1 hour**
BAKE **12 minutes per pizza**
OVEN **475°F**
MAKES **4 servings**

1   package active dry yeast
1¼ cups warm water (105°F to 115°F)
2   to 2¼ cups all-purpose flour
1½ cups semolina flour
3   tablespoons olive oil
2   teaspoons salt
2   teaspoons sugar
1   tablespoon butter
10 ounces morel mushrooms, cleaned and sliced ½ inch thick
½   cup sliced shallots (4 medium)
¼   cup dry white wine
2   teaspoons snipped fresh thyme
8   ounces thin asparagus spears, cleaned, trimmed, and cut into 2-inch pieces
    Cornmeal
2   cups shredded Gruyère cheese (8 ounces)
    Olive oil
    Cracked black pepper

1. In a large mixing bowl combine yeast and the water. Let stand until yeast is dissolved, about 5 minutes. **2.** Add 2 cups of the all-purpose flour, the semolina flour, the 3 tablespoons olive oil, the salt, and sugar. Beat with an electric mixer on low or by hand until combined, scraping sides of bowl. Turn dough out onto a lightly floured surface. Knead in enough of the remaining all-purpose flour to make a smooth elastic dough (6 to 8 minutes total). Shape dough into a ball. Place dough in a lightly oiled large bowl, turning once to oil surface. Cover; let rise in a warm place until nearly double in size (1 to 1½ hours). **3.** Meanwhile, in a large skillet melt butter over medium-high heat. Add mushrooms; cook and stir for 2 to 3 minutes or just until mushrooms begin to soften. Add shallots, wine, and thyme. Cook and stir for 4 to 6 minutes or until shallots are tender. Add asparagus; cook and stir for 2 minutes. Remove from heat. **4.** Preheat oven to 475°F. Grease and dust 2 extra-large baking sheets with cornmeal. Punch dough down and divide in half. On a lightly floured surface roll one portion of the dough to ⅛-inch thickness (don't worry if it's not perfectly round). Transfer to one of the prepared baking sheets. **5.** Brush lightly with additional olive oil. Top with half of the mushroom mixture and half of the cheese; sprinkle with pepper. Bake in oven on lowest rack about 12 minutes or until crispy and brown. Assemble second pizza with the remaining dough, mushroom mixture, and cheese; bake as directed.

EACH SERVING *458 cal, 18 g fat, 35 mg chol, 694 mg sodium, 54 g carb, 3 g fiber, 18 g pro.*

Broccoli Raab, Garlic, and Mushroom Pizza with Golden Raisins

Sicilians are fond of taming the pleasant bitterness of broccoli raab—what they call rapini—with the sweetness of golden raisins and a little heat from crushed red pepper. That combination is sometimes eaten as a vegetable side dish or incorporated with pasta to make a main dish. Here it serves as a topping for pizza.

PREP **1 hour**
BAKE **10 minutes**
OVEN **500°F**
MAKES **4 servings**

1   pound broccoli raab or Broccolini, tough stems and large leaves removed
⅓   cup golden raisins or currants
2   tablespoons olive oil
3   cloves garlic, thinly sliced
1   to 2 anchovy fillets
8   ounces cremini mushrooms or button mushrooms, sliced (about 3 cups)
¼   teaspoon crushed red pepper
1   crust (half recipe) Pizza Dough
     Cornmeal
¾   cup ricotta cheese
1   cup grated Pecorino-Romano cheese

1. Place a baking stone or large inverted baking sheet in the oven and preheat to 500°F.

2. Cook broccoli raab in boiling salted water for 4 minutes. Remove broccoli raab and plunge into a bowl of ice water. Drain well. Chop into bite-size pieces; set aside.

3. In a bowl pour enough hot water over raisins to cover; set aside.

4. In a large skillet heat oil over low heat. Add garlic; cook just until golden. Add anchovies, smashing them with the back of a spoon. Add mushrooms and crushed red pepper. Cook over medium-high heat about 3 minutes or until mushrooms are barely tender. Remove from heat; stir in broccoli raab.

5. On a lightly floured surface roll or stretch Pizza Dough into a 13-inch circle, about ¼ inch thick. Place the dough on a pizza peel or inverted baking sheet that has been sprinkled with cornmeal.

6. Drain raisins well; add to broccoli raab mixture. Using a slotted spoon, spoon broccoli raab mixture onto crust. Drop small spoonfuls of ricotta cheese onto pizza. Sprinkle with the Pecorino-Romano cheese.

7. Transfer pizza to the pizza stone. Bake for 10 to 15 minutes or until crust is golden brown.

Pizza Dough In a small bowl stir togetheer 1½ cups warm water (105°F to 115°F) and 2 teaspoons honey. Sprinkle yeast over water mixture; let stand a few minutes or until slightly floamy. Stir to dissolve yeast. In a food processor fitted with the plastic blade combine 4 cups all-purpose or bread flour and 2 teaspoons kosher salt. Cover. With food processor running, slowly add ¼ cup olive oil and the yeast mixture through the feed tube. Process just until dough forms a ball and all of the flour is incorporated. Transfer to a floured surface. Knead dough for 2 to 3 minutes or until no longer sticky, adding the remaining flour, 1 tablespoon at a time, as needed. Place dough in an oiled large bowl. Turn once to oil surface of dough. Cover; let rise in a warm place until double in size (1 to 1½ hours). Punch dough down. Divide dough into 2 portions. Use immediately or place each dough portion in a freezer bag that has been coated nonstick cooking spray. Seal, label, and freeze for up 3 months. Thaw in refrigerator before using.

EACH SERVING *302 cal, 13 g fat, 23 mg chol, 426 mg sodium, 35 g carb, 3 g fiber, 13 g pro.*

Fresh Tomato Pizza with Oregano and Mozzarella

This is pizza perfection: a thin, crisp crust topped with the very best of basic ingredients—ripe tomatoes, fresh mozzarella, garlic, oregano, and prosciutto. Out of the oven, the heat from the pizza brings out the peppery flavor of the arugula without wilting it.

PREP **20 minutes**
BAKE **15 minutes**
OVEN **475°F**
MAKES **4 servings**

2   cups cherry tomatoes
1   tablespoon olive oil
1   sprig fresh oregano
1   clove garlic, sliced
     All-purpose flour
1   1-pound ball fresh pizza
     dough, at room temperature
8   ounces fresh mozzarella
     cheese, sliced ¼ inch thick
¼   teaspoon sea salt
1   cup baby arugula (optional)
2   ounces very thinly sliced
     prosciutto, cut into strips
     (optional)

1. Place a 15×10×1-inch baking pan on the lowest rack of the oven. Preheat oven to 475°F.

2. For sauce, in a food processor combine cherry tomatoes, 1 tablespoon olive oil, the oregano, and garlic. Process just until tomatoes are coarsely chopped (do not puree). Set sauce aside.

3. Lightly sprinkle flour on an 18-inch-long piece of parchment paper. On the paper roll pizza dough into a 14×8-inch rectangle. Spread the sauce over the dough, leaving a 2-inch border around edges.

4. Carefully remove preheated pan from the oven. Place pizza (still on parchment) into the pan and return to the lowest rack of the oven. Bake for 10 minutes. Top with cheese. Bake about 5 minutes more or until pizza is crisp on the bottom. Sprinkle with sea salt. If desired, top with baby arugula and prosciutto.

EACH SERVING *487 cal, 24 g fat, 40 mg chol, 684 mg sodium, 48 g carb, 3 g fiber, 17 g pro.*

Edible Heirlooms

If you frequent farmers' markets, you've seen signs touting "heirloom" fruits and vegetables. Although there is some disagreement about what constitutes an heirloom, in general it is a plant that originated before 1951, when hybridization came into being. The seeds from the fruit of an heirloom plant can be dried, saved, and planted next year. This can't be done with hybrids, whose seeds are sterile.

There are many good reasons to grow and/or buy heirlooms. Here are a few of them:

Variety Heirloom fruits and vegetables haven't had all of their distinctive characteristics bred out of them, so the varieties available of a particular type of produce—tomatoes, for instance—is dizzying.

Flavor When plants are hyrbridized, traits such as disease-resistance, yield, and sturdiness for shipping are often chosen over flavor. Fans of heirlooms tout their superior flavor and quality.

Biogenetic Diversity As the number of types of plants grown for commercial production has narrowed and plant species die out, it creates a vulnerability in the food supply if there is a large plague or crop failure. Keeping diversity in the food chain is a smart thing to do.

Frugality Each year, after the crop is harvested, the seeds can be saved and stored to grow next year's garden. Many gardeners even join seed exchanges to swap seeds with other heirloom gardeners so they can try fun, new (old) varieties.

Roasted Indian Cauliflower, *recipe page 271*

little salads & sides

IT'S THEIR TIME TO SHINE At almost every meal, it's the main course that gets all of the fuss and attention. But with fresh vegetables and fruits naturally taking on the starring role in salads and side dishes, these serve-alongs step to the front of the stage and really sing.

Butter Lettuce and Spring Pea Salad with Mustard Vinaigrette

Dressed with a mustard-dill vinaigrette, this salad is delicious served with grilled salmon or roasted chicken. If you don't mind the calories or expense, definitely include the toasted macadamia nuts. They add a delightful crunch and buttery flavor.

START TO FINISH **30 minutes**
MAKES **6 servings**

2   cups shelled fresh peas or frozen peas
1   tablespoon snipped fresh dillweed
1   tablespoon lemon juice
1   tablespoon cider vinegar
2   teaspoons Dijon mustard
¼   teaspoon salt
¼   teaspoon freshly ground black pepper
3   tablespoons olive oil
2   small heads Belgian endive
1   large head butter or Bibb lettuce, separated into leaves
    Freshly ground black pepper
3   tablespoons chopped macadamia nuts, toasted (optional)
    Chive blossom florets* or snipped fresh chives (optional)

1. Fill a medium saucepan with water. Bring to boiling over high heat. Add peas; cook for 1 minute, stirring once. Immediately drain in a colander. Rinse with cold water. Drain peas again and set aside.
2. For mustard vinaigrette, in a medium bowl combine dillweed, lemon juice, vinegar, mustard, salt, and the ¼ teaspoon pepper. Slowly add the oil in a thin stream, whisking until fully blended. Add peas to vinaigrette; toss to coat.

3. Slice endive in half lengthwise and remove core. Slice endive lengthwise into thin strips. Add endive to pea mixture; lightly toss to mix.
4. Arrange lettuce on a platter; top with pea mixture. Sprinkle with additional pepper. If desired, top with nuts and chive blossom florets.
*Tip Break the chive blossom from the stem to get florets.
EACH SERVING *107 cal, 7 g fat, 0 mg chol, 142 mg sodium, 8 g carb, 3 g fiber, 3 g pro.*

Strawberry and Arugula Salad with Manchego Fricos

Italian for "little trifles," a frico is a lacy wafer of crispy fried cheese. They're made by cooking little piles of finely shredded cheese in a skillet until the cheese starts to bubble and brown slightly around the edges. Sometimes a bit of flour or herbs are mixed in. They are absolutely delicious as a garnish for a salad or soup. You can make them with Parmesan or cheddar as well. Here they're made with Manchego, a Spanish sheep's milk cheese.

PREP **15 minutes**
COOK **9 minutes**
MAKES **6 servings**

1   cup shredded Manchego cheese, shredded (4 ounces)
3   tablespoons olive oil
3   tablespoons balsamic vinegar
¼   teaspoon kosher salt
¼   teaspoon freshly ground black pepper
3   cups strawberries, halved and/or quartered
4   cups baby arugula

1. For fricos, heat a medium nonstick skillet over medium heat. Sprinkle one-third of the cheese over the bottom of the skillet, shaking the skillet so the cheese is in an even layer. Cook for 2 to 3 minutes or until cheese browns around the edges. Remove skillet from heat for 30 to 40 seconds or until cheese is set. Using a spatula and fork, carefully turn frico over, return to heat, and cook for 1 to 2 minutes more or until underside is golden. Slide frico out of pan onto a wire rack. Repeat with the remaining cheese to make 3 fricos.

2. For salad, in a large bowl combine olive oil, balsamic vinegar, salt, and pepper. Add strawberries and arugula; toss to coat. Transfer salad to 6 serving plates or a large platter.
3. Break fricos into pieces and serve with salad.

EACH SERVING *165 cal, 13 g fat, 17 mg chol, 192 mg sodium, 8 g carb, 2 g fiber, 6 g pro.*

Kohlrabi-Carrot Salad with Dill Vinaigrette

Kohlrabi is one of those vegetables that tends to stump even experienced cooks. It's been said that it looks like a cross between a spaceship and an octopus. Although its appearance suggests it's a root vegetable that grows underground, it is actually a swollen stem that grows above the ground. The peel is tough and should be removed, but the flesh is crisp and juicy with a mild flavor that is a bit like a broccoli stem with a hint of radish.

PREP **20 minutes**
CHILL **2 hours**
MAKES **6 servings**

4   medium kohlrabi* (about 1½ pounds total), peeled and chopped (3 cups)
1   medium red and/or green sweet pepper, cut into bite-size strips
½   cup coarsely chopped carrot (1 medium)
1   medium shallot, thinly sliced, or ½ of a small onion, thinly sliced
1   recipe Dill Vinaigrette

1. In a large bowl combine kohlrabi, sweet pepper strips, carrot, and shallot. Add Dill Vinaigrette; toss gently to coat.
2. Cover and chill for 2 hours, stirring occasionally to coat with dressing. Stir before serving.

Dill Vinaigrette In a small screw-top jar combine ¼ cup cider vinegar, 2 teaspoons extra virgin olive oil, 1 teaspoon sugar, 1 teaspoon snipped fresh dill or ¼ teaspoon dried dillweed, ¼ teaspoon celery seeds, ⅛ teaspoon salt, and ⅛ teaspoon ground black pepper. Cover and shake well to combine. Use immediately or cover and chill for up to 1 week.

*Tip If desired, substitute 3 cups chopped green cabbage (about 12 ounces) for the kohlrabi.

EACH SERVING *48 cal, 2 g fat, 0 mg chol, 73 mg sodium, 7 g carb, 3 g fiber, 2 g pro.*

Potato Salad with Caramelized Onions and Roasted Chile Vinaigrette

This recipe is perfect for a late-summer or early fall barbecue. Dutch yellow potatoes are a type of baby yellow potato with a very thin skin that doesn't require peeling. If you can't find them, you could substitute baby red potatoes. Mildly flavored roasted Anaheim chiles appear in the vinaigrette and are also mixed in with the roasted and dressed potatoes.

PREP **30 minutes**
ROAST **25 minutes**
OVEN **425°F**
MAKES **12 servings**

3 pounds Dutch yellow potatoes, halved
5 tablespoons olive oil
 Kosher salt and freshly ground black pepper
1 large sweet onion, thinly sliced
1 tablespoon butter
½ cup seasoned rice vinegar
2 tablespoons sugar
1½ pounds fresh Anaheim chiles,* roasted,** cooled, then coarsely chopped
1 clove garlic, peeled
⅓ cup canola oil
 Kosher salt and freshly ground black pepper
 Fresh cilantro

1. Preheat oven to 425°F. For potato salad, in a shallow roasting pan toss together potatoes and 3 tablespoons of the olive oil. Season with salt and black pepper. Roast potatoes, uncovered, for 25 to 30 minutes or until they can easily be pierced with a fork. Let cool.

2. Meanwhile, to caramelize onions, in a large skillet heat the remaining 2 tablespoons olive oil and the butter. Add onion slices; cook about 15 minutes or until golden, stirring frequently.

3. For vinaigrette, in a blender combine vinegar, sugar, ½ cup of the roasted chiles, and the garlic. Cover and blend until well combined. With blender running, slowly add canola oil in a steady stream through hole in the top until vinaigrette is thickened. Season with salt and black pepper.

4. In a large bowl gently toss roasted potatoes, caramelized onions, and the remaining chopped chiles. Add 1 cup of the vinaigrette; gently toss to combine. Sprinkle salad with cilantro. Pass remaining vinaigrette.

*Tip Because hot chile peppers contain volatile oils that can burn your skin and eyes, avoid contact with chiles as much as possible. When working with chile peppers, wear plastic or rubber gloves. If your bare hands do touch the chile peppers, wash your hands well with soap and water.

**Tip To roast peppers, preheat oven to 425°F. Arrange peppers on a baking sheet, allowing space between peppers. Roast about 20 minutes or until skins are blistered and browned.

EACH SERVING *284 cal, 15 g fat, 3 mg chol, 202 mg sodium, 35 g carb, 5 g fiber, 4 g pro.*

Corn and Blueberry Salad

Sweet corn and blueberries are an unexpected pair, but their flavors come together effortlessly in this lime- and cumin-laced salad. The sweetness of the corn and blueberries—together with a honey dressing—is balanced by a bit of heat from jalapeño.

PREP **25 minutes**
CHILL **6 to 24 hours**
MAKES **6 to 8 servings**

6   ears fresh sweet corn
1   cup fresh blueberries
1   small cucumber, sliced
¼   cup finely chopped red onion
¼   cup snipped fresh cilantro
1   jalapeño pepper, seeded and finely chopped*
2   tablespoons lime juice
2   tablespoons olive oil
1   tablespoon honey
½   teaspoon salt
½   teaspoon ground cumin

1. Fill a large pot with salted water; bring to boiling. Meanwhile, remove husks from ears of corn. Scrub with a stiff brush to remove silks; rinse. Add corn to boiling water. Cook, covered, about 5 minutes or until tender. Remove corn from boiling water. When cool enough to handle, cut corn from cobs.

2. In a serving bowl combine corn, blueberries, cucumber, red onion, cilantro, and jalapeño pepper.

3. For dressing, in screw-top jar combine lime juice, oil, honey, salt, and cumin. Cover and shake well to combine. Drizzle dressing over salad; toss to coat. Cover and chill for 6 to 24 hours.

***Tip** Because hot chile peppers contain volatile oils that can burn your skin and eyes, avoid contact with chiles as much as possible. When working with chile peppers, wear plastic or rubber gloves. If your bare hands do touch the chile peppers, wash your hands well with soap and water.

EACH SERVING *152 cal, 6 g fat, 0 mg chol, 211 mg sodium, 26 g carb, 3 g fiber, 4 g pro.*

The Buzz About Honey

All honey is sweet, but the nectar source has a bearing on its flavor, color, and body. Sometimes the honey comes from a single source and sometimes the bees do their own blending, depending on the different flowers they visit. There are more than 300 unique types of honey in the United States. Most grocery-store honey comes from clover, but small-scale beekeepers offer unique types.

Here's a sampling of the more common varieties:

Alfalfa Light in color with a mild flavor and aroma.

Avocado Dark in color with a rich, buttery taste.

Blueberry Light amber in color with a full, round flavor.

Buckwheat Dark and full-bodied and higher in antioxidants than other types.

Eucalyptus Strong flavor with a subtle medicinal scent.

Orange blossom Light in color with a fresh scent and light citrus taste.

Sage Light in color with a full body and mild flavor.

Tupelo A premium amber honey with a heavy body and mild flavor.

Wildflower This is often a blend from miscellaneous and unknown flower sources.

6 Fresh Ideas for Blueberries

Consumption of this native North American fruit has risen dramatically in recent years, thanks to the discovery that blueberries are among the highest in antioxidants of all fruits and vegetables.

1 Blueberry-Brie Quesadillas

Brush one side of four 7- to 8-inch flour tortillas with melted butter. Place tortillas, buttered sides down, on a large baking sheet. Layer thin slices of Brie on half of each tortilla. Sprinkle about ¼ cup fresh blueberries over cheese. Fold tortillas in half. Bake in a 400°F oven about 10 minutes or until lightly browned and cheese is melted. In a blender or food processor blend 1 cup fresh raspberries with ¼ cup honey. Serve quesadillas with raspberry sauce. Makes 4 servings.

2 Savory Blueberry Sauce

In a small saucepan heat 1 tablespoon olive oil over medium-high heat. Cook 1 small onion, chopped, in hot oil for about 3 minutes. Add 1½ cups fresh blueberries, ¼ cup cider vinegar, 1 teaspoon sugar, and 1 teaspoon fresh thyme leaves. Cook for 5 minutes or until thickened. Season with ¼ teaspoon each salt and freshly ground black pepper. Serve over grilled or roasted pork, lamb, or chicken. Makes about 1¼ cups.

3 Sweet Blueberry Sauce

In a small saucepan combine 1½ cups fresh blueberries and ½ to ¾ cup sugar. Cook, stirring occasionally, over medium heat until mixture comes to a boil. Reduce heat and simmer uncovered, stirring occasionally, until berries are tender and sauce thickens slightly, about 8 minutes. Remove from the heat and let cool. Then refrigerate until cold before using. Serve over ice cream, yogurt, pancakes, or waffles. Makes about 1 cup.

4 Blueberry Fizz

Divide a 2-liter bottle of chilled ginger ale between 2 half-gallon jars or pitchers. Add ½ cup fresh blueberries, half of a sliced lemon, half of a sliced lime, and 1 tablespoon crystallized ginger to each jar. Cover and chill 2 hours. Just before serving, fill jars with ice. To serve, fill each glass half full with blueberry mixture and ice. Fill glass with additional chilled plain ginger ale. Makes 12 servings.

5 Greens with Blueberries, Red Onion, and Goat Cheese Croutons

Divide 8 cups baby greens among 6 salad plates. Divide 1½ cups fresh blueberries, ⅓ cup slivered red onion, and ⅓ cup chopped toasted hazelnuts among plates. For croutons, toast 6 baguette slices under broiler. Spread each slice with soft goat cheese and broil until cheese is golden-brown. Drizzle each salad with balsamic vinaigrette (or olive oil, balsamic vinegar, salt, and pepper). Serve with croutons. Makes 6 servings.

6 Blueberry Fool

In a shallow dish use a potato masher to mash 1 cup fresh blueberries (or puree berries in a small food processor). Stir ⅛ teaspoon cinnamon into mashed berries. In a medium bowl combine ½ cup chilled whipping cream and 1 tablespoon sugar; beat with an electric mixer until cream is very thick. Fold in mashed blueberries. In six 6-ounce dessert dishes layer whipped cream mixture alternately with 1½ cups fresh blueberries, ending with whipped cream. Serve immediately or chill for up to 2 hours. Makes 6 servings.

Savory Blueberry Sauce, *page 250*

Beets and Greens Salad

Most beet salads call for roasted beets, which take a bit of time to cook. The beets in this recipe are cooked with cider vinegar and sugar in the microwave in about 10 minutes, so you can enjoy this hearty side salad on even the busiest weeknight.

START TO FINISH **30 minutes**
MAKES **4 servings**

6   small golden and/or red beets
½   cup cider vinegar
2   tablespoons sugar
2   tablespoons water
1   small baguette, sliced
       diagonally
4   ounces semisoft cheese with
       garlic and fine herbs
¼   cup extra virgin olive oil
½   teaspoon salt
½   teaspoon ground black pepper
8   cups mixed salad greens
⅓   cup dried cranberries
       Shelled roasted pumpkin seeds
       (optional)

1. Trim greens from beets. Place whole beets in a casserole dish. Add vinegar, sugar, and the water. Microwave, covered, on high for 9 to 12 minutes or until tender, stirring once. Slice stems from beets and slip off skins. Slice beets; reserve cooking liquid.

2. Meanwhile for toasts, preheat broiler. Spread baguette slices with cheese. Broil 4 inches from the heat about 3 minutes or until cheese is melted and bread edges are toasted; set aside.

3. For dressing, in a small bowl whisk together the reserved cooking liquid, the oil, salt, and pepper. In a large bowl toss beets, salad greens, and cranberries. Drizzle with dressing; toss to coat. If desired, sprinkle with pumpkin seeds. Serve with toasts.

EACH SERVING *581 cal, 24 g fat, 22 mg chol, 1,070 mg sodium, 74 g carb, 6 g fiber, 19 g pro.*

Persimmon, Blood Orange, and Pomegranate Salad

If you're looking for a special salad to serve at Thanksgiving or Christmas, this beautiful blend of jewel-tone fall and winter fruits with greens is a lovely choice. The orange-and-spice Pine Nut-Persimmon Vinaigrette infuses the salad with rich, nutty flavor.

START TO FINISH 50 minutes
MAKES 6 servings

1   pomegranate
2   large ripe Fuyu persimmons, mangoes, or papayas
5   cups mesclun, arugula, baby arugula, or mixed salad greens
6   tablespoons thinly sliced scallions or green onions (3)
1   recipe Pine Nut-Persimmon Vinaigrette
4   medium blood and/or navel oranges, peeled and thinly sliced*

1. Score an "X" into the top of the pomegranate. Break apart into quarters. Working in a bowl of cool water, immerse each quarter; use your fingers to loosen the seeds from the white membrane. Discard peel and membrane. Drain the seeds; set aside.

2. Cut each persimmon in half; remove core. Slice into ¼- to ½-inch slices.

3. In a large bowl combine mesclun and scallions. Drizzle with ½ cup of the Pine Nut-Persimmon Vinaigrette; toss to coat.

4. To serve, arrange mesclun mixture on 6 chilled salad plates. Arrange persimmons and oranges on top of greens, tucking a few in and under leaves. Sprinkle with pomegranate seeds. Pass the remaining Pine Nut-Persimmon Vinaigrette.

Pine Nut-Persimmon Vinaigrette
Remove the core from 1 large ripe Fuyu persimmon; cut in half. Scoop out pulp (should have about ⅓ cup). Discard skin. Place pulp in a blender or food processor. Cover and blend or process until smooth. Add ⅓ cup olive oil; ¼ cup red or white wine vinegar; 3 tablespoons pine nuts, toasted; 1½ teaspoons finely shredded blood orange peel or orange peel; 2 tablespoons blood orange juice or orange juice; 1 tablespoon honey; ½ of a large shallot, cut up; ½ teaspoon Dijon mustard; dash ground cinnamon or ground allspice; and a dash freshly ground black pepper. Cover and blend or process until smooth. Makes about 1¼ cups.

*Tip If desired, substitute 2 pink or red grapefruit for the oranges or use a combination of oranges and grapefruit. Or use 2 to 3 cups bottled sectioned citrus fruit in place of the oranges. Drain the fruit before adding it to the salad.

EACH SERVING *238 cal, 15 g fat, 0 mg chol, 18 mg sodium, 26 g carb, 3 g fiber, 2 g pro.*

Citrus Salad

This salad hints at ambrosia salad, that 1950s potluck standby of citrus, coconut, marshmallows, and maraschino cherries. This lighter, fresher, and more savory version swaps in crisp Bibb lettuce for the marshmallows and cherries and an herb-mustard vinaigrette for the whipped cream.

PREP 20 minutes
MAKES 6 to 8 servings

3   oranges
¼   cup extra virgin olive oil
1   tablespoon snipped fresh tarragon
1   tablespoon Dijon mustard
2   heads Bibb lettuce, torn
1   pink grapefruit, peeled and thinly sliced
2   clementines, peeled and separated into segments
2   tablespoons snipped chives
½   cup unsweetened flaked coconut, toasted

1. For dressing, squeeze juice from 1 orange and transfer to a small bowl. Whisk in oil, tarragon, and mustard.
2. Peel and thinly slice the remaining 2 oranges.
3. Place lettuce in a large bowl. Drizzle with dressing; toss to coat. Add orange slices, grapefruit slices, and clementine segments. Lightly toss to mix. Arrange salad on platter. Sprinkle with chives and toasted coconut.
EACH SERVING *211 cal, 15 g fat, 0 mg chol, 67 mg sodium, 19 g carb, 5 g fiber, 3 g pro.*

The Power of the Peel

Citrus peel is heady stuff. It's loaded with natural oils and hence, lots of flavor. So often the peels are simply tossed in the compost pile or down the disposal. Next time you're peeling a citrus fruit to use the juicy flesh, take a minute to carefully remove just the outer part (not the bitter white pith) and put that peel to good use.

Savor the flavor of citrus in one of these aromatic ways:

Citrus Vinegar In a microwave-safe glass bowl combine 2 cups white wine vinegar and the zest from 2 lemons (¼ cup) or a combination of citrus zests. Microwave on high for 2 minutes. Let stand 10 minutes. Remove zest. Pour into a clean bottle or jar. Add a thin strip of lemon or citrus peel and, if you like, 1 dried red chile. Cover tightly with a nonmetal lid and store in a cool dark place for up to 6 months. Remove chile after several days, if desired.

Citrus Cider In a 6-inch square of double-thickness cheesecloth place 8 inches of cinnamon stick, broken; 8 whole cloves; several strips of lemon and orange peel; and 3 slices of fresh ginger. Bring corners together and tie with 100%-cotton kitchen string. In a 3½- to 4-quart slow cooker combine 2 quarts apple cider, 1 cup fresh orange juice, ½ cup fresh lemon juice, and ¼ cup honey. Add spice bag to slow cooker. Cover; cook on low for 5 to 6 hours or on high for 2½ to 3 hours. Remove spice bag and discard.

Smashed Peas and Edamame with Ricotta Toasts

This unusual side dish has double the good green stuff—garden peas and edamame. They're cooked, pureed, and flavored with garlic, mint, lemon, kosher salt, and lots of freshly ground black pepper before being spread on warm ricotta toast. Delicious with a roasted chicken.

START TO FINISH 30 minutes
MAKES 8 servings

1   pound fresh shelled peas or one 16-ounce package frozen baby sweet peas
1   12-ounce package frozen shelled edamame (sweet soybeans)
1   tablespoon olive oil
4   cloves garlic, sliced
¼   cup snipped fresh mint
2   tablespoons lemon juice
1   to 2 teaspoons freshly ground black pepper
½   teaspoon kosher salt
½   of a 1-pound baguette, sliced and toasted
1   cup ricotta cheese
    Kosher salt and freshly ground black pepper
    Extra virgin olive oil (optional)

1. In large pot cook peas and edamame in a small amount of boiling water for 5 minutes or until tender. Drain in a colander. Transfer peas and edamame to a food processor; cover and process until almost smooth. Transfer pureed mixture to a serving bowl.
2. In small skillet heat oil over medium heat. Add garlic; cook for 1 to 2 minutes or until tender. Add the garlic, mint, lemon juice, 1 to 2 teaspoons pepper, and ½ teaspoon salt to pureed pea mixture.

3. For ricotta toasts, spread baguette slices with the ricotta cheese. Arrange on baking sheet. Broil 4 inches from heat for 1 to 2 minutes or until ricotta is warm. Sprinkle with salt and pepper.
4. If desired, drizzle peas with olive oil and sprinkle with additional black pepper. Serve with ricotta toasts.
EACH SERVING *274 cal, 11 g fat, 16 mg chol, 458 mg sodium, 30 g carb, 6 g fiber, 0 g pro.*

Artichokes with Tarragon Drizzle

Although you could serve these gorgeous grilled artichokes as an appetizer, in parts of the country where they are grown—most notably California's coastal areas—they are more popular than potatoes as a side dish for dinner.

PREP 25 minutes
COOK 20 minutes
GRILL 12 minutes
MAKES 8 to 10 servings

4   to 5 large whole artichokes or 12 to 15 baby artichokes
⅔   cup extra virgin olive oil
⅓   cup white wine vinegar
⅓   cup thinly sliced green onions or scallions
2   tablespoons snipped fresh tarragon or 2 teaspoons dried tarragon, crushed
2   tablespoons Dijon mustard
    Sea salt or salt
    Ground black pepper
    Extra virgin olive oil
    Snipped fresh tarragon (optional)
2   lemons, each cut into 8 to 10 wedges

1. Wash large artichokes; trim stems if desired, and remove loose outer leaves. Snip off the sharp leaf tips. If using baby artichokes, remove outer leaves to reach pale green or yellow leaves on bottom half. Cut darker green portion of leaves off top half of artichoke; discard. Cut off stem and trim any remaining green from base of baby artichokes.

2. In a large pot bring a large amount of lightly salted water to boiling; add artichokes. Return to boiling; reduce heat. Simmer, covered, for 20 to 30 minutes for large artichokes or 10 minutes for baby artichokes or until a leaf pulls out easily.

3. Place artichokes in a large bowl of ice water to cool completely. Drain artichokes upside down on paper towels. Cut artichokes in half from tops through stems; use a spoon to scoop out the fibrous cores, leaving the hearts and leaves intact.

4. For tarragon drizzle, in a screw-top jar combine the ⅔ cup oil, the vinegar, green onions, 2 tablespoons snipped tarragon, and the mustard. Cover and shake well. Season with salt and pepper.

5. Brush artichoke halves with additional olive oil. For a charcoal or gas grill, place artichokes, cut sides down, on the rack of a covered grill directly over medium heat. Grill for 7 minutes; turn artichokes and grill for 5 to 7 minutes more.

6. On a serving platter place grilled artichokes, cut sides up. Shake tarragon drizzle; pour some over artichokes. If desired, sprinkle with snipped tarragon. Serve with lemon wedges. Pass the remaining tarragon drizzle.

EACH SERVING *131 cal, 11 g fat, 0 mg chol, 153 mg sodium, 8 g carb, 4 g fiber, 3 g pro.*

Roasted Radishes with Chive
Vinaigrette, *recipe page 262*

Roasted Radishes with Chive Vinaigrette

pictured page 261

The ruling assumption about radishes is that they are only to be eaten raw. True enough, a really crisp, crunchy, peppery radish needs nothing more than a sprinkling of salt to be enjoyed at its prime. However, a hot oven works the same magic on radishes as it does on other vegetables. They become sweeter and mellower, with a fuller flavor.

PREP **15 minutes**
ROAST **30 minutes**
OVEN **425°F**
MAKES **6 servings**

1½ pounds radishes, trimmed, scrubbed, and halved
3 tablespoons olive oil
2 tablespoons white wine vinegar
1 tablespoon snipped fresh chives
½ teaspoon Dijon mustard
¼ teaspoon ground black pepper
⅛ teaspoon salt

1. Preheat oven to 425°F. In a medium bowl toss radishes with 1 tablespoon of the olive oil. Place the radishes in a 15×10×1-inch baking pan. Roast, uncovered, for 30 to 35 minutes or until tender and lightly browned, stirring once.

2. For chive vinaigrette, in a screw-top jar combine the remaining 2 tablespoons olive oil, the white wine vinegar, chives, mustard, pepper, and salt. Drizzle vinaigrette over radishes; toss to coat.

EACH SERVING *80 cal, 7 g fat, 0 mg chol, 103 mg sodium, 4 g carb, 2 g fiber, 1 g pro.*

Sweet Curry Carrots with Chive Yogurt

Carrots are tossed with curried honey toward the end of the roasting time to create a sweet and spicy caramelized exterior. A cool topping of creamy Greek yogurt flavored with chives spooned over the warm carrots makes the dish.

PREP **20 minutes**
ROAST **25 minutes**
OVEN **425°F**
MAKES **6 to 8 servings**

1½ pounds carrots with tops, trimmed (about 10)
1   tablespoon olive oil
½   teaspoon salt
3   tablespoons honey
1   tablespoon curry powder
⅔   cup plain Greek low-fat yogurt
¼   cup snipped fresh chives
     Snipped chives (optional)

1. Preheat oven to 425°F. Scrub carrots and, if desired, peel. Halve any large carrots lengthwise. Line a 15×10×1-inch baking pan with foil. Toss carrots with oil. Spread carrots in the prepared pan. Sprinkle with ¼ teaspoon of the salt.
2. Roast carrots for 15 minutes. Meanwhile, in a small microwave-safe bowl microwave honey on high for 30 seconds. Whisk in curry powder; set aside.
3. Remove carrots from oven. Drizzle with honey mixture; toss to coat. Roast about 10 minutes more or until carrots are tender when pierced with a fork and glazed, turning occasionally. Transfer to a serving bowl.

4. For chive yogurt, in a small bowl combine yogurt, chives, and the remaining ¼ teaspoon salt. Spoon over with roasted carrots. If desired, sprinkle with additional snipped chives.
EACH SERVING *121 cal, 3 g fat, 1 mg chol, 283 mg sodium, 21 g carb, 4 g fiber, 4 g pro.*

Lemon-Tarragon Peas

You can serve this side dish as either a warm vegetable or a cold salad. To serve it as a cold salad, substitute olive oil for the butter. Chill in the refrigerator before serving with fresh lemon or lime wedges.

PREP **15 minutes**
COOK **12 minutes**
MAKES **6 servings**

½   cup water
3½ cups shelled fresh English peas
1½ cups whole fresh sugar snap pea pods and/or snow pea pods
1   tablespoon butter, softened
1   tablespoon snipped fresh tarragon
2   teaspoons finely shredded lemon peel
½   teaspoon freshly cracked black pepper
¼   teaspoon salt

1. In a medium saucepan bring the water to boiling. Add shelled English peas. Return to boiling; reduce heat. Simmer, covered, for 8 minutes. Add the whole sugar snap peas. Cook, covered, about 4 minutes or just until crisp-tender; drain.
2. Add butter, tarragon, lemon peel, pepper, and salt to the peas. Toss gently until butter melts. Serve immediately.
EACH SERVING *91 cal, 2 g fat, 4 mg chol, 19 mg sodium, 14 g carb, 5 g fiber, 5 g pro.*

What's in the Box This Week?

Community supported agriculture (CSA) is a model of production in which customers buy a share in a small-scale farm. They pay at the beginning of each growing season for weekly portions of the harvest. Demand for shares in many CSAs has grown so much that there are waiting lists. It's a wonderful way to eat healthfully (many CSAs are organic) and completely in sync with the seasons. There are likely many CSAs to choose from in your area. Ask friends, neighbors, and coworkers who participate in one about how theirs works and what kind of produce they get. Or look online—most CSAs now have websites and online newsletters.

Consider these things before joining a CSA:

Be open You will receive vegetables in your CSA box that you may never have heard of, let alone eaten. You might have to do some research on how to prepare them.

Quantities vary CSA farmers try to fill up the weekly baskets with a good variety of produce in reasonable quantities. They don't want to skimp—but they don't want to drown you in cabbage either. Consider the size of your family and ask up front how much produce they expect to deliver each week and how it varies from the beginning of the season to the end.

Share the share If you don't think you can use all of the produce that arrives each week, consider buying a share with a friend or coworker.

Go with the flow Understand that farming is a risky business. There will be droughts, rain, hail, and probably pests. Consider whether the likelihood that you will get fabulous fresh produce almost every week is worth the time or two you won't.

French Green Beans with Shallot Butter

French green beans—also called haricots verts (ah-reek-koh VEHR)—
are longer, skinnier, and more tender than traditional American green
beans. This recipe exemplifies the principle that when you have fresh,
high-quality ingredients, you don't need to do much to them. Tossed
with a simple shallot butter, these tiny green beans can be served at the
most elegant dinner.

PREP **5 minutes**
COOK **5 minutes**
MAKES **4 servings**

1   pound fresh French green
    beans (haricot verts), ends
    trimmed
2   tablespoons butter
2   tablespoons minced shallot
¼   teaspoon salt
¼   teaspoon freshly ground black
    pepper

1. Place steamer basket in a large
saucepan; add enough water to
reach just below the basket. Add
beans to basket; bring water to
boiling. Cover and reduce heat.
Steam beans for 3 to 4 minutes or
until crisp-tender.

2. In a large skillet melt butter over
medium-high heat. Add shallots,
salt, and pepper; cook for 1 minute.
Stir in beans until well coated. Serve
immediately.

EACH SERVING *85 cal, 6 g fat,
16 mg chol, 212 mg sodium, 8 g carb,
2 g fiber, 2 g pro.*

Green and Wax Beans with Shiitake Mushrooms

Crisp, garlicky bread crumbs crown this mushroom and fresh green bean sauté. You can prepare the dish ahead through Step 2—just cover and chill the beans in the refrigerator and store the completely cooled bread crumbs in a tightly sealed container. When you're ready to finish the dish, microwave the beans on high for 1 minute—then proceed with Step 3.

PREP **15 minutes**
BAKE **5 minutes**
COOK **19 minutes**
OVEN **350°F**
MAKES **8 servings**

1   cup coarse soft bread crumbs
1   clove garlic, minced
¼   teaspoon salt
⅛   teaspoon ground black pepper
1   pound fresh green beans, ends trimmed
1   pound fresh wax beans, ends trimmed
2   tablespoons olive oil
½   cup minced shallots (4 medium)
½   pound fresh shiitake mushrooms, stems removed, sliced
1   teaspoon snipped fresh thyme or ¼ teaspoon dried thyme, crushed
2   cloves garlic, minced
¼   teaspoon ground black pepper
⅔   cup chicken broth

1. For crumb topping, preheat oven to 350°F. In a small bowl combine bread crumbs, 1 clove minced garlic, salt, and ⅛ teaspoon pepper. Spread crumb mixture on a baking sheet. Bake for 5 to 10 minutes or until golden.

2. Meanwhile, fill a large pot with salted water; bring to boiling. Add green and wax beans; return to boiling. Reduce heat; cook for 6 to 8 minutes or until crisp-tender. Drain and set aside.

3. In a large skillet heat olive oil over medium heat. Add shallots; cook about 3 minutes or until tender. Add mushrooms; cook for 5 minutes more. Add thyme, the 2 cloves minced garlic, and ¼ teaspoon pepper. Cook for 3 minutes. Add the green and wax beans and the chicken broth. Bring to a boiling; cook for 2 minutes. Spoon bean mixture into serving dish. Sprinkle with crumb topping.

EACH SERVING *95 cal, 4 g fat, 0 mg chol, 201 mg sodium, 13 g carb, 4 g fiber, 3 g pro.*

Roasted Tomato-Bread Toss

Chunks of toasted bread, olives, and roasted tomatoes are tossed with a simple dressing of olive oil, balsamic vinegar, garlic, salt, and pepper. The juice from the tomatoes soaks into the bread, so not a sweet drop is wasted. It couldn't be any simpler.

PREP **15 minutes**
ROAST **20 minutes**
OVEN **400°F**
MAKES **8 servings**

2   pounds cherry or grape tomatoes (about 6 cups)
6   cups torn baguette or Italian bread (12 ounces)
2   to 3 tablespoons olive oil
½   cup pitted kalamata and/or green olives
2   tablespoons balsamic vinegar*
4   cloves garlic, minced
½   teaspoon kosher salt
½   teaspoon freshly ground black pepper

1. Position one oven rack in the upper third of the oven. Preheat oven to 400°F. Line 15×10×1-inch baking pan with parchment paper. Arrange tomatoes in a single layer in the prepared pan. Place bread in large bowl. Drizzle 2 to 3 tablespoons oil over bread pieces. Toss to coat. In a second 15×10×1-inch baking pan arrange bread in a single layer.
2. Roast tomatoes on the upper rack and bread on the lower rack for 20 to 25 minutes. Roast tomatoes just until skins begin to split and wrinkle, gently stirring once. Roast bread until lightly toasted, stirring once.
3. Add bread and olives to tomatoes in pan; gently toss to mix. In a small bowl combine the remaining 2 tablespoons olive oil, the balsamic vinegar, garlic, salt, and pepper. Drizzle vinegar mixture over tomatoes, olives, and bread. Toss to coat.

*Tip For a richer flavor, in a small saucepan heat ⅓ cup balsamic vinegar over medium heat until boiling. Boil gently, uncovered, for 6 to 8 minutes or until reduced to 2 tablespoons, watching carefully at the end because vinegar will reduce quickly.
EACH SERVING *215 cal, 10 g fat, 0 mg chol, 494 mg sodium, 28 g carb, 3 g fiber, 5 g pro.*

Roasted Indian Cauliflower *also pictured page 240*

When cauliflower is roasted, the tips of the florets take on a delicately crisp texture and toasty flavor while the interior becomes tender and buttery. Plain, roasted cauliflower is wonderful. Seasoned with Indian spices, it's divine.

PREP **15 minutes**
ROAST **30 minutes**
OVEN **425°F**
MAKES **8 servings**

2   tablespoons peanut oil
2   teaspoons yellow or black mustard seeds
2   teaspoons sugar
2   teaspoons grated fresh ginger
1½   teaspoons ground turmeric
1½   teaspoons ground cumin
1   teaspoon ground coriander
½   teaspoon salt
¼   teaspoon crushed red pepper
1   medium head cauliflower (about 1 pound), cored and cut into florets
2   small bunches baby carrots with tops (about 10 ounces total), tops trimmed
2   tablespoons chopped fresh cilantro
1   lime, cut into 8 wedges

1. Preheat oven to 425°F. Line a 15×10×1-inch baking pan with foil; set aside. In a large bowl stir together oil, mustard seeds, sugar, ginger, turmeric, cumin, coriander, salt, and crushed red pepper.

2. Add cauliflower and carrots to bowl; toss to coat. Transfer to prepared baking pan. Roast about 30 minutes or until tender and vegetables begin to brown on edges, stirring twice.

3. Transfer to a serving dish. Sprinkle with cilantro. Serve with lime wedges to squeeze over vegetables.

EACH SERVING *71 cal, 4 g fat, 0 mg chol, 188 mg sodium, 8 g carb, 2 g fiber, 2 g pro.*

The Magic of Roasting

In the oven, vegetables are transformed from their humble selves into something far sweeter and more delicious. Sometimes the simplest seasoning—olive oil, salt, and pepper—is all the freshest veggies need before cooking.

Bring out the best flavor in these vegetables with a turn in the oven:

Tomatoes Cut ripe plum tomatoes in half lengthwise; scoop out the seeds and center membranes. Arrange in a shallow roasting pan and drizzle with olive oil. Season with fresh thyme leaves, salt, and pepper. Roast in a 375°F oven for 45 minutes.

Cipollini onions Cook whole onions in boiling water for 30 seconds; drain and cool. Remove skins. Place onions in a roasting pan. Toss with olive oil and balsamic vinegar. Season with salt and pepper. Roast in a 475°F oven for 30 minutes, turning twice. If desired, drizzle with additional balsamic vinegar.

Green beans In a roasting pan toss trimmed green beans with olive oil, salt, and pepper. Roast in a 450°F oven for 25 to 30 minutes or until tender, stirring twice. If desired, toss with fresh snipped dill and squeeze with fresh lemon, if desired.

Cabbage Cut a small green cabbage into 1-inch-thick rounds. Arrange rounds on a large rimmed baking sheet. Brush generously with olive oil and season with salt and pepper. Sprinkle with fennel or caraway seeds. Roast in a 450°F oven for 30 to 35 minutes or until tender and edges turn golden brown.

Roasted Vegetables and Chickpeas

With two kinds of potatoes, carrots, and protein-rich chickpeas, this is almost a meal in itself. Serve it with some hearty bread and it might be. It also pairs well with pork roast or chops or roasted chicken.

PREP **30 minutes**
ROAST **45 minutes**
OVEN **425°F**
MAKES **8 servings**

1 pound carrots, peeled and cut into 2-inch pieces
1 pound sweet potatoes, peeled and cut into chunks
1 pound red or russet potatoes, cut into cubes
1 large red onion, peeled, halved, and cut into 1-inch wedges
1 15-ounce can chickpeas (garbanzo beans), rinsed and drained
6 cloves garlic, minced
2 to 3 tablespoons vegetable oil or olive oil
1 tablespoon snipped fresh rosemary or 1 teaspoon dried rosemary, crushed
1 teaspoon packed brown sugar or granulated sugar
½ teaspoon kosher salt
½ teaspoon freshly ground black pepper

1. Preheat oven to 425°F. In a shallow roasting pan combine carrots, sweet potatoes, red potatoes, onion, chickpeas, and garlic. In a small bowl combine the oil, rosemary, sugar, salt, and pepper. Drizzle over vegetables; toss well to coat.

2. Roast, uncovered, about 45 minutes or until vegetables are lightly browned and tender, stirring twice.

EACH SERVING *223 cal, 4 g fat, 0 mg chol, 301 mg sodium, 42 g carb, 7 g fiber, 6 g pro.*

Shoestring Sweet Potatoes and Beets

These colorful fries are pretty to look at and tasty to eat. Save them for a meal when the main dish is fairly simple. They're not hard to make, but they do require a little bit of effort. It's very important to thoroughly dry the beet strips before putting them in the hot oil to avoid messy spattering.

PREP **30 minutes**
COOK **2 minutes per batch**
MAKES **4 to 6 servings**

2   small sweet potatoes
1   medium beet
1   teaspoon coarse salt
     Vegetable oil for deep-fat
     frying
     Thyme sprigs with tender
     stems* (optional)
     Coarse salt (optional)

1. Peel sweet potatoes and beet. Cut lengthwise into long thin strips. (Use a julienne cutter or a mandoline to make the thin vegetable strips.) Place strips of each vegetable in separate bowls. Toss each with ½ teaspoon coarse salt.

2. In a 4-quart Dutch oven or deep-fryer heat 2 to 3 inches of oil to 365°F. To prevent splattering, spread beets on a paper towel and pat dry. Carefully add beets and potatoes, about one-fourth at a time, to the hot oil. Fry about 2 minutes per batch, until crisp and golden brown, stirring gently once or twice. Using a slotted spoon, carefully remove fries from hot oil to paper towels to drain. If desired, carefully add thyme sprigs to hot oil with the vegetables (thyme sprigs will spatter briefly when added to hot oil). Transfer to platter. If desired, sprinkle with additional coarse salt.

*Tip If you have thyme with tougher stems, remove the thyme leaves from the stem and sprinkle over the fries on the platter.

EACH SERVING *406 cal, 41 g fat, 0 mg chol, 522 mg sodium, 11 g carb, 2 g fiber, 1 g pro.*

Skillet Salt-Roasted Potatoes

Coarse, inexpensive kosher salt is used to season the potatoes and to create and hold an even heat as they roast on the stove top. The fennel-infused salt can be sprinkled over the cooked potatoes, or saved in an airtight container and use for seasoning steamed vegetables or fish.

PREP **15 minutes**
COOK **35 minutes**
STAND **10 minutes**
MAKES **4 to 6 servings**

2   pounds red and/or yellow small new potatoes
2   cups kosher salt
1   to 2 tablespoons fennel or caraway seeds
1   tablespoon olive oil

1. Scrub potatoes; set aside. Pour salt into the bottom of a very large heavy cast-iron skillet or Dutch oven, spreading evenly. Heat over medium heat about 5 minutes or until hot. Sprinkle evenly with fennel seeds.

2. Add potatoes to hot salt in skillet, pressing potatoes into salt slightly. Cover skillet. Cook for 35 to 40 minutes or until tender. Remove skillet from heat. Let stand, covered, for 5 minutes.

3. Remove potatoes from skillet with tongs and brush excess salt from potatoes (reserve salt mixture). Transfer potatoes to a serving platter. Drizzle with olive oil. Cover with foil and let stand for 5 minutes. Serve with reserved salt mixture.

EACH SERVING *129 cal, 3 g fat, 0 mg chol, 331 mg sodium, 25 g carb, 3 g fiber, 3 g pro.*

The Importance of Salt and Pepper

Salt and pepper are fundamental seasonings. Salt enhances flavor, making food come alive. Pepper gives food a smoky spice and aroma—from a tinge of heat to a sharp and citrusy hit. The coarser the grind, the bolder the flavor. As basic as they are, quality and flavor differences are discernible in different types. Using good-quality salt and pepper can improve the flavor of food significantly—especially that of garden-fresh vegetables, whose essence you want to intensify, not mask.

Stock your pantry with several types of salt and whole black peppercorns:

Table salt This finely textured and inexpensive salt has additives to make it free-flowing. It is best for salting water for cooking pasta and vegetables.

Kosher salt Many cooks feel that the large grains of this salt adhere to food better than table salt. It is additive free and has a naturally pure flavor.

Coarse salt This very large-grained salt is good for sprinkling on vegetables before roasting.

Sea salt Making salt by evaporating sea water is a more expensive process than mining. Sea salt has a distinctive flavor. It can be fine or coarse grained.

Flaked salt Maldon, an English sea salt, is the most common type of flaked salt. Its clean taste and appearance make it a good finishing salt for seasoning foods right before serving.

Whole black peppercorns Tellicherry and Lampong are among the best varieties of black pepper, but even basic black peppercorns have great flavor—slightly hot with a hint of sweetness—when freshly ground.

Braised Cabbage with Spicy Croutons

Sometimes it takes just a little something special to dress up a humble vegetable. In this dish, homemade croutons spiced with garlic and crushed red pepper enliven a very simple braise. Placing the cabbage wedges in the hot skillet before the water is added to the pan to finish the cooking process gives the wedges a lovely caramelized edge.

PREP **10 minutes**
COOK **18 minutes**
MAKES **6 to 8 servings**

2 tablespoons olive oil
1 tablespoon butter
⅓ of a 12-ounce baguette, torn into coarse crumbs (2 cups)
¼ teaspoon garlic powder
¼ teaspoon crushed red pepper
1 small head green cabbage, cut into 6 wedges
 Salt and ground black pepper
½ cup water
 Snipped fresh parsley
 Lemon wedges

1. For croutons, in a very large skillet heat 1 tablespoon of the olive oil and the butter over medium-high heat. Add bread, garlic powder, and crushed red pepper. Cook and stir for 3 to 5 minutes or until golden brown. Remove croutons from skillet with slotted spoon; cool in a single layer on paper towels.

2. Add cabbage to the skillet, overlapping wedges if necessary. Sprinkle with salt and black pepper. Add the water; bring to boiling. Reduce heat; simmer, covered, about 15 minutes or until tender.

3. Place cabbage on a platter; drizzle the remaining 1 tablespoon olive oil over cabbage. Sprinkle with croutons and parsley; serve with lemon wedges.

EACH SERVING *141 cal, 7 g fat, 5 mg chol, 254 mg sodium, 19 g carb, 4 g fiber, 4 g pro.*

Braised Brussels Sprouts with Crispy Shallots

These crispy green sprouts are lightly browned in butter, then braised in white wine and broth before a final dash of cider vinegar is added to the pan to create a slightly syrupy sauce. A topping of fried shallot rings adds crunch and flavor.

START TO FINISH **40 minutes**
MAKES **6 servings**

2   pounds Brussels sprouts
3   tablespoons butter
1   teaspoon kosher salt
½   teaspoon dry mustard
¼   cup dry white wine
½   cup vegetable broth or
      mushroom broth
2   tablespoons olive oil
1   cup thinly sliced shallots
      (8 medium)
      Kosher salt
¼   cup cider vinegar
      Ground black pepper

1. Trim Brussels sprouts.* In an extra-large skillet heat butter over medium-high heat. Add Brussels sprouts; toss to coat. Sprinkle with 1 teaspoon salt and dry mustard. Cook and stir for 3 to 5 minutes or until sprouts are lightly browned.
2. Carefully add wine to skillet, stirring to scrape up any crusty browned bits. Add broth. Reduce heat to medium-low. Cook, covered, for 10 to 12 minutes or just until sprouts are tender, stirring occasionally.
3. Meanwhile, in a large skillet heat oil over medium heat. Add shallots, breaking apart into individual rings. Cook for 10 to 12 minutes or until deep brown and crisp, stirring frequently. Using tongs, transfer shallots to a paper towel-lined plate. Season with additional salt.

4. Gently stir vinegar into sprout mixture. Increase heat to medium-high. Cook, uncovered, about 2 minutes or until most of the liquid is evaporated. Remove from heat. Season with additional salt and pepper. Transfer Brussels sprouts to a serving bowl; top with shallots.
*Tip To trim Brussels sprouts, cut off the stems just at the spot where the leaves start to grow. Remove dark green outer leaves until the tender, light green leaves are uniformly exposed.

EACH SERVING *182 cal, 11 g fat, 15 mg chol, 580 mg sodium, 17 g carb, 6 g fiber, 6 g pro.*

Caramelized Carrots

Caramelization is the process of cooking and browning the sugars in a fruit or vegetable (or even meat). It results in an intensification of the sweetness and the creation of a nutty flavor and beautiful brown color. There are lots of natural sugars in carrots, making them ideal for caramelization. You can steam them, but they won't taste like this.

PREP 20 minutes
COOK 22 minutes
MAKES 8 servings

2   pounds whole small carrots with tops, peeled and halved lengthwise
2   tablespoons olive oil
¼   teaspoon salt
4   cloves garlic, thinly sliced
⅔   cup whipping cream
⅛   teaspoon cayenne pepper
     Snipped fresh Italian (flat-leaf) parsley

1. In a very large skillet cook carrots, cut sides down, in hot oil. Sprinkle with salt. Cook, covered, for 10 minutes. Flip carrots; add garlic to skillet. Cook, covered, about 10 minutes more or until carrots are tender and both sides are golden brown, gently shaking skillet occasionally to prevent sticking. Transfer carrots to serving plate; cover and keep warm.
2. Add whipping cream and cayenne pepper to skillet. Bring to boiling. Reduce heat; boil gently, uncovered, for 2 to 4 minutes until cream is slightly thickened. Pour over carrots. Serve immediately.
EACH SERVING 146 cal, 11 g fat, 27 mg chol, 160 mg sodium, 12 g carb, 3 g fiber, 2 g pro.

Cool-Weather Crops

Fruits and vegetables fall into two broad categories—warm-weather crops and cool-weather crops. While warm-weather crops really only have one season, cool-weather crops can (but don't always) have two—one in the spring and one in the fall. For instance, carrots are at peak in spring—sweet and crunchy in fresh slaws—and again in the fall, when they nestle in with other root vegetables in hearty braises. For the purposes of categorizing in this book (see the Produce Guide, page 328), the cool-weather crops are placed in one season—either spring or fall.

The most common vegetables that are in season in spring and fall:

Beets
Broccoli
Carrots
Cauliflower
Garlic
Kohlrabi
Lettuces
Mushrooms (certain types are specific to either spring or fall)
Onions
Peas
Potatoes
Salad greens
Spinach

Roasted Sweets and Greens

These simple and satisfying wedges are seasoned with garlic and paired with crunchy hazelnuts, then finished as they come out of the oven with peppery arugula and a splash of vinegar.

PREP **10 minutes**
ROAST **34 minutes**
OVEN **400°F**
MAKES **4 servings**

1½ to 2 pounds sweet potatoes, scrubbed
1 tablespoon olive oil
½ teaspoon salt
¼ teaspoon ground black pepper
¼ cup chopped hazelnuts
2 cloves garlic, minced
2 cups arugula
¼ cup cider vinegar

1. Preheat oven to 400°F. Scrub potatoes thoroughly with a brush; pat dry. Cut sweet potatoes in half lengthwise, then cut into wedges. Place in a 15×10×1-inch baking pan. Toss sweet potatoes with oil and sprinkle with salt and pepper.

2. Roast sweet potatoes for 15 minutes. Using a spatula, gently turn sweet potatoes over; roast about 15 minutes more or until tender. Sprinkle with hazelnuts and garlic. Roast for 4 to 5 minutes or until nuts are toasted. Remove from oven. Top sweet potatoes with arugula; drizzle with vinegar.

EACH SERVING *236 cal, 9 g fat, 0 mg chol, 387 mg sodium, 37 g carb, 6 g fiber, 4 g pro.*

Special Deliveries

There are a growing number of sources of fresh, locally produced food, and cooperatives are one of them. A cooperative is an organization of vendors—farmers and food producers—from whom cooperative members (who pay an annual fee) can place orders online through the cooperative's website. The vendors deliver the orders to a central location, where members then pick them up and pay for them. Multiple vendors offer fresh fruits and vegetables, meats, bread, baked goods, dried beans, nuts, eggs, cheese, grains and cereals, honey, jam—even handmade soaps and candles.

Joining a cooperative is a commitment. Consider the following:

Quality Because it is produced on a small scale locally and not trucked in from thousands of miles away, it's very likely that the flavor and nutrition of the food available through your cooperative will be much better quality than you can get at a supermarket.

Price Joining a cooperative may or may not save you money. You do have to pay an annual membership fee, and the cost of the food can vary widely. Study the prices on the cooperative's website to see if it will decrease or increase your food bill.

Comfort When you go to pick up your apples or your grass-fed beef, you will get to meet the grower or farmer in person. For many people, knowing who produces their food—being able to ask questions—is reassuring.

Convenience While it's handy to order your groceries from home and just pick it all up at once, most cooperatives have a fairly narrow time frame for pick up. If your schedule is extremely busy or not very predictable, it may prove too difficult or frustrating.

Sherried Cherry Crisp, *recipe page 300*

desserts

CELEBRATE FRUIT Berries, cherries, peaches, plums, apricots, apples, figs, and melons at peak season need almost no embellishment to show off their succulent natural sweetness. But it never hurts to throw a little butter, sugar, flour, whipped cream, chocolate—and even marshmallows—into the mix.

Rosemary Almond Cake with Strawberries and Mascarpone

Inspired by an Italian cake that contains cornmeal for crunch and rosemary for flavor, this version also features toasted almonds, which pair deliciously with the strawberries. The sign of a good strawberry? It's reasonably small and red all the way through—a sure sign of sweetness and lots of juice.

PREP **20 minutes**
BAKE **25 minutes**
COOL **15 minutes**
OVEN **350°F**
MAKES **8 to 10 servings**

²⁄₃ cup all-purpose flour
⅓ cup yellow cornmeal
1½ teaspoons baking powder
¼ teaspoon salt
²⁄₃ cup granulated sugar
½ cup coarsely chopped almonds, toasted
1½ teaspoons snipped fresh rosemary
½ cup butter, softened
3 eggs
½ cup ricotta cheese
3 cups quartered and/or halved fresh strawberries
¼ cup Orange-Vanilla Sugar
3 to 4 tablespoons orange juice
1 8-ounce container mascarpone cheese

1. Preheat oven to 350°F. Grease a 9×1½-inch round cake pan. Line bottom of pan with parchment paper or waxed paper. Grease paper and lightly flour pan; set aside. In a small bowl combine the flour, cornmeal, baking powder, and salt; set aside.
2. In a food processor combine ²⁄₃ cup granulated sugar, almonds, and rosemary. Cover and process until almonds are finely ground.
3. In a large mixing bowl beat the butter with an electric mixer on medium to high for 30 seconds. Gradually add the sugar-almond mixture, beating on medium for 1 to 2 minutes or until well combined and fluffy, scraping sides of bowl occasionally. Add eggs, one at a time, beating well after each addition. Stir in the ricotta cheese until combined. Sprinkle flour mixture over egg mixture; stir just until combined. Spread batter into the prepared pan.
4. Bake for 25 to 30 minutes or until a toothpick inserted near the center comes out clean. Cool in pan on a wire rack for 15 minutes. Remove cake from pan. Cool completely on a wire rack.

5. Meanwhile, in a medium bowl combine strawberries and the ¼ cup Orange-Vanilla Sugar. Allow to stand at room temperature until sugar dissolves and creates a syrup, stirring occasionally. In a small bowl stir enough orange juice into mascarpone cheese to make a spoonable consistency.
6. Place cake on a serving platter and top with strawberries; pour syrup over strawberries. Serve with mascarpone cheese.

Orange-Vanilla Sugar In a food processor combine 2 cups sugar and 1 tablespoon finely shredded orange peel. Scrape seeds from ½ of a vanilla bean; add to food processor. Cover and process until very fine granules form. Store in an airtight container in the refrigerator for up to 1 month. Use to sprinkle over fresh fruit or substitute for sugar in cake and cookie recipes.

EACH SERVING *483 cal, 32 g fat, 144 mg chol, 362 mg sodium, 43 g carb, 3 g fiber, 13 g pro.*

Strawberry Pavlova with Mint

The story goes that this classic dessert was created by a chef in New Zealand in honor of Russian ballerina Anna Pavlova after she toured that country in the 1920s. It is an ethereal, crisp meringue with a soft, marshmallowy center topped with whipped cream and seasonal fruit. Here it happens to be strawberries, but it lends itself to other berries, cherries, peaches, or—in the winter—pomegranate seeds.

PREP 40 minutes
STAND 30 minutes
BAKE 90 minutes
COOL 60 minutes
OVEN 250°F
MAKES 8 servings

6	egg whites
	Pinch salt
	Pinch cream of tartar
1½	cups sugar
1	teaspoon lemon juice
½	teaspoon vanilla
2½	teaspoons cornstarch
4	cups strawberries
2	tablespoons sugar
10	mint leaves
1½	cups whipping cream
½	cup crème fraîche

1. Allow egg whites to stand at room temperature for 30 minutes. Meanwhile, line a baking sheet with parchment paper or foil. Draw a 9-inch circle on the paper or foil. Invert paper or foil so the circle is on the reverse side.

2. Preheat oven to 250°F. For meringue, in a large mixing bowl beat egg whites, salt, and cream of tartar with an electric mixer on medium until soft peaks form (tips curl). Add the 1½ cups sugar, 1 tablespoon at a time, beating on high until stiff peaks form (tips stand straight). Beat in lemon juice and vanilla. Sift cornstarch over egg white mixture; using a rubber spatula, gently fold cornstarch into egg white mixture.

3. Spread meringue over circle on paper or foil, building up edges slightly to form a shell. Bake for 1½ hours (do not open door). Turn off oven; let meringue dry in oven with door closed for 1 hour.

4. For filling, 20 minutes before serving, clean, hull, and slice the strawberries. Place strawberries in a large bowl. Toss berries with the 2 tablespoons sugar. Tear mint leaves; gently stir mint into strawberry mixture. Let stand for 20 minutes.

5. Meanwhile, in a large mixing bowl beat the whipping cream and crème fraîche with an electric mixer on medium (or beat with a whisk or rotary beater) until soft peaks form (tips curl).

6. Place meringue shell on a large platter. Spread the cream mixture into the meringue shell. Spoon the strawberry mixture over the cream mixture. Serve immediately.

EACH SERVING *404 cal, 22 g fat, 82 mg chol, 83 mg sodium, 49 g carb, 1 g fiber, 4 g pro.*

Rhubarb Hand Tarts

Flaky pastry encases a winning combination of rhubarb and apples in these turnover-style tarts. A bit of flavor magic happens when the two fruits come together. The sweetness of the apples mellows the rhubarb, while the tartness of the rhubarb helps perk up the apple flavor.

PREP **50 minutes**
BAKE **30 minutes**
COOL **30 minutes**
OVEN **375°F**
MAKES **8 tarts**

1   cup sugar
2   tablespoons quick-cooking tapioca
1   teaspoon fresh ginger
     Pinch ground nutmeg
3   cups ½-inch slices fresh rhubarb or frozen sliced rhubarb
1   cup sliced, peeled tart apples
2   cups all-purpose flour
½   teaspoon salt
½   cup shortening
7   to 9 tablespoons ice water
     Milk
     Coarse sugar

1. Line a large baking sheet with foil; grease foil and set aside.

2. In a large saucepan stir together the 1 cup sugar, the tapioca, ginger, and nutmeg. Stir in rhubarb and apples until coated. Let stand about 15 minutes or until a syrup begins to form, stirring occasionally. Cover and cook over medium heat for 15 minutes or just until fruit is softened, stirring occasionally. Remove from heat. Let cool for 30 minutes.

3. Meanwhile, preheat oven to 375°F. In a large bowl combine flour and salt. Using a pastry blender, cut in shortening until pieces are pea size. Sprinkle 1 tablespoon of the water over part of the mixture; gently toss with a fork. Push moistened mixture to side of bowl. Repeat, using 1 tablespoon of the water at a time, until all the dough is moistened. Divide dough in half. On a lightly floured surface roll out each portion of pastry to a 12-inch square. Cut each portion into four 6-inch squares.

4. Spoon about ¼ cup of the cooked rhubarb mixture onto half of one pastry square, leaving a 1-inch border around edge of pastry. Brush edges of square with water. Fold pastry over filling, forming a rectangle. Press edges gently to seal. Brush edges lightly with water again. Fold edges up and over about ¼ inch. Press edges with tines of a fork to seal again. Place tart on prepared baking sheet. Repeat with remaining squares of pastry and rhubarb filling.

5. Prick tops two or three times with the tines of a fork for steam to escape. Pat down tops to get rid of excess air around filling. Brush tops with milk and sprinkle with coarse sugar. Bake for 30 to 35 minutes or until golden brown. Cool on wire rack about 30 minutes; serve warm.

EACH TART *344 cal, 13 g fat, 0 mg chol, 149 mg sodium, 54 g carb, 2 g fiber, 3 g pro.*

Mango-Carambola Compote with Sugared Biscuits and Orange Cream

This recipe turns the idea of shortcake upside down. Instead of splitting a sweet biscuit and filling it with fruit, here the biscuit is laid on top of a melange of warm fruit in individual dessert dishes and then topped with orange-flavor whipped cream.

PREP 25 minutes
BAKE 13 minutes
COOK 10 minutes
COOL 15 minutes
OVEN 425°F
MAKES 8 servings

1   cup all-purpose flour
¼   cup sugar
1   teaspoon baking powder
¼   teaspoon salt
¾   cup whipping cream
1   teaspoon grated fresh ginger
1   teaspoon finely shredded lime peel
1   tablespoon whipping cream
1   tablespoon sugar
1   teaspoon ground cinnamon
3   medium mangoes, seeded, peeled, and sliced
1   medium carambola (star fruit), thinly sliced crosswise
½   cup orange juice
¼   cup sugar
1   tablespoon lime juice
1   sprig lemon verbena or lemon thyme (optional)
1   recipe Orange Cream
     Ground cinnamon (optional)

1. Preheat oven to 425°F. In a large bowl whisk together flour, ¼ cup sugar, the baking powder, and salt. In a liquid measuring cup combine the ¾ cup cream, the ginger, and the lime peel. Add cream mixture to flour mixture, stirring with a wooden spoon until a dough forms (it will seem too sticky at first, but keep stirring and it will firm up). Drop dough in 8 mounds on a baking sheet. Brush tops with the 1 tablespoon cream. Sprinkle with the 1 tablespoon sugar and 1 teaspoon cinnamon. Bake about 13 minutes or until golden. Transfer biscuits from baking sheet to a wire rack. Cool.

2. For compote, in a medium saucepan combine mangoes, carambola, orange juice, ¼ cup sugar, lime juice, and, if desired, lemon verbena. Bring to boiling; reduce heat. Simmer, uncovered, about 10 minutes or until fruit has softened but isn't mushy. Remove from heat; cool slightly (about 15 minutes). Discard lemon verbena (if using).

3. To serve, spoon warm compote into shallow dessert dishes. Add a biscuit to each dish and top with Orange Cream. If desired, sprinkle with additional cinnamon.

Orange Cream In a chilled medium mixing bowl combine ¾ cup whipping cream, 1 to 2 tablespoons orange liqueur, and 1 tablespoon powdered sugar. Beat with an electric mixer on medium until soft peaks form (tips curl).

EACH SERVING *341 cal, 18 g fat, 64 mg chol, 153 mg sodium, 44 g carb, 2 g fiber, 3 g pro.*

Hummingbird Cupcakes

The beloved Southern recipe for Hummingbird Cake gets a makeover. This departs from the classic in size—going from an imposing, multilayer cake to cupcakes—but also swaps in fresh pineapple for canned and shredded sweet potato for mashed banana. Why it has been called Hummingbird Cake remains a mystery, but it could have something to do with the fact that hummingbirds (and many humans) are drawn to intense sweetnesss.

PREP 45 minutes
BAKE 20 minutes
COOL 5 minutes
OVEN 350°F
MAKES 18 cupcakes

2 cups all-purpose flour
1 cup granulated sugar
2 teaspoons baking powder
½ teaspoon salt
¼ teaspoon ground cinnamon
¼ teaspoon ground cloves
1 cup mashed ripe bananas (3 medium)
2 eggs, lightly beaten
½ cup vegetable oil
1 teaspoon vanilla
1 cup shredded, peeled uncooked sweet potato (1 medium)
1 cup finely chopped fresh pineapple
1 recipe Marshmallow-Cream Cheese Frosting
½ cup raw chip coconut or flaked coconut, toasted*

1. Preheat oven to 350°F. Grease and lightly flour eighteen 2½-inch muffin cups or line with paper bake cups. Set pans aside.

2. In a very large bowl combine flour, granulated sugar, baking powder, salt, cinnamon, and cloves. Stir in bananas, eggs, oil, and vanilla just until combined. Fold in sweet potato and ½ cup of the pineapple. Divide batter evenly among the muffin cups.

3. Bake about 20 minutes or until tops spring back when lightly touched. Cool in pans on wire racks for 5 minutes. Remove cupcakes from pans. Cool completely on racks.

4. Spread Marshmallow-Cream Cheese Frosting on cupcakes. Sprinkle with toasted coconut. Top with the remaining pineapple just before serving.

Marshmallow-Cream Cheese Frosting In a large bowl let one 3-ounce package cream cheese stand at room temperature for 30 minutes. Beat cream cheese with an electric mixer on medium to high until fluffy. Add 3 cups powdered sugar, 1 cup marshmallow creme, and 1 teaspoon coconut flavoring. Beat on low until combined. Beat on high for 30 seconds.

*Tip To toast coconut, spread chips or flakes in a shallow baking pan. Bake in a preheated 350°F oven for 5 to 7 minutes or just until golden, shaking the pan once or twice. Watch closely to prevent overbrowning.

EACH CUPCAKE *306 cal, 9 g fat, 26 mg chol, 139 mg sodium, 55 g carb, 1 g fiber, 3 g pro.*

6 Fresh Ideas for Mint

Mint is one of those garden plants that is truly prolific. If you happen to have planted this perennial herb somewhere in your yard, it is a very good thing to have some creative ways to use it.

1 Mint Yogurt Sauce

In a small bowl combine ¼ cup mint leaves, cut into strips; 6 ounces plain Greek yogurt; ½ of a medium peeled cucumber, grated; ½ cup crumbled feta cheese; ¼ teaspoon salt; ¼ teaspoon sugar; and ¼ teaspoon black pepper. Serve with grilled chicken, fish, or burgers. Makes about 1¼ cups.

2 Minted French Green Beans

Rinse and trim 8 ounces haricots verts or other small thin green beans. Place in a covered dish with 2 tablespoons water. Microwave on high for 2 minutes. Drain and rinse under cold water (or plunge into ice water). Drain well. In a medium bowl toss beans with 1 tablespoon minced shallot, 2 teaspoons olive oil, and 2 teaspoons snipped fresh mint. Season to taste with salt and pepper. Cover and chill for 2 hours. Makes 2 to 3 servings.

3 Classic Mint Julep

In a cocktail shaker combine 1 teaspoon sugar and 2 fresh mint leaves; crush the mint with back of a spoon. Add 2 ounces bourbon and a handful of ice cubes. Cover and shake until sugar is dissolved and drink is very cold. Fill an 8-ounce glass with crushed ice. Strain liquid into glass. Garnish with mint sprigs. Makes 1 serving.

4 Mint-Herb Pesto

In a blender or food processor combine ½ cup each of lightly packed arugula, mint, and basil; ¼ cup extra virgin olive oil; 2 tablespoons toasted pine nuts; 1 tablespoon lemon juice; and 2 cloves minced garlic. Cover and blend or process until smooth, scraping down sides as needed. Add ¼ cup shredded pecorino cheese and ½ teaspoon crushed red pepper. Cover and blend or process just until combined. Season to taste with salt and pepper. Toss with hot cooked pasta or vegetables. Makes about ⅔ cup.

5 Peach-Mint Green Tea

Bring 2 cups of cold water just to boiling in a large saucepan. Remove from heat and add 5 green tea bags. Steep, covered for 5 minutes. Remove bags. Stir in 12 ounces peach nectar, ½ cup slightly crushed mint leaves, and 3 tablespoons sugar. Cover and chill for 2 to 24 hours. Strain and serve over ice. Makes 5 servings.

6 Feta-Mint Rice

In a large saucepan cook ¼ cup chopped onion in 1 tablespoon olive oil until tender. Stir in 1 cup long grain rice; cook and stir for 1 minute. Slowly add 2 cups chicken broth. Bring to boiling; reduce heat. Cover and simmer for 15 to 20 minutes or until rice is tender and liquid is absorbed. Stir in ½ cup crumbled feta cheese, 3 tablespoons fresh mint, and ½ teaspoon pepper. Serve warm. Garnish with fresh mint leaves if you like. Serve with grilled lamb or beef. Makes 4 servings.

Classic Mint Julep

Roasted Peach Pies with Butterscotch Sauce

These pies are simply thick-sliced peaches baked in a biscuitlike crust. The only added sweetness comes from the Butterscotch Sauce so that the flavor of the peaches isn't masked. This recipe makes two 7-inch pies or one 9-inch pie. Look for small pie pans online or at a specialty kitchen store.

PREP **40 minutes**
CHILL **30 minutes**
BAKE **33 minutes**
OVEN **450°F/350°F**
MAKES **6 to 8 servings**

1   cup all-purpose flour
½   teaspoon baking powder
¼   teaspoon salt
¼   cup unsalted butter
½   cup sour cream
1   tablespoon milk
6   small or 4 medium peaches
1   recipe Butterscotch Sauce
      Vanilla ice cream (optional)
      Freshly ground nutmeg (optional)
      Fresh mint leaves (optional)

1. In a large bowl combine flour, baking powder, and salt. Using a pastry blender, cut in butter until mixture resembles coarse cornmeal. Stir in sour cream and milk just until combined. Cover and chill for at least 30 minutes or up to 2 days.
2. Preheat oven to 450°F. For two 7-inch pies, divide dough in half. On a lightly floured work surface roll each half from center to edges into a circle 8½ inches in diameter. Transfer each pastry circle to a 7-inch pie tin. (For a 9-inch pie, do not divide dough, roll to an 11-inch circle, and transfer to a 9-inch pie plate.) Trim crusts even with top of pie tins. With a lightly floured fork, press sides of crust into pie plate. Line with a double thickness of foil that has been coated with nonstick cooking spray to prevent pastry from sticking. Bake for 8 minutes. Remove foil; bake for 5 to 6 minutes more or until crust is golden; let cool. Reduce oven temperature to 350°F.
3. Cut peaches into thick slices, slicing around the pit. Add peaches to cooled crusts. Cover edges of pies with foil.

4. Bake for 20 to 25 minutes or just until peaches are tender. Transfer to a rack. While pies are still warm, drizzle with ¼ cup of the Butterscotch Sauce. Serve immediately. If desired, serve with ice cream and sprinkle with nutmeg and mint. Pass the remaining warm Butterscotch Sauce.
Butterscotch Sauce In a small saucepan melt ¼ cup unsalted butter over medium heat. Stir in ⅓ cup packed brown sugar and 1 tablespoon light-color corn syrup. Bring to boiling over medium heat. Boil gently, uncovered, for 5 minutes, stirring frequently. Carefully stir in 2 tablespoons whipping cream. Cool slightly. Serve warm.
EACH SERVING *357 cal, 21 g fat, 56 mg chol, 142 mg sodium, 41 g carb, 2 g fiber, 4 g pro.*

Chilled Peach Soup with Blueberries and Prosecco

A splash of Prosecco—a dry sparkling Italian wine—gives this fruity dessert soup a bit of effervescence. You can use champagne or any other kind of dry sparkling white wine in its place.

PREP 25 minutes
COOK 10 minutes
CHILL 3 to 4 hours
MAKES 6 to 8 servings

2½ pounds fresh ripe peaches, peeled and coarsely chopped (about 6 cups)
1½ cups orange juice
3 tablespoons honey
2 tablespoons lime juice
2 tablespoons grated fresh ginger
⅛ teaspoon ground cardamom
1 6- to 7-ounce carton vanilla Greek yogurt
1½ cups fresh blueberries
⅔ cup chilled Prosecco or sparkling apple cider
6 to 8 thin slices unpeeled fresh peach (optional)
2 tablespoons chopped crystallized ginger (optional)

1. In a 4- to 5-quart Dutch oven combine chopped peaches, orange juice, honey, lime juice, ginger, and cardamom. Bring to boiling; reduce heat. Simmer, uncovered, for 10 to 15 minutes or until peaches are tender, stirring frequently. Remove from heat; let cool slightly.
2. Place half of the peach mixture in a food processor or blender. Cover and process or blend until smooth; transfer to a large bowl. Repeat with the remaining peach mixture. Cover and chill for 3 to 4 hours or until well-chilled.
3. Before serving, whisk in yogurt. Stir in blueberries and Prosecco. Serve soup in chilled bowls. If desired, garnish with peach slices and sprinkle with candied ginger.
EACH SERVING *214 cal, 1 g fat, 0 mg chol, 16 mg sodium, 47 g carb, 4 g fiber, 5 g pro.*

Going to Market

From 1994—when the USDA began publishing the *National Directory of Farmers' Markets*—to 2012, the number of farmers' markets in the United States increased from 1,755 to 7,864. That's an increase of almost 78 percent. Farmers' markets have become sources of fresh vegetables as well as for other local products such as meat, eggs, cheese, honey, and baked goods. Shoppers fill their baskets and sip cups of hot coffee as they browse and socialize. To find all of the farmers' markets in your area, visit localharvest.org.

Tips for smart shopping:

Rise and shine Farmers' markets are the least crowded right when they open—and that's early. That's when they have the best selection as well.

Plan ahead If you are familiar with what's available during any given season, you can anticipate what the market will offer and plan meals accordingly.

Be spontaneous Trying new things or being unable to resist those gorgeous strawberries is part of the fun of going to famers' markets. Remember, you sacrificed sleep for this.

Five-Berry Compote with Mint and Orange Infusion

Dessert doesn't get any lighter than this ambrosial bowl of berries and cherries in a mint-scented infusion of white wine, black tea, pomegranate juice, and sugar. It's just the thing to serve after a hearty meal, when something sweet sounds good but something rich doesn't.

PREP **25 minutes**
STAND **10 minutes**
COOL **2 hours**
CHILL **2 hours**
MAKES **8 servings**

½	cup water
3	orange pekoe tea bags
3	4-inch sprigs fresh mint
1	cup fresh strawberries, hulled and halved lengthwise
1	cup fresh golden raspberries
1	cup fresh red raspberries
1	cup fresh blackberries
1	cup fresh blueberries
1	cup pitted, halved fresh sweet cherries
1	750-milliliter bottle Sauvignon Blanc
⅔	cup sugar
½	cup pomegranate juice
1	teaspoon vanilla
	Fresh mint sprigs (optional)

1. For infusion, in a small saucepan bring the water to boiling. Add tea bags and the 3 mint sprigs; stir until mint wilts. Cover pan; remove from heat. Let stand for 10 minutes.
2. In a large bowl combine strawberries, golden raspberries, red raspberries, blackberries, blueberries, and cherries; set aside.
3. For syrup, in a medium saucepan combine wine, sugar, and pomegranate juice. Pour infusion through a fine-mesh sieve into the saucepan with the wine. Squeeze tea bags to release liquid; discard mint sprigs and tea bags. Cook and stir until sugar is dissolved. Remove from heat; stir in vanilla. Let cool to room temperature. Pour over fruit mixture. Cover and chill for 2 hours.

4. To serve, spoon mixture into shallow bowls. If desired, garnish with mint sprigs.
*Tip For a nonalcoholic version, substitute 3½ cups white grape juice for the Sauvignon Blanc wine and reduce the sugar to ⅓ cup.
EACH SERVING *203 cal, 0 g fat, 0 mg chol, 3 mg sodium, 34 g carb, 4 g fiber, 1 g pro.*

Apricot Upside-Down Cakes

A mixture of butter, brown sugar, and apricot juice bubbles away in the bottom of each muffin cup—along with the fresh apricot half—to create a delightfully sticky apricot syrup that soaks into the cardamom-scented cake. You may find yourself reaching for more than one.

PREP **20 minutes**
BAKE **20 minutes**
COOL **10 minutes**
OVEN **350°F**
MAKES **18 mini cakes**

Nonstick cooking spray
¾ cup packed brown sugar
¼ cup butter
2 tablespoons 100%-juice apricot juice
¾ teaspoon ground cinnamon
9 small apricots, halved and pitted
2 cups all-purpose flour
1 cup ground pistachio nuts
1 tablespoon baking powder
1 teaspoon ground cardamom
½ teaspoon salt
½ cup butter, softened
1 cup granulated sugar
2 eggs
1 teaspoon vanilla
1 cup 100%-juice apricot juice

1. Preheat oven to 350°F. Lightly coat eighteen 2½-inch muffin cups with cooking spray; set aside.
2. In a small saucepan combine brown sugar, the ¼ cup butter, the 2 tablespoons juice, and the cinnamon. Cook and stir over low heat until sugar is dissolved. Place about 2 teaspoons of the brown sugar mixture in each prepared muffin cup. Arrange apricots in the muffin cups, cut sides down; set aside.
3. In a medium bowl combine flour, pistachio nuts, baking powder, cardamom, and salt; set aside. In a large mixing bowl beat the ½ cup softened butter with an electric mixer on medium to high for 30 seconds. Gradually add granulated sugar, beating on medium until combined. Add eggs, one at a time, beating well after each addition. Beat in vanilla. Alternately add the flour mixture and the 1 cup apricot juice, beating on low just until combined. Spoon batter into prepared muffin cups, filling each about three-fourths full.

4. Bake for 20 to 25 minutes or until a wooden toothpick inserted in centers comes out clean. Cool for 10 minutes on a wire rack. Using a knife, loosen sides of cakes from pan. Invert cakes onto a serving platter. Cool for 10 minutes. Serve warm.
EACH MINI CAKE *261 cal, 12 g fat, 41 mg chol, 205 mg sodium, 37 g carb, 2 g fiber, 4 g pro.*

Sherried Cherry Crisp *also pictured page 282*

The season for tart red cherries is very brief, but it is worth a little time and effort spent seeking them out at farmers' markets or pick-your-own orchards. There is nothing quite like the flavor of a warm tart cherry crisp or pie with rivulets of melting vanilla ice cream. This recipe can be made with sweet cherries, but it won't be quite as lip-puckering.

PREP **25 minutes**
STAND **30 minutes**
BAKE **50 minutes**
OVEN **375°F**
MAKES **6 servings**

½ cup dried tart red cherries
⅓ cup dry sherry or port wine
4 cups fresh* or frozen unsweetened pitted tart red cherries or sweet cherries
½ cup granulated sugar
1 to 2 tablespoons all-purpose flour**
1 teaspoon finely shredded orange peel
2 to 4 tablespoons orange juice**
¾ cup all-purpose flour
½ cup regular rolled oats
½ cup packed brown sugar
½ teaspoon salt
½ teaspoon vanilla
⅓ cup cold butter, cut up

1. In a small bowl soak the dried cherries in sherry for 30 minutes. If using frozen cherries, let cherries thaw for 30 to 45 minutes or until cherries are partially thawed. Meanwhile, lightly grease a 1½-quart baking dish or deep-dish pie plate; set aside.
2. Preheat oven to 375°F. In a medium bowl combine cherries, granulated sugar, flour, orange peel, and orange juice. Stir in dried cherries with sherry. Pour mixture into prepared dish.
3. For topping, in a large bowl combine the ¾ cup flour, the oats, brown sugar, and salt. Sprinkle with vanilla. Using a pastry blender, cut in butter until mixture resembles coarse crumbs. Sprinkle topping over the cherry mixture.

4. Bake about 50 minutes or until filling is bubbly over entire surface and topping is golden brown. Serve warm.
***Tip** You will need 1¼ to 1½ pounds of fresh cherries to get 4 cups pitted cherries.
****Tip** If using fresh cherries, use 1 tablespoon all-purpose flour and ¼ cup orange juice. If using frozen cherries, use 2 tablespoons all-purpose flour and 2 tablespoons orange juice.
EACH SERVING *427 cal, 11 g fat, 27 mg chol, 295 mg sodium, 78 g carb, 4 g fiber, 4 g pro.*

Salted Caramel Flan with Blackberries

The reason this flan is so incredibly rich and silky: It's made with sweetened condensed milk and seven egg yolks. The intensely sweet caramel sauce is offset by a sprinkling of salt right before serving—and the acidity of the berries offers a welcome relief from all that fabulous richness.

PREP **30 minutes**
BAKE **65 minutes**
COOL **1 hour**
CHILL **2 hours**
OVEN **325°F**
MAKES **6 servings**

¾   cup sugar
1½   cups milk
1   14-ounce can sweetened condensed milk
3   eggs
4   egg yolks
2   teaspoons vanilla
     Gray sea salt or kosher salt
1   pint fresh blackberries

1. Preheat oven to 325°F. Place six 6-ounce custard cups at least ½ inch apart in a 3-inch deep baking pan; set aside.

2. To caramelize sugar, place ½ cup of the sugar in a large skillet. Place skillet over medium-high heat and cook until sugar starts to melt, shaking skillet occasionally. Do not stir. When sugar starts to melt, reduce heat to low and cook about 5 minutes or until all of the sugar is melted, stirring as needed with a wooden spoon. Working quickly, pour syrup into custard cups, dividing syrup evenly among cups. Tilt cups to distribute caramel evenly over the bottoms of the cups. Set aside.

3. In a medium saucepan combine the remaining ¼ cup of sugar, the milk, and the condensed milk. Cook and stir over medium heat until mixture is simmering. Remove from heat; set aside.

4. In a large bowl whisk eggs and egg yolks until combined. Gradually add milk mixture, whisking well. Stir in vanilla. Strain mixture through a fine-mesh sieve into a pitcher or large liquid measuring cup. Divide mixture among custard dishes.

5. Pull out oven rack; set pan with custard cups on rack. Using a tea kettle, slowly pour hot water into the baking pan around the cups until the water reaches about halfway up the sides of the custard cups. Slowly and carefully slide oven rack back into the oven.

6. Bake flans for 65 to 70 minutes or until barely set in the centers. Remove pan from oven; transfer to a cooling rack. Let flans cool in the hot water for about 1 hour. Remove flans from water. Cover and chill for at least 2 hours.

7. To serve, run a small knife around the edges of one flan. Quickly turn custard cup over a serving plate. Shake plate and custard cup to release the flan. Remove custard cup. Using a small rubber spatula, scrape excess caramel from the cup over the flan. Repeat with remaining flans. Sprinkle each flan with salt. Spoon blackberries over flans; serve immediately.

EACH SERVING *437 cal, 13 g fat, 243 mg chol, 447 mg sodium, 69 g carb, 3 g fiber, 13 g pro.*

Panna Cotta with Peaches in Lime Syrup

"Panna cotta" means "cooked cream" in Italian. It's similar to custard but has a much lighter texture because it is thickened with gelatin instead of eggs. It is sometimes flavored with herbs, chocolate, or espresso and served with fruit and syrup made from fruit juice or wine.

PREP **20 minutes**
STAND **5 minutes**
CHILL **4 to 24 hours**
MAKES **8 servings**

1   envelope unflavored gelatin
¼   cup water
½   cup sugar
2   cups half-and-half or light cream
2   cups whole-fat or 2% plain Greek yogurt
1   teaspoon vanilla
1   recipe Lime Syrup
3   to 4 medium peaches, cut into wedges
     Thin lime slices (optional)
     Coarsely chopped pistachio nuts (optional)

1. Place 8 small glasses in a shallow baking pan; set aside.
2. In a small bowl sprinkle gelatin over the water. Do not stir. Let stand for 5 minutes.
3. Meanwhile, in a medium saucepan stir together sugar and ½ cup of the half-and-half. Heat over medium heat until hot but not boiling. Add gelatin mixture and stir until gelatin is dissolved. Remove from heat. Whisk in yogurt until smooth. Stir in the remaining 1½ cups half-and-half and vanilla. Pour into glasses. Cover and chill for 4 to 24 hours or until set.*
4. Meanwhile, prepare Lime Syrup. In a medium bowl toss peaches with the Lime Syrup. To serve, top panna cottas with peaches and some of the syrup. If desired, top with lime slices and pistachios.

Lime Syrup In a small saucepan combine 1 cup sugar, ½ cup water, and 3 tablespoons lime juice. Bring to boiling, stirring to dissolve sugar. Reduce heat and simmer, uncovered, about 8 minutes or until slightly thickened. Syrup will continue to thicken as it cools.
*Tip Speed-Set Method: Prepare as directed, except cover and freeze for 20 minutes before transferring to the refrigerator to chill for 1½ hours or until set.

EACH SERVING *336 cal, 13 g fat, 32 mg chol, 49 mg sodium, 48 g carb, 1 g fiber, 9 g pro.*

Watermelon Granita

A granita is a Sicilian invention of fruit and juice, sugar, and ice—a tasty antidote to the hot Italian summer sun. No matter where you live, this sweet and icy treat is a thoroughly refreshing way to finish a meal.

PREP 25 minutes
FREEZE 8 hours
MAKES 8 servings

2 cups cubed, seeded watermelon
½ cup sugar
1 envelope unflavored gelatin
⅓ cup cranberry juice
Thin watermelon slices, cut into wedges (optional)

1. Place watermelon in a blender or food processor. Cover and blend or process until smooth. (You should have 3 cups pureed melon.) Stir in sugar.
2. In a small saucepan sprinkle gelatin over cranberry juice. Let stand for 5 minutes. Stir mixture over low heat until gelatin is dissolved.
3. Stir the gelatin mixture into the melon mixture. Pour into an 8×8×2-inch baking pan. Cover and freeze about 2 hours or until firm.
4. Break up frozen mixture and place in a chilled large mixing bowl. Beat with an electric mixer on medium to high until fluffy. Return to pan. Cover and freeze about 6 hours or until firm.
5. To serve, break up granita with a fork. Scoop into dessert dishes. If desired, garnish with sliced watermelon pieces.
Tip Break up granita; transfer to a freezer container. Seal, label, and freeze for up to 1 month.
EACH SERVING *83 cal, 0 g fat, 0 mg chol, 3 mg sodium, 20 g carb, 1 g fiber, 1 g pro.*

Shared Work, Shared Reward

The greenest spots in many communities are its community gardens. The American Community Gardening Association (ACGA) defines a community garden quite simply: "any piece of land gardened by a group of people." Community gardens can be urban, suburban, or rural. They grow tangibles—fruits, flowers, and vegetables—and intangibles such as a sense of accomplishment. They can provide fresh food for the gardeners who work in it, as well as for a school, hospital, neighborhood, or retirement community. To find a community garden near you, visit the ACGA website at communitygarden.org.

Here are a few great things community gardens do:

- Produce nutritious food
- Beautify neighborhoods
- Reduce family food budgets
- Encourage self-reliance
- Build community
- Establish green space
- Improve quality of life
- Conserve resources
- Create opportunities for exercise, recreation, therapy, and education

Brownies with Brandied Cherries

There is something magical about the combination of chocolate and cherries. (Think Black Forest Torte or chocolate-covered cherries.) This recipe combines sweet cherries that are briefly cooked and soaked in sugar and brandy with a dense, super-chocolaty rich brownie.

PREP 25 minutes
BAKE 25 minutes
COOL 45 minutes
OVEN 325°F
MAKES 4 servings

⅔ cup sugar
½ cup brandy
1 cup fresh sweet cherries, stemmed, pitted, and halved
   Unsweetened cocoa powder
½ cup butter
1 cup sugar
¾ cup unsweetened cocoa powder
1 teaspoon vanilla
½ teaspoon salt
2 eggs
⅓ cup all-purpose flour
   Vanilla gelato or vanilla ice cream (optional)

1. For brandied cherries, in a small saucepan combine the ⅔ cup sugar and the brandy. Bring to boiling; add cherries. Reduce heat; simmer, uncovered for 3 minutes. Remove from heat; let cool.

2. Preheat oven to 325°F. Grease an 8×8×2-inch baking pan. Line pan with foil, leaving about 1 inch of the foil extending over the edges of the pan. Grease the foil; sprinkle with cocoa powder.

3. In a small saucepan melt butter over low heat. Transfer melted butter to a medium bowl. Add the 1 cup sugar, the ¾ cup cocoa powder, the vanilla, and salt. Using a wooden spoon, stir until cocoa powder is completely incorporated. Add eggs, one at a time, beating with a wooden spoon just until combined. Add flour; stir just until combined. Spread batter in the prepared pan.

4. Bake about 25 minutes or until edges start to pull away from sides of pan. Cool brownies for 45 minutes (they will still be slightly warm). Use foil to lift uncut brownies from pan. Cut warm brownies into 16 squares. Place 1 brownie square in each of 4 shallow dessert dishes. Top with brandied cherries. If desired, serve with gelato. Let remaining brownies cool completely. Store cooled brownies in an airtight container at room temperature for up to 3 days or freeze for up to 1 month.

EACH SERVING *379 cal, 7 g fat, 39 mg chol, 134 mg sodium, 66 g carb, 2 g fiber, 2 g pro.*

Meringue with Seared Pineapple

This dessert is very much like a pavlova (see recipe, page 287), except instead of a whipping cream filling, it has a Pineapple-Lime Curd filling crowned with caramelized pineapple. The curd filling will cause the meringue to soften a little, so assemble just before serving.

PREP **30 minutes**
STAND **30 minutes**
BAKE **35 minutes**
COOL **1 hour**
OVEN **300°F**
MAKES **10 servings**

5   eggs
2   teaspoons vanilla
¼   teaspoon cream of tartar
¾   cup granulated sugar
1   recipe Pineapple-Lime Curd
2   tablespoons butter
½   fresh pineapple, peeled, cored, and sliced
2   tablespoons packed brown sugar
     Sliced key limes (optional)
     Fresh mint (optional)

1. Separate egg yolks and whites. Set yolks aside for Pineapple-Lime Curd. For meringue, let whites stand at room temperature 30 minutes. Preheat oven to 300°F. Line a baking sheet with parchment paper. In large mixing bowl beat egg whites, vanilla, and cream of tartar with an electric mixer on medium until soft peaks form. Beating on high, add granulated sugar, 1 tablespoon at a time, until stiff peaks form (about 8 minutes total).
2. Spread meringue on prepared baking sheet to make a large oval (about 13×9 inches), building up edges slightly. Bake for 35 minutes. Turn oven off; let stand for 1 hour. Carefully lift meringue off paper and transfer to serving platter.
3. Meanwhile, prepare Pineapple-Lime Curd.
4. In a very large skillet melt butter over medium heat. Add pineapple slices; cook in hot butter about 8 minutes or until browned, turning once. Sprinkle with brown sugar. Cook, uncovered, for 1 to 2 minutes more or until sugar is dissolved.

5. To assemble, fill meringue with Pineapple-Lime Curd; top with seared pineapple slices. Drizzle with juice from seared pineapple. If desired, garnish with lime slices and mint.

Pineapple-Lime Curd In a medium saucepan combine ¾ cup granulated sugar and 1 tablespoon cornstarch. Stir in ⅓ cup water, ¼ cup lime juice, and ¼ cup frozen pineapple juice concentrate, thawed. Cook and stir over medium heat until thickened and bubbly. In a medium bowl whisk together the 5 reserved egg yolks from the meringue until smooth. Gradually whisk half of the hot mixture into the yolks. Return yolk-juice mixture to saucepan. Cook and stir until mixture thickens and comes to a gentle boil. Cook and stir for 2 minutes more. Remove from heat; stir in ½ cup butter, cut up, until melted. Transfer to a bowl. Cover and chill for at least 30 minutes.

EACH SERVING *297 cal, 14 g fat, 136 mg chol, 118 mg sodium, 41 g carb, 0 g fiber, 4 g pro.*

Wine-Country Cake with Roasted Grapes

A generous glug of fruity white wine infuses this moist pecan-and-spice cake with flavor. The grapes "roast" in the oven as the cake bakes. Serve it with a full-body, full-flavor coffee.

PREP 25 minutes
BAKE 80 minutes
COOL 2 hours
OVEN 325°F
MAKES 20 servings

3⅔ cups all-purpose flour
¼   teaspoon ground mace
⅛   teaspoon salt
1   cup butter, softened
1⅔ cups packed brown sugar
1⅓ cups granulated sugar
4   eggs
1⅓ cups fruity white wine, such as Viansa Frescolina Tocai, Imbianco Barbera Blanc, or Moscato D'Asti
1   cup coarsely chopped pecans, toasted
3   cups small red seedless grapes, stemmed, rinsed, and patted dry
2   tablespoons butter, melted
1   tablespoon granulated sugar

1. Preheat oven to 325°F. Grease a 13×9×2-inch baking pan; set aside. In a medium bowl stir together flour, mace, and salt; set aside.

2. In a large mixing bowl beat the 1 cup butter with an electric mixer on medium to high for 30 seconds. Add brown sugar and the 1⅓ cups granulated sugar. Beat until combined, scraping sides of bowl occasionally. Beat in eggs until combined. Alternately add flour mixture and wine to butter mixture, beating on low after each addition just until combined. Stir in pecans. Pour batter into the prepared baking pan, spreading evenly. Sprinkle with 2 cups of the grapes.

3. Bake for 40 minutes. Sprinkle with the remaining 1 cup grapes. Bake about 40 minutes more or until a toothpick inserted in the center comes out clean.

4. Immediately brush hot cake with the 2 tablespoons melted butter and sprinkle with the 1 tablespoon granulated sugar. Cool in pan on a wire rack.

EACH SERVING *380 cal, 16 g fat, 65 mg chol, 127 mg sodium, 55 g carb, 1 g fiber, 4 g pro.*

Blackberry-Lemon Ice Cream Sandwiches with Pistachio Shortbread

Vanilla ice cream and lemon sorbet are swirled together with fresh blackberries and lemon peel for the filling in these itty-bitty ice cream sandwiches. They are so much fun—and can be made up to a month ahead of serving and stored in the freezer.

PREP **30 minutes**
FREEZE **6 to 8 hours**
BAKE **20 minutes**
STAND **5 minutes**
OVEN **325°F**
MAKES **18 mini ice cream sandwiches**

1   cup vanilla ice cream, softened
½   cup lemon sorbet, softened
¾   cup fresh blackberries
½   teaspoon finely shredded lemon peel
2   cups all-purpose flour
½   cup packed brown sugar
½   cup ground pistachio nuts
1   cup butter
     Coarsely chopped pistachio nuts (optional)

1. Line a 9×5×3-inch loaf pan with foil, leaving about 1 inch foil extending over edges of pan. In a chilled medium bowl combine softened ice cream, softened sorbet, blackberries, and lemon peel. Quickly swirl ingredients together, breaking up berries slightly. Spread in the prepared loaf pan; smooth top to make an even layer. Cover and freeze for 4 to 6 hours or until firm.

2. For shortbread, preheat oven to 325°F. In a large bowl combine flour, brown sugar, and the ½ cup ground pistachio nuts. Using a pastry blender, cut in butter until mixture resembles fine crumbs and starts to cling together. Shape into a ball and knead until smooth. On an ungreased cookie sheet pat or roll dough into a 9-inch square. Using a fluted pastry wheel or knife, cut dough into 36 squares (1½ inches each), but do not separate. Bake for 20 to 25 minutes or just until bottom starts to turn brown. Cool for 5 minutes. While shortbread is still warm, use the pastry wheel or knife to recut each square and trim edges. Transfer squares to a wire rack; let cool.

3. To assemble ice cream sandwiches, remove ice cream mixture from the freezer. Let stand at room temperature for 5 minutes. Using the foil, lift ice cream mixture from pan. Using a long knife and working quickly, cut into eighteen 1½-inch squares. Using a small metal spatula, place an ice cream square on the bottom sides of half the cookies. Top each with another cookie, top sides up. If desired, roll ice cream sides in chopped pistachio nuts, pressing lightly so nuts adhere. Wrap each ice cream sandwich in plastic wrap and return to freezer. Freeze at least 2 hours or until firm.

Make-Ahead Tip Ice cream sandwiches can be made ahead and stored in a covered container in the freezer for up to 1 month.

EACH MINI ICE CREAM SANDWICH *209 cal, 13 g fat, 31 mg chol, 99 mg sodium, 22 g carb, 1 g fiber, 3 g pro.*

Lemon Shortcake
with Plums

Instead of individual shortcakes, this recipe is made into one large lemony shortcake filled and topped with glazed plums and whipped cream with mascarpone. It's luscious and a little messy to cut, but a thing of beauty to bring out at the end of a meal.

PREP **25 minutes**
BAKE **23 minutes**
OVEN **400°F**
MAKES **8 servings**

2	cups all-purpose flour
¼	cup sugar
1	tablespoon baking powder
1	tablespoon finely shredded lemon peel
½	teaspoon salt
½	cup butter, cut up
½	cup milk
1	egg, lightly beaten
2	teaspoons whipping cream
2	teaspoons sugar
7	plums, thinly sliced
6	tablespoons sugar
1	tablespoon lemon juice
1	cup recipe Mascarpone Whipped Cream

1. Preheat oven to 400°F. Grease a 9×1½-inch round cake pan; set aside. In a medium bowl combine flour, the ¼ cup sugar, the baking powder, lemon peel, and salt. Using a pastry blender, cut in butter until mixture resembles coarse crumbs. Add milk and egg, tossing with a fork just until flour mixture is moistened. On a floured surface knead dough by folding and gently pressing it just until dough holds together. Pat into pan. Brush top with the 2 teaspoons whipping cream; sprinkle with the 2 teaspoons sugar. Bake for 23 to 25 minutes or until golden. Let cool on a wire rack.

2. In a medium saucepan combine 1 of the sliced plums, the 6 tablespoons sugar, and the lemon juice. Cook over medium heat about 8 minutes or until tender. Stir in the remaining plums; let cool.

3. To serve, remove shortcake from baking pan; split horizontally in half. Place bottom half of shortcake on a platter. Top with half of the Mascarpone Whipped Cream and half of the plum mixture. Add the top half of the shortcake, the remaining Mascarpone Whipped Cream, and the remaining plum mixture.

Mascarpone Whipped Cream
In a small mixing bowl combine ½ cup mascarpone cheese, ¼ cup whipping cream, 2 tablespoons sugar, and 1 teaspoon vanilla. Beat with an electric mixer on medium until combined. In a large mixing bowl beat 1¼ cups whipping cream with an electric mixer on medium until soft peaks form (tips curl). Fold mascarpone mixture into the whipped cream.

EACH SERVING *430 cal, 22 g fat, 79 mg chol, 347 mg sodium, 53 g carb, 1 g fiber, 6 g pro.*

Quince Skillet Tart with Savory Prosciutto Pastry

Quince, which tastes like a cross between an apple and a pear, must be peeled and cooked to bring out its best flavor. Apples make a wonderful substitute in this tart, but it won't have the same golden caramel color you'll get if you use quince. This unusual tart is not overly sweet—you could actually serve it as an appetizer or first course as well as dessert.

PREP **30 minutes**
COOK **20 minutes**
BAKE **30 minutes**
COOL **25 minutes**
OVEN **375°F**
MAKES **12 servings**

½   cup butter
6   cups thickly sliced, peeled quince or cooking apples (5 to 6 quince or apples)
⅔   cup sugar
2   teaspoons finely snipped fresh sage or 1 teaspoon dried sage leaves, crushed
1   recipe Savory Prosciutto Pastry
¼   cup shredded Manchego or sharp cheddar cheese (1 ounce) (optional)
    Snipped fresh sage (optional)

1. Preheat oven to 375°F. For filling, in a large oven-going skillet with flared sides melt butter over medium heat. Stir in quince slices, sugar, and sage. Cook over medium heat until bubbly, stirring occasionally. Reduce heat to medium-low. Cook, uncovered, about 20 minutes more or until fruit is very tender (if using quince, mixture will thicken and turn a deep golden brown), stirring occasionally. Remove from heat.
2. On a lightly floured surface use your hands to slightly flatten Savory Prosciutto Pastry dough. Roll dough from center to edge into a 10-inch circle. Cut slits in the center of the pastry. Carefully wrap pastry circle around rolling pin. Unroll pastry over the filling in the skillet, being careful not to stretch the pastry.
3. Bake about 30 minutes or until pastry is golden and filling is bubbly. Cool in skillet on a wire rack for 5 minutes. Invert onto a large serving plate. Lift off skillet. Replace any fruit slices left in skillet. If desired, sprinkle with cheese and sage. Cool for 20 minutes more. Serve warm.

Savory Prosciutto Pastry In a medium bowl stir together 1½ cups all-purpose flour, 2 tablespoons sugar, and a pinch ground black pepper. Using a pastry blender, cut in ½ cup cold butter until pieces are pea size. Stir in ⅓ cup finely chopped prosciutto. In a small bowl use a fork to lightly beat 1 egg; stir the egg and the 1 tablespoon cold water into flour mixture. Stir until all the flour mixture is moistened, adding another 1 tablespoon water if necessary. Gather mixture into a ball, kneading gently until it holds together.

EACH SERVING *275 cal, 16 g fat, 59 mg chol, 159 mg sodium, 31 g carb, 1 g fiber, 3 g pro.*

White Wine-Poached Pears with Vanilla Crème Fraîche, *recipe page 318*

White Wine-Poached Pears with Vanilla Crème Fraîche *pictured page 317*

Vanilla bean paste is made by infusing vanilla beans in a thick sugar syrup into which the vanilla beans are then scraped. It has a more intense vanilla flavor and aroma than extract because it is not diluted by alcohol—and you get the beautiful flecks of the vanilla beans in your baked goods or desserts. Look for it at specialty food stores or online.

PREP **10 minutes**
COOK **15 minutes**
MAKES **4 servings**

3   cups dry white wine
1   cup sugar
1   cup water
4   strips orange peel
3   inches stick cinnamon
2   whole star anise
4   firm ripe pears, peeled and
       cored
¼   cup crème fraîche
¼   cup whipping cream
1   teaspoon vanilla bean paste or
       vanilla extract

1. In a large heavy saucepan combine wine, sugar, the water, orange peel, cinnamon, and star anise. Bring to boiling. Add pears to saucepan. Return to boiling; reduce heat. Simmer, covered, for 15 to 20 minutes or until pears are tender.
2. For vanilla crème fraîche, in a small bowl whisk together crème fraîche, whipping cream, and vanilla bean paste until light.
3. To serve, remove pears from syrup; reserve syrup. Cut pears lengthwise in half. Divide pear halves among 4 shallow dessert dishes. Spoon about ¼ cup syrup over each. Top with vanilla crème fraîche. Serve immediately.

EACH SERVING *373 cal, 11 g fat, 41 mg chol, 18 mg sodium, 53 g carb, 5 g fiber, 1 g pro.*

Buttered Apples in Maple Syrup Custard

A wedge of apple pie served with a slice of cheddar cheese is a favorite combination of some pie eaters, particularly in the Northeast. This dessert extrapolates on that idea with layers of sautéed apples and sharp white cheddar topped with an airy custard.

PREP **30 minutes**
BAKE **25 minutes**
STAND **30 minutes**
OVEN **350°F**
MAKES **8 servings**

¾   cup milk
3   tablespoons sugar
2   teaspoons all-purpose flour
¼   teaspoon freshly grated
      nutmeg
      Large pinch kosher salt
2   tablespoons unsalted butter
5   to 7 Granny Smith apples,
      peeled, cored, and sliced
      ½ inch thick (about 8 cups)
1   small lemon
4   ounces extra-sharp white
      cheddar cheese, cut into
      ½-inch cubes
4   eggs, separated
2   tablespoons sugar
2   tablespoons all-purpose flour
½   teaspoon kosher salt
¾   cup pure maple syrup
3   tablespoons unsalted butter,
      melted
¼   cup whipping cream
½   teaspoon vanilla
      Pure maple syrup (optional)
      Whipped cream (optional)

1. Let milk stand at room temperature for 30 minutes. Preheat oven to 350°F. In a small bowl combine 3 tablespoons sugar, 2 teaspoons flour, nutmeg, and a large pinch of salt.

2. In large skillet melt 1 tablespoon of the butter; add half of the apples (do not overcrowd pan) and sprinkle with half of the sugar mixture. Cook over high heat; shaking and turning occasionally until apples are well browned. Squeeze half of the lemon over the apples, using your fingers to catch any seeds. Transfer to a buttered 9×2-inch quiche dish or deep-dish pie plate. Sprinkle with half of the cheese. Repeat with the remaining 1 tablespoon butter, apples, sugar mixture, and lemon; place on top of the first apple-cheese layer. Sprinkle with remaining cheese.

3. For custard, in a large bowl whisk together the egg yolks, 2 tablespoons sugar, 2 tablespoons flour, and ½ teaspoon salt. Whisk in ¾ cup maple syrup, the melted butter, the ¾ cup room-temperature milk, ¼ cup whipping cream, and vanilla.

4. In a separate clean large bowl whisk the egg whites with a clean whisk until soft mounds form. Whisk in the egg yolk mixture just until blended. Pour over the apples, stirring gently to distribute custard throughout.

5. Bake for 25 to 30 minutes or until custard is browned, set on top, and jiggles just in the center when gently shaken. (Interior temperature when tested with an instant-read thermometer should read 160°F.) Set on a wire rack to cool. Serve warm or at room temperature. If desired, stir a little maple syrup into whipped cream; serve with apples and custard.

EACH SERVING *374 cal, 18 g fat, 152 mg chol, 276 mg sodium, 48 g carb, 3 g fiber, 8 g pro.*

Stirred Custard with Fresh Figs and Sherry-Caramel Sauce

Perfectly ripe, succulent figs float in a delicate custard swirled with a sherried caramel sauce. Figs don't ripen well after being picked, so be sure the figs you choose are ripe. They should be plump and feel heavy in your hand and should be tender but not mushy.

PREP 25 minutes
COOL 15 minutes
CHILL 2 hours
MAKES 8 servings

5   egg yolks, lightly beaten
1½   cups whole milk
¼   cup granulated sugar
1½   teaspoons vanilla
¾   cup packed brown sugar
½   cup butter, cut up
½   cup whipping cream
2   tablespoons light-color corn
     syrup
2   tablespoons dry sherry
8   fresh figs or 4 peaches, halved,
     pitted, and sliced

1. In a medium heavy saucepan combine egg yolks, milk, and granulated sugar. Cook and stir continuously with a heatproof rubber scraper over medium heat just until sauce thickens and coats the back of the scraper. Remove from heat. Stir in vanilla.

2. Quickly cool custard by placing saucepan in a large bowl of ice water for 1 to 2 minutes, stirring constantly. Pour custard mixture into a medium bowl. Cover the surface with plastic wrap to prevent a skin from forming. Chill for at least 2 hours before serving. Do not stir.

3. Meanwhile, for sherry-caramel sauce, in a medium heavy saucepan combine brown sugar, butter, whipping cream, and corn syrup. Bring to boiling over medium-high heat, whisking occasionally. Reduce heat to medium. Boil gently, uncovered, for 3 minutes more. Remove from heat. Stir in sherry. Cool for 15 minutes.

4. To serve, halve figs. Spoon custard into 8 dessert dishes. Top each with 2 fig halves, cut sides up. Drizzle with some of the sherry-caramel sauce. (Remaining sauce can be refrigerated in a covered container for up to 2 weeks. Serve over ice cream, cake, or fruit.)

Tip Another time serve the stirred custard with raspberries, blackberries, blueberries, and/or halved or quartered strawberries.

EACH SERVING *379 cal, 22 g fat, 171 mg chol, 142 mg sodium, 44 g carb, 1 g fiber, 4 g pro.*

Pumpkin and Sweet Potato Pie with Toasted Marshmallows

Looking for something different for Thanksgiving? This creamy pie, served warm with melty, toasted marshmallows on top, is absolutely irresistible. The fabulous crust is made from crumbled fig bar cookies, butter, and flour. One forkful and you are in for a whole piece.

PREP **30 minutes**
BAKE **50 minutes**
COOL **1 hour**
OVEN **350°F**
MAKES **8 servings**

8   fig bar cookies (6 ounces)
½   cup all-purpose flour
¼   cup butter, melted
1   3-ounce package cream
    cheese, softened
3   eggs
¾   cup mashed cooked sweet
    potatoes
¾   cup fresh or canned pureed
    pumpkin (see recipe for
    Pumpkin Puree, page 154)
⅓   cup packed brown sugar
⅓   cup whipping cream
¼   cup granulated sugar
1   tablespoon molasses
2   teaspoons grated fresh ginger
1   teaspoon vanilla
1   teaspoon ground cinnamon
½   teaspoon salt
½   teaspoon grated whole nutmeg
    or ¼ teaspoon ground nutmeg
⅛   teaspoon ground ancho or
    chipotle chile powder
1½ cups tiny marshmallows

1. Preheat oven to 350°F. For crust, in a medium bowl combine cookies and flour. Using your fingers, crumble the cookies with the flour. Pour melted butter over the crumb mixture. Stir to combine. Press into the bottom and up the sides of a 9-inch pie plate. Bake about 10 minutes or until set. Let cool on a wire rack.

2. For filling, in a large mixing bowl beat cream cheese with an electric mixer on medium for 30 seconds. Add eggs, sweet potatoes, pumpkin, brown sugar, whipping cream, granulated sugar, molasses, ginger, vanilla, cinnamon, salt, nutmeg, and chile powder. Beat until well combined. Pour filling into crust.

3. Bake for 40 to 45 minutes or until a knife inserted near the center comes out clean.

4. Remove pie from oven. Spread marshmallows evenly over top of pie. Turn oven to broil. Broil pie 4 to 5 inches from the heat for 1 minute or just until marshmallows are puffed and beginning to brown.

5. Cool on a wire rack about 1 hour before serving warm.

Make-Ahead Tip Prepare pie as directed, except do not top with the marshmallows. Cool at room temperature for up to 2 hours. Chill for longer storage. Serve with whipped cream.

EACH SERVING *357 cal, 16 g fat, 110 mg chol, 348 mg sodium, 49 g carb, 2 g fiber, 5 g pro.*

Spiced Butternut Squash Loaf with Mascarpone Icing

Here's a twist on pumpkin bread—it just calls for a different kind of squash. Butternut squash is naturally sweet in the same way that pumpkin is—and both provide flavor and moistness to quick breads. The rich mascarpone icing dresses up the loaf for tea.

PREP **25 minutes**
BAKE **50 minutes**
COOL **2 hours**
OVEN **350°F**
MAKES **12 servings**

1¾ cups all-purpose flour
1   teaspoon baking soda
1   teaspoon baking powder
1   teaspoon ground ginger
½   teaspoon salt
½   teaspoon ground cinnamon
½   cup butter, softened
1   cup packed brown sugar
¼   cup granulated sugar
3   eggs
¼   cup milk
1   cup butternut squash puree*
1   cup powdered sugar
⅓   cup mascarpone cheese
2   tablespoons milk

1. Preheat oven to 350°F. Grease the bottom and ½ inch up the sides of a 9×5×3-inch loaf pan; set aside. In a medium bowl whisk together flour, baking soda, baking powder, ginger, salt, and cinnamon. Set flour mixture aside.

2. In a large mixing bowl beat butter with an electric mixer on medium to high for 30 seconds. Gradually add brown sugar and granulated sugar, beating on medium until combined. Add eggs, one at a time, beating well after each addition. Alternately add ¼ cup milk and squash puree, beating on low until combined. Gradually add flour mixture, beating on low just until combined. Spoon batter into prepared pan.

3. Bake for 50 to 60 minutes or until a wooden toothpick inserted in center comes out clean. Cool in pan on a wire rack for 10 minutes. Remove from pan. Cool completely on wire rack.

4. For icing, in a medium bowl combine powdered sugar, mascarpone cheese, and 2 tablespoons milk. Beat with an electric mixer on medium until smooth. Spread over top of cake.

*Tip For butternut squash puree, place a 1½-pound piece butternut squash, cut side down, in a baking dish. Bake in a 350°F oven for 45 to 50 minutes or until very tender. Cool. Using a metal spoon, scrape squash from peel. Use a potato masher or fork to mash squash until nearly smooth.

EACH SERVING *317 cal, 12 g fat, 75 mg chol, 341 mg sodium, 49 g carb, 1 g fiber, 5 g pro.*

Lemon-Vanilla Tart

A sizeable shot of vanilla brings out the sweet, flowery side of lemons in this custard tart topped with oven-candied lemon slices. They are so simple to make—and so delicious—you might make a batch just for you.

PREP **40 minutes**
BAKE **33 minutes**
OVEN **450°F/350°F**
MAKES **8 servings**

1   recipe Tart Pastry
½   cup sugar
1   tablespoon all-purpose flour
2   eggs
4   teaspoons finely shredded lemon peel
6   tablespoons lemon juice
¼   cup butter, melted
1   tablespoon vanilla
1   recipe Oven-Candied Lemon Slices

1. Prepare Tart Pastry. Preheat oven to 450°F. Wrap the pastry circle around a rolling pin. Ease pastry into a 9-inch tart pan with removable bottom without stretching the pastry. Press pastry into fluted sides of tart pan. Trim edges even with the pan. Line pastry with a double thickness of foil. Bake for 8 minutes. Remove foil. Bake for 5 to 6 minutes more or until crust is golden. Cool on wire rack. Reduce oven temperature to 350°F.

2. In a medium bowl combine sugar and flour. Add eggs. Beat with an electric mixer on medium to high about 3 minutes or until mixture is light in color and slightly thickened. Stir in lemon peel, lemon juice, butter, and vanilla. Pour into baked pastry shell. Place tart pan on a baking sheet.

3. Bake tart on baking sheet for 20 to 25 minutes or until filling is set and lightly browned. Cool on a wire rack. To serve, remove sides of pan and top tart with Oven-Candied Lemon Slices.

Tart Pastry In a medium bowl cut ½ cup cold butter into 1¼ cups all-purpose flour until pieces are the size of small peas. In a small bowl combine 1 lightly beaten egg yolk and 1 tablespoon ice water.

Gradually stir the yolk mixture into the flour mixture. Add 2 to 4 tablespoons additional water, 1 tablespoon at a time, until all the dough is moistened. Shape into a ball. If necessary, cover dough with plastic wrap and chill for 30 to 40 minutes or until dough is easy to handle. On a lightly floured surface roll out dough to an 11-inch circle.

Oven-Candied Lemon Slices
Preheat oven to 275°F. Line a 15×10×1-inch baking pan with parchment paper. Cut 2 small lemons crosswise into ⅛- to ¼-inch slices. Arrange lemon slices in a single layer in pan. Sprinkle with ¼ cup sugar. Bake for 45 to 50 minutes or until lemons are almost dry and covered with a sugary glaze. While still warm, loosen slices from paper to prevent sticking.

EACH SERVING *338 cal, 19 g fat, 125 mg chol, 143 mg sodium, 40 g carb, 3 g fiber, 5 g pro.*

Broiled Grapefruit Tart

There are many more interesting ways to enjoy grapefruit than the standard half with breakfast. Baking releases its natural juices, which form a flavorful glaze for the fruit. The tart is sprinkled with sugar and broiled briefly right before serving.

PREP 15 minutes
CHILL 2 hours
BAKE 28 minutes
BROIL 2 minutes
OVEN 425°F
MAKES 8 servings

1¾ cups all-purpose flour
½   teaspoon salt
⅓   cup shortening
¼   cup unsalted butter, cut into pieces
3   to 4 tablespoons ice water
3   ruby red grapefruit
¼   cup orange or citrus marmalade
⅓   cup finely crushed tea biscuit or butter cookies
6   tablespoons sugar

1. In a medium bowl stir together flour and salt. Using a pastry blender, cut in shortening and butter until pieces are pea size. Sprinkle 1 tablespoon of the water over part of the flour mixture; toss with a fork. Push moistened pastry to side of the bowl. Repeat moistening flour mixture, using 1 tablespoon of the water at a time, until flour mixture is moistened. Gather flour mixture into a ball, kneading gently until it holds together. Gently flatten dough into a disk. Wrap in plastic wrap and chill for at least 2 hours.
2. Preheat oven to 425°F. On a lightly floured surface roll pastry from center to edges into a circle about 12 inches in diameter. Wrap pastry circle around rolling pin. Ease pastry into a 12-inch pizza pan. Flute edge. Bake for 8 minutes.
3. Meanwhile, cut a thin slice from both ends of 1 grapefruit. Place a cut end on a cutting board and cut away the peel and the white part of the rind. Cut sections from membranes. Place sections on paper towels; pat dry. Repeat with the remaining 2 grapefruits.
4. Spread marmalade over partially baked crust. Sprinkle with crushed cookies. Arrange grapefruit on crust; sprinkle with 3 tablespoons of the sugar.
5. Bake for 20 to 22 minutes or until crust is browned. Remove tart from oven; turn on broiler. Sprinkle tart with the remaining 3 tablespoons sugar. Broil for 2 to 3 minutes or until top is browned. Let cool on a wire rack.

EACH SERVING *225 cal, 10 g fat, 10 mg chol, 114 mg sodium, 32 g carb, 1 g fiber, 3 g pro.*

produce guide

GET THE PICK OF THE BUSHEL Whether you grow your own or pick up produce at the farmer's market or grocery store, just-harvested, in-season fruits and vegetables are delicious and nutritionally superior. Here's how to choose top-quality produce—and how to bring out its best qualities with proper preparation and storage once you get it home.

spring

THE GARDEN'S OPENING SEASON The cool temperatures of spring yield special seasonal flavors: the pungency of greens, the sweetness of peas, and the mild meatiness of mushrooms.

Artichokes

About: The spiky, grenadelike appearance of an artichoke may make it look inedible and foreboding, but this vegetable is easy to prepare and a treat to eat. Two parts of the artichoke are edible. Enjoy the soft fleshy parts at the base of each leaf as well as the dense mild heart, which is the very inside base of the artichoke. The edible flower of the artichoke plant can't be eaten raw—it must be cooked. It is most commonly boiled or steamed, but you can also braise, bake, or grill it. Enjoy cooked artichoke hot or cold, au naturel or with dipping sauces. Hollandaise and artichoke is a classic pairing. The heart can also be pickled or preserved in oil and is a delicious component for dips or added to pizza. Almost exclusively grown in California, artichokes provide calcium, iron, and potassium.

Varieties: There are several varieties of artichokes, but the Green Globe, with a deep green color and a round but slightly elongated shape, is most common. Green globes are available in baby to large sizes.

Selecting: Look for firm, heavy artichokes with tightly closed heads. The size of the artichoke doesn't matter as it does with some veggies; there is no flavor difference between large and small artichokes. To test for freshness, press the leaves together to produce a squeaking sound. Their peak season is March through May.

Storing: Place unwashed artichokes in a plastic bag in your refrigerator. They can be stored for up to 4 days but are best if used immediately after purchase.

Preparing Artichokes

1. Cut off the bottom stem using a sharp chef's knife.

2. Cut off about 1 inch from the top.

3. Remove the fuzzy "choke" with a spoon.

Asparagus

About: Slender and juicy, the spears of asparagus are one of the culinary joys of springtime. This fast-growing vegetable (it can grow up to 10 inches in a 24-hour period) grows straight up out of the ground, rising from the soil like a small green missile. It is delicious raw or cooked. You can steam, roast, sauté, or grill it. Asparagus is a favorite of gardeners, food lovers, and nutritionists. It is a perennial—it comes back year after year. Its unique fresh flavor and succulent texture complement so many recipes, and it has the highest folic acid content of any vegetable. Asparagus is such a revered vegetable that cities across Europe and in the United States have festivals to honor the harvest of this spring vegetable.

Varieties: Asparagus comes in green and purple varieties. Purple asparagus may be a bit less tender than its green cousin. You may also find white asparagus in stores in spring. This isn't a different variety but is created by growing the spears without light. White asparagus is considered a delicacy, especially in Europe. It has a milder flavor and is more tender than green asparagus.

Selecting: Look for firm, straight, bright green spears that are not limp. Diameter has no impact on tenderness but color does. The greener it is, the more tender it is. Asparagus is grown in four sizes—jumbo, extra-large, large, and standard. Stir-fry thin spears and grill the thick ones. Regardless of size, the tips of any asparagus should be closed tightly.

Storing: Asparagus is best used immediately after purchase. It is, in fact, more perishable than other vegetables. You can store asparagus in your refrigerator for several days by trimming the bases of the spears, loosely covering them with a plastic bag, and then standing them up in some water. Place in the refrigerator. Wash spears right before use.

Preparing Asparagus

1. Snap off the woody base of the asparagus where it bends.

2. Or simply cut off the woody end with a paring knife.

3. If desired, remove the tough outer skin from the lower part of the spear using a vegetable peeler.

Broccoli

About: Broccoli is a member of the Brassica family, whose crunchy cousins include cauliflower, Brussels sprouts, cabbage, collard greens, kale, and kohlrabi. Broccoli is as versatile as it is delicious. Eat it raw or cooked. Bake it, steam it, or sauté it. It plays a starring role as a side dish or partners well with beef or chicken in stir-fry or with cheese in soup. Or go simple: drizzle spears with balsamic vinegar, minced garlic, and broil it.

Varieties: There are two kinds of broccoli. Sprouting broccoli is available in the early spring. Also known as Italian broccoli, it has loose leafy stems with no central head. The other type produces a big head. This is what you usually buy at the grocery store. Each section of the head is called a floret.

Selecting: Look for firm, heavy broccoli heads that have a rich green color. Avoid any that are pale green or yellow. Check the cut end of the stalk; if it's fresh and moist, the broccoli head will be at its peak.

Storing: Broccoli is best used immediately after purchase, but you can store it in an open plastic bag in your refrigerator crisper for up to 10 days.

Broccoli Raab

About: This green, leafy vegetable has small broccolilike buds that look like loose broccoli florets. But broccoli raab is more closely related to the turnip than to broccoli. The leaves and buds are edible. In Italy, it is called rapini. The flavor of broccoli raab is nutty with a tinge of bitterness. It gets more bitter-tasting the older it is and the longer it sits after picking, so buy it young and cook it immediately. Sauté with olive oil and garlic, then add a sprinkle of crushed red pepper and a splash of lemon juice for a fast and flavorful side dish. Broccoli raab is vitamin-packed with A, C, and K, potassium, and iron.

Selecting: Choose firm, rich green small stems with tightly packed flower heads. Do not buy if the flower heads have any yellow on them or if the leaves are wilting.

Storing: Store broccoli raab in a plastic bag or wrapped in a moist paper towel in the refrigerator for up to 5 days.

Carrots

About: Carrots, the sweetest of all the root vegetables, are one of the few true vegetables that can be found in every course, from appetizers to dessert. In its purest form, this robust root can simply be scrubbed, peeled, and crunched on raw. Slice, dice, or shred carrots into salads. Eat them steamed, stewed, sautéed, and roasted. Or shred them, stir into batter, and bake into moist, orange-flecked cakes and muffins. Although carrots won't help you see in the dark like your mom may have told you, they are chock-full of vitamin A, beta-carotene, and calcium.

Cooking carrots actually makes the calcium more available for digestion by your body.

Varieties: Garden-variety orange carrots range from petite to large. But this versatile veggie also comes in yellow, purple, and red varieties. Cook them together to make a colorful side dish or stew. Carrots generally produce long, tapered roots, but there are varieties that buck that trend and come in round-as-radish shapes.

Selecting: Look for firm, smooth carrots with a bright color. If the greens are still attached, they should be fresh, not dry or wilted. Carrots that do still have the greens attached generally taste better. Avoid carrots with cracks or that feel soft or wilted, or those with greenish skin at the top. Smaller carrots have better flavor than large ones. Choose carrots that are less than 1 inch in diameter if possible. Don't be fooled by "baby" carrots, sold peeled and prewashed in plastic bags. They aren't baby carrots at all but rather pieces of larger carrots that have simply been cut down and shaped.

Storing: Remove any greens that may still be attached to the carrots. The carrots can then be stored in a perforated plastic bag in the refrigerator for several weeks.

ROBUST ROOTS Carrots are a cool-weather crop that peaks twice a year—in both spring and fall. Spring carrots are sweeter and have a more delicate flavor than fall carrots. Both types have a lot of sugar, which helps protect them from freezing.

Cauliflower

About: Cauliflower was once so rare, it was considered a delicacy in France. Now it's available everywhere. Its distinctive large white head is actually a tight group of flower buds, which is called the curd because of its lumpy appearance. A cousin to broccoli (both are members of the Brassica family), cauliflower can be eaten raw. Or like broccoli, it can be prepared many delicious ways: roasted, boiled, fried, or steamed. For a quick and easy side dish, try pan-frying small florets with oil and garlic, then top with chives, lemon, and Parmesan. Cauliflower is a good source of vitamin C.

Varieties: When growing cauliflower, the large leaves that surround the head are wrapped and tied over the top of the curd to keep it white. There are nonwhite varieties of cauliflower that taste the same but offer a rainbow of choices: orange, lime green, purple. Together they make a stunningly colorful crudités platter.

Selecting: Choose cauliflower heads that are firm and tightly compact. Avoid any that are discolored, shriveled, or have dried-out leaves attached.

Storing: Store wrapped in plastic in the vegetable crisper of your refrigerator for up to 5 days. Keep it away from apples, melons, peaches,

pears, plums, and mangoes, all of which produce ethylene gas as they ripen. Ethylene gas can cause cauliflower florets to turn yellow and the leaves to wither and shed.

Kohlrabi

About: Kohlrabi looks like an extraterrestrial but has a deliciously earthy taste—similar to broccoli stem but milder and sweeter. And although it looks like a root crop, this round vegetable grows suspended on a sturdy stalk. A relative of cabbage and member of the Brassica family, kohlrabi can be eaten raw or cooked. Peel off the outer skin with a paring knife to reveal the crisp, juicy center. Grate or chop kohlrabi and use raw in salads or cooked in soups or stewed lightly in cream. After cutting, sprinkle with salt; allow to sit for 5 minutes to remove excess liquid.

Varieties: Kohlrabi comes in green and purple varieties.

Selecting: Look for kohlrabi that's 2 to 4 inches in diameter. It should be firm and brightly colored with no splitting, cracking, or shriveling. The larger the kohlrabi, the tougher the flesh. If the kohlrabi is sold with the leaves attached, choose those with fresh-looking and not wilted leaves.

Storing: Trim off leaves attached to the kohlrabi. You can eat the leaves; store them in a plastic bag with a slightly moistened paper towel. Place the kohlrabi in a storage bag in the refrigerator. It will store for about a week.

Leeks

About: Leeks are the regal relative of the onion (Allium) family. Both the leaves and bulb are bigger than that of scallions, but they have a milder onion flavor than scallions or storage onions. They won't overpower a dish in the way that onions might. Leeks are versatile and can be eaten raw (usually chopped up for salads or used as a garnish) as well as cooked. They can be baked, grilled, or sautéed on their own as a side dish or added to roasts, sautés, braises, soups, and stews for flavor. The edible parts of the leek are the white bulb (the part that grows underground) and the lightest green part of the leaves. The dark and fibrous upper part of the leek is discarded. Leek soup is popular, as is the classic French leek and potato soup, called vichyssoise, which is served cold. Leeks are a good source of fiber, iron, and vitamins K, C, and A.

Varieties: There are early, mid-, and late-harvest leek varieties. Wild leeks are called ramps and have a stronger onion flavor than their cultivated cousins.

Selecting: Leeks are generally about 1 foot long with thick green leaves and a 1- to 2-inch-diameter white bulb. Look for leeks with long stems that are graduated white to green. The roots should still be attached. Bulbs and stems should be firm and fresh-looking with no soft spots. White bulbs should not have any cracks, cuts, or bruises. Avoid leeks with yellowed or withered leaves or those that are mostly all green. Smaller leeks generally have the best flavor. Very large leeks may be fibrous.

Storing: Wrap unwashed leeks with a plastic bag and place in the refrigerator. Leave the green leafy tops intact while in storage; this helps to preserve moisture. Stored in this manner, leeks can stay fresh for up to 2 weeks.

Trimming and Cleaning Leeks

1. Trim off the stem and leaf ends of the leek.

2. Cut leeks in half lengthwise, then slice.

3. Place the sliced leeks in a salad spinner filled with water; swirl the pieces in water to clean. Spin dry.

Lettuces and Salad Greens

About: There are four types of head lettuces: butterhead, crisphead, leaf, and romaine. Buttery texture and loosely clasped leaves characterize butterhead lettuces such as Boston, Bibb, and Buttercrunch. The crisphead family—fathered by iceberg lettuce—is known for its crisp and clean taste. Romaine is known for its elongated head and sturdy leaves. Leaf lettuces grow in loose heads. Most varieties of lettuce—especially dark green and red-leaf, are high in vitamins A and C, folate, and other nutrients. Salad greens have very distinct flavors, from bitter and peppery to tangy. Many salad greens—such as escarole and radicchio—can be cooked.

Selecting: For head types, choose dense, heavy heads with bright coloring and no browning on the outer leaves. For looseleaf types, select crisp, not wilting leaves.

Storing: Rinse lettuce, dry on paper towels (or roll up in a clean dish towel), and store in a plastic bag in the crisper. Head lettuce lasts up to 2 weeks; Butterhead stores for 10 days, and looseleaf can be kept for about 1 week. Salad greens should be used within 3 or 4 days. Rinse and dry before using.

GREEN LOOSELEAF Mild and pliable, the leaves have ruffled surfaces.

ROMAINE Sturdy and refreshing with slight bitter herb flavor.

RED BIBB Ruffled, mild, tender leaves make it a great choice for salads.

RED LOOSELEAF Mild-flavor leaves add color to salads.

BIBB Delicate loose leaves with buttery flavor and tender texture.

ICEBERG Dense, crisp heads can be sliced into wedges. Leaves can be used as wraps.

CURLY ENDIVE Bitter-flavored, it's best blended with other greens.

MÂCHÉ Also known as corn salad, it has a delicate flavor.

BELGIAN ENDIVE A chicory with crunchy, slightly bitter leaves.

OAKLEAF Delicate flavor with tender leaves.

ARUGULA Peppery and slightly bitter.

RADICCHIO Enlivens with color and slightly bitter notes.

BEET GREENS Leaves have an earthy taste like the root on which they grow.

WATERCRESS Little leaves have tangy, peppery flavor.

ESCAROLE Use its sturdy leaves in salads when they are young. Also good sautéed.

MIZUNA Its tender, peppery leaves are popular in Japanese cuisine.

FRISÉE Great texture with a bitter flavor.

Mushrooms

About: Mushrooms tend to grow where the sun doesn't shine much, like the deep woods. They are among the first things to pop out of the wet ground in spring—although both spring and fall have specific varieties. (They are grouped here together in order to talk about their common points.) Used in the cuisines of many cultures, mushrooms are sometimes referred to as meaty because of their dense, fleshy texture. There are many types of edible fungi and they come in various shapes, colors, textures, and flavors. Fragile fungi add an earthy and nutty flavor to dishes. Most edible mushrooms can be fried, boiled, sautéed, or eaten raw.
Note: There are many types of edible mushrooms and many types of inedible mushrooms. In fact, some inedible types are poisonous. Be sure to buy mushrooms from reputable sources, especially if they are gathered in the wild. Most mushrooms have a stem, a cap, and gills.

Varieties: Some mushrooms, such as button and cremini, are available year-round. Other mushrooms are seasonal, especially those that are gathered in the wild. Some of the other more common varieties include portobello, shiitake, morel, chanterelle, and oyster.

Selecting: When buying mushrooms—no matter the variety—look for these qualities: Mushrooms should have fresh-looking, firm flesh without blemishes or spots. They should be moist but not at all slimy—or overly dry. They should have an earthy but clean smell and tight gills.

Storing: As with selecting, most mushrooms have similar storage requirements to stay fresh. Store in a loosely covered container or paper bag in the refrigerator and use within a few days. If you purchase packaged button mushrooms, remove the plastic wrap covering the tray and wrap the entire container with paper towels and store in the refrigerator. Do not clean mushrooms until right before you use them. Brush with a damp paper towel but do not soak in water or they will get mushy. The exception to this rule is morels: Gently brush away any excess soil. If the morels are dirty, soak gently in water to remove soil, bugs, and other natural matter. Pat dry and store in a loosely covered container in the refrigerator. Use as soon as possible.

Peas (English)

About: Round, verdant green, garden or English peas are sweet and delicious. These are the peas that grow inside a pod, lined up like teeth in a broad smile, but the pod is not edible. Fresh garden peas burst with sweetness and have a satisfying crunch. In fact, many gardeners eat them fresh from the vine, raw, for the best flavor. Picked at peak perfection in early spring, they should be eaten as soon after harvest as possible. Because of their sweet, subtle flavor, they require little embellishment. Drop in boiling water, drain, then add a little butter and salt. Simple, easy, and delicious. Peas are a good source of fiber, iron, and protein. Here's some simple pea math: 1 pound of peas in the pod yields about 1 cup of shelled peas.

Varieties: There are many new and old (heirloom) types of English peas. Petits pois are very small English peas.

Selecting: English pea pods should be firm, bright green, and bulging with peas. The stem and tip should be soft and green. Overly large pods contain starchy peas.

Storing: Because all peas have a short shelf life, you should use them as soon as possible after purchase. Store peas in a plastic bag in the crisper section of your refrigerator. In this manner, they sometimes last up to 1 week. You can also freeze peas for later use. Shell peas just before using them.

Prepping Peas

1. Cut both ends of the pea pod and remove the string.

2. Pop open the pea pod.

3. Run your thumb down the length of the pea pod and pop out the peas.

Radishes

About: Radishes are the speed demons of the garden. Small radishes are ready to harvest in spring as little as three weeks after planting seeds. They are also a fall crop. Whether you pluck them fresh from the ground or pick up a bundle at a produce stand, they are easy and quick to prepare. Wash them under cold water, cut off the root end and the leafy green foliage top and the radish is ready to join other fresh veggies on a crudités platter. Radishes have a distinctive flavor; they are crunchy, peppery, and jazz up salads and sandwiches. The tops are edible too. Dice radishes for a tasty soup garnish. They're full of vitamin B, riboflavin, and calcium.

Varieties: Most people think of radishes as small, round, and red, but there are also round varieties in different colors such as white and purple. Radishes also come in tapered varieties. Popular red-and-white French radishes are tapered. These shapely radishes are beautiful sliced or served whole. Long white radishes, called daikon radishes, are popular in Japanese cuisine. These radishes are larger, carrot-shape, and have a milder flavor.

Selecting: Look for bright color and firm, plump skin. Avoid radishes with nicks, bruises, or cracks. If sold with their leaves attached, the foliage should not be excessively wilted.

Storing: Remove any foliage attached to the radishes. Store in a plastic bag in the refrigerator where they will stay fresh for 3 to 5 days.

Rhubarb

About: The stocky red, green, or red-tinged green stems (also called petioles) of the rhubarb plant are early risers in the spring garden—and they show up in produce sections not long after. Rhubarb looks a little like celery and has the same texture when raw: crunchy and juicy. It's easy to harvest—just pull it from the ground—and is a snap to dice into pieces for recipes; just cut with a sharp knife. Rhubarb is usually sold in bunches. Stems may have the large leaves still attached, which are inedible and, in fact, poisonous. The leaves cannot be eaten in any form, cooked or raw. This perennial vegetable is frequently referred to as a fruit. It has a tart flavor so it's often used in recipes that call for a lot of sugar: jams, crisps, pies, and even wine. You can eat rhubarb raw (add small pieces to salads or puree for margaritas), but it is generally served cooked. It does not hold its shape when cooked for a long time. Rhubarb is rich in vitamin C and fiber.

Varieties: There are many varieties of rhubarb and they are mostly differentiated by the stem color and size. There are thick- and thin-stemmed varieties. The color of the stems can range from light green to cherry red. Some of the darker red rhubarb retains its red color after it is cooked.

Selecting: Look for crisp red, green, or dark pink stalks that are firm and smooth. Avoid stalks that have black ends or spots on them. A deeper color often indicates how sweet the taste, although flavor varies by variety. Larger stalks are not necessarily sweeter than thin ones. If the leaves are still attached, they should be fresh and not wilted.

Storing: Before storing, remove any leaves from stalks and discard. Store rhubarb in plastic bags in refrigerator. In this manner, they will remain fresh for a few days. You can also cut the stalks into 1- or 2-inch lengths, place in a storage bag, and freeze for later use.

Preparing Rhubarb

1. Wash stems and trim off leaves.

2. Cut off the bottoms of the stems.

3. Dice into small pieces for cooking or freezing.

Scallions

About: Scallions are the baby brother in the onion (Allium) family. They also go by the name green onions or clumping onions. Scallions are a type of onion that is harvested young; a mature scallion is about the size of a pencil. You can eat the white part, which is the bulb and grows underground. The leaves are hollow and flavorful—much like chives. They are also edible. Scallions can add a pungent onion bite without overpowering a meal. Chopped scallions can be added raw to soups, salads, or marinades and are an integral part of many Asian dishes. They can also be sautéed or grilled. To prepare scallions, remove the bottom ¼ inch of the bulb where the root is joined. Trim off the very tops of the green leaves and remove any yellow or wilted leaves. Then chop the bulb and stalk together.

Varieties: There are different scallion varieties, but most are indistinguishable from each other, differing mostly in size and harvest time.

Selecting: Scallions are sold in bunches, usually rubber-banded together. Look for scallions with bright green leaves and firm white bottoms. Choose scallions with the roots still intact. Avoid any bunches that feel limp or show any trace of slime on the leaves or bulb.

Storing: If you have purchased a clump of scallions, remove the

rubber band holding them together and stand them up in jar with an inch or two of water. Then place a plastic bag over the scallions and place the whole thing in the refrigerator. Stored in this manner, scallions will last about 1 week.

Spinach

About: Spinach is a lush, leafy green that is so full of good things. This power veggie contains iron, calcium, and antioxidants. It's a healthful and delicious alternative to iceberg lettuce on sandwiches. Spinach even makes a great smoothie—just drop raw leaves into a blender with orange juice and your favorite fruit; it's a super way to get a helping of veggies at breakfast. Other ways to enjoy spinach: sauté it, drop it into boiling soup, or eat it raw as a salad green. It is excellent in fritattas and omelets. Eat spinach fresh or steamed to get the most nutrients. Spinach is easy to grow, sprouting quickly in cool seasons (spring and fall). It must be harvested before the summer heat makes plants bolt or winter's frost kills it. Sold in bunches or prewashed bags, this leafy green couldn't be easier to prepare. Baby spinach is simply immature spinach. It's slightly more tender than mature spinach and doesn't require stemming.

Selecting: Look for fresh, moist, green leaves. Avoid yellow, muddy, shriveled leaves or any that are beginning to feel slimy.

Storing: Do not wash spinach until you are ready to use it. Place unwashed leaves in plastic bags and store in your refrigerator for several days. To prepare, cut the stems off the bunch of spinach, then wash the leaves in a salad spinner. Or swirl the leaves in a bowl of cool water, changing the water several times if necessary. Dry on paper towels or on a clean kitchen towel.

SUGAR PEAS

SNOW PEAS

Sugar Peas and Snow Peas

About: Sugar peas (sometimes called sugar snap peas) and snow peas are a two-for-one treat: You eat both the pods and the peas inside. Unlike English peas, which you need to shell, these peas grow in tender, stringless pods. The pods of sugar peas are fleshy, sweet, and as tender as the peas inside. Since the whole pod of a sugar pea is edible, this may be one of the most kid-friendly treats, especially in the garden: Pick and pop into the mouth. Snow peas are frequent ingredients in stir-fry recipes.

Varieties: If growing peas, there are specific varieties that do best in warm and cool areas. Harvest sugar peas after the peas have filled out inside the pods. Many specific varieties have the word "sugar" in them (Sugar Ann, Super Sugar Snap), which indicates the sublime sweetness of these peas.

Selecting: Snow peas should be selected with flat, bright green pods with small peas just barely visible inside.

Sugar peas should be fresh, bright green, and smooth with no marks or blemishes. Peas within the pods are generally not visible.

Storing: Because all peas have a short shelf life, you should use them as soon as possible after purchase. Store peas in a plastic bag in the crisper section of your refrigerator, where they can last up to 1 week. You can also freeze fresh peas for later use.

summer

WARM UP TO THE TASTE OF SUMMER As the temperatures rise and the growing season lengthens, the flavors of produce intensify. Sweet fruits, savory peppers, and ripe, juicy tomatoes burst with sun-kissed goodness.

Apricots

About: Picked fresh from the tree or picked up at the produce market, fresh apricots are a delicious, healthful summer treat. These beautiful, golden-yellow fruits have smooth skins and sweet, succulent meat. They are packed with beta-carotene, vitamins A and C, and fiber. Close relatives of plums, apricots are generally eaten fresh or processed into jams or jellies. The fruit can also be dried, making them great little energy boosters you can tuck into trail mix or your kids' sack lunches. Dried apricots can be used in chutneys and stuffings and complement pork and chicken dishes. Apricots are ideal for dieters; they have fewer calories than other fruits. Three apricots contain only 50 calories. The apricot pit is actually a nut that contains a high content of vitamin B17. Although bitter, the pit can be ground and swallowed with a teaspoon of juice or honey.

Varieties: There are three apricot harvests, depending on the varieties, which are early, midseason, and late. Apricot varieties vary by size and color.

Selecting: Look for firm, unblemished fruit that has a rich yellow-orange color and sweet aroma. There should be no trace of green on the skin. Apricots bruise easily so most are sold unripe. Overly soft or squishy fruit is best avoided. Smell them; they should be sweetly fragrant.

Storing: Place apricots in a brown paper bag out of direct sunlight to ripen them. Check for ripeness every day because fruit quality can deteriorate quickly. When ripe, apricots can be stored in the refrigerator for a day or two.

Skinning and Pitting Apricots

1. Place apricots in boiling water for 15 to 20 seconds, then place into ice water.

2. Peel loosened skin from the fruit with a paring knife.

3. Cut apricots in half. Remove the pit with the tip of the paring knife.

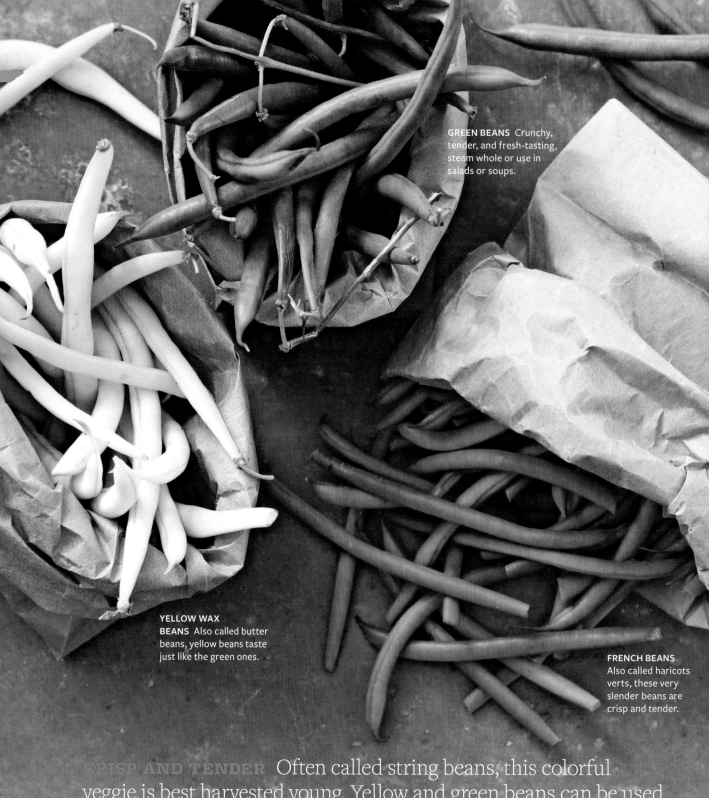

GREEN BEANS Crunchy, tender, and fresh-tasting, steam whole or use in salads or soups.

YELLOW WAX BEANS Also called butter beans, yellow beans taste just like the green ones.

FRENCH BEANS Also called haricots verts, these very slender beans are crisp and tender.

CRISP AND TENDER Often called string beans, this colorful veggie is best harvested young. Yellow and green beans can be used interchangeably in recipes.

Avocado

About: Native to Central Mexico, this tasty fruit (yes, it's a fruit) is commonly called "alligator pear" because of its thin, dark green rubbery skin or "butterfruit" because of its rich, creamy flesh. The flesh is removed and can be sliced and eaten raw or mashed into a creamy paste. Use avocados soon after you cut them or they will brown; a little lemon juice sprinkled over the cut fruit helps slow discoloration. Avocados are a good source of fiber, potassium, and vitamins C and K. Half of an avocado contains 160 calories and 15 grams of heart-healthy unsaturated fat, with only 2 grams of saturated fat.

Varieties: There are several varieties of avocado, some of which you may never see in a store unless you live in warm regions such as California or Florida. In northern regions, you are most likely to see Hass, which is the most common variety. Other avocados varieties include Zutano, Bacon, and Fuerto.

The SlimCado is a variety that has 35% fewer calories and 50% less fat than regular avocados.

Selecting: Look for solid, heavy avocados that have no blemishes or nicks. Avocados ripen after they are picked, so the harder they are, the fresher they are. Buy hard avocados and ripen them at home because by the time they are ripe in the store, they are often bruised. It takes 2 to 5 days for an avocado to ripen.

Storing: Place avocados in a brown paper bag and ripen at room temperature. A ripe avocado yields slightly when gently squeezed. Once ripe, they can be stored in the refrigerator for up to 10 days. To hasten ripening, place an apple or banana in the paper sack with your avocados. (Both release ethylene gas as they ripen, which speeds the ripening of the avocado.) Keep out of direct sunlight.

Halving and Seeding an Avocado

1. Cut the avocado in half lengthwise.

2. Twist the avocado to pop open the halves.

3. Insert a spoon beneath the seed and pop it out.

Beans

About: When summer temperatures start to climb, it's a sure sign that bean season is about to kick into high gear. Often lumped together in the category of "string beans," green, French, and yellow wax beans all have similar traits and can be used interchangeably in recipes (yellow wax beans are often called butter beans—different from the legume of the same name). All beans are at their best when harvested young from either bushes or vines trained up trellises. Beans make delicious additions to salads and soups, or as a side dish on their own, steamed and tossed with butter and salt.

Varieties: There are several varieties of beans. French beans, also called haricots verts, are thin, crisp, and tender. Several varieties of green beans aren't green; these beans come in yellow and purple. Generally these beans taste the same as green beans. When these beans are cooked, they lose their color and look just like green beans. In the garden, there are bush and pole beans, which refers to the way they grow and has nothing to do with their taste.

Selecting: Look for beans that are firm with a fresh color. A fresh bean should snap easily when bent. Small, thin beans generally have the best flavor.

Storing: Beans stay fresh in your refrigerator in a plastic bag for up to a week.

STRAWBERRIES

BLACKBERRIES

BLUEBERRIES

RED RASPBERRIES

Berries

About: Summer is the season when Mother Nature's candy store opens for business, producing a variety of flavorful and brightly colored berries. Some of her most popular offerings include strawberries, blackberries, blueberries, raspberries, and strawberries. These soft, sweet, and fragile fruits require gentle handling. Ideal for eating fresh, of course, they are also seemingly tailor-made for tarts, sorbets, and jellies and jams. They're low in calories, high in fiber, and contain essential vitamins and minerals. The pigments that give berries their bold, jewel-like colors are also good for your health. These phytochemicals and flavonoids are believed to be helpful in preventing some forms of cancer.

Varieties: Check your area for locally grown berries, pick-your-own berry farms, and farmers' markets. You can grow many berries in your garden, some of which are compact enough to excel in containers. These berries are perennial plants, meaning they will come back year after year.

- **Strawberries** These ruby fruits contain more antioxidants than most other fruits and vegetables. Only blackberries and walnuts score higher. Strawberries are generally red, but there are white varieties. Try tiny alpine strawberries on ice cream.
- **Raspberries** Available in red and golden varieties, raspberries are succulent and are thought to have anticancer benefits due to high antioxidant and anti-inflammatory phytonutrients.
- **Boysenberries** A cross between a raspberry and a blackberry, this berry is high in anthocyanin, a natural antioxidant. It is especially juicy and sweet.
- **Blackberries** Dark and juicy blackberries are high in antioxidants, and the dark pigment, anthocyanin, helps with inflammation.
- **Blueberries** From small wild varieties to the big commercially grown blueberries, this wonder berry has so many health benefits; recently it has been shown to help with memory loss.

Selecting: Look for berries that are firm, with a bright color and pleasant fragrance. Avoid any that are overly soft or showing any signs of gray moldy spots or blemishes. Some berries, such as strawberries, are sold with their caps intact. Look for ones on which the caps are still fresh and green. If purchasing a prepackaged pint or quart of berries, try to check the bottom of the pile for rot or mold.

Storing: All berries are best used as soon as possible after purchase. Store berries unwashed in a tightly wrapped container in your refrigerator for several days. Wash right before using. To freeze for longer storage, wash berries in cool water, then dry gently and thoroughly on clean paper towels. Arrange berries in a single layer on a rimmed baking sheet. Freeze berries on baking sheet until firm, then transfer to resealable plastic freezer bags and store in the freezer. Blueberries are the exception to this method. They should be frozen before being washed. Washing them before freezing toughens the skins. Before using, give the frozen berries a quick rinse in cold water, then dry on paper towels.

SWEET AND JUICY Whether eaten out of hand, sprinkled on hot or cold cereal, whipped into a smoothie, or cooked into jam or pies, berries offer bright color, sweet flavor, and powerful nutrition.

Cherries

About: Dangling from trees like beautiful Chinese lanterns, cherries are one of nature's true delicacies. Available in sour and sweet varieties, there's a cherry for every purpose. Sour cherries are ideal for jams, jellies, syrups, and pies. They are also the cherries that are dried (with sugar added). Sweet cherries can be enjoyed right off the tree and are the cherries most often sold in produce sections. Both types of cherries pack a punch when it comes to antioxidants, beta-carotene, fiber, potassium, magnesium, iron, and vitamins C and E.

Varieties: Select fresh cherries for a specific purpose.

- **Sweet** Ideal for eating fresh, sweet cherries are available midsummer. Cherry fans love the sweeter-than-sweet Rainier, a yellow-red blushed skin with yellow flesh. Sweet Ann is a white-flesh variety. Dark red sweet cherries include the popular Bing and dark Hudson. Look for local growers in regions where cherries are raised for lesser known, but equally sweet varieties.

- **Sour** Tart cherries are used for pies and crisps and require sweetening. There are two types of tart cherries—amarelle and morello. Amarelle cherries only have red pigment in the skin, with opaque flesh. Canned pie filling is usually made with Montmorency cherries, an amarelle cherry. Morello cherries are red throughout.

Selecting: Cherries should be plump with bright, shiny skins. Avoid cherries that are soft or have deep blemishes. Cherries with the stems attached last longer than those without. In general, the darker the cherry, the sweeter it is. Sour cherries can be firmer to the touch than sweet cherries.

Storing: Store unwashed cherries in a plastic bag in your refrigerator. They can last for up to 4 days stored in this manner. Wash right before using. To freeze for longer storage, wash and dry on clean paper towels. Freeze in a single layer on a rimmed baking sheet, then transfer to sealable plastic bags and store in freezer.

Removing a Cherry Pit

1. Pull out the stem.

2. Insert a clean paper clip into the cherry. Twist it around the pit to loosen it.

3. Pull out the pit. You can also use a cherry pitter.

Cucumbers

About: Cucumbers are a member of the gourd family and are the fourth most widely cultivated vegetable in the world behind tomatoes, cabbage, and onions. Use cucumbers cut up in leafy salads, on sandwiches, and au naturel with a bit of salt. Cucumbers pair well with dill and mint.

Varieties: Cucumbers are grouped as slicers or picklers. Slicers are long, thin, smooth, and are best eaten fresh. Picklers are generally shorter and have spines or bumps on their skin. Although you can also eat picklers fresh, these are the varieties most commonly used in canning to make dill and sweet pickles. The best pickling cucumbers are Kirbys because they are small and easy to pack into jars. There are some varieties of cucumbers that are seedless (or virtually so). The most common of these is the long, slender English (or hothouse) cucumber.

Selecting: Choose firm cucumbers with no blemishes or marks on the skin. They should feel heavy for their size. Small cucumbers are generally crisper with smaller seeds than large ones.

Storing: Cucumbers can be stored for up to 7 days if placed in a perforated plastic bag in your refrigerator.

Eggplant

About: As beautiful as it is delicious, eggplant is a close relative of the tomato and grows in a similar manner, hanging from the vine in the height of summer. When cooked, the flesh becomes tender and develops a rich, complex flavor. Used in Indian, Mediterranean, Middle Eastern, and French cooking, eggplant is also a great replacement for meat because of its rich and hearty taste. Eggplant is the star of dishes such as eggplant Parmesan, ratatouille, and baba ghanoush. Eggplant is rich in antioxidants and high in fiber.

Varieties: Eggplants come in a wide range of colors, sizes, and shapes. The classic purple, patent leather-shiny, egg-shape eggplant is most recognizable. The most common varieties of this type are Black Magic, Black Beauty, and Black Bell. Eggplants also come in lighter purple colors. Some are streaked. Shapes vary, including long cylindrical and small round varieties. Colors range from dark purple and burgundy to bright white. Try white eggplants called Albino and White Beauty.

Selecting: Choose eggplants that are firm and feel heavy for their size. Avoid any eggplants with bruises, cracks, or signs of shriveling. If the skin gives slightly when you press your fingernail against it, the eggplant is ripe. Small eggplants tend to be sweeter and more tender than large ones.

Storing: Eggplants are best consumed as soon as possible, but you can store them for a day or two by putting them in a perforated plastic bag in your refrigerator.

Long, slender Japanese-type eggplants have thinner skin than standard eggplants and won't store as long. The two most common varieties of Japanese eggplant are Millionaire and Orient Express.

Figs

About: Native to Turkey, figs are now grown and savored around the world. Fig varieties vary in color and texture, but they all have deliciously sweet flesh that surrounds nutty, crunchy seeds. You can eat figs fresh or dried. Dried figs can be used in muffins, cakes, oatmeal, and energy bars. Fresh figs are lovely in salads and even poached in wine or fruit juice. Or just eat them in their purest form, fresh, out of hand.

Varieties: There are hundreds of fig varieties, and many are regionally supplied. California-grown Black Mission figs have purplish-black skin and intensely sweet red flesh. Other common varieties include pale green-yellow Kadota figs; mild-tasting Brown Turkey figs; and large, gold-skinned, nutty-flavored Calimyrna figs.

Selecting: Figs come in a variety of colors and types, so know what color your fig should be before you buy. Look for figs with smooth, dry skin that has no blemishes or cracks. Ripe figs will be firm but give slightly to the touch. Avoid any overly soft or mushy fruit.

Storing: Use figs as soon as possible after purchase. You can place them in a plastic bag in your refrigerator to preserve them for a few days.

CONCORD GRAPES The grapes with the true "grape" taste. They contain seeds.

RED GRAPES Rosy-hued, seedless, and sweet.

GREEN GRAPES A favorite variety, Thompson Seedless, is sweet and seedless.

CHAMPAGNE GRAPES The smallest variety of seedless grapes.

Grapes

About: One of the world's original fast foods, grapes have been an important part of diets for more than 8,000 years. Grapes are generally broken into three types: table, wine, and raisin. All three share a variety of important health benefits including the presence of antioxidants, anti-inflammatory qualities, and cardiovascular and blood sugar benefits. One of the more interesting recent discoveries is that grapes contain a phytonutrient called resveratrol. Resveratrol has been shown to reduce heart disease, lower the risk of cancer, and is believed to help slow aging and increase longevity. Most of the beneficial elements in grapes are found on the skin and in the seeds.

Varieties: There are a variety of table grapes in a variety of colors: green, red, and blue-black. Green-skin Thompson Seedless and red Blush Seedless and Flame Seedless are, as their names suggest, without seeds and are a favorite with kids.

Selecting: Look for plump grapes that are held firmly to the stem. Darker varieties of grapes should be fully colored, with little green on the skin. Avoid any grapes that are soft or shriveled. A powdery white coating on grapes is natural and is called the bloom.

Storing: Store unwashed grapes in a plastic bag in the refrigerator. They should last about a week. Don't store grapes near pungent vegetables such as leeks because they can absorb odors.

Herbs

About: Herbs are a class of plants that offer a variety of seasoning possibilities. They are generally classified as woody-stemmed (such as rosemary and thyme) or soft-stemmed (such as basil, mint, and parsley). Some herbs, such as chives, rosemary, thyme, and sage, also produce edible flowers. Depending on the herb, different parts of the plant are used. The leaves of basil, cilantro, and oregano are used to season fresh and cooked food. Both the leaves and seeds of dill and cilantro (the seeds are called coriander) are used.

Selecting: When selecting herbs, avoid any that are wilted or have blemishes or soft spots. All herbs should have a fresh fragrance.

Storing: Place herbs in a plastic bag with a slightly damp paper towel and store in the refrigerator for up to 1 week. You can also store fresh herbs by standing upright in a glass filled with a bit of water and lightly tented with a plastic bag in the refrigerator (except for basil, which should be stored in water at room temperature). This storage method can extend the life of fresh herbs for more than a week.

MINT Try flavor variations such as spearmint, chocolate mint, and orange mint.

PARSLEY Parsley comes in two forms: curly-leaf (on the right) and flat-leaf (on the left).

THYME Fragrant thyme has tiny leaves that are rich in flavor. Used in Mediterranean dishes.

SAGE Perfect with chicken and pork dishes, sage is also a standby herb for stuffings.

ROSEMARY Aromatic rosemary seasons pizza, pasta sauces, and pork and chicken dishes.

OREGANO An important herb in Mediterranean cuisine.

BASIL Has hints of cinnamon, anise, and clove. Grind into pesto or stir into soups and sauces.

FRENCH TARRAGON Has a sweet anise flavor that pairs with poultry and eggs.

DILL Ferny, airy dill leaves add flavor to fish, potato, and egg dishes.

CILANTRO Bright green leaves add flavor to Mexican and Asian foods.

MARJORAM Sweet-spicy leaves add flavor to roasts and stews.

Mangoes

About: Tropical fruit lovers all over the world swoon over the sweet flavor of mangoes. This hefty round or oblong fruit is known for two things: its great flavor and its oddly shaped large seed, which to novices can seem to be a cutting conundrum. Mangoes are best eaten fresh and are key ingredients in smoothies, chutneys, and fruit salads. Mango salsa is a refreshing topper for fish dishes. Mango is a good source of vitamin A and fiber. The mango is the national fruit of India, which is also the country that produces the most mangoes.

Varieties: Mangoes come in different colors, ranging from yellow-orange, yellow, or green. Although there are many varieties, most mangoes available in American produce sections are Tommy Atkins, which is a variety that has a longer shelf life and ships well. In tropical areas, look for other mango varieties in local produce stands and farmers' markets.

Selecting: Choose ripe mangoes by giving them the squeeze test; they should yield a bit. Give them the smell test too. They should have a slightly fruity scent at their stem ends. Avoid overly ripe and mushy mangoes and those with obvious bruises or blemishes.

Storing: Keep unripe mangoes on the kitchen counter, where they will ripen at room temperature. As they ripen, they will become softer and sweeter. To speed ripening, place them in a paper bag. Once ripe, move mangoes to the refrigerator, where the cool temperature will slow down the ripening process. You can also peel and slice mangoes and keep them in the refrigerator in a sealed container for several days.

Dicing a Mango

1. Hold the mango so the "eye" (a small dimple at the base) is looking at you. Cut off the sides of the mango, avoiding the large seed.

2. Slice a checkerboard pattern into the mango, taking care not to slice through the skin.

3. Invert the mango slice so that the dices stand out. Insert the knife next to the skin and slice off the dices.

Melon

About: What would a summer picnic be without some ice-cold melon to pass around to family and friends? A native of North Africa and Asia, melons have been enjoyed for thousands of years. Over time, as the melon was transported around the world, new hybrids were created that were sweeter and easier to grow. Although there are many different types of melons, the three most commonly available include watermelon, cantaloupe, and honeydew. Because they all have a high water content, they are low in calories. Cantaloupe and honeydew are both high in vitamin C, and watermelon contains the powerful antioxidant lycopene that has been linked to cancer reduction and the risk of heart attack. Serve cut melon as an appetizer, draped with a piece of paper-thin prosciutto. Use a melon baller to scoop out a melon, then fill the empty shell and use it as a serving bowl. A medium cantaloupe or honeydew (about 2½ pounds) yields about 6 cups cubed melon.

Varieties: Commercially grown cantaloupe, watermelon, and honeydew are available in stores. Look for heirloom varieties at farmers' markets.

Selecting: Look for melons with firm, unblemished skin. They should also feel firm and heavy but be slightly soft near the stem end. A ripe cantaloupe also has a fresh cantaloupe fragrance. Cantaloupes should have a rich yellow-orange flesh. A ripe watermelon is creamy yellow on the underside, where it sat on the ground. Look for honeydew melons with creamy yellow skin and concentric "sugar cracks" around the blossom end, which indicate high sugar content. They should also feel firm, although a ripe melon will be slightly soft near the stem.

Storing: Uncut melons can be stored at room temperature for up to 1 week. Cut melons can be stored covered in the refrigerator for 4 or 5 days.

CANTALOUPE
Sweet, juicy slices
pair well with
salty food, such
as prosciutto.

WATERMELON
Seedless varieties of
this iconic picnic food
are easiest to eat.

HONEYDEW Pale
green flesh is sweet
and succulent, with a
slightly floral flavor.

ZUCCHINI Also called courgette, zucchini is best eaten small. The flowers can be used in a variety of recipes, from soups to appetizers.

YELLOW SQUASH This mild squash has the highest levels of beta carotene of the summer squash varieties due to its brightly colored skin.

PATTYPAN This saucer-shape squash is best eaten when about 2 inches in diameter. Larger ones can be chopped and used in place of yellow squash.

Summer Squash

About: Prolific and delicious, summer squash varieties are available in pound after pound of interesting and sculptural fruit during the height of summer. They can be long, straight, and thin like traditional green zucchini or yellow summer squash. Or they can come in a variety of other shapes, such as the flying saucer-shape pattypan. Slice or chop into salads to add texture and heft, stir into soups and sauces, and combine with other vegetables. They also make great grillmates; just slice lengthwise into strips, brush with olive oil, season, and grill until lightly browned. Summer squash is low in calories and a good source of fiber, potassium, vitamins C and A, and beta-carotene.

Selecting: When shopping for summer squash, look for those with glossy, unblemished skin. They should feel heavy for their size. Small- to medium-size squash are best—about 6 inches long or wide (if it is a pattypan variety). When it comes to summer squash, bigger is not better. Smaller squash are sweeter and more tender than larger ones, which can get starchy and bland if overmature.

Storing: Store unwashed summer squash in a plastic bag in your refrigerator. In this manner, they will generally last up to 5 days.

Nectarines

About: Nectarines are essentially fuzz-free peaches. Although they may resemble plums because of their bright, shiny skin, a nectarine is actually a smooth-skinned peach. In fact, they are such close relatives that it's almost impossible to tell a peach tree from a nectarine tree in the orchard. Nectarines are generally a bit sweeter than peaches, but you can use them in the same way that you use peaches. Try them in pies and chutneys. Nectarines provide vitamins A and C, and potassium. They are also a good source of beta-carotene.

Varieties: Like peaches, nectarines come in both freestone (the flesh separates from the pit easily) and clingstone varieties (the flesh has a tendency to cling to the pit). Like peaches, there are yellow- and white-flesh varieties of nectarines.

Selecting: Look for fruit with unblemished skin that feels firm, but not hard, to the touch. If the fruit is soft, it may already be too ripe. Avoid nectarines that are obviously bruised or with skin that has a withered appearance.

Storing: To ripen, store at room temperature in a paper bag out of direct sunlight. Most nectarines will ripen quickly in this manner. Ripe

nectarines will feel slightly soft and have a fresh nectarine fragrance. You can store ripe nectarines for several days in a perforated plastic bag in your refrigerator.

Okra

About: A Southern specialty, okra deserves to be used more frequently in other parts of the country. This elegant, podlike vegetable is also called lady's fingers or gumbo. (Okra contains a natural thickener that helps thicken gumbo.) Okra is the edible green seedpod of a tall tropical plant related to both hibiscus and cotton. It excels in hot climates and is easy to grow in home gardens. Okra plants are prolific producers. Slice the pods in half and you'll see that it has seeds inside, like peppers. The whole okra pod can be consumed. There are dozens of ways to prepare okra. It can be fried, pickled, grilled, sautéed, baked, and stirred into soups, stews, and gumbo. Okra is also an excellent health food. It's rich in fiber, vitamins A, C, and K as well as iron, calcium, manganese, and magnesium.

Varieties: Most okra varieties produce slender pods that range in color from dark to light green. But there are okra varieties with dramatic difference in pod size, ranging from squat to long, slender pods that measure more than a foot long. There are also several varieties that produce red or scarlet-streaked pods. Look for heirloom varieties at local farmers' markets.

Selecting: Okra pods should feel firm and dry. If they are mushy or slimy or have blemishes, avoid them.

Check the skin coating; it should have a peach-fuzz appearance.

Storing: Place okra in a paper bag and store in your refrigerator. Don't let okra get too cold or it will rot quickly. Stored in this manner it will last 2 to 3 days.

Peaches

About: What could be more refreshing than biting into a fresh, tree-ripened peach and having its sweet juice run down your chin? First cultivated in China thousands of years ago, the peach traveled across the globe with early explorers and put down roots wherever the climate was ideal. Since then, peaches have played starring roles in pies, cobblers, cakes, ice cream, juices, salsas, and jams. They can also be grilled, poached, or roasted. They are an excellent source of vitamins A, C, E, and K as well as antioxidants and dietary fiber.

Varieties: There are hundreds of peach varieties. Clingstone peaches are softer and sweeter than freestone varieties (the flesh of freestone peaches doesn't cling to the pit as it does with clingstones). There are Asian white-flesh peaches and flat, white-flesh heirloom peaches called donut peaches.

Selecting: Look for unblemished fruit that's firm but yields under slight pressure. The fruit should be aromatic. Avoid peaches that have green patches on the skin because they have been harvested too young.

Storing: If your peaches aren't ripe when you buy them, place them in an open brown paper bag on the kitchen counter. Don't let them touch; this can cause overripening and spoilage at the contact points. Ripening happens quickly. Ripe peaches last about 3 days at room temperature. Move ripe peaches to the refrigerator (in a perforated plastic bag) to extend their life another day or two.

Peeling and Pitting a Peach

 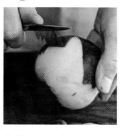 

1. Place peaches in boiling water for 15 to 20 seconds, then place into ice water.

2. Remove the loosened skin using a paring knife.

3. Cut in half and remove the pit using your fingers or the tip of a sharp knife.

Peppers (Sweet)

About: Used in salads, salsas, stir-fries, and sauces, as well as for roasting, baking, and grilling, sweet peppers (also called bell peppers) are one of the most versatile vegetables in the garden and kitchen. Sweet peppers have a classic bell shape with thick, fleshy skin. Their mild flavor and deep, glossy colors add visual zing and satisfying crunch to salads, sandwiches, and wraps. For a quick appetizer, cut different-color sweet peppers into strips and serve with dipping sauces. A common ingredient in Mexican and Italian dishes, sweet peppers add fine flavor to tomato-based sauces. In fact, tomatoes and peppers are a classic pairing. Their thick skin and boxy shape make them ideal for stuffing and baking. Sweet peppers are also a good source of vitamins C and A. Although sweet peppers contain the health-benefitting compound capsaicin, they don't carry as much as the hot varieties.

Varieties: Sweet peppers are available in a rainbow of colors: green, white, yellow, red, orange, and chocolate brown. On the plant all varieties start out green, but as they mature they develop their full color. From small heart-shape fruits to elongated varieties, sweet peppers offer a range of sizes and shapes. Other types of sweet peppers include small pimientos, cahucha (a sweet pepper used in Cuban dishes), and the long and slender bull's horn.

Selecting: Choose peppers whose skins are smooth, taut, firm, glossy, and exhibit bright color. If the

stems are still attached, they should be green and flexible, not dry and brittle. Avoid peppers with bruises or soft spots.

Storing: Store peppers unwashed and unwrapped in your refrigerator for up to 2 weeks.

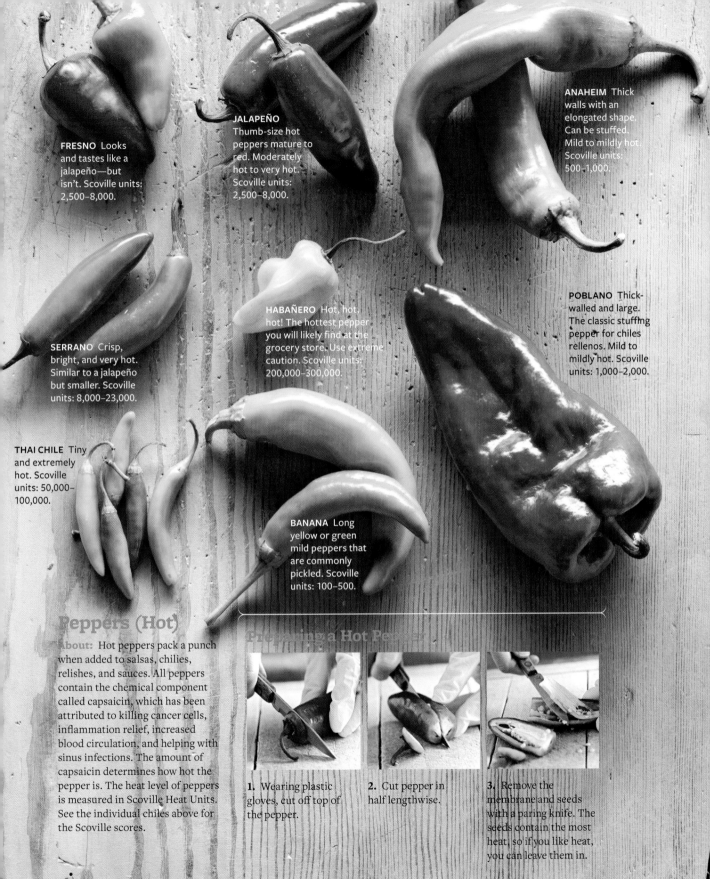

FRESNO Looks and tastes like a jalapeño—but isn't. Scoville units: 2,500–8,000.

JALAPEÑO Thumb-size hot peppers mature to red. Moderately hot to very hot. Scoville units: 2,500–8,000.

ANAHEIM Thick walls with an elongated shape. Can be stuffed. Mild to mildly hot. Scoville units: 500–1,000.

SERRANO Crisp, bright, and very hot. Similar to a jalapeño but smaller. Scoville units: 8,000–23,000.

HABAÑERO Hot, hot, hot! The hottest pepper you will likely find at the grocery store. Use extreme caution. Scoville units: 200,000–300,000.

POBLANO Thick-walled and large. The classic stuffing pepper for chiles rellenos. Mild to mildly hot. Scoville units: 1,000–2,000.

THAI CHILE Tiny and extremely hot. Scoville units: 50,000–100,000.

BANANA Long yellow or green mild peppers that are commonly pickled. Scoville units: 100–500.

Peppers (Hot)

About: Hot peppers pack a punch when added to salsas, chilies, relishes, and sauces. All peppers contain the chemical component called capsaicin, which has been attributed to killing cancer cells, inflammation relief, increased blood circulation, and helping with sinus infections. The amount of capsaicin determines how hot the pepper is. The heat level of peppers is measured in Scoville Heat Units. See the individual chiles above for the Scoville scores.

Preparing a Hot Pepper

1. Wearing plastic gloves, cut off top of the pepper.

2. Cut pepper in half lengthwise.

3. Remove the membrane and seeds with a paring knife. The seeds contain the most heat, so if you like heat, you can leave them in.

Pineapple

About: Hawaii may be the first place you think of when you see a ripe pineapple, but this sweet, delicious fruit is actually native to the Caribbean and South America. It's a member of the bromeliad family (which is a tropical flower), and the single fruit is actually a series of small fruitlets that have fused together. Pineapple can be consumed fresh or juiced or made into ice cream, yogurt, and baked goods. Pineapple is high in Vitamin C, thiamin, and the trace mineral manganese, which is important for energy production and antioxidant defenses. One medium pineapple (4 pounds) will yield about 4½ cups peeled and cubed pineapple.

Varieties: The most commonly grown pineapple in the world for commercial purposes is a variety called Smooth Cayenne. When buying pineapple in nontropical locations, this is most likely the variety you will get.

Selecting: Choose pineapples that feel plump and firm and have a strong, sweet fragrance. The green leaves of the fruit should look fresh and not dried out. Ripe pineapples can have a golden-yellow color rising from the base of the plant. The higher the yellow color occurs on the pineapple, the sweeter it is. Also, check the base of the fruit. If it yields to pressure, your pineapple is probably ripe. Avoid fruit with blemishes or spots of mold.

Storing: Use pineapple as soon as possible after purchase. Store and ripen on your kitchen counter at room temperature for a few days or prolong shelf life slightly by putting the entire fruit in a perforated plastic bag in the refrigerator. (Look for perforated plastic bags in the aisle of your supermarket that has storage bags, plastic wrap, aluminum foil. They are sometimes called "produce bags.")

Cutting and Coring Pineapple

1. Cut off the base and the top of the pineapple.

2. Slice off the rough sides.

3. Cut into large wedges. Slice off the fibrous core on the inside edge of each wedge.

Plums

About: Plums are the jewels of summer, rich and ripe and available in a variety of brilliant colors, including black, red, yellow, pink, and green. Each has a slightly different flavor, but when ripe, they are all sweet and juicy. Plums are close relatives of almonds and peaches and are generally divided into three main categories: American, Japanese, and European. All plums are loaded with antioxidants, vitamin C, beta-carotene, and carotenoids. Dried plums are sold as prunes.

Varieties: Stanley is one of the most common plum varieties used to make prunes. There are also hybrids of plums crossed with other fruits. A plumcot is an equal blend of an apricot and a plum. A pluot has predominantly plum parentage.

Selecting: No matter what variety you are buying, look for firm, unblemished fruit. Some plums have a gray-white cast to their skins. It's called the bloom and is perfectly natural. It is sign that the fruit is mature and has not been overly handled. Plums have thin skin, so examine closely for cuts and bruises.

Storing: Plums will ripen at room temperature, so if you have purchased unripe fruit, place it in a paper sack at room temperature for a

few days. Check frequently because it can go from unripe to overripe very quickly. Once ripe, plums can be stored in the refrigerator for 2 or 3 days.

Sweet Corn

About: It's hard to imagine a summer picnic or barbecue without a heaping platter of butter-slathered ears of sweet corn on the center of the table. The sweetness factor is the primary reason this is a favorite vegetable with kids of all ages. Sweet corn can be boiled, steamed, roasted, or grilled or the kernels can be removed from the cob to use in many recipes. Sweet corn begins to convert its sugars to starch just moments after harvest, so pick and prepare as soon as possible. (The old adage is that you should start boiling the pot of water, then head out to the garden to pick the corn.) If you don't have a plot of corn in the backyard, you can still enjoy the sweet flavor by cooking it as soon as you buy it. How sweet is sweet corn? An ear of corn has about the same calories as an apple and less than one-fourth the sugar. It is also loaded with lutein and zeaxanthin, two phytochemicals that promote healthy vision. And sweet corn also provides a moderate amount of fiber and vitamin A. Sweet corn is generally cooked, but it can be eaten raw, right off the cob.

Varieties: Super-sweet hybrid varieties such as the award winning Honey 'N Pearl have four to ten times the sugar content of standard varieties. Most sweet corn varieties produce either yellow, white, or bicolored kernels. A farmstand favorite is Peaches & Cream.

Selecting: Look for firm, filled ears with green husks and tight rows of kernels filled out on the cob completely. The silk should also be fresh. Check for earworm caterpillars inside the husk.

Storing: It's best to use sweet corn as soon after picking as possible, but you can hold it for a few days if you place it, husk and all, in the refrigerator. (The husk helps protect the corn and keep it from drying out.) Some super-sweet hybrids will lose sweetness as time passes.

Cutting Kernels Off of the Cob

1. Shuck the corn (remove the leaves and silk).

2. Cut off the stem.

3. Set the corn on the stem end and slice off the kernels.

Swiss Chard

About: Nutritious and beautiful Swiss chard is a close relative of beets. The dark green leaves have the same sweet, earthy flavor that beets have. Swiss chard has high levels of vitamins A, K, and C and is rich in calcium and potassium. The leaves also contain two carotenoids—lutein and zeaxanthin—that research indicates can be helpful to protect eyes against vision problems and macular degeneration. Although it can be eaten raw, it's best boiled or sautéed because cooking reduces the oxalic acid in the leaves. Oxalic acid is what gives Swiss chard and beet greens a sharp flavor. Be sure to cook quickly. The longer Swiss chard is processed, the more nutrients and flavor it loses. Swiss chard leaves are dark green, although the stalks can be white, red, orange, or yellow.

Varieties: Bright Light Swiss chard has multicolor, red, and yellow stems and ribs.

Selecting: Choose leaves that are fresh and brightly colored with firm stems. Avoid those that are wilted or have holes or brown spots on the foliage.

Storing: Store unwashed Swiss chard and refrigerate in plastic bags. Stored in this manner, Swiss chard stays fresh up to 5 days.

GRAPE TOMATOES

ROMA OR PLUM TOMATOES

HEIRLOOM TOMATOES

PEAR TOMATOES

CHERRY TOMATOES

SLICING TOMATOES

Tomatillos

About: From their name you would think tomatillos are just small tomatoes, but in reality they are very different in taste and habit from tomatoes. The tomatillo plant develops lots of small greenish, berrylike fruits that are enclosed in paperlike husks. When the husk turns brown, it is the sign that the tomatillo is ripe. Their flavor is tart and lemony. A native of Mexico, tomatillos can be eaten raw, blanched, and roasted. They are the key ingredient in salsa verde and also lend their mild flavor to sauces, chili, tacos, enchiladas, and other Mexican favorites. Tomatillos are high in vitamin C and provide potassium and dietary fiber.

Varieties: Tomatillos offer several color options: green, purple, and yellow. Toma Verde—the most common variety—has green fruits that turn yellow when ready to eat.

Selecting: Select dry, firm tomatillos with tightly fitting papery husks. Avoid those that feel soft, show signs of mold, or have very loose husks.

Storing: Store tomatillos in the refrigerator in an open paper bag in your crisper drawer for up to 3 weeks.

Tomatoes

About: One of the true treats of the summer garden, a sun-ripened tomato has no equal when harvested fresh from the vine. Savor fresh from the garden and eaten raw or cook them in soups, stews, and sauces. They are also easy to preserve to enjoy during winter. You can freeze, can, and dry tomatoes to enjoy later. Packed with vitamins C, A, and K, they also contain a hefty dose of lycopene, a powerful antioxidant. Tomatoes became a staple of North American dining tables in the 1880s, their popularity coinciding with seeds becoming commercially available. By the early 20th century, more than 150 named varieties were available as breeders scrambled to develop meatier, juicer fruits.

Tomatoes are generally classified in several categories depending on use: paste or plum, cherry (salad), and beefsteak (slicing). They also come in different colors, including red, pink, purple, orange, yellow, striped, and bicolor.

Varieties: Tomatoes come in many sizes and colors. For salads, soups, or popping into your mouth for a fast snack, cherry tomatoes are ideal. Try round and red Sweet Million or small, pear-shape Yellow Pear. Roma tomatoes are the best tomatoes for making paste and sauce. Heirloom tomatoes such as Beefsteak and Brandywine are ideal for eating fresh. Called slicing tomatoes, these hefty and flavorful fruits are best served in sun-warmed slices with a drizzle of olive oil or balsamic vinegar.

You can find all sorts of exotic and colorful heirloom varieties at farmers' markets and grocery-store produce sections. Unusually colored tomatoes such as Green Zebra, a striped variety, or Ruffled Yellow, a yellow tomato ideal for stuffing, are fun to try. If you want fresh-from-the-vine tomatoes, grow Patio, a small-space tomato that excels in containers.

Selecting: Choose firm (but not hard) tomatoes that are fragrant and richly colored for their variety. They should be blemish-free, heavy for their size, and give slightly to gentle pressure.

Storing: Store tomatoes in a cool, dark place where they will last 2 to 4 days. Do not refrigerate and do not place in direct sunlight.

fall & winter

SAVOR THE SEASON'S FINALE Fall produce is the magical culmination of the growing season's warm sun and quenching rains. Sweet and tart fruits and earthy root crops take center stage. In winter, dark leafy greens and bright citrus shine.

Apples

About: The old adage "An apple a day keeps the doctor away" is based on the health benefits that are naturally packed into every apple. At about 95 calories a serving, apples are an ample source of antioxidants and fiber (each apple delivers 4 grams of fiber). To get that fiber boost, eat apples with the peels on; two-thirds of the fiber is in the peel. A recent study also links the consumption of apples to a lower risk of death from coronary heart disease and cardiovascular disease. Luckily, this wonder fruit is available everywhere and at all times of the year. However, apples are generally harvested in autumn.

Varieties: Hundreds of varieties vary from sweet to tart. Depending on your taste—whether you like sweet or tart, crisp or tender—most apples are good eaten fresh. Certain types are better than others for baking and cooking, however. Honey Crisp and Fuji are delicious raw but aren't as good for cooking. Some popular all-purpose apples include Granny Smith, Jonagold, McIntosh, Golden Delicious, Jonathon, Royal Gala, Cortland, and Braeburn.

Selecting: Look for fruit that has firm, unwrinkled skin with no soft spots or nicks. The fruit should have a fresh apple fragrance.

Storing: Apples are best stored in a cool, dark location. If you have a lot of apples, store them in a root cellar or cool basement. Storage time varies by apple variety. For smaller amounts, refrigerate apples in plastic bags for up to 2 weeks.

Peeling and Coring an Apple

1. Cut the skin off with a paring knife.

2. Cut the apple in four wedges.

3. Cut the core out of each piece. Chop or slice as called for in the recipe.

MCINTOSH

BRAEBBURN

GOLDEN DELICIOUS

JONATHAN

CORTLAND

GRANNY SMITH

Beets

About: Beets are one of the few vegetables of which all parts of the plant are edible. Prized for their sweet, earthy roots, beets also offer vitamin-packed leaves that can be boiled, sautéed, and used raw in salads. The pigments that give beet roots their color are called betalains, which function as powerful antioxidants and anti-inflammatory compounds. It is believed that nutrient-rich beets help protect against heart disease and colon cancer. Because beets contain more natural sugar than starch, they are particularly tasty when roasted in a hot oven or on the grill. Roasting concentrates the sugar rather than allowing it to leach out into the cooking water when beets are boiled. Beets can be cooked by boiling, steaming, roasting, grilling, and sautéeing. Beets are also frequently canned and pickled.

Varieties: Although beet roots are generally red, there are also flashier varieties, including yellow, white, and striped. There are many varieties of red beets, ranging in flavor from sweet to almost bitter. If you like to can beets, try Gladiator. Thin-skinned yellow or golden beets are milder in flavor than red beets. The Italian heirloom beet Chioggia has a surprising red-and-white bulls-eye in the center, which makes for beautiful slices. Related to the red beets are the white-flesh, sucrose-storing sugar beets. These are not eaten; they are processed to make white table sugar.

Selecting: Look for firm, brightly colored beets that are less than 2 inches in diameter. The smaller the beet the sweeter it is. If beets are sold with their greens attached, check that the greens are fresh and not wilted. The taproot of the beet (the long, thin root at the bottom of the beet) should still be attached to the bulb.

Storing: Both the bulblike root and the leaves of beets are usable. To store, remove the leaves from the beet about 2 inches above the bulb. Do not remove the taproot. Place the trimmed beets into plastic bags in your refrigerator for up to 10 days. The greens can be stored separately in a plastic bag for several days. Wash both the root and the leaves right before using.

Brussels Sprouts

About: At first glance, a stalk of Brussels sprouts appears more alien than edible. Hundreds of tiny cabbage-like heads (which are actually tiny buds) cling tightly to a tall, thick stalk with a few large, blue-green leaves sprouting from the top. It's a strange-looking plant. (You rarely see Brussels sprouts sold on the stalks in produce sections, although farmers' markets may sell them this way.) Yet Brussels sprouts are one of the tastiest members of the cabbage, or Brassica, family. They have a sweet, nutty flavor. In the garden their flavor actually improves after they've been exposed to an early frost. Brussels sprouts are a good source of fiber and vitamins C and A. They are also packed with antioxidants and are believed to be helpful in fighting colon and prostate cancer as well as cardiovascular disease. Although Brussels sprouts can be used in a variety of ways in the kitchen, they are at their best when roasted in olive oil and/or balsamic vinegar in a hot oven. You can grill, steam, and sauté them too. Overcooked Brussels sprouts are nutritionally inferior and emit a sulfurous smell. To help them cook evenly, trim just a tiny piece off the bottom and cut them in half.

Varieties: There are many varieties of Brussels sprouts. Jade Cross is a popular early-maturing variety. Most Brussels sprouts are green, but there are purple varieties, such as Falstaff.

Selecting: Buy firm, bright green Brussels sprouts in tight heads. If possible, buy Brussels spouts still attached to the stem. Avoid any Brussels sprouts that are yellow, soft, or beginning to open.

Storing: Store unwashed Brussels sprouts in a plastic bag in your refrigerator for 1 week to 10 days. Store on-stem sprouts in a cool place for up to 2 weeks.

RED CABBAGE
Has a hearty flavor
and contains more
vitamins and disease-
fighting chemicals
than green cabbage.

BOK CHOY Has a light,
crisp flavor and is ideal for
stir-fry recipes.

NAPA CABBAGE Also called
Chinese cabbage; its flavor is
similar to bok choy or celery;
ideal for stir-fry or spring rolls.

GREEN CABBAGE Firm,
dense heads add crunch
and rich flavor to slaws,
sauerkraut, and soups.

Cabbage

About: The workhorse of the
vegetable world, cabbage lends itself
to almost any recipe, from soups
and stews to salads and sauerkraut.
This hearty, cold-weather plant
has played an important role in
European diets since the Middle
Ages. Closely related to broccoli,
cauliflower, and Brussels sprouts,
cabbage comes in a greater variety
of shapes, sizes, and colors than
any of its cousins. Some of the
most popular types include red,
green, savoy, napa, and bok choy.
All of them contain hefty doses of
vitamins C and K, beta-carotene,
potassium, and antioxidants.

Selecting: Look for cabbage that
feels heavy for its size with a bright
color depending on type (red, green,
etc). Avoid any that show signs
of discoloration or rotting. Savoy
types have looser heads, so will feel
lighter.

Storing: Place cabbage in a plastic
bag and store in your refrigerator.
Cabbage will last 1 week to 10 days
stored in this manner. Savoy cabbage
will only store for 3 to 5 days.

Celery Root

About: This gnarly, pock-marked, pale white root is easy to pass by in the produce aisle. Yet this bulbous root of the wild celery plant has a wonderful, nutty flavor that tastes like a culinary hybrid of celery and parsley. A popular vegetable in Europe, celery root can be a substitute for potatoes in soups, stews, and other dishes. It's particularly good mashed with potatoes and garlic. Celery root contains vitamins C and K and phosphorous and is a good source of fiber. Wash the root vigorously before using. Peel off the rough exterior with a potato peeler or a paring knife until the white interior is exposed.

Selecting: The bulbous root should be firm, dense, and light brown. Avoid roots with green spots or a green cast. The root should not be slimy.

Storing: Wrap celery root loosely in plastic wrap and keep in the refrigerator for up to 2 weeks.

Citrus Fruit

About: Breakfast across America wouldn't be nearly as sweet without the jolt of sunshine provided by a glass of cold orange or grapefruit juice. The other members of the citrus clan are equally bright and charming. Lemons provide juice for summer's favorite drink, lemonade, as well as zest for pies, cookies, and other lemony baked goods. Limes are a requisite ingredient for many mixed drinks (you can't make a good margarita without one). Tiny key limes are the ingredient that differentiates key lime pie from just lime pie. Kaffir lime is used in Asian dishes. Lime's acidy juice "cooks" raw fish in ceviche. Tangerines, especially clementines, are easy to eat out of hand; they peel effortlessly and the small sections are just the right size for popping into the mouth. Grapefruits offer sweet and sour fruit in golden to ruby red colors. This oversize citrus makes delicious, healthful, and low-calorie juice. All members of the citrus family contain high levels of immune-boosting vitamin C. Most citrus fruit is consumed fresh or as juice, but it also adds a healthy zing to vinaigrettes, steamed vegetables, and meat dishes. Marmalade, a sort of citrus jam, is made with oranges and sometimes lemon or grapefruit.

Varieties: Always juicy and sometimes sweet or tart (or both), the citrus family offers lots of variety.

- **Oranges:** These sunny orbs generally fall into two categories, those used for juice, such as Valencia, and those for fresh eating, such as navel oranges.
- **Clementines:** A seedless tangerine, clementines are easy to peel and separate.
- **Lemons:** Bright yellow lemons vary in flavor. Easy-to-grow Meyer lemon is a bit milder than varieties such as Eureka.
- **Limes:** These tart fruits vary in their acidity depending on the variety. The Persian lime is one of the most common varieties and bears a slightly acidic flavor. Key limes have thinner skins and are smaller in size.
- **Tangerines:** This category includes clementines and tangelos.
- **Grapefruits:** More astringent than other citrus, these are low in calories and have a bracing, refreshing taste. Varieties include Ruby Red, Duncan, Pink, and Flame.

Selection: Look for firm, smooth-textured skin with no blemishes. The fruit should also feel heavy for its size. Avoid bruised or wrinkled skin. The skin should not be dull.

Storage: Oranges can be stored at room temperature for up to a week. Or store in the refrigerator for 2 weeks. Clementines can be stored at room temperature for up to 3 days. They will last a little longer stored in the refrigerator. Store lemons and limes for up to 1 week at room temperature. It's best, however, to place them in a tightly sealed storage bag in your refrigerator. Stored in this manner they can last several weeks. The flavor will lessen the longer you store them. Grapefruit can be stored at room temperature for up to 1 week or in the refrigerator for 2 weeks.

Peeling and Sectioning an Orange

1. Slice off the top and bottom of the orange.

2. Slice off the skin and bitter pith.

3. Holding the orange over a bowl, slide the knife between the membranes. The sections will drop into the bowl.

Collard Greens

About: A loose-leafed member of the cabbage family, collard greens are prized for their nutritious dark green, edible leaves. Collard greens are a key ingredient in many Southern recipes. In fact, Southerners often serve collard greens with black-eyed peas on New Year's Day to ensure good luck in the coming year. Because collards have a mild flavor—kind of a cross between cabbage and kale—that blends well with stronger flavors, they are often paired with salty meats such as bacon and smoked ham. Collards are known to help lower cholesterol and improve cancer protection. They are packed with vitamins K, A, and C as well as a host of nutrients such as calcium, iron, and manganese. Like other members of the cabbage family, the flavor of collards often improves during cool weather.

Varieties: There are several heirloom varieties of collards, including Morris Heading, Champion, and Georgia. In warm climates some collard varieties are winter hardy. Flavor varies from variety to variety. Collards can be raised as both a spring and a fall crop.

Selecting: Choose collards with crisp, dark green leaves. Avoid yellow or wilted collards.

Storing: Collards store longer than most other greens. Wrap unwashed leaves in a moist paper towel and place in a sealed plastic bag where

they will last up to 5 days in a crisper drawer in the refrigerator. When ready to use, wash well, giving several passes through cold water. The leaves are wavy and have a tendency to hold soil.

Cranberries

About: Native Americans were the first people to discover the culinary uses of the cranberry and shared their knowledge with the early New England settlers, who quickly incorporated this crisp and tangy berry into their own repertoire. Today, cranberry sauce is a required side dish at Thanksgiving dinners. The tart flavor, sweetened with sugar, is an ideal complement to poultry dishes such as turkey. When boiling cranberries for sauce, cook only until the berries burst. In addition to sauces, cranberries can be dried and used in salads and baked goods; they are a delicious alternative to raisins. Cranberries make excellent chutneys and can be pressed for juice. Often described as a "superfruit," cranberries contain five health-supportive phytonutrients which are thought to have anticancer and anti-inflammatory properties. They also contain vitamin C, fiber and manganese.

Varieties: Many different varieties of this American native are grown in cranberry-producing states based on what grows best in each location. Massachusetts grows mostly Early Blacks and Howes, while Wisconsin and Oregon grow mostly Stevens.

Selecting: Look for cranberries that are firm to the touch with a smooth, shiny dark red color. Avoid any that are soft, squishy, or blemished. A ripe cranberry should bounce if you drop it.

Storing: Cranberries will last up to 2 months stored in plastic bags in your refrigerator. Be sure to remove any soft or decaying berries before storing. To freeze for longer storage, place whole unopened bags of cranberries in the freezer. For bulk cranberries, wash under cold running water, then dry thoroughly on clean paper towels. Freeze in a single layer on a rimmed baking sheet, then transfer to resealable plastic bags and store in freezer.

Fennel Bulb

About: There are two kinds of fennel: herb fennel, whose ferny leaves and anise-flavor seeds are used as seasonings, and vegetable fennel, whose bulbous base is used as a vegetable. The vegetable fennel is known by several aliases: fennel bulb, Florence fennel, and finocchio. The two kinds share the same botanical name, but only Florence fennel forms the large white bulb at the base of its plant. (Florence fennel has the same type of foliage as herbal fennel but doesn't have the same type of seeds.) For fennel lovers, it's all about the bulb, which has a licorice- or aniselike flavor. In fact, it was once used to make absinthe liquor. The crisp, aromatic bulb can be prepared several ways: stewed, grilled, sautéed, stir-fried, and eaten raw. Fennel is an excellent source of potassium. It also contains vitamin A, folic acid, calcium, phosphorous, and magnesium.

Selecting: Select smooth, unblemished bulbs with bright green leaves. Avoid any bulbs that are split or those that show signs of flowering. Give the bulb a sniff: A fresh anise scent should be evident.

Storing: Use fennel as soon as possible after purchase because it tends to lose flavor over time. Fennel bulbs can be stored, fresh-looking fronds attached, for up to 5 days in a plastic bag in your refrigerator. If the fronds do not look fresh, remove before storing.

Preparing a Fennel Bulb

1. Cut off the stalk and leaves on the top of the bulb and the root end on the bottom.

2. Cut the bulb into quarters

3. Cut out the fibrous core.

Garlic

About: Fragrant and pungent garlic adds rich flavor to a variety of foods. It's so popular, in fact, that this member of the onion family often gets top billing on recipes, including garlic-mashed potatoes, garlic bread, and garlic chicken. This flavorful vegetable is actually used more like an herb and a seasoning. When roasted, garlic takes on a mild, nutty flavor and a spreadable consistency. Use hot and spicy raw garlic in salad dressings and sauces to add heat and flavor. Garlic also provides many health benefits. It has an abundance of antioxidants.

Selecting: Choose garlic heads that are firm with no soft cloves. Avoid those with nicks or blemishes. Watch for dark, powdery patches under the skin. This indicates a common mold that ruins the cloves.

Storing: Store garlic in a cool, dry location with plenty of air circulation. If you have a lot of garlic, place the cloves in mesh bags and hang from a basement or pantry ceiling. Stored properly, unpeeled garlic can last 3 months. If the cloves sprout, they are still edible, but remove the green growth before using.

Peeling the Skin from Garlic

 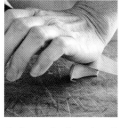 

1. Pull a clove out of the garlic head.

2. Press the flat edge of a chef's knife onto the clove.

3. Remove the papery skin.

Kale

About: The ruffly dark green or purple leaves of kale look rather humble and unassuming—just another leafy green. Yet this frilly member of the cabbage family is a powerhouse of health benefits that few other vegetables can equal. Kale is packed with vitamins A, K, and C as well as fiber, sulfur, iron, calcium, magnesium, omega fatty acids, and powerful antioxidants such as carotenoids and flavonoids. Eat fresh crisp leaves in a hearty salad topped with hard-cooked eggs and a tangy vinaigrette—it's a complete, protein-packed meal. Or enjoy roasted kale chips as a crunchy snack (so much healthier than potato chips). You can even drink your daily kale—blended into a smoothie. Like other members of the cabbage family, the flavor of kale—earthy and pleasantly bitter—improves during the cool months or after a frost.

Varieties: Most kale varieties fall into one of three main groups: curly kale, which has frilly edges; Tuscan kale (also called dinosaur kale), with oblong, bubbly surfaced leaves; and winter kale, which comes in green and purple hues.

Selecting: Look for crisp, dark green leaves with crisp edges. Small- to medium-size leaves have the most flavor. Avoid kale with wilted, slimy, or yellow leaves.

Storing: All lettuces and salad greens are delicate and highly perishable. Kale has a bit more staying power than most. Wrap and refrigerate—unwashed—for only a day or two.

Preparing Fresh Kale

1. Pull the leafy part off the rib of the leaf.

2. Discard the rib.

3. Chop the leaves into the size your recipe calls for.

Kumquats

About: Kumquats are the smallest fruits of the citrus group and are believed to be natives of China. They look like tiny oranges: They have orange skin and flesh and are the size of large olives. The most surprising thing about kumquats (unlike other citrus fruits) is that they are consumed whole, skin and all. Another surprising thing: The peel is the sweet part and the fruit is sour. Their in-the-mouth appeal is the sweet-and-sour blast you get when you bite down on one. (Although kumquats are eaten whole, it's recommended that you don't eat the seeds.) Serve fresh kumquats as you would grapes. They can be eaten alone as a snack, sliced into salads, and served with cheese. Kumquats can be cooked and used to make sweet preserves and marmalade, just like other citrus. Cook them with ginger and garlic to make a lovely chutney, a citrusy addition to savory dishes. They can also be dried, candied, and pickled.

Varieties: Kumquat varieties come in two shapes: round and oval. Oval-shape Nagami is the most common variety in the United States. One of the sweetest varieties is the round-shape Meiwa.

Selecting: Look for large, bright orange fruit that is firm to the touch. The skin should not be withered or wrinkled. If the skin shows any traces of green, it is not ripe, so avoid it.

Storing: Kumquats can be stored at room temperature for several days. Or you can store them in the refrigerator in a plastic bag for up to 2 weeks.

Mustard Greens

About: A leafy green member of the Brassica family, this spicy green can be eaten raw in salads alone or combined with other greens. Use it raw on sandwiches as a way to add flavor without calories. Although steamed or boiled mustard greens are popular, sautéeing these greens is a better way to eat them because they retain more of their nutritional value. These delicious greens may lower cholesterol and may have cancer-preventative and anti-inflammatory qualities. Mustard greens are a spring and fall crop.

Varieties: Mustard greens come in a variety of leaf types and flavors. Southern Giant Curled offers bright green curled leaves. Giant Red is a dark red-purple leaf variety. The very frilly leaves of Green Wave offer a spicy-hot flavor.

Selecting: Choose mustard greens with crisp, dark green leaves. Avoid yellow or wilted leaves.

Storing: Wrap unwashed mustard greens in a moist paper towel and place in a sealed plastic bag. They last for 3 to 4 days in the refrigerator. When ready to use, wash well, giving several passes through cold water to remove any clinging soil.

PEARL ONIONS A close relative to the leek, true pearl onions are sweeter than regular onions. They come in white, yellow, and red.

YELLOW The hot, complex taste of yellow onions makes them good for cooking. The flavor is due to high sulfur levels.

WHITE Clean, tangy white onions are ideal for eating raw or cooking.

CIPOLLINI The bulb of the grape hyacinth. A wild Italian onion, it has a flat saucer shape. The cooked taste is mild and sweet.

RED Sweet enough to eat raw, red onions come in a variety of sizes.

Onions

About: Both home cooking and haute cuisine would be far less interesting without onions. Onions are sautéed into soups and stews, caramelized with sweet butter, spooned on vegetables or meat dishes, and chopped fresh for salads and sandwiches. Onions are infamous for causing cooks to cry when the bulbs are chopped. (To avoid this, chill the onions in the refrigerator for 10 to 15 minutes [but do not store in the refrigerator] before chopping.) Different color onions offer a range of flavors. All sauté to a rich brown and sweeten when cooked. Sweet onion varieties such as Maui, Vidalia and Walla Walla contain the most natural sugar. All onions are members of the Allium family, which makes onions, scallions, leeks, and chives cousins. Onions contain antioxidants that fight cancer, lower cholesterol, and reduce blood clots.

Selecting: Choose onions that are firm and have brightly colored outer skin. Avoid onions with soft spots or bruises or those that have begun to sprout.

Storing: Store onions in a cool, dark, well-ventilated spot for up to 4 weeks (do not refrigerate). You can also stuff them into mesh bags and hang them from a basement or closet ceiling. Do not store in plastic bags. Cut onions can be stored in a sealed container for up to 1 week.

Pears

About: Pears have enjoyed a long, glamorous history, reaping rave reviews even in ancient times. In *The Odyssey,* Homer refers to the pear as a gift of the gods. Succulent and shapely, the pear was also revered for its long storage life, an important trading commodity in the ancient world. A fresh, juicy pear is a special treat, but cooked pears are equally delicious. Pears are also a low-calorie fruit (about 100 calories per medium pear), and are a good source of vitamin C and fiber.

Varieties: Pears come in a variety of colors (green, yellow, red) and shapes (from squatty to long and elegant). Varieties include Bosc, Asian, Bartlett, Anjou, Comice, Red Bartlett, and Seckel. Firm varieties, such as Bosc and Anjou, are best choices for poaching, baking, and grilling. Their dense flesh holds its shape. Softer pears, such as Yellow Bartlett, Red Bartlett, and Comice, are not good candidates for cooking because they become squishy and their flavor diminishes. Eat these varieties fresh.

Selecting: Look for pears with no bruises or cuts. Avoid fruit that is too soft because this indicates the fruit is overripe. Pears should be firm and heavy with a slight "give" to the skin if pressed. Choice pears may also have a strong, sweet aroma at room temperature.

Storing: Let pears ripen in a cool, dark place. They can also be refrigerated for several days, but do not store them in plastic bags. All pears bruise easily when ripe, so use them as soon as they are ready.

Persimmon

About: Once a favorite of Native Americans, persimmons are still found growing wild along the East Coast. The persimmons most commonly sold at the grocery store in the fall, however, are Japanese varieties—Hachiya and Fuyu (shown in the photo, right). These are grown in California and the South. These sweet fall fruits boast about half the vitamin C and one-fourth of the fiber you need each day. They also contain important antioxidants such as beta-carotene, lycopene, lutein, and vitamin A. Persimmons require very little preparation before using—just be sure they are ripe first. Simply wash in cool water and cut out the cap with a paring knife. Quarter to eat fresh or chop or puree according to recipe directions.

Varieties: Hachiya persimmons are most commonly used in baking. Acorn-shape and very soft, Hachiyas have a bitter flavor if eaten before completely ripe. Fuyu persimmons look more like a flattened tomato and can be eaten out of hand or incorporated into recipes.

Selecting: Hachiya and Fuyu persimmons are both generally available from October through February. Hachiya persimmons should have a deep solid orange color with no dark spots. Fuyu persimmons have a bright yellow-orange color and should be firm to the touch.

Storing: Both types of persimmon store best at room temperature. When ripe, they should be consumed as soon as possible. Hachiya persimmons are ready to eat when they are soft and about

to burst. Depending on their state of ripeness when you buy them, Hachiya persimmons can be stored for up to 1 week at room temperature. Fuyu persimmons will stay firm up to 3 weeks stored at room temperature. Use Fuyus as soon as they begin to soften.

Pomegranate

About: The tough, leathery skin of the pomegranate is deceiving: Inside the hard exterior you'll find a buried treasure of sweet juice and seeds. Pomegranates are an ancient tree fruit that has been cherished since biblical times. It's native to Iran and northern India and is usually about the size of an orange. Cutting open a pomegranate reveals a multitude of crimson kernels, called arils. You can eat the whole aril raw as a delicious snack or sprinkle these ruby jewels onto salads or soups. The juice from the seeds has a pleasant sweet-sour taste; pomegranate juice has become very popular recently in the United States. Grenadine syrup is thickened, sweetened pomegranate juice. Pomegranates are high in fiber, vitamin C, and potassium as well as polyphenols, a type of antioxidant that has been linked with reduced risk of heart disease and some cancers.

Varieties: There are many varieties of pomegranates. A variety called Wonderful offers large red fruits with red arils. In the United States it is the most widely consumed pomegranate. Grenada is smaller, deeper red, and less tart than the Wonderful variety.

Selecting: Look for large, heavy pomegranates with firm, smooth, shiny skin. Avoid those with wrinkled skin or with scarred spots on the skin. Small fruits have less juice, so look for large pomegranates.

Storing: Pomegranates can be placed in a storage bag and kept fresh in the refrigerator for up to 8 weeks. The seeds can also be frozen for later use. Pomegranates can be stored at room temperature for up to 1 week. Once cut, use a pomegranate within 2 to 3 days.

Removing Pomegranate Seeds

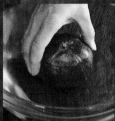

1. Cut off the top and bottom of the fruit.

2. Score the rind in four sections, taking care not to cut into the fruit.

3. Set the fruit into a bowl of water.

4. Holding the fruit underwater, break along the scores into four pieces.

5. With a slotted spoon, remove the floating skin and membrane.

6. With a strainer, remove the pomegranate seeds.

PURPLE AND BLUE Originally from South America, these colorful tubers have a nutty flavor. The flesh ranges from blue and purple to white.

ROUND WHITE These versatile potatoes have medium starch level and white flesh. A good all-purpose potato.

LONG WHITE These oval-shape potatoes have a medium starch level and thin skin. They are firm and creamy when cooked.

ROUND RED Firm, round red potatoes hold their shape when cooked, so they are ideal for roasting or for potato salad.

RUSSET Thick-skin large russet potatoes make excellent baked or mashed potatoes. White-flesh russets are high in starch.

YELLOW Yellow-flesh potatoes such as Yukon gold have a buttery flavor and creamy texture.

FINGERLING Small, narrow "finger-shape" potatoes measure 2 to 4 inches long. Varieties come in red, purple, yellow, and gold. Great for potato salads and roasting.

Potatoes

About: Probably the most important and widely distributed vegetable in the world, potatoes of various sizes, shapes, and colors continue to spread their impact on cuisines around the globe. First discovered in Peru, this versatile, nutrient-rich tuber is prized for its flavor and its ability to be fried, baked, boiled, grilled, mashed, roasted, and stir-fried. In American markets, potatoes are generally broken into different categories based on their size and the consistency of their flesh. For example, russet potatoes are prized for baking and for french fries, while sweeter, smaller potatoes such as Yukon gold are generally best used for mashed potatoes and boiled and served whole. New potatoes, available in the spring, are simply small potatoes harvested early in the growing season. Potatoes are a great source of vitamins C and B6, copper, potassium, manganese, and fiber. They also contain compounds said to lower blood pressure and improve cardiovascular function.

Selection: Choose potatoes that are firm to the touch with no soft spots or green coloration of the skin. Avoid potatoes that have started to sprout. The "eyes" of the potatoes should always be removed, because they contain toxins.

Storing: Potatoes store best in a cool, dark, well-ventilated location at a temperature between 40°F and 50°F. If you buy potatoes in plastic bags, remove them from the bag and store in an open paper sack or cardboard box. Do not wash potatoes before storing them. This will speed the process of decay. Never store potatoes in the refrigerator or freeze uncooked potatoes. If your potatoes begin to sprout, you can use them; just cut off the sprouts and use potatoes soon as possible.

Pumpkins

About: Pumpkins are the most literary member of the squash family, appearing in all sorts of poems, legends, and fairy tales. Of course, these orange orbs of autumn can also play a starring role in the kitchen. Fresh pumpkin is sweet and delicious and can be used in recipes from soup to nuts (literally, because you can eat the seeds roasted to crisp, nutty perfection). Look for pumpkin varieties developed specifically for culinary use. (To make puree from fresh pumpkin, see page 154.) Pumpkins are a good source of vitamins A, C, and E, as well as dietary fiber.

Varieties: Although all varieties of pumpkin can be eaten, some of the most delicious include Long Island Cheese, Small Sugar, Baby Bear and Baby Pam, Rouge Vif D'Etampes, New England Pie, Musque de Provence, Winter Luxury, and Autumn Crown.

Selecting: Choose pumpkins that feel heavy for their size. Small pumpkins are generally better because they have sweeter flesh. The best pumpkins will still have their stems intact and the skin will have a dull, matte finish. Shiny pumpkins indicate that they were harvested too early. Eliminate any pumpkins with soft spots or deep gashes.

Storing: Store in a cool, dry location that remains somewhere between 45°F to 60°F. Avoid moist, humid locations such as basements to discourage mold and rot. Stored in this manner, most pumpkins will last about 1 month. In the refrigerator (if you have space) pumpkins can last 3 months or

more. You can also disinfect the skin of the pumpkin to help it last longer. Mix 1 tablespoon of chlorine bleach in 1 gallon of water. Rub the bleach mixture over the entire pumpkin, then dry it completely. This should kill mold spores that might be on the pumpkin skin.

Quince

About: Looking a bit like a misshapen pear, the quince—while not seen frequently in American markets—has been around since the time of the ancient Greeks, when it was used as a ritual item in wedding ceremonies because the fruit symbolized love and happiness. Quince has a yellow skin and is rather lumpy in appearance. Because the flesh has a slightly sour flavor, it has historically been made into refreshing jams, jellies, and marmalades. Quince is high in fiber, vitamin C, and potassium, which helps reduce the risk of high blood pressure. Quinces can be prepared for use very much like apples. Quarter, then cut out the core and seeds from each piece. Peel the skin.

Varieties: Perfumed and pineapple are the two main types of quince. The pineapple quince has a somewhat pear shape, and the perfumed quince has a shape more like a football. Both turn yellow when ripe.

Selecting: Avoid soft fruit or those that have deep bruises or blotches. Because quince is generally processed into jams and jellies, light bruising on the skin is not a problem. Choose fruits that are hard and firm.

Storing: Place fruit in a plastic bag and store in the refrigerator. In this manner, quinces can last up to 2 weeks. They can also be stored at room temperature for about a week.

RUTABAGA First discovered growing wild in Sweden, this hearty root crop is often called Swede in Europe.

TURNIPS Prized for their delicious roots and vitamin-rich greens, turnips can be eaten raw, chopped and added to soups, and boiled.

PARSNIPS Close relatives to carrots, parsnips get sweeter when cooked. Add them to mashed potatoes for a little zing.

Root Vegetables

About: Root crops such as rutabagas, turnips, and parsnips get little respect from those who have never tasted these humble yet delicious vegetables. Plentiful in the produce aisles and farmers' markets during fall and winter, all three can be roasted, boiled, pureed, mashed, and used in stews and soups. They are terrific when mashed with each other (with a little cream, butter, salt, and pepper)—or with potatoes and/or carrots. Before using any of these root vegetables, scrub, peel, and trim both ends.

Selecting: Look for parsnips that measure between 5 and 10 inches long; larger parsnips will have a woody, bitter core. Choose parsnips that have an even color, firm flesh, and no soft spots or shriveled areas. Rutabagas should be smooth, unblemished, and feel heavy for their size. Avoid ones with soft spots. Smaller rutabagas (around 3 to 5 inches in diameter) are generally the sweetest. Choose turnips that feel heavy for their size, and—if possible—still have some fresh-looking green leaves attached. Small- and medium-size turnips are the sweetest.

Storing: Store parsnips as you would carrots, in a plastic bag in the vegetable drawer of your refrigerator. They can last up to 2 weeks. Rutabagas can be stored for about 2 weeks in the refrigerator or in a cool, dark, well-ventilated location. Stored at room temperature, rutabagas last about 1 week. Place turnips in a cool, dark, dry, well-ventilated area. In the refrigerator, turnips can last up to 2 weeks if you keep them loosely wrapped.

Shallots

About: The mildest member of the onion family, shallots have a rich, spicy flavor somewhere between garlic and onions. They are ideal for vinaigrettes, sauces, rice dishes, and other recipes where a milder onion flavor is preferred. To prepare, remove the flaky outer skin and chop the shallot as you would a garlic clove. The pale purple-white bulbs contain vitamin A, copper, iron, and more antioxidants per weight than onions.

Varieties: Some top varieties include Pikant, which produces large, French-style bulbs; Picador, which has reddish-brown skin with white flesh; Ambition, which is a red shallot with a long storage life; and Saffron, which has copper skin and a pale yellow interior.

Selecting: Look for shallots that are heavy and firm to the touch and have dry, papery skins. They should have no soft spots. Also avoid any that have sprouted, which indicates that they are old. Old shallots have a strong flavor that tastes more like onions.

Storing: Store in a dark, well-ventilated space, preferably hanging them in a mesh bag from the ceiling of a dry basement or garage. They can last 2 months.

Sweet Potato

About: You might be surprised to learn that the sweet potato is more closely related to the morning glory than it is to a true potato. This tropical vine develops sweet, edible tuberous roots that are yellow, orange, red, purple, or brown, depending on variety. In the supermarket the terms sweet potato and yam are often used interchangeably, but they are the roots of two different species. In North America, virtually all roots by these names are sweet potatoes. Sweet potatoes offer a wide range of culinary possibilities. They can be fried, baked, roasted, boiled, mashed, and grilled. They are also a nutritional rich food that contains vitamins A and C, fiber, and potassium, plus phytochemicals that promote eye health.

Varieties: There are orange and white-flesh varieties available. Two common orange-flesh varieties are Beauregard and Evangeline. Two common white-flesh varieties include O'Henry and Bonita.

Selecting: Look for sweet potatoes that feel firm to the touch and don't have any cracks, bruises, or soft spots. Avoid any that have been stored in the refrigerated section of your grocery store.

Storing: Do not place sweet potatoes in the refrigerator. The intense cold turns the starch in the potato into a sugar, which actually gives them an unpleasant flavor. Instead, store them in a cool, dark, well-ventilated location that remains between 50°F and 60°F. Store loosely—not in plastic bags or piled on top of one another.

BUTTERNUT This attractive squash has bright orange flesh like a pumpkin and a sweet and nutty flavor.

SPAGHETTI SQUASH When cooked, the flesh breaks into ribbons of spaghettilike strands.

DELICATA Growing to 8 or 9 inches long, Delicata has orange-yellow flesh. The seeds can be roasted.

ACORN Nutty and sweet when baked. White, golden, and striped varieties are also occasionally available.

Winter Squash

About: Unlike its relatives yellow summer squash and zucchini, winter-squash varieties develop hard outer shells that protect the flesh inside. The shells also lengthen the shelf life of winter squash, making them an ideal vegetable to store during the colder months. The flesh of winter squash can be baked, boiled, roasted, and sautéed. It can be served as a side dish by itself or featured in soups, pasta, pies, casseroles, and a host of other dishes. Winter squash have more nutrients than summer squash, with greater levels of beta-carotene.

Selecting: Select spaghetti squash that has a hard, bright yellow shell. If your fingernail can puncture the skin, it is unripe. Delicata squash should have solid, blemish-free flesh. Choose butternut squash that feel dense and heavy with no blemishes or soft spots. The color should be flat, not shiny. Look for squash that still has the stem attached. The stem helps keep the flesh moist. Select acorn squash with smooth, dry, unblemished skin. As acorn squash ages, the skin turns an orange-yellow mottled color, so select those that have as little mottling on them as possible for the sweetest, most finely textured flesh.

Storing: Most winter squash do best stored in a cool, dry location between 50°F and 60°F. They'll last several months this way. The exception is Delicata, which should be used as quickly as possible. Don't store near apples, pears, onions, or potatoes, which give off ethylene gas that will spoil squash. Once cut, wrap in plastic wrap and refrigerate for several days.

index

A

Almonds
Avocado and Blood Orange Salad with Almonds and Chili Oil, 187
Cheese and Almond Guacamole, 55
Rosemary Almond Cake with Strawberries and Mascarpone, 284
Anaheim Chicken and Mango Salad, 175
Ancho-Avocado Butter, 56

Appetizers
Baked Poppers, 194
Butternut-Sage Crostini with Ricotta and Hazelnuts, 45
Cheese and Almond Guacamole, 55
Crispy Fried Okra with Creole Remoulade, 61
Eggplant Rolls, 46
Grilled Arugula Bruschetta, 43
Lemon-Avocado Dip, 56
Lemon-Garlic Olives, 156
Mixed Peppers in a Gougère Crust, 42
Quince Skillet Tart with Savory Prosciutto Pastry, 315
Roasted Cherry Tomato Pizza Poppers, 40
Stuffed Endive with Pear, Walnut, and Goat Cheese, 49
Stuffed Mushrooms with Lemon-Pea Hummus, 52
Toasted Baguette with Herbed Butter and Radish, 39
Wasabi-Vinegar Kale Chips, 53
White Bean Dip with Garlic and Cilantro, 156
Zucchini Fritters with Caper Mayonnaise, 58

Apples, 368
Buttered Apples in Maple Syrup Custard, 319
Chicken and Lentils in Apple-Curry Sauce, 102
Muenster, Cabbage, and Apple Sandwiches, 220
peeling and coring, 368
Puffed Apple Pancake, 16
Rhubarb Hand Tarts, 288
Short Ribs with Port Wine, Apples, Figs, and Onions, 75
Zucchini, Cheddar, and Sage Crust Pizza with Chicken and Apples, 235

Apricots, 346
Apricot Upside-Down Cakes, 299
Golden Grilled Chicken Thighs with Apricots, 109
skinning and pitting, 346
Spinach Salad with Indian-Spiced Chickpeas, Apricots, and Onions, 183
Aromatic Beef Stew with Butternut Squash, 73
Aromatic Pork with Baby Zucchini and Figs, 90

Artichokes, 330
Artichokes with Tarragon Drizzle, 259
Herbed Spinach Torte in Potato Crust, 35
Pork Roast with Baby Artichokes, 79
preparing, 330

Arugula, 339
Eggplant Rolls, 46
Grilled Arugula Bruschetta, 43
Mint-Herb Pesto, 292
Orecchiette in Creamed Corn with Wilted Tomatoes and Arugula, 160
Roasted Sweets and Greens, 281
Spring Greens Soup, 203
Strawberry and Arugula Salad with Manchego Fricos, 245

Asparagus, 332
English Muffin and Asparagus Bake, 30
Grilled Asparagus Soup with Chili Croutons, 213
Ham and Asparagus-Stuffed Chicken, 96
Ham-Asparagus and Cheese Strata, 31
Morel and Asparagus Crispy Pizzas, 236
preparing, 332
Prosciutto-Wrapped Asparagus Panini, 226

Avocados, 349
Ancho-Avocado Butter, 56
Avocado, Prosciutto, and Egg Sandwiches, 222
Avocado and Blood Orange Salad with Almonds and Chili Oil, 187
Avocado BLT Sandwiches, 56
Avocado-Cilantro Cream, 56
Avocado-Grapefruit Salad, 56
Cheese and Almond Guacamole, 55
Chilled Avocado Soup, 56

Fresh Sweet Corn Soup with Toasted Corn Guacamole, 202
halving and seeding, 349
Lemon-Avocado Dip, 56
Quinoa-Nectarine Gazpacho with Crispy-Spice Tortilla Strips, 212
Succotash Salad with Buttermilk Avocado Dressing, 177

B

Bacon
Avocado BLT Sandwiches, 56
Frizzled Egg Spinach Salad, 190
Grilled Bacon, Cheddar, and Hot Pepper Jelly Sandwich, 194
Grilled Bacon-Wrapped Turkey Tenderloins with Glazed Plums, 112
Watercress and Radish Salad on Smoky White Bean-Bacon Croutons, 171
Wild Rice-Stuffed Acorn Squash with Cranberries, Pecans, and Pancetta, 144
Baked Poppers, 194
Balsamic Vinegar, Melon in, 24
Barley-Sweet Corn Chopped Salad with Lime-Cumin Vinaigrette, 185
Basil, 357
Basil-Infused Olive Oil, 110
Basil Lemonade, 110
Basil Mayonnaise, 110
Basil Pesto, 43
Basil-Tomato Grilled Cheese, 110
Creamy Basil-Scrambled Eggs, 110
Mint-Herb Pesto, 292
Penne with Five Herbs and Ricotta Salata, 159
Pesto Vinaigrette, 110
Thai Gremolata, 209
Warm Glass Noodles with Edamame, Basil, and Chicken, 100
Beans, 349. *See also* Green beans; Lentils
Barley-Sweet Corn Chopped Salad with Lime-Cumin Vinaigrette, 185
Braised Collards and Black-Eyed Peas with Andouille Sausage and Couscous, 91
Chilled Cucumber-Chickpea Soup, 208

Green and Wax Beans with Shiitake
 Mushrooms, 267
Heirloom Tomato Salad with Grilled
 Tuna and Cannellini, 179
Roasted Vegetables and
 Chickpeas, 272
Skillet Pork Chops with Butter Beans,
 Peas, and Charred Scallions, 84
Smashed Peas and Edamame with
 Ricotta Toasts, 256
Spinach Salad with Indian-Spiced
 Chickpeas, Apricots, and Onions, 183
Succotash Salad with Buttermilk
 Avocado Dressing, 177
Warm Glass Noodles with Edamame,
 Basil, and Chicken, 100
Watercress and Radish Salad
 on Smokey White Bean-Bacon
 Croutons, 171
White Bean and Roasted Garlic Soup
 with Escarole, 205
White Bean Dip with Garlic and
 Cilantro, 156
Beef
Aromatic Beef Stew with Butternut
 Squash, 73
Burger with Pickled Beets and Fried
 Egg, 217
Flank Steak and Plum Salad with
 Creamy Chimichurri Dressing, 167
Quick Paprika Steaks with Tomato
 Gravy, 72
Shepherd's Pie with Root Vegetable
 Mash, 94
Short Ribs with Port Wine, Apples,
 Figs, and Onions, 75
Soy-Glazed Flank Steak with
 Blistered Green Beans, 70
Beet greens, 339
Omelet with Wilted Greens, 28
Roasted Beet Salad with Shredded
 Greens, Golden Raisins, and Pine
 Nuts, 197
Beets, 371
Beets and Greens Salad, 252
Burger with Pickled Beets and Fried
 Egg, 217
Pepper-Poached Salmon and Herbed
 Beets, 118
Roasted Beet Salad with Shredded
 Greens, Golden Raisins, and Pine
 Nuts, 197
Shoestring Sweet Potatoes and
 Beets, 273
Berries, 351. See also specific berries
Biscuits, Blueberry Cream, with
 Blueberry Sauce, 17
Blackberries, 351
Blackberry-Lemon Ice Cream
 Sandwiches with Pistachio
 Shortbread, 311

Five-Berry Compote with Mint and
 Orange Infusion, 296
Roast Duck with Blackberry-Orange
 Sauce, 114
Salted Caramel Flan with
 Blackberries, 303
Blueberries, 351
Blueberry-Brie Quesadillas, 250
Blueberry Cream Biscuits with
 Blueberry Sauce, 17
Blueberry Fizz, 250
Blueberry Fool, 250
Chilled Peach Soup with Blueberries
 and Prosecco, 295
Corn and Blueberry Salad, 249
Five-Berry Compote with Mint and
 Orange Infusion, 296
Greens with Blueberries, Red Onion,
 and Goat Cheese Croutons, 250
Lemon-Ricotta Blueberry Pancakes
 with Black and Blue Sauce, 15
Savory Blueberry Sauce, 250
Sweet Blueberry Sauce, 250
Bok choy, 372
Parchment-Baked Halibut with Asian
 Vegetables, 124
Bourbon-Soaked Pork Chops with
 Squash Hash, 89
Boysenberries, 351
Braised Brussels Sprouts with Crispy
 Shallots, 278
Braised Cabbage with Spicy
 Croutons, 276
Braised Collards and Black-Eyed Peas
 with Andouille Sausage and
 Couscous, 91
Brandied Cherries, Brownies with, 306
Breads
Blueberry Cream Biscuits with
 Blueberry Sauce, 17
Butternut-Sage Crostini with Ricotta
 and Hazelnuts, 45
Cheesy Roasted Garlic-Topped
 Flatbread, 156
Cranberry-Buttermilk Muffins, 20
Grilled Arugula Bruschetta, 43
Grilled Panzanella, 191
Homemade Croutons, 191
Real Garlic Bread, 156
Roasted Tomato-Bread Toss, 268
Smashed Peas and Edamame with
 Ricotta Toasts, 256
Spiced Butternut Squash Loaf with
 Mascarpone Icing, 324
stale, uses for, 191
Toasted Baguette with Herbed Butter
 and Radish, 39
Watercress and Radish Salad
 on Smokey White Bean-Bacon
 Croutons, 171

Broccoli, 332
Pappardelle with Spring Vegetables
 and Hazelnuts, 163
Turkey Lettuce Wraps with Spicy
 Peanut Sauce, 113
Broccoli raab, 333
Broccoli Raab, Garlic, and Mushroom
 Pizza with Golden Raisins, 237
Broiled Grapefruit Tart, 326
Brownies with Brandied Cherries, 306
Bruschetta, Grilled Arugula, 43
Brussels sprouts, 371
Braised Brussels Sprouts with Crispy
 Shallots, 278
Brussels Sprouts, Walnuts, Fennel,
 and Pearl Onions Over Bacon-Swiss
 Polenta, 148
Brussels Sprouts and Noodle Stir-Fry
 with Cilantro and Almonds, 155
Brussels Sprouts and Spicy Fennel
 Sausage Pizza, 232
Burger with Pickled Beets and Fried
 Egg, 217
Butter, Ancho-Avocado, 56
Buttered Apples in Maple Syrup
 Custard, 319
Butter Lettuce and Spring Pea Salad
 with Mustard Vinaigrette, 242
Butternut-Sage Crostini with Ricotta
 and Hazelnuts, 45
Butternut Squash Soup with Thai
 Gremolata, 209

C

Cabbage, 372
Braised Cabbage with Spicy
 Croutons, 276
Fish Tacos with Cabbage and Chile
 Pepper Slaw, 127
Muenster, Cabbage, and Apple
 Sandwiches, 220
Parchment-Baked Halibut with Asian
 Vegetables, 124
Quinoa and Caraway-Crusted Tuna
 Steaks with Wilted Red Cabbage
 Slaw, 134
roasting, 271
Seared Scallops with Meyer Lemon
 Beurre Blanc and Warm Savoy-
 Citrus Slaw, 137
Cakes
Apricot Upside-Down Cakes, 299
Hummingbird Cupcakes, 291
Rosemary Almond Cake with
 Strawberries and Mascarpone, 284
Wine-Country Cake with Roasted
 Grapes, 309
Cantaloupe, 358, 359
Caramelized Pork with Melon, 77

Cantaloupe (*continued*)
Chilled Melon Soup with Grilled
Shrimp, 24
Creamy Melon Cooler, 24
Melon and Champagne Slush, 24
Melon in Balsamic Vinegar, 24
Melon-Radish Salad with Creamy
Watercress Dressing, 24
Melon Ribbons and Raspberries with
Anise Syrup, 21
Melon with Smoked Salmon, 24
Carambola-Mango Compote with
Sugared Biscuits and Orange
Cream, 289
Caramel Flan, Salted, with
Blackberries, 303
Caramelized Carrots, 279
Caramelized Onion, Thyme, and Winter
Squash Pizza, 227
Caramelized Pork with Melon, 77
Carrots, 335
Caramelized Carrots, 279
French Garden Soup with Cheese
Croutons, 201
Kohlrabi-Carrot Salad with Dill
Vinaigrette, 246
Pappardelle with Spring Vegetables
and Hazelnuts, 163
Pork Roast with Baby Artichokes, 79
Pulled Pork with Kohlrabi-Carrot
Slaw, 83
Roasted Indian Cauliflower, 271
Roasted Vegetables and
Chickpeas, 272
Sweet Curry Carrots with Chive
Yogurt, 263
Cashews and Cherries, Honey-Soaked
Quinoa Salad with, 184
Cauliflower, 335
Cauliflower, Roasted Indian, 271
Celery root, 373
Celery Root Soup with Parsley Oil, 206
Shepherd's Pie with Root Vegetable
Mash, 94
Char-Grilled Spring Onion, Pineapple,
and Shrimp Pizzas, 231
Cheese. *See also* Mozzarella; Ricotta
cheese
Baked Poppers, 194
Basil-Tomato Grilled Cheese, 110
Blueberry-Brie Quesadillas, 250
Broccoli Raab, Garlic, and Mushroom
Pizza with Golden Raisins, 237
Brussels Sprouts and Spicy Fennel
Sausage Pizza, 232
Caramelized Onion, Thyme, and
Winter Squash Pizza, 227
categories of, 159
Char-Grilled Spring Onion,
Pineapple, and Shrimp Pizzas, 231
Cheese and Almond Guacamole, 55

Cheesy Roasted Garlic-Topped
Flatbread, 156
choosing, 159
Chorizo, Kale, and Sweet Potato
Galette, 228
Farro-Stuffed Peppers, 143
Feta-Mint Rice, 292
French Garden Soup with Cheese
Croutons, 201
Greens with Blueberries, Red Onion,
and Goat Cheese Croutons, 250
Grilled Bacon, Cheddar, and Hot
Pepper Jelly Sandwich, 194
Ham-Asparagus and Cheese
Strata, 31
Kale-Goat Cheese Frittata, 27
Marshmallow-Cream Cheese
Frosting, 291
Mixed Peppers in a Gougère Crust, 42
Morel and Asparagus Crispy
Pizzas, 236
Muenster, Cabbage, and Apple
Sandwiches, 220
Penne with Five Herbs and Ricotta
Salata, 159
Prosciutto-Wrapped Asparagus
Panini, 226
Pumpkin Parmesan Risotto, 154
Roasted Garlic-Parmesan Polenta, 156
Rosemary Almond Cake with
Strawberries and Mascarpone, 284
Rustic Phyllo Pie with Mustard
Greens and Fresh Goat Cheese, 140
Smoky Grilled Vegetable Torte, 151
Spiced Butternut Squash Loaf with
Mascarpone Icing, 324
Spinach-Tarragon Supper Soufflé, 147
Strawberry and Arugula Salad with
Manchego Fricos, 245
Stuffed Endive with Pear, Walnut,
and Goat Cheese, 49
Zucchini, Cheddar, and Sage Crust
Pizza with Chicken and Apples, 235
Cherries, 352
Brownies with Brandied Cherries, 306
Five-Berry Compote with Mint and
Orange Infusion, 296
Honey-Soaked Quinoa Salad with
Cherries and Cashews, 184
Pan-Seared Chicken with Cherry-
Tarragon Sauce, 104
removing pit from, 352
Sherried Cherry Crisp, 300
Chicken
Anaheim Chicken and Mango
Salad, 175
Chicken and Lentils in Apple-Curry
Sauce, 102
Chicken with Melted Tomatoes, 103
Golden Grilled Chicken Thighs with
Apricots, 109

Ham and Asparagus-Stuffed
Chicken, 96
Honey Roast Chicken with Spring
Peas and Shallots, 105
Lemony Grilled Chicken with Green
Bean-Potato Salad, 178
Lime and Tangerine Chicken
Breasts, 98
Lime-Marinated Chicken and
Tomatillo-Corn Salsa, 108
Pan-Seared Chicken with Cherry-
Tarragon Sauce, 104
Roast Chicken with Fiery Lemon
Glaze, 99
Roast Chicken with Roasted Treviso,
Potatoes, Rosemary, and
Oranges, 107
Smoked Chicken Salad with Broken
Raspberry Vinaigrette, 174
Succotash Salad with Buttermilk
Avocado Dressing, 177
Warm Glass Noodles with Edamame,
Basil, and Chicken, 100
Zucchini, Cheddar, and Sage Crust
Pizza with Chicken and Apples, 235
Chicken Sausage, Fingerling Potato, and
Leek Packets, 97
Chile peppers, 363
Anaheim Chicken and Mango
Salad, 175
Ancho-Avocado Butter, 56
Baked Poppers, 194
Cheese and Almond Guacamole, 55
Fire-Roasted Jalapeño Pesto, 194
Fresh Sweet Corn Soup with Toasted
Corn Guacamole, 202
Green Curry-Style Vegetables with
Sizzled Tofu and Rice, 138
Grilled Bacon, Cheddar, and Hot
Pepper Jelly Sandwich, 194
Hot Chile Mayonnaise, 194
Hot Pepper Jelly, 194
Jalapeño Marinade, 194
Potato Salad with Caramelized
Onions and Roasted Chile
Vinaigrette, 248
preparing, 363
Stuffed Poblano Chiles with Chorizo
Gravy, 87
varieties and heat levels, 55
Chilled Avocado Soup, 56
Chilled Cucumber-Chickpea Soup, 208
Chilled Melon Soup with Grilled
Shrimp, 24
Chilled Peach Soup with Blueberries
and Prosecco, 295
Chives
Roasted Radishes with Chive
Vinaigrette, 262
Sweet Curry Carrots with Chive
Yogurt, 263

Chocolate
  Brownies with Brandied Cherries, 306
Chorizo, Kale, and Sweet Potato
  Galette, 228
Cilantro, 357
  Avocado-Cilantro Cream, 56
  Brussels Sprouts and Noodle Stir-Fry
    with Cilantro and Almonds, 155
  culinary ideas for, 155
  White Bean Dip with Garlic and
    Cilantro, 156
Citrus, 374. *See also specific types*
  Citrus Salad, 255
  peels, cooking with, 255
  varieties of, 374
Classic Mint Julep, 292
Clementines, 374
  Citrus Salad, 255
  Shrimp with Peppered Citrus
    Fruits, 135
Coconut
  Citrus Salad, 255
  Hummingbird Cupcakes, 291
Collard greens, 375
  Collards, Braised, and Black-Eyed
    Peas with Andouille Sausage and
    Couscous, 91
Community gardens, 305
Community supported agriculture
  (CSA), 265
Cooperatives, joining, 281
Coriander
  cooking with, 155
  Coriander-Paprika Spice Rub, 208
Corn, 365
  Barley-Sweet Corn Chopped Salad
    with Lime-Cumin Vinaigrette, 185
  Corn and Blueberry Salad, 249
  cutting kernels off the cob, 365
  Farro-Stuffed Peppers, 143
  Fresh Sweet Corn Soup with Toasted
    Corn Guacamole, 202
  Grilled Romaine Salad with Tomato
    and Corn Tumble, 193
  Lime-Marinated Chicken and
    Tomatillo-Corn Salsa, 108
  Orecchiette in Creamed Corn with
    Wilted Tomatoes and Arugula, 160
  Stuffed Poblano Chiles with Chorizo
    Gravy, 87
  Succotash Salad with Buttermilk
    Avocado Dressing, 177
Cornmeal
  Crispy Fried Okra with Creole
    Remoulade, 61
  Lemon-Ricotta Blueberry Pancakes
    with Black and Blue Sauce, 15
  Polenta with Eggs and Zucchini, 26
  Roasted Garlic-Parmesan Polenta, 156

Couscous
  Braised Collards and Black-Eyed
    Peas with Andouille Sausage and
    Couscous, 91
  Moroccan Lamb Chops with
    Couscous and Minted Kumquats, 93
Cranberries, 375
  Cranberry-Buttermilk Muffins, 20
  Wild Rice-Stuffed Acorn Squash
    with Cranberries, Pecans, and
    Pancetta, 144
Creamy Basil-Scrambled Eggs, 110
Creamy Melon Cooler, 24
Crepes with Strawberries and Lemony
  Crème Fraîche, 12
Crispy Fried Okra with Creole
  Remoulade, 61
Crostini, Butternut-Sage, with Ricotta
  and Hazelnuts, 45
Croutons, Homemade, 191
Cucumbers, 352
  Chilled Cucumber-Chickpea
    Soup, 208
  Cucumber Sangria, 65
  Grilled Panzanella, 191
  Quick Pickled Cucumber Salad, 218
Cupcakes, Hummingbird, 291

D

Desserts. *See also* Cakes
  Blackberry-Lemon Ice Cream
    Sandwiches with Pistachio
    Shortbread, 311
  Blueberry Fool, 250
  Broiled Grapefruit Tart, 326
  Brownies with Brandied Cherries, 306
  Buttered Apples in Maple Syrup
    Custard, 319
  Chilled Peach Soup with Blueberries
    and Prosecco, 295
  Five-Berry Compote with Mint and
    Orange Infusion, 296
  Lemon Shortcake with Plums, 312
  Lemon-Vanilla Tart, 325
  Mango-Carambola Compote with
    Sugared Biscuits and Orange
    Cream, 289
  Melon in Balsamic Vinegar, 24
  Meringue with Seared Pineapple, 308
  Panna Cotta with Peaches in Lime
    Syrup, 304
  Pumpkin and Sweet Potato Pie with
    Toasted Marshmallows, 322
  Quince Skillet Tart with Savory
    Prosciutto Pastry, 315
  Rhubarb Hand Tarts, 288
  Roasted Peach Pies with Butterscotch
    Sauce, 294
  Salted Caramel Flan with
    Blackberries, 303

Sherried Cherry Crisp, 300
Spiced Butternut Squash Loaf with
  Mascarpone Icing, 324
Stirred Custard with Fresh Figs and
  Sherry-Caramel Sauce, 321
Strawberry Pavlova with Mint, 287
Watermelon Granita, 305
White Wine-Poached Pears with
  Vanilla Crème Fraîche, 318
Dill, 357
  Grilled Zucchini Salad with
    Mozzarella and Dill, 188
  Kohlrabi-Carrot Salad with Dill
    Vinaigrette, 246
Dips and spreads
  Ancho-Avocado Butter, 56
  Basil Mayonnaise, 110
  Cheese and Almond Guacamole, 55
  Hot Chile Mayonnaise, 194
  Lemon-Avocado Dip, 56
  Quick Lemon Aïoli, 214
  Smashed Peas and Edamame with
    Ricotta Toasts, 256
  Toasted Corn Guacamole, 202
  White Bean Dip with Garlic and
    Cilantro, 156
Drinks
  Basil Lemonade, 110
  Blueberry Fizz, 250
  Citrus Cider, 255
  Classic Mint Julep, 292
  Creamy Melon Cooler, 24
  Cucumber Sangria, 65
  Dry Martini, 67
  Electric Lemonade, 67
  Ginger Peach Margaritas, 62
  Lemon-Lime Mint Iced Tea, 214
  Lemon Milkshake, 214
  Limoncello, 214
  Margarita, 67
  Melon and Champagne Slush, 24
  Peach-Mint Green Tea, 292
  Tom Collins, 67
  Watermelon Martinis, 66
Duck, Roast, with Blackberry-Orange
  Sauce, 114

E

Eggplant, 354
  Eggplant Rolls, 46
  Roasted Vegetable and Fresh
    Mozzarella Panini, 224
  Smoky Grilled Vegetable Torte, 151
Eggs
  Avocado, Prosciutto, and Egg
    Sandwiches, 222
  Burger with Pickled Beets and Fried
    Egg, 217
  buying, 27
  Creamy Basil-Scrambled Eggs, 110

English Muffin and Asparagus Bake, 30
Frizzled Egg Spinach Salad, 190
Ham-Asparagus and Cheese Strata, 31
Kale-Goat Cheese Frittata, 27
Omelet with Wilted Greens, 28
Polenta with Eggs and Zucchini, 26
Spicy Poached Eggs in Tomato
Sauce, 33
Spinach-Tarragon Supper Soufflé, 147
Electric Lemonade, 67
Endive, 339
stuffed, additional ideas for, 49
Stuffed Endive with Pear, Walnut,
and Goat Cheese, 49
English Muffin and Asparagus Bake, 30
Escarole, 339
Escarole, White Bean and Roasted
Garlic Soup with, 205

F

Farmers' markets, 295
Farro-Stuffed Peppers, 143
Fennel, 376
Brussels Sprouts, Walnuts, Fennel,
and Pearl Onions over Bacon-Swiss
Polenta, 148
Grilled Trout with Fennel and
Citrus, 130
preparing, 376
Seared Halibut with Fennel Puree
and Olive, Hazelnut, and Parsley
Gremolata, 126
Feta-Mint Rice, 292
Figs, 354
Aromatic Pork with Baby Zucchini
and Figs, 90
Short Ribs with Port Wine, Apples,
Figs, and Onions, 75
Stirred Custard with Fresh Figs and
Sherry-Caramel Sauce, 321
Fire-Roasted Jalapeño Pesto, 194
Fish. *See also* Salmon
buying and storing, 131
Fish Tacos with Cabbage and Chile
Pepper Slaw, 127
Grilled Halibut and Leeks with
Mustard Vinaigrette, 122
Grilled Trout with Fennel and
Citrus, 130
Heirloom Tomato Salad with Grilled
Tuna and Cannellini, 179
Parchment-Baked Halibut with Asian
Vegetables, 124
Quinoa and Caraway-Crusted Tuna
Steaks with Wilted Red Cabbage
Slaw, 134
Seared Halibut with Fennel Puree
and Olive, Hazelnut, and Parsley
Gremolata, 126

Seared Tuna with Grapefruit-Orange
Relish, 131
Swordfish with Pickled Onion, Olive,
and Orange Salsa, 129
testing for doneness, 131
Five-Berry Compote with Mint and
Orange Infusion, 296
Flan, Salted Caramel, with
Blackberries, 303
Flank Steak and Plum Salad with
Creamy Chimichurri Dressing, 167
French Garden Soup with Cheese
Croutons, 201
French Green Beans with Shallot
Butter, 266
French Toast, Savory, 191
Fresh Sweet Corn Soup with Toasted
Corn Guacamole, 202
Fresh Tomato Pizza with Oregano and
Mozzarella, 239
Frittata, Kale-Goat Cheese, 27
Fritters, Zucchini, with Caper
Mayonnaise, 58
Frizzled Egg Spinach Salad, 190
Frosting, Marshmallow-Cream
Cheese, 291
Fruits. *See also* Citrus; *specific fruits*
berries, about, 351
heirloom, about, 239

G

Galette, Chorizo, Kale, and Sweet
Potato, 228
Garlic, 376
Cheesy Roasted Garlic-Topped
Flatbread, 156
Garlic Soup, 156
Lemon-Garlic Olives, 156
Market-Stand Pasta Salad with Garlic
and Shallot Dressing, 168
peeling skin from, 376
Real Garlic Bread, 156
Roasted Garlic-Parmesan Polenta, 156
White Bean and Roasted Garlic Soup
with Escarole, 205
White Bean Dip with Garlic and
Cilantro, 156
Ginger-Green Tea Waffles with Summer
Peach Sauce, 19
Ginger Peach Margaritas, 62
Golden Grilled Chicken Thighs with
Apricots, 109
Grains. *See also* Cornmeal; Polenta; Rice
Barley-Sweet Corn Chopped Salad
with Lime-Cumin Vinaigrette, 185
Farro-Stuffed Peppers, 143
Honey-Soaked Quinoa Salad with
Cherries and Cashews, 184

Quinoa and Caraway-Crusted Tuna
Steaks with Wilted Red Cabbage
Slaw, 134
Quinoa-Nectarine Gazpacho with
Crispy-Spice Tortilla Strips, 212
Granita, Watermelon, 305
Grapefruit, 374
Avocado-Grapefruit Salad, 56
Broiled Grapefruit Tart, 326
Citrus Salad, 255
Seared Scallops with Meyer Lemon
Beurre Blanc and Warm Savoy-
Citrus Slaw, 137
Seared Tuna with Grapefruit-Orange
Relish, 131
Shrimp with Peppered Citrus
Fruits, 135
Grapes, 355
Grapes, Roasted, Wine-Country Cake
with, 309
Green beans, 348, 349
French Garden Soup with Cheese
Croutons, 201
French Green Beans with Shallot
Butter, 266
Frizzled Egg Spinach Salad, 190
Green and Wax Beans with Shiitake
Mushrooms, 267
Lemony Grilled Chicken with Green
Bean-Potato Salad, 178
Minted French Green Beans, 292
roasting, 271
Soy-Glazed Flank Steak with
Blistered Green Beans, 70
Green Curry-Style Vegetables with
Sizzled Tofu and Rice, 138
Greens. *See also specific types*
Avocado-Grapefruit Salad, 56
Beets and Greens Salad, 252
Greens with Blueberries, Red Onion,
and Goat Cheese Croutons, 250
Persimmon, Blood Orange, and
Pomegranate Salad, 253
salad, types of, 338–39
Smoked Chicken Salad with Broken
Raspberry Vinaigrette, 174
Warm Salad with Lamb Chops and
Mediterranean Dressing, 172
Gremolata
about, 209
Seared Halibut with Fennel Puree
and Olive, Hazelnut, and Parsley
Gremolata, 126
Thai Gremolata, 209
variations on, 209
Grilled Arugula Bruschetta, 43
Grilled Asparagus Soup with Chili
Croutons, 213
Grilled Bacon, Cheddar, and Hot Pepper
Jelly Sandwich, 194

Grilled Bacon-Wrapped Turkey
  Tenderloins with Glazed Plums, 112
Grilled Halibut and Leeks with Mustard
  Vinaigrette, 122
Grilled Panzanella, 191
Grilled Romaine Salad with Tomato and
  Corn Tumble, 193
Grilled Salmon and Oyster
  Mushrooms, 119
Grilled Trout with Fennel and Citrus, 130
Grilled Zucchini Salad with Mozzarella
  and Dill, 188

H

Halibut
  Grilled Halibut and Leeks with
    Mustard Vinaigrette, 122
  Parchment-Baked Halibut with Asian
    Vegetables, 124
  Seared Halibut with Fennel Puree
    and Olive, Hazelnut, and Parsley
    Gremolata, 126
Ham
  Avocado, Prosciutto, and Egg
    Sandwiches, 222
  Ham and Asparagus-Stuffed
    Chicken, 96
  Ham-Asparagus and Cheese Strata, 31
  Prosciutto-Wrapped Asparagus
    Panini, 226
  Savory Prosciutto Pastry, 315
Hazelnuts
  Butternut-Sage Crostini with Ricotta
    and Hazelnuts, 45
  Roasted Sweets and Greens, 281
Heirloom fruits and vegetables, 239
Heirloom Tomato Salad with Grilled
  Tuna and Cannellini, 179
Herbs, 356. *See also specific types*
  Herbed Chanterelle Risotto with
    Thyme Browned Butter, 152
  Herbed Spinach Torte in Potato
    Crust, 35
  Penne with Five Herbs and Ricotta
    Salata, 159
  Toasted Baguette with Herbed Butter
    and Radish, 39
  varieties of, 356–357
Honey, 249
  Honey Roast Chicken with Spring
    Peas and Shallots, 105
  Honey-Soaked Quinoa Salad with
    Cherries and Cashews, 184
  varieties of, 249
Honeydew, 358, 359
  Cucumber Sangria, 65
  Melon Ribbons and Raspberries with
    Anise Syrup, 21
Hot Chile Mayonnaise, 194
Hot Pepper Jelly, 194

Hummingbird Cupcakes, 291
Hummus, Lemon-Pea, Stuffed
  Mushrooms with, 52

I-K

Ice cream
  Blackberry-Lemon Ice Cream
    Sandwiches with Pistachio
    Shortbread, 311
  Lemon Milkshake, 214
Jalapeño Marinade, 194
Jelly, Hot Pepper, 194
Kale, 377
  Chorizo, Kale, and Sweet Potato
    Galette, 228
  Kale-Goat Cheese Frittata, 27
  Omelet with Wilted Greens, 28
  preparing, 377
  Wasabi-Vinegar Kale Chips, 53
Kohlrabi, 336
  Kohlrabi-Carrot Salad with Dill
    Vinaigrette, 246
  Pulled Pork with Kohlrabi-Carrot
    Slaw, 83
Kumquats, 378
  Kumquats, Minted, and Couscous,
    Moroccan Lamb Chops with, 93

L

Lamb
  Lamb Meatballs on Flatbread with
    Quick Pickled Cucumber Salad, 218
  Moroccan Lamb Chops with
    Couscous and Minted Kumquats, 93
  Shepherd's Pie with Root Vegetable
    Mash, 94
  Warm Salad with Lamb Chops and
    Mediterranean Dressing, 172
Leeks, 336
  Chicken Sausage, Fingerling Potato,
    and Leek Packets, 97
  Grilled Halibut and Leeks with
    Mustard Vinaigrette, 122
  Pappardelle with Spring Vegetables
    and Hazelnuts, 163
  trimming and cleaning, 336
Lemons, 374
  Basil Lemonade, 110
  Electric Lemonade, 67
  Lemon-Avocado Dip, 56
  Lemon-Garlic Olives, 156
  Lemon-Lime Mint Iced Tea, 214
  Lemon Milkshake, 214
  Lemon-Ricotta Blueberry Pancakes
    with Black and Blue Sauce, 15
  Lemon Shortcake with Plums, 312
  Lemon-Tarragon Peas, 265
  Lemon-Vanilla Tart, 325
  Lemon Vinaigrette, 214

Lemony Grilled Chicken with Green
    Bean-Potato Salad, 178
  Limoncello, 214
  Preserved Lemons, 214
  Quick Lemon Aïoli, 214
  Roast Chicken with Fiery Lemon
    Glaze, 99
  Seared Scallops with Meyer Lemon
    Beurre Blanc and Warm Savoy-
    Citrus Slaw, 137
Lentils
  Chicken and Lentils in Apple-Curry
    Sauce, 102
  Rosemary Salmon over Roasted Root
    Vegetables and Lentils, 121
Lettuce
  Anaheim Chicken and Mango
    Salad, 175
  Avocado BLT Sandwiches, 56
  Barley-Sweet Corn Chopped Salad
    with Lime-Cumin Vinaigrette, 185
  Butter Lettuce and Spring Pea Salad
    with Mustard Vinaigrette, 242
  Citrus Salad, 255
  Flank Steak Plum Salad with Creamy
    Chimichurri Dressing, 167
  Grilled Romaine Salad with Tomato
    and Corn Tumble, 193
  Honey-Soaked Quinoa Salad with
    Cherries and Cashews, 184
  Turkey Lettuce Wraps with Spicy
    Peanut Sauce, 113
  types of, 338–39
  Warm Salad with Lamb Chops and
    Mediterranean Dressing, 172
Limes, 374
  Barley-Sweet Corn Chopped Salad
    with Lime-Cumin Vinaigrette, 185
  Cucumber Sangria, 65
  Ginger Peach Margaritas, 62
  Lemon-Lime Mint Iced Tea, 214
  Lime and Tangerine Chicken
    Breasts, 98
  Lime-Marinated Chicken and
    Tomatillo-Corn Salsa, 108
  Watermelon Martinis, 66
Limoncello, 214

M

Mangoes, 358
  Anaheim Chicken and Mango
    Salad, 175
  dicing, 358
  Mango-Carambola Compote with
    Sugared Biscuits and Orange
    Cream, 289
Maple Syrup Custard, Buttered Apples
  in, 319
Margaritas, Ginger Peach, 62
Marinade, Jalapeño, 194

Marjoram, 357
Market-Stand Pasta Salad with Garlic
   and Shallot Dressing, 168
Marshmallow-Cream Cheese
   Frosting, 291
Marshmallows, Toasted, Pumpkin and
   Sweet Potato Pie with, 322
Martinis, Watermelon, 66
Mayonnaise
   Basil Mayonnaise, 110
   Hot Chile Mayonnaise, 194
Meat. *See* Beef; Lamb; Pork
Meatballs, Lamb, on Flatbread with
   Quick Pickled Cucumber Salad, 218
Melon, 358. *See also specific types*
   Melon in Balsamic Vinegar, 24
   Melon-Radish Salad with Creamy
      Watercress Dressing, 24
   Melon Ribbons and Raspberries with
      Anise Syrup, 21
   Melon with Smoked Salmon, 24
   varieties of, 358
Meringue
   Meringue with Seared Pineapple, 308
   Strawberry Pavlova with Mint, 287
Mint, 356
   Classic Mint Julep, 292
   Cucumber Sangria, 65
   Electric Lemonade, 67
   Feta-Mint Rice, 292
   Lemon-Lime Mint Iced Tea, 214
   Minted French Green Beans, 292
   Mint-Herb Pesto, 292
   Mint Yogurt Sauce, 292
   Peach-Mint Green Tea, 292
   Strawberry Pavlova with Mint, 287
Mixed Peppers in a Gougère Crust, 42
Morel and Asparagus Crispy Pizzas, 236
Moroccan Lamb Chops with Couscous
   and Minted Kumquats, 93
Mozzarella
   Eggplant Rolls, 46
   English Muffin and Asparagus Bake, 30
   Fresh Tomato Pizza with Oregano
      and Mozzarella, 239
   Grilled Arugula Bruschetta, 43
   Grilled Zucchini Salad with
      Mozzarella and Dill, 188
   Roasted Cherry Tomato Pizza
      Poppers, 40
   Roasted Vegetable and Fresh
      Mozzarella Panini, 224
   Rustic Swiss Chard and Mozzarella
      Tart, 139
Muenster, Cabbage, and Apple
   Sandwiches, 220
Muffins, Cranberry-Buttermilk, 20
Mushrooms, 340
   Broccoli Raab, Garlic, and Mushroom
      Pizza with Golden Raisins, 237
   Frizzled Egg Spinach Salad, 190

Green and Wax Beans with Shiitake
   Mushrooms, 267
Grilled Salmon and Oyster
   Mushrooms, 119
Herbed Chanterelle Risotto with
   Thyme Browned Butter, 152
Herbed Spinach Torte in Potato
   Crust, 35
Morel and Asparagus Crispy
   Pizzas, 236
Smoky Grilled Vegetable Torte, 151
Spring Greens Soup, 203
Stuffed Mushrooms with Lemon-Pea
   Hummus, 52
Mustard greens, 378
Mustard Greens and Fresh Goat
   Cheese, Rustic Phyllo Pie with, 140
Mustard-Rubbed Pork Loin with
   Rhubarb Sauce, 81

Nectarines, 361
Nectarine-Quinoa Gazpacho with
   Crispy-Spice Tortilla Strips, 212
Noodles, Warm Glass, with Edamame,
   Basil, and Chicken, 100
Nuts
   Avocado and Blood Orange Salad
      with Almonds and Chili Oil, 187
   Blackberry-Lemon Ice Cream
      Sandwiches with Pistachio
      Shortbread, 311
   Brussels Sprouts, Walnuts, Fennel,
      and Pearl Onions over Bacon-Swiss
      Polenta, 148
   Butternut-Sage Crostini with Ricotta
      and Hazelnuts, 45
   Cheese and Almond Guacamole, 55
   Honey-Soaked Quinoa Salad with
      Cherries and Cashews, 184
   Roasted Sweets and Greens, 281
   Rosemary Almond Cake with
      Strawberries and Mascarpone, 284
   Spicy Peanut Sauce, 113
   Stuffed Endive with Pear, Walnut,
      and Goat Cheese, 49
   Thai Gremolata, 209
   Wild Rice-Stuffed Acorn Squash
      with Cranberries, Pecans, and
      Pancetta, 144
   Wine-Country Cake with Roasted
      Grapes, 309

Oils
   Basil-Infused Olive Oil, 110
   for dressings, 187
Okra, 361

Okra, Crispy Fried, with Creole
   Remoulade, 61
Olives
   Lemon-Garlic Olives, 156
   Roasted Tomato-Bread Toss, 268
   Seared Halibut with Fennel Puree
      and Olive, Hazelnut, and Parsley
      Gremolata, 35
   Swordfish with Pickled Onion, Olive,
      and Orange Salsa, 129
   Zucchini, Cheddar, and Sage Crust
      Pizza with Chicken and Apples, 235
Omelet with Wilted Greens, 28
Onions, 379
   Brussels Sprouts, Walnuts, Fennel,
      and Pearl Onions over Bacon-Swiss
      Polenta, 148
   Caramelized Onion, Thyme, and
      Winter Squash Pizza, 227
   Char-Grilled Spring Onion,
      Pineapple, and Shrimp Pizzas, 231
   Potato Salad with Caramelized
      Onions and Roasted Chile
      Vinaigrette, 248
   roasting, 271
   Short Ribs with Port Wine, Apples,
      Figs, and Onions, 75
   Swordfish with Pickled Onion, Olive,
      and Orange Salsa, 129
Oranges, 374
   Avocado and Blood Orange Salad
      with Almonds and Chili Oil, 187
   Citrus Salad, 255
   Grilled Trout with Fennel and
      Citrus, 130
   peeling and sectioning, 374
   Persimmon, Blood Orange, and
      Pomegranate Salad, 253
   Roast Chicken with Roasted
      Treviso, Potatoes, Rosemary,
      and Oranges, 107
   Roast Duck with Blackberry-Orange
      Sauce, 114
   Seared Scallops with Meyer Lemon
      Beurre Blanc and Warm Savoy-
      Citrus Slaw, 137
   Seared Tuna with Grapefruit-Orange
      Relish, 131
   Swordfish with Pickled Onion, Olive,
      and Orange Salsa, 129
Orecchiette in Creamed Corn with
   Wilted Tomatoes and Arugula, 160
Oregano, 357
Organic food, defined, 39

Pancakes
   Lemon-Ricotta Blueberry Pancakes
      with Black and Blue Sauce, 15
   Puffed Apple Pancake, 16

Pancetta, Cranberries, and Pecans, Wild Rice-Stuffed Acorn Squash with, 144
Panna Cotta with Peaches in Lime Syrup, 304
Pan-Seared Chicken with Cherry-Tarragon Sauce, 104
Panzanella, Grilled, 191
Pappadams, Toasted, 183
Pappardelle with Spring Vegetables and Hazelnuts, 163
Parchment-Baked Halibut with Asian Vegetables, 124
Parsley, 356
Parsley Oil, Celery Root Soup with, 206
Parsnips, 385
Pasta. *See also* Couscous
  Brussels Sprouts and Noodle Stir-Fry with Cilantro and Almonds, 155
  Market-Stand Pasta Salad with Garlic and Shallot Dressing, 168
  Orecchiette in Creamed Corn with Wilted Tomatoes and Arugula, 160
  Pappardelle with Spring Vegetables and Hazelnuts, 163
  Penne with Five Herbs and Ricotta Salata, 159
  Warm Glass Noodles with Edamame, Basil, and Chicken, 100
Pastry dough
  Olive Oil Galette Dough, 228
  Savory Prosciutto Pastry, 315
  Savory Tart Pastry, 139
  Tart Pastry, 325
Pavlova, Strawberry, with Mint, 287
Peaches, 362
  Chilled Peach Soup with Blueberries and Prosecco, 295
  Ginger-Green Tea Waffles with Summer Peach Sauce, 19
  Ginger Peach Margaritas, 62
  Panna Cotta with Peaches in Lime Syrup, 304
  Peach-Mint Green Tea, 292
  Peachy Po-Boy, 221
  peeling and pitting, 362
  Roasted Peach Pies with Butterscotch Sauce, 294
Peanuts and peanut butter
  Spicy Peanut Sauce, 113
  Thai Gremolata, 209
Pears, 380
  Roast Pork Loin with Pears, Thyme, and Shallots, 82
  Stuffed Endive with Pear, Walnut, and Goat Cheese, 49
  White Wine-Poached Pears with Vanilla Crème Fraîche, 318
Peas
  Butter Lettuce and Spring Pea Salad with Mustard Vinaigrette, 242
  English, about, 340

French Garden Soup with Cheese Croutons, 201
Honey Roast Chicken with Spring Peas and Shallots, 105
Lemon-Tarragon Peas, 265
Pappardelle with Spring Vegetables and Hazelnuts, 163
Skillet Pork Chops with Butter Beans, Peas, and Charred Scallions, 84
Smashed Peas and Edamame with Ricotta Toasts, 256
snow and sugar snap, about, 345
Stuffed Mushrooms with Lemon-Pea Hummus, 52
Pecans
  Wild Rice-Stuffed Acorn Squash with Cranberries, Pecans, and Pancetta, 144
  Wine-Country Cake with Roasted Grapes, 309
Penne with Five Herbs and Ricotta Salata, 159
Peppercorns
  Pepper Poached Salmon and Herbed Beets, 118
  seasoning with, 275
  Shrimp with Peppered Citrus Fruits, 135
Peppers, 362. *See also* Chile peppers
  Farro-Stuffed Peppers, 143
  Grilled Panzanella, 191
  Hot Pepper Jelly, 194
  Mixed Peppers in a Gougère Crust, 42
  Parchment-Baked Halibut with Asian Vegetables, 124
  Roasted Vegetable and Fresh Mozzarella Panini, 224
  Smoky Grilled Vegetable Torte, 151
Persimmons, 380
  Persimmon, Blood Orange, and Pomegranate Salad, 253
Pesto
  Basil Pesto, 43
  Caramelized Onion, Thyme, Winter Squash, and Pesto Pizza, 227
  Dried Tomato Pesto, 224
  Fire-Roasted Jalapeño Pesto, 194
  Mint-Herb Pesto, 292
  origins of, 43
  Pesto Vinaigrette, 110
  variation on, 43
Pies
  Pumpkin and Sweet Potato Pie with Toasted Marshmallows, 322
  Roasted Peach Pies with Butterscotch Sauce, 294
  Rustic Phyllo Pie with Mustard Greens and Fresh Goat Cheese, 140
Pineapple, 364
  Char-Grilled Spring Onion, Pineapple, and Shrimp Pizzas, 231

cutting and coring, 364
Green Curry-Style Vegetables with Sizzled Tofu and Rice, 138
Hummingbird Cupcakes, 291
Meringue with Seared Pineapple, 308
Pistachio Shortbread, Blackberry-Lemon Ice Cream Sandwiches with, 311
Pizza Dough, 237
Pizzas
  Broccoli Raab, Garlic, and Mushroom Pizza with Golden Raisins, 237
  Brussels Sprouts and Spicy Fennel Sausage Pizza, 232
  Caramelized Onion, Thyme, and Winter Squash Pizza, 227
  Caramelized Onion, Thyme, Winter Squash, and Pesto Pizza, 227
  Char-Grilled Spring Onion, Pineapple, and Shrimp Pizzas, 231
  Fresh Tomato Pizza with Oregano and Mozzarella, 239
  Morel and Asparagus Crispy Pizzas, 236
  Roasted Cherry Tomato Pizza Poppers, 40
  Zucchini, Cheddar, and Sage Crust Pizza with Chicken and Apples, 235
Plums, 364
  Flank Steak and Plum Salad with Creamy Chimichurri Dressing, 167
  Grilled Bacon-Wrapped Turkey Tenderloins with Glazed Plums, 112
  Lemon Shortcake with Plums, 312
Polenta
  Brussels Sprouts, Walnuts, Fennel, and Pearl Onions over Bacon-Swiss Polenta, 148
  Polenta with Eggs and Zucchini, 26
  Roasted Garlic-Parmesan Polenta, 156
  Smoky Grilled Vegetable Torte, 151
Pomegranate, 381
  Pomegranate, Persimmon, and Blood Orange Salad, 253
Pork. *See also* Bacon; Ham; Sausages
  Aromatic Pork with Baby Zucchini and Figs, 90
  Bourbon-Soaked Pork Chops with Squash Hash, 89
  Brussels Sprouts and Spicy Fennel Sausage Pizza, 232
  Caramelized Pork with Melon, 77
  Mustard-Rubbed Pork Loin with Rhubarb Sauce, 81
  Pork Roast with Baby Artichokes, 79
  Pulled Pork with Kohlrabi-Carrot Slaw, 83
  Roast Pork Loin with Pears, Thyme, and Shallots, 82
  Skillet Pork Chops with Butter Beans, Peas, and Charred Scallions, 84

Potatoes, 383. *See also* Sweet potatoes
Celery Root Soup with Parsley Oil, 206
Chicken Sausage, Fingerling Potato, and Leek Packets, 97
Frizzled Egg Spinach Salad, 190
Herbed Spinach Torte in Potato Crust, 35
Lemony Grilled Chicken with Green Bean-Potato Salad, 178
Pork Roast with Baby Artichokes, 79
Potato Salad with Caramelized Onions and Roasted Chile Vinaigrette, 248
Roast Chicken with Roasted Treviso, Potatoes, Rosemary, and Oranges, 107
Roasted Vegetables and Chickpeas, 272
Skillet Salt-Roasted Potatoes, 275
Spring Greens Soup, 203
varieties of, 382–83
Zucchini Fritters with Caper Mayonnaise, 58
Poultry. *See* Chicken; Duck; Turkey
Preserved Lemons, 214
Prosciutto
Avocado, Prosciutto, and Egg Sandwiches, 222
Prosciutto-Wrapped Asparagus Panini, 226
Savory Prosciutto Pastry, 315
Puffed Apple Pancake, 16
Pulled Pork with Kohlrabi-Carrot Slaw, 83
Pumpkin, 384
Pumpkin and Sweet Potato Pie with Toasted Marshmallows, 322
Pumpkin Parmesan Risotto, 154

Quesadillas, Blueberry-Brie, 250
Quick Lemon Aïoli, 214
Quick Paprika Steaks with Tomato Gravy, 72
Quince, 384
Quince Skillet Tart with Savory Prosciutto Pastry, 315
Quinoa
Honey-Soaked Quinoa Salad with Cherries and Cashews, 184
Quinoa and Caraway-Crusted Tuna Steaks with Wilted Red Cabbage Slaw, 134
Quinoa-Nectarine Gazpacho with Crispy-Spice Tortilla Strips, 212

Radicchio, 339
Roast Chicken with Roasted Treviso, Potatoes, Rosemary, and Oranges, 107
Warm Salad with Lamb Chops and Mediterranean Dressing, 172
Radishes, 343
Melon-Radish Salad with Creamy Watercress Dressing, 24
Roasted Radishes with Chive Vinaigrette, 262
Toasted Baguette with Herbed Butter and Radish, 39
Watercress and Radish Salad on Smoky White Bean-Bacon Croutons, 171
Raisins
Broccoli Raab, Garlic, and Mushroom Pizza with Golden Raisins, 237
Moroccan Lamb Chops with Couscous and Minted Kumquats, 93
Roasted Beet Salad with Shredded Greens, Golden Raisins, and Pine Nuts, 197
Raspberries, 351
Five-Berry Compote with Mint and Orange Infusion, 296
Melon Ribbons and Raspberries with Anise Syrup, 21
Smoked Chicken Salad with Broken Raspberry Vinaigrette, 174
Real Garlic Bread, 156
Rhubarb, 343
Mustard-Rubbed Pork Loin with Rhubarb Sauce, 81
preparing, 343
Rhubarb Barbecue Sauce, 83
Rhubarb Hand Tarts, 288
Rice
Feta-Mint Rice, 292
Green Curry-Style Vegetables with Sizzled Tofu and Rice, 138
Herbed Chanterelle Risotto with Thyme Browned Butter, 152
Herbed Wild Rice, 129
Pumpkin Parmesan Risotto, 154
Wild Rice-Stuffed Acorn Squash with Cranberries, Pecans, and Pancetta, 144
Ricotta cheese
Broccoli Raab, Garlic, and Mushroom Pizza with Golden Raisins, 237
Butternut-Sage Crostini with Ricotta and Hazelnuts, 45
Herbed Spinach Torte in Potato Crust, 35
Lemon-Ricotta Blueberry Pancakes with Black and Blue Sauce, 15

Smashed Peas and Edamame with Ricotta Toasts, 256
Risotto
Herbed Chanterelle Risotto with Thyme Browned Butter, 152
Pumpkin Parmesan Risotto, 154
Roast Chicken with Fiery Lemon Glaze, 99
Roast Chicken with Roasted Treviso, Potatoes, Rosemary, and Oranges, 107
Roast Duck with Blackberry-Orange Sauce, 114
Roasted Beet Salad with Shredded Greens, Golden Raisins, and Pine Nuts, 197
Roasted Cherry Tomato Pizza Poppers, 40
Roasted Garlic-Parmesan Polenta, 156
Roasted Indian Cauliflower, 271
Roasted Peach Pies with Butterscotch Sauce, 294
Roasted Radishes with Chive Vinaigrette, 262
Roasted Sweets and Greens, 281
Roasted Tomato-Bread Toss, 268
Roasted Vegetable and Fresh Mozzarella Panini, 224
Roasted Vegetables and Chickpeas, 272
Roast Pork Loin with Pears, Thyme, and Shallots, 82
Rosemary, 357
Rosemary Almond Cake with Strawberries and Mascarpone, 284
Rosemary Salmon over Roasted Root Vegetables and Lentils, 121
Rustic Phyllo Pie with Mustard Greens and Fresh Goat Cheese, 140
Rustic Swiss Chard and Mozzarella Tart, 139
Rutabagas, 385

Sage, 356
Salad dressings. *See also specific salad recipes*
Lemon Vinaigrette, 214
oils and vinegars for, 187
Pesto Vinaigrette, 110
Salads. *See also* Slaws
Anaheim Chicken and Mango Salad, 175
Avocado and Blood Orange Salad with Almonds and Chili Oil, 187
Avocado-Grapefruit Salad, 56
Barley-Sweet Corn Chopped Salad with Lime-Cumin Vinaigrette, 185
Beets and Greens Salad, 252
Butter Lettuce and Spring Pea Salad with Mustard Vinaigrette, 242
Citrus Salad, 255

Corn and Blueberry Salad, 249
Flank Steak and Plum Salad with
    Creamy Chimichurri Dressing, 167
Frizzled Egg Spinach Salad, 190
Greens with Blueberries, Red Onion,
    and Goat Cheese Croutons, 250
Grilled Panzanella, 191
Grilled Romaine Salad with Tomato
    and Corn Tumble, 193
Grilled Zucchini Salad with
    Mozzarella and Dill, 188
Heirloom Tomato Salad with Grilled
    Tuna and Cannellini, 179
Honey-Soaked Quinoa Salad with
    Cherries and Cashews, 184
Kohlrabi-Carrot Salad with Dill
    Vinaigrette, 246
Lemony Grilled Chicken with Green
    Bean-Potato Salad, 178
Market-Stand Pasta Salad with Garlic
    and Shallot Dressing, 168
Melon-Radish Salad with Creamy
    Watercress Dressing, 24
Persimmon, Blood Orange, and
    Pomegranate Salad, 253
Potato Salad with Caramelized
    Onions and Roasted Chile
    Vinaigrette, 248
Quick Pickled Cucumber Salad, 218
Roasted Beet Salad with Shredded
    Greens, Golden Raisins, and Pine
    Nuts, 197
Smoked Chicken Salad with Broken
    Raspberry Vinaigrette, 174
Spinach Salad with Indian-Spiced
    Chickpeas, Apricots, and
    Onions, 183
Strawberry and Arugula Salad with
    Manchego Fricos, 245
Succotash Salad with Buttermilk
    Avocado Dressing, 177
Warm Salad with Lamb Chops and
    Mediterranean Dressing, 172
Watercress and Radish Salad
    on Smoky White Bean-Bacon
    Croutons, 171
Salmon
Grilled Salmon and Oyster
    Mushrooms, 119
Melon with Smoked Salmon, 24
Pepper-Poached Salmon and Herbed
    Beets, 118
Rosemary Salmon over Roasted Root
    Vegetables and Lentils, 121
Salt, seasoning with, 275
Salted Caramel Flan with
    Blackberries, 303
Sandwiches
Avocado, Prosciutto, and Egg
    Sandwiches, 222
Avocado BLT Sandwiches, 56

Basil-Tomato Grilled Cheese, 110
Grilled Bacon, Cheddar, and Hot
    Pepper Jelly Sandwich, 194
Lamb Meatballs on Flatbread with
    Quick Pickled Cucumber Salad, 218
Muenster, Cabbage, and Apple
    Sandwiches, 220
Peachy Po-Boy, 221
Prosciutto-Wrapped Asparagus
    Panini, 226
Pulled Pork with Kohlrabi-Carrot
    Slaw, 83
Roasted Vegetable and Fresh
    Mozzarella Panini, 224
Sangria, Cucumber, 65
Sauces. *See also* Pesto
Avocado-Cilantro Cream, 56
Mint Yogurt Sauce, 292
Rhubarb Barbecue Sauce, 83
Savory Blueberry Sauce, 250
Sweet Blueberry Sauce, 250
Sausages. *See also* Chicken Sausage
Braised Collards and Black-Eyed
    Peas with Andouille Sausage and
    Couscous, 91
Brussels Sprouts and Spicy Fennel
    Sausage Pizza, 232
Chorizo, Kale, and Sweet Potato
    Galette, 228
Market-Stand Pasta Salad with Garlic
    and Shallot Dressing, 168
Stuffed Poblano Chiles with Chorizo
    Gravy, 87
Savory Blueberry Sauce, 250
Scallions, 344
Scallions, Charred, Butter Beans, and
    Peas, Skillet Pork Chops with, 84
Scallops, Seared, with Meyer Lemon
    Beurre Blanc and Warm Savory-Citrus
    Slaw, 137
Seafood. *See* Fish; Scallops; Shrimp
Seared Halibut with Fennel Puree
    and Olive, Hazelnut, and Parsley
    Gremolata, 126
Seared Scallops with Meyer Lemon
    Beurre Blanc and Warm Savory-Citrus
    Slaw, 137
Seared Tuna with Grapefruit-Orange
    Relish, 131
Shallots, 386
Braised Brussels Sprouts with Crispy
    Shallots, 278
French Green Beans with Shallot
    Butter, 266
Honey Roast Chicken with Spring
    Peas and Shallots, 105
Market-Stand Pasta Salad with Garlic
    and Shallot Dressing, 168
Roast Pork Loin with Pears, Thyme,
    and Shallots, 82

Shellfish. *See* Scallops; Shrimp
Shepherd's Pie with Root Vegetable
    Mash, 94
Sherried Cherry Crisp, 300
Sherry-Caramel Sauce and Fresh Figs,
    Stirred Custard with, 321
Shoestring Sweet Potatoes and Beets, 273
Shortbread, Pistachio, Blackberry-Lemon
    Ice Cream Sandwiches with, 311
Shortcake, Lemon, with Plums, 312
Short Ribs with Port Wine, Apples, Figs,
    and Onions, 75
Shrimp
Char-Grilled Spring Onion,
    Pineapple, and Shrimp Pizzas, 231
Chilled Cucumber-Chickpea Soup,
    208
Chilled Melon Soup with Grilled
    Shrimp, 24
Peachy Po-Boy, 221
Shrimp with Peppered Citrus
    Fruits, 135
Skillet Pork Chops with Butter Beans,
    Peas, and Charred Scallions, 84
Skillet Salt-Roasted Potatoes, 275
Slaws
Quinoa and Caraway-Crusted Tuna
    Steaks with Wilted Red Cabbage
    Slaw, 134
Seared Scallops with Meyer Lemon,
    Beurre Blanc, and Warm Savory-
    Citrus Slaw, 137
Smashed Peas and Edamame with
    Ricotta Toasts, 256
Smoked Chicken Salad with Broken
    Raspberry Vinaigrette, 174
Smoky Grilled Vegetable Torte, 151
Soufflé, Spinach-Tarragon Supper, 147
Soups
Butternut Squash Soup with Thai
    Gremolata, 209
Celery Root Soup with Parsley Oil, 206
Chilled Avocado Soup, 56
Chilled Cucumber-Chickpea
    Soup, 208
Chilled Melon Soup with Grilled
    Shrimp, 24
Chilled Peach Soup with Blueberries
    and Prosecco, 295
French Garden Soup with Cheese
    Croutons, 201
Fresh Sweet Corn Soup with Toasted
    Corn Guacamole, 202
Garlic Soup, 156
Grilled Asparagus Soup with Chili
    Croutons, 213
Quinoa-Nectarine Gazpacho with
    Crispy-Spice Tortilla Strips, 212
Spring Greens Soup, 203
White Bean and Roasted Garlic Soup
    with Escarole, 205

Soy-Glazed Flank Steak with Blistered Green Beans, 70
Spiced Butternut Squash Loaf with Mascarpone Icing, 324
Spice Rub, Coriander-Paprika, 208
Spicy Poached Eggs in Tomato Sauce, 33
Spinach, 344
    Chicken and Lentils in Apple-Curry Sauce, 102
    Frizzled Egg Spinach Salad, 190
    Herbed Spinach Torte in Potato Crust, 35
    Omelet with Wilted Greens, 28
    Skillet Pork Chops with Butter Beans, Peas, and Charred Scallions, 84
    Spinach Salad with Indian-Spiced Chickpeas, Apricots, and Onions, 183
    Spinach-Tarragon Supper Soufflé, 147
    Spring Greens Soup, 203
Spring Greens Soup, 203
Squash. *See also* Pumpkin; Zucchini
    Aromatic Beef Stew with Butternut Squash, 73
    Bourbon-Soaked Pork Chops with Squash Hash, 89
    Butternut-Sage Crostini with Ricotta and Hazelnuts, 45
    Butternut Squash Soup with Thai Gremolata, 209
    Caramelized Onion, Thyme, and Winter Squash Pizza, 227
    Farro-Stuffed Peppers, 143
    Smoky Grilled Vegetable Torte, 151
    Spiced Butternut Squash Loaf with Mascarpone Icing, 324
    summer, about, 360
    Wild Rice-Stuffed Acorn Squash with Cranberries, Pecans, and Pancetta, 144
    winter, about, 387
Stew, Aromatic Beef, with Butternut Squash, 73
Stirred Custard with Fresh Figs and Sherry-Caramel Sauce, 321
Strata, Ham-Asparagus and Cheese, 31
Strawberries, 351
    Crepes with Strawberries and Lemony Crème Fraîche, 12
    Five-Berry Compote with Mint and Orange Infusion, 296
    Rosemary Almond Cake with Strawberries and Mascarpone, 284
    Strawberry and Arugula Salad with Manchego Fricos, 245
    Strawberry Pavlova with Mint, 287
Stuffed Endive with Pear, Walnut, and Goat Cheese, 49
Stuffed Mushrooms with Lemon-Pea Hummus, 52

Stuffed Poblano Chiles with Chorizo Gravy, 87
Succotash Salad with Buttermilk Avocado Dressing, 177
Sweet Blueberry Sauce, 250
Sweet Curry Carrots with Chive Yogurt, 263
Sweet potatoes, 386
    Chorizo, Kale, and Sweet Potato Galette, 228
    Hummingbird Cupcakes, 291
    Pumpkin and Sweet Potato Pie with Toasted Marshmallows, 322
    Roasted Sweets and Greens, 281
    Roasted Vegetables and Chickpeas, 272
    Shepherd's Pie with Root Vegetable Mash, 94
    Shoestring Sweet Potatoes and Beets, 273
Swiss chard, 365
    Omelet with Wilted Greens, 28
    Rustic Phyllo Pie with Mustard Greens and Fresh Goat Cheese, 140
    Rustic Swiss Chard and Mozzarella Tart, 139
Swordfish with Pickled Onion, Olive, and Orange Salsa, 129

T

Tacos, Fish, with Cabbage and Chile Pepper Slaw, 127
Tangerines, 374
    Lime and Tangerine Chicken Breasts, 98
    Shrimp with Peppered Citrus Fruits, 135
Tarragon, 357
Tarts
    Broiled Grapefruit Tart, 326
    Chorizo, Kale, and Sweet Potato Galette, 228
    Lemon-Vanilla Tart, 325
    Mixed Peppers in a Gougère Crust, 42
    Quince Skillet Tart with Savory Prosciutto Pastry, 315
    Rhubarb Hand Tarts, 288
    Rustic Swiss Chard and Mozzarella Tart, 139
Tea
    Lemon-Lime Mint Iced Tea, 214
    Peach-Mint Green Tea, 292
Thyme, 356
Toasted Baguette with Herbed Butter and Radish, 39
Tofu, Sizzled, and Rice, Green Curry-Style Vegetables with, 138

Tomatillos, 367
    Fish Tacos with Cabbage and Chile Pepper Slaw, 127
    Lime-Marinated Chicken and Tomatillo-Corn Salsa, 108
Tomatoes, 367
    Avocado BLT Sandwiches, 56
    Basil-Tomato Grilled Cheese, 110
    Chicken with Melted Tomatoes, 103
    Dried Tomato Pesto, 224
    Eggplant Rolls, 46
    Fresh Tomato Pizza with Oregano and Mozzarella, 239
    Grilled Panzanella, 191
    Grilled Romaine Salad with Tomato and Corn Tumble, 193
    Heirloom Tomato Salad with Grilled Tuna and Cannellini, 179
    Orecchiette in Creamed Corn with Wilted Tomatoes and Arugula, 160
    Pappardelle with Spring Vegetables and Hazelnuts, 163
    Penne with Five Herbs and Ricotta Salata, 159
    Quick Paprika Steaks with Tomato Gravy, 72
    Roasted Cherry Tomato Pizza Poppers, 40
    Roasted Tomato-Bread Toss, 268
    roasting, 271
    Spicy Poached Eggs in Tomato Sauce, 33
Tortes
    Herbed Spinach Torte in Potato Crust, 35
    Smoky Grilled Vegetable Torte, 151
Tortillas
    Anaheim Chicken and Mango Salad, 175
    Blueberry-Brie Quesadillas, 250
    Crispy-Spice Tortilla Strips, 212
    Fish Tacos with Cabbage and Chile Pepper Slaw, 127
Trout, Grilled, with Fennel and Citrus, 130
Tuna
    Heirloom Tomato Salad with Grilled Tuna and Cannellini, 179
    Quinoa and Caraway-Crusted Tuna Steaks with Wilted Red Cabbage Slaw, 134
    Seared Tuna with Grapefruit-Orange Relish, 131
Turkey
    Grilled Bacon-Wrapped Turkey Tenderloins with Glazed Plums, 112
    Turkey Lettuce Wraps with Spicy Peanut Sauce, 113
Turnips, 385

V

Vegetables. *See also specific vegetables*
cool-weather crops, 279
Green Curry-Style Vegetables with
Sizzled Tofu and Rice, 138
heirloom, about, 239
Market-Stand Pasta Salad with Garlic
and Shallot Dressing, 168
roasting, 271
root, about, 385
root, types of, 385
Rosemary Salmon over Roasted Root
Vegetables and Lentils, 121
Vinaigrettes
Lemon Vinaigrette, 214
oils and vinegars for, 187
Pesto Vinaigrette, 110
Vinegar, for salad dressings, 187
Vinegar, Citrus, 255

W

Waffles, Ginger-Green Tea, with
Summer Peach Sauce, 19
Walnuts
Brussels Sprouts, Walnuts, Fennel,
and Pearl Onions Over Bacon-Swiss
Polenta, 148
Stuffed Endive with Pear, Walnut,
and Goat Cheese, 49
Warm Glass Noodles with Edamame,
Basil, and Chicken, 100

Warm Salad with Lamb Chops and
Mediterranean Dressing, 172
Wasabi-Vinegar Kale Chips, 53
Watercress, 339
Grilled Salmon and Oyster
Mushrooms, 119
Grilled Trout with Fennel and
Citrus, 130
Melon-Radish Salad with Creamy
Watercress Dressing, 24
Pepper Poached Salmon and Herbed
Beets, 118
Watercress and Radish Salad
on Smokey White Bean-Bacon
Croutons, 171
Watermelon, 358, 359
Watermelon Granita, 305
Watermelon Martinis, 66
White Bean and Roasted Garlic Soup
with Escarole, 205
White Bean Dip with Garlic and
Cilantro, 156
White Wine-Poached Pears with Vanilla
Crème Fraîche, 318
Wild rice
Herbed Wild Rice, 129
Wild Rice-Stuffed Acorn Squash
with Cranberries, Pecans, and
Pancetta, 144
Wine-Country Cake with Roasted
Grapes, 309

Y-Z

Yogurt
Creamy Melon Cooler, 24
Mint Yogurt Sauce, 292
Sweet Curry Carrots with Chive
Yogurt, 263
Zucchini, 360
Aromatic Pork with Baby Zucchini
and Figs, 90
Grilled Zucchini Salad with
Mozzarella and Dill, 188
Polenta with Eggs and Zucchini, 26
Roasted Vegetable and Fresh
Mozzarella Panini, 224
Smoky Grilled Vegetable Torte, 151
Stuffed Poblano Chiles with Chorizo
Gravy, 87
Zucchini, Cheddar, and Sage Crust
Pizza with Chicken and Apples, 235
Zucchini Fritters with Caper
Mayonnaise, 58

product differences

Most of the ingredients called for in the recipes in this book are available in most countries. However, some are known by different names. Here are some common American ingredients and their possible counterparts:

- Sugar (white) is granulated, fine granulated, or castor sugar.
- Powdered sugar is icing sugar.
- All-purpose flour is enriched, bleached or unbleached white household flour. When self-rising flour is used in place of all-purpose flour in a recipe that calls for leavening, omit the leavening agent (baking soda or baking powder) and salt.
- Light-color corn syrup is golden syrup.
- Cornstarch is cornflour.
- Baking soda is bicarbonate of soda.
- Vanilla or vanilla extract is vanilla essence.
- Green, red, or yellow sweet peppers are capsicums or bell peppers.
- Golden raisins are sultanas.

volume and weight

The United States traditionally uses cup measures for liquid and solid ingredients. The chart below shows the approximate imperial and metric equivalents. If you are accustomed to weighing solid ingredients, the following approximate equivalents will be helpful.

- 1 cup butter, castor sugar, or rice = 8 ounces = ½ pound = 250 grams
- 1 cup flour = 4 ounces = ¼ pound = 125 grams
- 1 cup icing sugar = 5 ounces = 150 grams
- Canadian and U.S. volume for a cup measure is 8 fluid ounces (237 ml), but the standard metric equivalent is 250 ml.
- 1 British imperial cup is 10 fluid ounces.
- In Australia, 1 tablespoon equals 20 ml, and there are 4 teaspoons in the Australian tablespoon.
- Spoon measures are used for smaller amounts of ingredients. Although the size of the tablespoon varies slightly in different countries, for practical purposes and for recipes in this book, a straight substitution is all that's necessary. Measurements made using cups or spoons always should be level unless stated otherwise.

common weight range replacements

Imperial / U.S.	Metric
½ ounce	15 g
1 ounce	25 g or 30 g
4 ounces (¼ pound)	115 g or 125 g
8 ounces (½ pound)	225 g or 250 g
16 ounces (1 pound)	450 g or 500 g
1¼ pounds	625 g
1½ pounds	750 g
2 pounds or 2¼ pounds	1,000 g or 1 Kg

oven temperature equivalents

Fahrenheit Setting	Celsius Setting	Gas Setting
300°F	150°C	Gas Mark 2 (very low)
325°F	160°C	Gas Mark 3 (low)
350°F	180°C	Gas Mark 4 (moderate)
375°F	190°C	Gas Mark 5 (moderate)
400°F	200°C	Gas Mark 6 (hot)
425°F	220°C	Gas Mark 7 (hot)
450°F	230°C	Gas Mark 8 (very hot)
475°F	240°C	Gas Mark 9 (very hot)
500°F	260°C	Gas Mark 10 (extremely hot)
Broil	Broil	Grill

*Electric and gas ovens may be calibrated using celsius. However, for an electric oven, increase celsius setting 10 to 20 degrees when cooking above 160°C. For convection or forced air ovens (gas or electric), lower the temperature setting 25°F/10°C when cooking at all heat levels.

baking pan sizes

Imperial / U.S.	Metric
9×1½-inch round cake pan	22- or 23×4-cm (1.5 L)
9×1½-inch pie plate	22- or 23×4-cm (1 L)
8×8×2-inch square cake pan	20×5-cm (2 L)
9×9×2-inch square cake pan	22- or 23×4.5-cm (2.5 L)
11×7×1½-inch baking pan	28×17×4-cm (2 L)
2-quart rectangular baking pan	30×19×4.5-cm (3 L)
13×9×2-inch baking pan	34×22×4.5-cm (3.5 L)
15×10×1-inch jelly roll pan	40×25×2-cm
9×5×3-inch loaf pan	23×13×8-cm (2 L)
2-quart casserole	2 L

u.s. / standard metric equivalents

⅛ teaspoon = 0.5 ml	
¼ teaspoon = 1 ml	
½ teaspoon = 2 ml	
1 teaspoon = 5 ml	
1 tablespoon = 15 ml	
2 tablespoons = 25 ml	
¼ cup = 2 fluid ounces = 50 ml	
⅓ cup = 3 fluid ounces = 75 ml	
½ cup = 4 fluid ounces = 125 ml	
⅔ cup = 5 fluid ounces = 150 ml	
¾ cup = 6 fluid ounces = 175 ml	
1 cup = 8 fluid ounces = 250 ml	
2 cups = 1 pint = 500 ml	
1 quart = 1 litre